Home

The Macmillan Company, New York

Introduction to *Home Furnishings*

Introduction to
Furnishings

Dorothy Stepat–De Van

Professor of Home Economics
Hunter College of the City University of New York

Collier-Macmillan Limited, London

THE MACMILLAN COMPANY
866 Third Avenue, New York, New York 10022
COLLIER–MACMILLAN CANADA, LTD.,
TORONTO, ONTARIO

Library of Congress catalog card number: 76–112852

First Printing

To My Very Understanding
Family and Friends

The original purposes of this book were to emphasize some of the relationships that we assumed existed between people and their homes and to provide background information that might lend confidence in making the many decisions that are involved in establishing a home.

Much has happened since the first edition went into print. We are employing new technologies in almost every area of housing and interior design. Many new products have appeared on the market. Our society has become much more aware of the home as it relates to individual needs and we have entered an age that makes all of us wonder about how the conquest of space will influence our way of life. The current war on poverty, further advances in technology, and new experiments in space are bound to have some effects on our future social structure.

All these developments serve to emphasize the deeper implications of home economics education and, in my opinion, will help to strengthen the goals and objectives of home economics. In the first edition of this book I mentioned that although we cannot teach people how to enjoy life, we can make them more conscious of the factors that contribute to the joy of living. It is becoming increasingly important for us to understand how a home environment can affect individual development and influence the relationships within a family. Until we can prove otherwise, I think we must assume that the atmosphere of a home is a very important element in creating a better society.

In the revised edition I have, of course, tried to bring the information up-to-date, but I have also put a little more emphasis on housing and furnishings for low-income groups. I had considered omitting Section VI on home projects in the revision, but decided against it because this area has become so important in working with low-income groups.

Preface to the Second Edition

Inadequate as this section may be, I feel that its inclusion serves to emphasize the growing interest in such projects.

In selecting illustrations, I have generally tried to include those that show items that are readily available or that suggest certain ideas that are adaptable. It would have been easy to use more museum sources to illustrate many points, but for the purposes of this book, these sources did not seem practical. Although design in mass-produced furnishings is certainly becoming more sophisticated, the task of finding good illustrations convinced me that we still have a long road ahead. I am grateful to the many individuals and companies that were so cooperative in submitting photographs. I am also most grateful to Bigelow-Sanford, Inc., for photographs of rug designs by Dorothy Liebes, internationally known textile designer. We have used them to embellish the opening section pages with the belief that her unique awareness of design will serve as a source of stimulation and inspiration for students.

This edition retains some of the basic material that was originally reviewed by such experts as Miss Gladys Miller, formerly of *New Homes Guide*; Mrs. Mary Davis Gillies of *McCall's*; Mr. George Kinley of William Marshall Ltd.; Miss Ruth Holman of the American Carpet Institute; and Mr. W. H. Hall of the Munsell Color Company. Once again, I should like to express my appreciation for their efforts.

Dorothy Stepat—De Van

The French use a delightful phrase *joie de vivre* or "joy of living." I believe that one of our functions in home economics is to help students appreciate this concept and to help them develop their own values and standards with relationship to it. We cannot teach people how to enjoy life but we can make them more conscious of the factors that contribute to the joy of living. Without a doubt, the atmosphere of the home is one of the elements that determine whether a family really lives or merely exists. It is important for a homemaker to understand how the home environment can influence personal development and affect relationships within a family.

The purposes of this book aim chiefly toward helping the student understand various aspects that must be considered in establishing a home. In no sense is it meant as a training text for interior designers. However, in every sense it is meant to help the young homemaker develop her own ideas about how her home should function and how it should look.

I have tried to present material that will encourage the student to examine purposes and needs and give her some degree of confidence in making decisions. I have also tried to include material that might stimulate interest in further study. No one book could possibly produce experts in this field. Nevertheless, I have tried to portray the nostalgia of the past and the challenge of the future, with the hope that the student will intensify her appreciation of both.

As a teacher, I have found my greatest rewards in watching students develop enthusiasm for the study of home furnishings. It really doesn't matter which aspect of the subject becomes most appealing; the important point is that the student should develop a better understanding and appreciation of the various ways in which a home environment can affect personal and family living.

Preface to the First Edition

With such various factors in mind, I have tried to prepare a text that will be useful for both the teacher and the student. This is a difficult subject to teach because we should not attempt to impose our own tastes and standards on students. We have broken with tradition in so many ways that perhaps the only safe rule about home furnishings is that we must "never say never." This does not imply, however, that "anything goes." It becomes increasingly important, therefore, to develop an awareness on the part of the student and then let her decide for herself.

In organizing the vast amount of material in this field I have tried to keep in mind that teachers have different ideas about how such a course should be presented. Therefore, each section and each chapter is an entity so that the teacher may rearrange the material to suit her needs. However, in each area I have tried to stress the important basic factors so there will be continuity no matter how the material is rearranged.

Many people have helped in the preparation of this book. I am indebted to Mrs. Judith Harlan of The Macmillan Company for her painstaking reviews of the original drafts. My colleagues at Hunter College have been most sympathetic and understanding. I should like to express my special appreciation to our department chairman at Hunter College,

Professor Gertrude Borgeson, for her encouragement and cooperation. Professor Anna McKellar has been of invaluable assistance in reading portions of the manuscript and in making many helpful comments.

I am also grateful to several other specialists for reading parts of the manuscript and for offering such useful suggestions. Miss Gladys Miller of *New Homes Guide*, Mrs. Mary Davis Gillies of *McCall's*, Mr. George Kinley of William Marshall, Ltd., and Miss Ruth Holman of the American Carpet Institute all offered many valuable comments and suggestions. Mr. W. H. Hall of the Munsell Color Company read the original draft of the section on color and was most helpful with his suggestions for revisions.

In addition, I should like to offer a special tribute to Miss Claire Boasi and Miss Kate Urquhart for excellent assistance in obtaining illustrations. Miss Boasi was also most helpful in choosing illustrations and in taking care of many details involved in organization. Without her diligent work I could not have prepared the finished manuscript.

Last, but not at all least, I should like to express my deep appreciation to several people who were responsible for the actual preparation of the manuscript. Mrs. Norma Oswald, Mrs. Janis Thomas, Mrs. Rosemary Kiely, Mrs. Gertrude Brady, and Mrs. Bette Brady were all most cooperative in this part of the project.

Dorothy Stepat—De Van

Contents

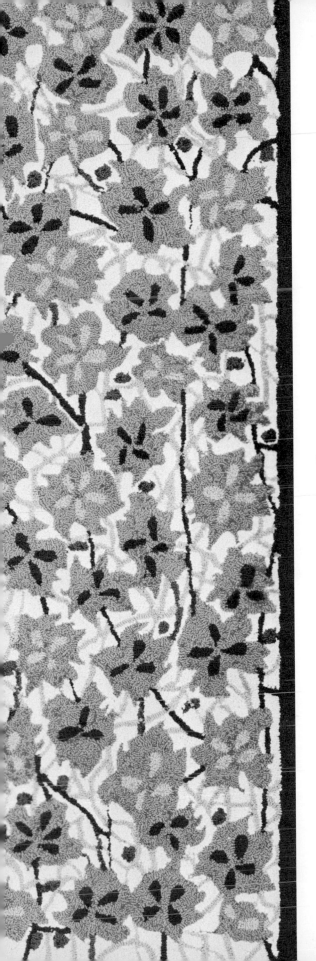

Section I
Planning a Home

Our relatively new centers for environmental studies are taking a fresh approach to the relationships between people and their physical surroundings. Although there has been considerable research in all phases of housing, leaders in this field are becoming more aware of the fact that satisfactory solutions to the problems involved require the combined efforts of specialists in many different areas. There is a pressing need for more collaboration among experts in fields such as sociology, psychology, architecture, home economics, and health.

It is difficult to determine the extent to which the physical aspects of a home influence the behavior and attitudes of an individual or a family. We must recognize that some people seem to lead happy, wholesome lives in surroundings that are far less than desirable whereas others who are fortunate enough to have superior housing find it impossible to maintain satisfying relationships. Nevertheless, there are indications that physical conditions do influence social attitudes and family activities. One recent study showed significant differences in attitudes and activities between families living in large and small houses.[1] Certainly physical aspects frequently determine the way in which a home will be furnished and the way in which a household will function. Before we begin any discussion of furnishings, therefore, it seems desirable to consider a few basic factors involved in the selection of a home.

Housing is a worldwide problem and there is a tremendous amount of housing that is neither safe nor sanitary. In most countries there are both short-range and long-range programs for improving conditions. However, our

1

Space for Living

[1] Donna Beth Downer, "The Influences of Attitudes on the Relationship Between the House and the Adult Social Activity," *Journal of Home Economics*, Vol. 61, No. 1 (January, 1969), pp. 17–21.

interdisciplinary approach to this problem reveals a new dilemma. We are becoming more cognizant of the fact that requirements vary with the individual and with the family at different stages of the life cycle, but there are also trends toward urbanization and more mass-produced housing. How, then, do we provide adaptable homes that truly meet needs and desires? Current research is attempting to provide some answers to this complex question.

There are no universally accepted standards with respect to what constitutes "adequate" housing. Many local communities have codes and laws that regulate building to some extent. Government-financed programs must meet certain specifications, but at the present time there is considerable controversy regarding this matter. Some authorities believe that standards are so low that we are merely creating new slums in a rather frantic effort to relieve the situation. The matter of minimum standards must be subject to a great deal of further research.

What constitutes "desirable" housing poses quite a different question. Standards in this matter will naturally vary with the individual and probably no two people have identical values. In addition to the many families that are forced to live in homes that are inadequate according to the most basic standards, there are many others who have homes that they do not consider desirable. Another recent study attempted to probe the housing values of families at different stages of development. By using an experimental house constructed for the purpose of the study it was possible to evaluate the reactions of different families to a specific amount and arrangement of space. The results indicated that desires change with the various stages of the family cycle.[2]

Most average families spend between one quarter and one third of their total income on either owning or renting a home. Often the choices about how this money will be spent are more restricted than they are in other major areas of family economics, such as food, automobiles, insurance, and recreation.

[2] D. B. Downer, R. H. Smith, and M. T. Lynch, "Values and Housing—A New Dimension," *Journal of Home Economics*, Vol. 60, No. 3 (March, 1968), pp. 173–176.

Influences on Choice

What determines where people live and what kind of housing they purchase? There has been limited research in this area but simple observation points to some of the reasons.

HABIT. Some of us are more migratory than others and perhaps more adaptable to different patterns of living. But many people find it difficult to change their way of life. There is an old cliché that goes, "It's a nice place to visit but I wouldn't want to live here." The city dweller says it about the farm and the small-towner says it about the big city, and the probable reason is that each has become accustomed to the particular advantages of his own pattern. It is difficult to generalize about the different patterns of living because they vary to some extent with specific places.

There are advantages and disadvantages to living in either a city or a small town. Space is, of course, at a premium in most cities. One room in a convenient section may cost as much as a whole house with considerable ground around it in another area. Generally there is a more impersonal quality to city living than there is in a small town. Naturally the opportunities for entertainment, recreation, and other activities vary a great deal.

Suburbia has been the answer for many families. Living in a small community close to a big city would seem to solve all the problems because one can have the advantages of both types of living. But some families have found that they also have the disadvantages of both types. The suburbanite who spends considerable time traveling to and from work may find that he cannot enjoy the advantages of either the city or his community.

WORK. A particular job or type of work may force people to live in a certain area. A doctor who has established a practice or a person who owns a business may be bound to some special locality. Teachers, farmers, salesmen, lawyers, and diplomats must live where they will have the greatest satisfactions from their work. Industries are somewhat centralized in various parts of the country. The unskilled worker has more choice but he still must face the problems of the labor market.

FAMILY TIES. Some people stay in the particular locality simply because all their relatives live there. There may be dependent parents who cannot be moved easily to a different community. For some people, breaking close family associations is unthinkable. To others who have different sets of values packing up and going may be a problem, but if the advantages outweigh the disadvantages they can do it.

Transplanting children from one community to another is often a difficult problem. Once youngsters have established themselves in school it isn't easy for them to become accustomed to a new way of life.

STATUS. Whether or not we like to face the fact, housing does represent a status symbol. In cities, people will often pay exorbitant rents for a tiny space simply because of a "good" address. Almost every town has a right and a wrong side of the tracks, even though there are no tracks. One can drive through almost any community and pick out the "elite" section.

Even in developments where hundreds of houses begin life on a par, owners begin to make improvements and the ball starts to roll. Some years ago it was the two-car garage and an outdoor patio that represented luxury and elegance. Now that these have become more generally available, the marks of the "upper strata" include a family swimming pool and an air-conditioned house. The sauna or Finnish bath is becoming a new status symbol. Who can tell what the next mark of distinction will be? Perhaps a private landing field for a family helicopter.

Needs in the Home

The primary purpose of shelter is, of course, to protect us from the elements, but beyond that we need and expect much more from our homes. Because what constitutes desirable living quarters is a very personal and individual matter, requirements and wants vary with each family. We are all consumers of shelter and we have a certain number of dollars to spend for housing. Our values determine how we spend those dollars and few of us can have all our wants satisfied. We sacrifice or compromise in one area to achieve something else that seems more important. One family might live in a small city apartment because it is convenient for the wage-earning father. Another similar family prefers to live some distance away from the city so that they have more space and a yard for the children, even though the father has to travel back and forth. In each case the family might spend the same amount of money on housing, but each family has different values.

There are, however, certain basic needs and desires that we would like our homes to fulfill. Most of us want some degree of comfort, privacy, and convenience. We want our homes to be functional. And most of us also want our homes to be beautiful.

STANDARDS. It has been pointed out that there are no real standards for adequate or desirable housing. Among the agencies and groups that either require or recommend certain qualities are the following:

Federal Housing Administration. This government agency was set up to insure mortgages and in an indirect manner it has established certain minimum standards. Before the FHA will approve a loan, the house must meet certain regulations. These cover:

1. Materials and products.
2. Structural design.
3. Construction.
4. Exterior and interior covering materials.
5. Mechanical equipment.
6. Water supply and sewage disposal.
7. General planning.
8. Plot planning.
9. General criteria.

In some categories the requirements are quite specific, but they represent minimum rather than desirable standards.

Minimum standards for housing are both necessary and important, but they also present a dangerous threat. Instead of being regarded as a base below which the level must not fall, in practice they tend to become acceptable as pat standards.

American Public Health Association. In 1938 the association's Committee on the Hygiene of Housing defined certain requirements in a report, "Basic Principles of Healthful Housing." In the introduction to the second edition, it is pointed out that the report is a formulation of "basic health needs which housing should subserve." It also says, "The Principles and Specific Requirements are believed to be fundamental minima required for the promotion of physical, mental, and social health essential in low-rent as well as high-cost housing, on the farm as well as in the city dwelling.'' In a more recent report it was noted that ''There is usually a considerable difference between 'optimum' and 'minimum' requirements; that there is a continuous, gradual movement from 'minimum' toward 'optimum.' Codes represent the level of conditions which the public and their representatives consider to be so economically, socially, and politically necessary and acceptable that they should be required by law for all people.''[3]

The Small Homes Council. A program of research on housing is conducted at the University of Illinois under the auspices of The Small Homes Council. This agency is more concerned with recommending desirable features than with setting minimum standards. The council publishes a wide variety of pamphlets on home planning and construction.

Other Organizations. Several agencies concerned with financing make recommendations for home construction—for example, The United States Saving and Loan League and the Metropolitan Life Insurance Company. In many communities local housing codes and building restrictions impose certain standards.

It has been pointed out that we are taking a new approach to housing research and several universities have established centers for environmental studies. Hopefully, these centers will provide more useful guidelines for better housing programs.

In 1956 a government organization, The Housing and Home Finance Agency, sponsored a Women's Congress on Housing to draw up recommendations for meeting the housing needs of middle-income families with children. Some of these included:

Parlor-type living room
Kitchen–family room with space for table and
 six chairs
Parents' bedroom with two closets
Two additional bedrooms with closet in each
Enclosed front foyer
Rear entry into laundry-utility area

Main bath with single lavatory
Guest coat closet
Linen closet-broom closet

If economically feasible, the congress suggested the following *additionally desirable* features:

Separate dining room
Den–study–guest room with closet
Second closet in the two additional bedrooms
Fireplace (in northern parts of the country)

A more recent study of forty households indicated that a considerable number of homemakers (40 per cent) ''found the following features unsatisfactory: amount of storage space, space for guests, provisions for individual privacy, protection against excessive noise, and space for family members to pursue individual interests.''[4]

Today most homes are designed for a pattern of living rather than for individual families. The requirements of each family vary with the different stages of family life. The beginning family with several young children will have different needs from those of the family with several teen-agers. The special needs of retired couples have received considerable attention in recent years.

SPACE. Space for specific needs and activities is of primary importance—but space is usually expensive in either bought or rented shelter. Except in luxury-type housing, some concessions must be made to costs. Also, space needs vary as a family grows and then decreases. In the early years of family life, young children can share bedrooms, but as they grow older, it is often more desirable that they have private rooms. When the children mature and leave home, the parents are often left with excess space.

The FHA sets the following minimum standards for a three-bedroom living unit.

Living room	170 sq. ft.
Dining room	95 sq. ft.
Kitchen	70 sq. ft.
Total bedrooms	280 sq. ft.
(Minimum per bedroom	80 sq. ft.)

[3] ''Basic Health Principles of Housing and Its Environment,'' *American Journal of Public Health,* Vol. 69, No. 5 (May, 1969), pp. 841–851.

[4] Freda Teitzel Vars, ''Factors Related to Housing Satisfaction,'' *Journal of Home Economics,* Vol. 61, No. 3 (March, 1969), pp. 164–166.

Remember that these are minimum standards. The total area for the rooms indicated adds up to 615 square feet. For a family of four, the Small Homes Council recommends 1,500 square feet, not including closets and bathrooms.

In the study by Downer, cited previously, the "small house" sample was chosen from a group living in two-story houses that had about 450 square feet of space on each floor plus an attic and a basement. The "large house" participants lived in units that had a minimum of 1,500 square feet in a one-story house and at least 850 square feet on each floor of a two-story house.[5]

Although adequate housing must include many features besides the proper amount of space, this is perhaps the most fundamental need. But the arrangement of available space is equally important. A matter of major concern today is planning for functionalism in this respect so that the normal activities of the family are served in the best possible manner.

SLEEPING. A comfortable place to sleep is both physically and psychologically important. It is basic and imperative, therefore, for every home to have adequate sleeping quarters. The ideal of a private room for each member of the family who might want one is not always feasible. When people have to share sleeping quarters, every effort must be made to ensure maximum comfort and privacy for each person.

EATING. There is a curious association between the manner in which we partake of food and the general level of "standards of living." The arrangements that a home provides for feeding family and friends is, strangely enough, both a good indication of the values placed upon family life and a symbol of status.

A separate room used exclusively for dining has almost become a thing of the past, although it should be noted that a dining room is one of the features listed as a desirable aspect for a home when the family can afford it.

A dining room affords the family a place to congregate; it also offers a place where friends may be entertained with ease and graciousness. The cost of maintaining such a room is often prohibitive, but if it is within

[5] Donna Beth Downer, op. cit., p. 18.

reason, the family should not overlook the values received.

Dual-purpose dining rooms are gaining in favor. Such an area may lend itself for use as an extra sitting room or as a sewing room. It may even be furnished to serve as a guest room, though such an arrangement may present several problems.

Various arrangements may be made in the home for providing meals of different types without a dining room. A snack bar in the kitchen for quick individual meals is sometimes useful. An alcove or a dining area as part of another room has become an accepted plan.

Outdoor eating and entertaining are part of the way of life in many areas of the country, and where the space and equipment for cookouts are available, this form of family dining and entertaining is both practical and enjoyable.

The kitchen is an important area in the home because of the specialized equipment and storage space. But it is such a major area of activity that the utilization and decoration of the room should be of primary concern to every family.

Some homes combine kitchen and laundry areas to economize on plumbing costs and for convenience purposes. In others, the kitchen is planned to become the "family" room or a second living room.

The kitchen of today is much more scientifically planned and executed than were yesterday's kitchens; even so, few families have the advantages of a kitchen that is efficient enough to meet all their needs in the best possible way. Although many studies have analyzed work-motion routines, storage needs, and the utilization of space, there are numerous homes being built with no recognition of the most practical arrangements.

There are also special kitchens planned for people with particular needs. The elderly person or the woman with a heart condition should have a kitchen that is designed to meet specific requirements.

PRIVACY AND HOBBIES. An ideal arrangement is to have a separate area for each member of the family. This is not always practical, but frequently some sort of compromise can be made whereby each person can at least use a corner or area that provides a feeling of privacy. When a family has several

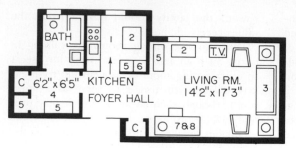

1. FOOD PREPARATION
2. EATING
3. SLEEPING
4. DRESSING
5. STORAGE
6. MAINTENANCE
7. HOBBY AREA
8. BUSINESS AREA
9. EXTRA SLEEPING
10. EXTRA LIVING AREAS

(a)

FIGURE 1-1 The plan for the studio apartment shown in (a) indicates how basic needs might be met in a small area. The apartment in (b) and the ranch-type house in (c) naturally allow more flexibility.

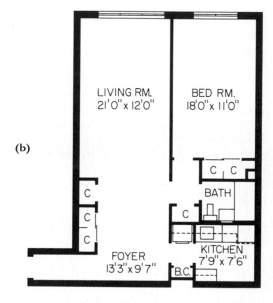

(b)

(c)

8

FIGURE 1-2 A one-room apartment can be elegant as well as functional. Lightweight furniture can be easily rearranged for entertaining. The game area may also be used as a work center. (*Designed by Barbara D'Arcy, A.I.D., Bloomingdale's, N.Y. Photo by Richard Averill Smith*)

children, it is usually necessary for them to share bedrooms. Even under these circumstances, various arrangements can be made to ensure the privacy of each individual. Every member of the household should have at least a corner that he can call his own, to do with as he wishes.

GROUP LIVING AND RECREATION: Certainly some area in the home must be devoted to the family as a group. The current tendency is to have two such areas—one a more formal "living room" and another "family room" designed for informal use or as an adjunct to the group living quarters. Such an area is of particular advantage when the family includes children of teen-age , or in

any other situation where there may be two distinct interpretations of group living. Even within a small family unit there may be different ideas of enjoyable group association. Two or more living areas in the home make it possible for people to enjoy a variety of activities.

PERSONAL NEEDS. Most families would prefer to have at least one-and-one-half bathrooms; a luxury standard would be a private bathroom for each member of the family. Prohibitive costs of space, fixtures, and plumbing have forced the development of various kinds of new arrangements in bathrooms to make them more useful. Building each fixture into a compartment and including two washbasins makes it possible to have a room that can accommodate more than one person at a time and yet afford some degree of privacy. Although this arrangement is not always the most desirable, it does at least extend the function of one bathroom to meet the needs of the family more adequately.

MAINTENANCE. Various activities may be involved in maintaining the home. In a private home, a special laundry area is desirable, as is some type of workroom. The laundry may be part of the kitchen and the workroom may be part of the garage, or both areas may be in the basement. Where space is available it is usually more desirable to have these areas separated.

STORAGE. Sufficient closet and storage space seems to be a problem in every home. Apartments are notable for having inadequate storage space. Even private houses fall short in this respect. An attic or a basement is, of course, very useful, but some homes have neither.

Each bedroom should have a large closet, and any room that will be shared should have at least two closets. In addition, there are general storage areas necessary for linens, cleaning equipment, and so on. A house with a yard will need storage facilities for lawn mower, hose, and garden equipment. When there are children in the family, such items as bicycles, wagons, and sleds must be kept someplace when they are not in use. A garage is usually suitable for the storage of much of this equipment, but it should be large enough so that it can also accommodate the car. Many families in private homes neglect to provide storage space for such outdoor equipment and large toys. Frequently the garage becomes a storeroom while the car is left outside because it simply won't fit.

BUSINESS CENTER. Every household needs a special area for the business of managing a home. All sorts of records, bills, and stationery supplies should be convenient and readily accessible. This office might be merely a drawer in a chest or a desk in the living room, but it should be well organized and completely equipped. File drawers are a great asset, and some companies have recognized the need for filing cabinets that are attractive in the home.

Good light, a comfortable chair, a typewriter, and an ample work surface are also desirable for the family office.

Choice of Housing

Although many families have extremely limited choices when it comes to making decisions about how they will use their allotments for shelter, there are still some choices that must be made:

1. To rent or buy.
2. House or apartment.
3. One home or two.
4. Modular housing.

TO RENT OR BUY. There are general advantages and disadvantages to either renting or owning shelter, but for individual families the advantages of one may far outweigh the disadvantages. Renting a home is obviously more desirable for a family that may have to move frequently because of the work of the wage earners. But even for a more static family, renting shelter may provide a more desirable solution because of the comparative freedom from responsibilities. Usually the renter is absolved from the costs and worry about major repairs and renovations. Although his rent may eventually be influenced by a change in tax rates and property values, his expenses for shelter are more fixed and steady than those of a homeowner. The family that rents shelter is also more at liberty to keep the size of the home related to the needs of the family as it grows and disperses over the years.

Ownership, on the other hand, has much in its favor, as is witnessed by the growing number of families who prefer to buy housing rather than to rent it. Even in cities there is growing interest, especially in the middle-income group, in cooperatively owned apartment houses.

Most people have the idea that it is cheaper in the long run to own a home rather than to rent one, but such is not always the case; in some areas of the country it may be cheaper to own than to rent, but in other areas the opposite is true. Undoubtedly, the family income and the amount that can be spent for shelter is another determining factor. Families in very low income-brackets are more likely to find the costs of ownership prohibitive.

Maintenance costs must be considered among the expenses for shelter. The ability of the homeowner to take care of the upkeep himself rather than to pay for the high costs of labor may well be another important consideration.

The homeowner may deduct some of his shelter expenses in computing his personal income tax, whereas the renter receives no such allowance; this may be an important consideration when comparing the economic advantages of ownership and rental.

The argument that after a period of years the homeowner has "something to show" for his money does not always stand up under close economic analysis. If the property value depreciates and he includes all the expenses of his investment he may be far worse off from the monetary standpoint than the renter who preferred to invest his capital in some other manner.

Aside from the seemingly unanswerable question of whether or not it is cheaper to own or to rent, there are other values that must be considered. Many families prefer the feelings of security and stability associated with homeownership. They sense a more integral relationship with the community, and they enjoy a certain "status", which is reflected not only in intangible ways but in a higher credit rating. Pride of ownership promotes greater interest in the appearance and maintenance of the home, but for the person who doesn't enjoy household tasks and chores these may soon become burdensome.

Most homeowners feel that through purchasing a home they can have a better quality of housing, with space and equipment more nearly designed to meet their needs.

HOUSE OR APARTMENT. The choice between a house and an apartment may be linked to the buy-or-rent problem because, in general, we buy houses and rent apartments. However, many people rent houses or buy apartments. In the past, owning an apartment usually meant that it was a cooperative venture with other tenants in the building. Today the condominium is becoming quite popular: one owns the apartment just as he might own a house. He may buy and sell without the approval of the other tenants. This approval is usually necessary in the cooperative.

We have already discussed some of the relative merits of living in the city, country, or suburbs, and location may be the deciding factor, but there are other considerations, too. A house usually offers the advantages of a yard, with more opportunity for outdoor living and more play area for children. There is usually more space and a feeling of more freedom and privacy. For some people, apartment living carries an air of confinement; for others the important factor in apartment living is freedom from chores and responsibilities.

ONE HOME OR TWO. Some families prefer to divide their housing allotment to cover a separate vacation home. Such an expense cannot be considered wholly shelter cost, because it can reduce the cost of vacations. But the costs of the regular home are likely to continue while the family is enjoying the vacation home. Of course, expense is an important factor to consider, but for many families two homes and two types of living have answered some of the questions already presented. An apartment that one rents during the year and a summer house that one owns may provide the advantages of almost all types of shelter. Vacation homes are often designed for easy maintenance so that it is possible to have the pleasures of ownership without the constant pressure of the chores.

MODULAR HOUSING. A relatively new concept in housing emphasizes the modular unit as a possible answer to some of our housing problems. A house or basic modules that can be transformed into apartments may be produced in a factory and transported to a building site where they are connected to utilities. Habitat, the complex shown at Expo '67 in Montreal, is a noted example of modular apartments.

Mobile homes, although not as new as apartment modules, are another example of modular housing. These units are becoming increasingly important—especially in meeting the housing needs of two particular groups— young married couples and elderly retired couples. Mobile homes differ from trailers in that they are usually larger and if they are to be moved at all, which is not usually the case, they must be hauled by professional transportation companies.

The average mobile home is 12 feet wide

(a)

(b)

FIGURE 1-3 Habitat '67 in Montreal represents a pioneer experiment in modular housing. Units of precast concrete were hoisted in place to create a new type of futuristic architecture. (*Courtesy of National Film Board of Canada*). *Photo by Central Mortgage & Housing Corporation*)

and 60 feet long and sells for about $5,700. There are expandable types that pull out to provide an additional 6 or 8 feet in width to a bedroom or a living room. The cost of a furnished mobile home is about $8 a square foot, as compared to about $14 a square foot for unfurnished conventional housing.

A recent report points out that in 1967 mobile homes represented about 32 per cent of the market in all single-family, privately constructed, nonfarm housing in this country.[6] In 1968 there were about 315,000 units produced—the major share of all single-family homes built for less than $15,000.

In some areas of the country, location sites for this type of housing have been well developed and aesthetically planned. The Cornell study recognizes that some communities have been reluctant to establish such sites because they fear a poor image. Nevertheless, the study recommends modular units for apartments and houses as one answer to the national housing shortage.

The houseboat is another type of mobile home that is becoming popular in certain areas. Some of these are quite luxurious, and living on the water seems to have a restful quality that appeals to many people. Although we have tended to think of a houseboat as a vacation home, it should be noted that even in colder climates there is a growing interest in the boat as an all-year-round home.

Owning a Home

Suppose one has decided that owning a home suits his needs. The next decisions are important ones that will not only involve considerable sums of money but also influence his personal and family life. There are so many things to consider about the home that plan-

[6] *The New Building Block*, Center for Housing and Environmental Studies (Ithaca, N.Y.: Cornell University, 1968).

ning and studying the project will take a great deal of time. Here again, one will have important decisions and choices, but he should bear in mind that there probably isn't any house that is perfect in every respect. One will usually have to make compromises between what he would like and what he can have, but if he weighs all the factors very carefully before he makes the decisions, he will certainly be more satisfied with his results.

The prospective homeowner may choose one of the following courses.

1. To buy a house that is already built.
2. To hire an architect to draw up custom plans.
3. To buy a plan and have a house built.
4. To buy a prefabricated house.

A HOUSE THAT IS ALREADY BUILT.
There are some advantages to buying a house that already exists, since, of course, one can see what he is purchasing. It may be brand new or a house that has been lived in by another family. In either case, it is helpful to note the relationship of the house to the land, the construction and the finishing. One can also see the space relationships and have a clearer picture of how they will meet the needs of the family.

A house that has already been occupied may have certain advantages by way of landscaping, storm windows, screens, and so on. Depending upon the age of the house, cracks from settling or needed repairs are evident. But one should try to find out the real reason the present owner wants to sell. If the house had some disadvantage for him, it may have some for the new owner, too.

A brand-new house will probably be more up-to-date in equipment and materials. However, all sorts of flaws may show up when one actually begins to heat it and use the plumbing. Buying from a reliable builder is, of course, essential, but one can almost always expect some unforeseen problems.

One may select a "model" home and have it built with some changes made from the original. This procedure will have some advantages in that one can adapt the house to meet specific needs, but the more changes, the more expensive the house will be. "Optional" features on a model house can increase the costs considerably.

FIGURE 1-4   Modular housing answers some of the current needs for economy, space, and comfort. (*Courtesy of Stirling Homes Corporation, Avon, N.Y.*)

(a) (above) Ceilings for the modules are made in a rather unique manner—upside down. After being constructed in giant forms, they are turned over by machine and set atop the modules on the moving production line.

(b) (below) Floor and wall units are carefully joined to form the basic module, which is moved down the production line on a rolling track.

(c) At the end of the production line, finished modules are covered with canvas and plastic sheets to protect them from the weather prior to being erected at the site. They are then loaded on haulers for transportation to the homesite.

(d) A module unit is dropped into position at the site. Each upper module is three feet longer than the lower unit in order to provide second floor overhang.

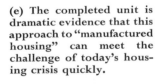

(e) The completed unit is dramatic evidence that this approach to "manufactured housing" can meet the challenge of today's housing crisis quickly.

FIGURE 1-5   (a) The use of the 10- or 12-foot "double-wides" or the expandable principle achieves greater living areas. The latter provides for greater length or width to be telescoped into the home while it is in transit and then expanded once the home has been located. (*Courtesy of Mobile Homes Manufacturers Association*)

(b) The site is important. Many developments feature paved roads, street lighting, various recreational areas, laundry facilities, and so on. Lawns and gardens are points of pride for many owners.

(c) Wall-to-wall carpeting, picture windows, and fireplaces can be found in many mobile homes.

(d) Separate dining areas with ceiling-to-floor cupboards are located near the functional kitchens.

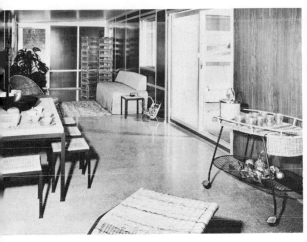

(e) Florida rooms or cabanas can be added after a home has been in place. These can serve a variety of functions—family or guest room, carport, or storage area. Frequently such a room can provide the appearance of a conventional stationary house.

(f) Bedrooms are designed to offer maximum storage in limited areas.

(g) Floor plans for typical mobile homes. The 12-foot-wide unit in (a) has a raised kitchen and two bedrooms. The plan shown in (b) has an expandable living room.

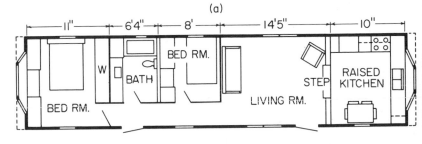

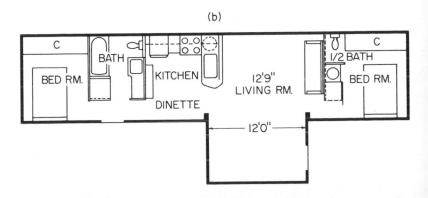

USING AN ARCHITECT. It is possible to engage an architect to draw up a custom-made plan. Then either the architect will be responsible for negotiating with a contractor to build the house or he will turn over his plans to the prospective owner for the actual execution. Naturally, a custom-designed house is more expensive because more special services are involved.

BUYING A PLAN. Various agencies and organizations offer house plans that one can buy. This is cheaper than actually engaging an architect, but it is necessary to engage the builder and rely upon him to interpret the plans properly. Also, it should be remembered that changes can quickly add to the estimated costs.

PREFABRICATED HOUSES. A prefabricated house can be purchased and assembled on the site chosen. Housing units purchased this way would seem to be the answer to the high costs of construction; indeed, the industry has developed to a point where preconstructed houses are no longer limited to the low-cost economy brackets. They are now acceptable in many areas that would previously approve of homes only in the "luxury" class. There is quite a wide range of types at different cost levels.

Although preconstructed homes may offer an answer to the high costs of building, haulage rates are also high. For the sake of efficiency, actual manufacturing of the units must take place in a central plant. When the parts are transported for any great distance, the shipping costs mount and sometimes overcome the economic advantages of this method of construction.

Choosing the Location

Whether one buys or rents a home, the community in which he settles will influence his pattern of living. There will probably be a closer association between one's family and the community if he owns property than if he rents it. In either case, the neighbors, the atmosphere, and the spirit of the area will have a direct bearing on whether or not one will be happy in a location. Each town or community has a particular personality, which may be extremely impersonal or extremely

group-minded. Those who prefer seclusion may find it difficult to avoid the community spirit. If, on the other hand, one enjoys group activities, a community that has little group-mindedness will be dull and unrewarding.

Beyond the spirit of the community there are several other practical features that one should evaluate. The general appearance, the accessibility of schools, churches, and shops, as well as noise and fumes from factories or other commercial establishments must all be considered. Is public transportation readily available or must one depend on a car? Are the services that provide electricity, gas, water, and refuse disposal dependable, and what are the costs? Who is responsible for the roads in winter? A community that looks like sheer delight in the summer may be a real problem in the winter if snowplows do not open the roads. Is there a public sewerage system or must one depend on septic tanks or cesspools? Are there sidewalks and if not will these be installed at some future date? Any of these improvements will affect present or future tax rates. Zoning regulations with regard to businesses that may or may not develop in the area should be of concern to the prospective homeowner because these will affect property values.

The House Itself

There are many features one should consider very carefully before buying a new home. The appearance of the house and whether or not it will meet the needs of the new owner are, of course, important. In addition, it pays to seek the unbiased opinions of people who are qualified to judge construction. The advice of reliable appraisers, real estate agents, contractors, architects, and building inspectors may cost money, but their training and experience in the technical aspects of construction can be of inestimable value to the average layman.

STYLE. The basic design of the house is, of course, closely tied in with construction costs. The majority of homes built today do not, as a rule, cling to traditional styles of architecture, although any home may interpret the "flavor" of some particular style. Except for houses in the luxury class, where costs are not a primary factor, the expense of duplicating many of the older and more familiar architectural styles is prohibitive. Besides, newer concepts of form and function in small homes have made it more desirable to adapt only certain styles of architecture and to develop new ones that are more suitable to modern building methods and materials. Thus, current home-building includes various designs that are inspired by traditional styles but that make no attempt to copy them in an authentic fashion. This approach to house design has given rise to numerous hybrid styles that almost defy classification. It has become the custom, therefore, to refer to the style of a house in several different ways. The architect or the builder may give it a name that is suggestive of its origin, or they may merely designate it by a number.

The basic form of the house is often used as a rather broad designation.

One-Story or Ranch Type. Although we have come to refer to the one-story house as a ranch-type home, the wide variety of styles often bears little, if any, resemblance to an actual ranch house. Colonial, Oriental, Spanish, and modern styles of architecture have all been interpreted in the single-story home.

Even in a fairly small home, the exterior of the one-story design presents broad, low lines that have popular appear. However, this type of house requires a sufficient amount of ground to show it off to best advantage, and it is not usually attractive when built on a small lot.

Split-Level. A popular style that has developed in recent years has part of the house on the ground floor and the other parts on two or more other levels. There have been many interpretations of the split-level form, including some that are very poorly planned. However, when the house is well designed, the arrangement offers practical advantages of conserving land and building expenses.

Although the split-level house would seem to be the answer to many problems, it can present other problems. The need to climb any steps at all may be a disadvantage in some situations. Also, it is a difficult house to design and to build. Usually, a split-level home looks more attractive on sloping terrain rather than flat ground. The exterior proportions may have a chopped-up appearance, especially in small homes built on too little ground.

Two-Story. For the economical use of ground and building materials, the house that is built up rather than spread out offers the most advantages. This form lends itself to a wide variety of treatments, which range from basic economy models to luxurious formal dwellings.

Some of the low-cost houses make use of one-and-one-half-story arrangements with the upper floor frequently unfinished. The lower floor provides a complete home, and the space in the upper story is available when the owner is ready to finish it.

Architects and builders are currently stressing the importance of relating the style of the house to the site upon which it will be built. The building and the surrounding terrain should enhance and complement each other. The outdoor living areas have become as important as the indoor living space. Although we need and want the enclosure offered by the walls of the house, we like the spirit and atmosphere of the interior flowing to the outside. The surrounding areas that will include terraces, patios, and swimming pools must, therefore, look like a continuity of the house and not just an afterthought.

The materials used to build the house are an integral part of the design. Texture and color must be chosen and arranged to enhance rather than detract from the basic lines. The general spirit or expressiveness of the house is also dependent on the actual substance in relation to the overall design. Wood, stone, metal, and glass are commonly used. In the future, plastics will probably play an important role.

All houses combine materials in one way or another, and there is a wide variety from which to choose. Just as in any form of art, the success of the design depends on sensitivity in selecting the medium. In housing design, a common mistake is to use too many different materials. Restraint and good taste in this respect separate the good from the mediocre.

The design of a house must be considered in relation to the neighborhood as well as its immediate vicinity. A huge formal mansion would certainly be out of place in a development of low-cost economy homes. A truly modern home looks incongruous when nestled in the peaceful hills of a sleepy country village. Yet does this mean we must be stereotyped in housing design? Not at all. It simply means that experiments with prototypes of future homes are more successful and more interesting if

(a)

(b)

(c)

FIGURE 1-6 Popular types of houses. (a) Ranch-type; (b) Split-level; (c) Two-story. (*Courtesy of* House Beautiful Building Manual, *Richard B. Pollman, designer. Irving E. Palmquist, A.I.A.*)

FIGURE 1-7 (a) The "Moon House," an experimental project, can be built for approximately $10,000, exclusive of land. The shingled multi-level dwelling is climate-controlled and has parking space for cars under the ground-level archway.

(b) The living-dining area leads via a moon-shaped door to a terrace. The room has walls and floors carpeted in indoor-outdoor carpeting, and a moon-shaped fireplace, table, and skylight. (*Courtesy of The Englander Company, a subsidiary of Union Carbide Corporation*)

they are isolated enough to be judged on their own merits. We look at any house in relation to its surroundings as well as in terms of its purpose. A house that is exaggerated or completely different may become only a sore thumb rather than a pace-setter in spite of all its advantages. A house plan that recognizes the setting, may incorporate many new ideas and innovations without becoming an architectural outcast in the community.

SPACE. Anyone who plans to buy or build a home should learn something about blueprints and about how space is represented on a small sheet of paper. Such a "map" of a house will reveal many things, but until one learns to interpret the plans in terms of *actual* space, it has little meaning. For example, consider a floor plan that includes a bedroom 10′ 0″ × 10′ 0″. Is it large or small? One should measure some of the rooms where he now lives. Then he takes a ruler and a plain sheet of paper and draws a scale plan of rooms that he really knows. One-quarter inch on the ruler should equal one foot of the actual measurements. At first, just an outline should be drawn, without any indication of doors, windows, and so on.

Now it is possible to see familiar living quarters represented, after a fashion, in a plan. Next, doors, windows, closets, radiators, juts in the walls, and electrical outlets should be placed. Figure 1-8 shows some of the symbols used in architectural plans. The space where the doors, windows, stairways, and electrical outlets are placed influence the way a home will function, so it pays to understand and interpret floor plans.

A primary concern in evaluating a floor plan should be the total amount of space, the number of rooms, and the size of each. One should evaluate them in terms of usefulness and costs. The plan should also point up the features of the functionalism of the house. The following points should be checked:

1. Does one have to go through any room to get to another?
2. Is there an entrance from the garage or parking area that facilitates unloading the car and bringing supplies into the kitchen?
3. Is there a closet near the main entrance where guests may deposit coats and hats?
4. Is the wall space in each room flexible for furniture arrangement, or is it broken up by windows and doors that limit the placement of larger pieces?
5. Is there sufficient space to entertain guests for meals or overnight?
6. Is there a utility area that can serve as a laundry, a workroom, and so on?
7. Is there sufficient storage space for both indoor and outdoor needs?
8. If living space is to be added in the future, how can the plan be adapted? Is it feasible to add another room? Can the attic or basement be converted to more useful space?

CONSTRUCTION. There are certain things that anyone can observe about the construction of a house, but by and large it takes a trained eye to judge hidden aspects. For example, it is easy to see whether or not the house seems to be run down and badly in need of repair. In an old house, peeling paint, cracked masonry, and sagging beams all indicate needed repair work. A more experienced eye is usually needed to evaluate other features.

Heating and Ventilation. Our forefathers had no central heating or air-conditioning units in the homes that they built, but they did realize the importance of a comfortable atmosphere in the home. With fireplaces and stoves they managed to keep rooms warm; in climates where hot weather is a major problem, the building materials and the arrangement of space in the home were geared to keeping the interior atmosphere comfortable. We can learn a great deal from people in tropical countries about natural methods of air conditioning. They build houses around central patios, keep roofs shaded with tall trees, and use shutters that are closed tight in the middle of the day to prevent the sun from heating the interior of the house. Stone and marble provide excellent insulating materials. But these methods are not always practical in contemporary building, where costs and the availability of space and materials almost dictate the designs of our houses. We rely, therefore, on mechanical methods of keeping interior atmospheres livable and comfortable.

Heating may be a major expense in the maintenance of a home. The heating unit should utilize the most economical fuel for

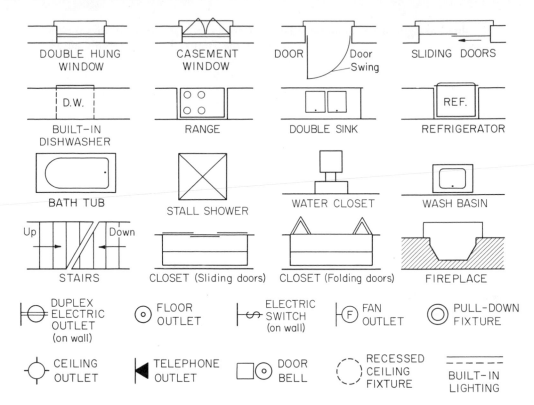

FIGURE 1-8 Architectural symbols are useful in understanding floor plans.

the particular area of the country. Gas and oil are commonly favored, but in certain localities other fuels, such as electricity, may be less expensive. The construction of walls, floors, and ceilings is closely related to the use of fuel. Poor insulating qualities increase costs in winter; good insulation not only reduces costs in cold weather but keeps the house cool during warm weather.

In some areas, air conditioning has become almost a necessity. Although the cost of a central unit is still prohibitive in many cases, room-size devices and exhaust fans in kitchens and bathrooms are relatively inexpensive.

The value of a house will be increased by the ease and economy of keeping the interior comfortable for year-round living. For areas where both heat and cold are problems, there are units that combine heating and cooling systems. If a house is considered in relation to resale value, it might be wise to invest in one that has an adequate control of interior temperatures. There is little doubt that in the future this aspect will assume greater importance.

Plumbing. The source of water supply and the condition of all pipes should be carefully checked. An inadequate or a worn system can be expensive to remedy. Sewerage may be taken care of by a community system or by a private septic tank, or cesspool. Whatever the system, it should be properly installed and adequate in size. It should be accessible for periodic cleanings, which will, of course, add to the cost of maintenance.

Wiring. The house must provide adequate current for all major appliances. The local utility company will probably be able to offer some assistance in this respect. If one plans to use electricity for a range or for air conditioning, dependability should be checked. In some areas, the current is often affected by storms. Of course, outlets should be convenient for lamps and appliances.

Acoustics. A noisy home can be a real problem, and one's first consideration should be location. He should beware of trains, buses, or commercial establishments in the immediate vicinity. A location close to an airport may be a drawback. A house in a busy district has certain property advantages, but it may also have the disadvantages of a nonresidential atmosphere.

Within the house, noise can be controlled in several ways. Some materials are more sound-absorbent than others. Ceiling tiles that absorb sound are a great advantage. Resilient materials on floors, counters, and furniture will also contribute to the "sound conditioning" of a home. Closets placed between bedrooms provide space between the room walls.

Odor. It is interesting to observe that some cultures are extremely aware of the interplay of *all* the senses. We tend to emphasize visual, tactile, and auditory sensations, but in the Orient the importance of the olfactory sensations is equally recognized. Incense, an aromatic substance, is burned to create an agreeable atmosphere. Odors certainly influence one's reactions to a particular home. They may be pleasant, soothing, exotic, or stimulating, or they may be repulsive. Too much of any aroma is not appealing, but a faint, suggestive odor can do wonders in creating an atmosphere. The smell of pine and cedar are familiar to many of us, and they usually have delightful associations.

Building materials sometimes provide the aromatic atmosphere. Natural substances, such as some woods, are noteworthy; certain synthetic materials may have rather clinical odors.

Facts About Financing

The generally accepted standard indicates that a family should purchase a house that is no more than two to two-and-one-half times the annual income. However, some authorities believe that with increased tax rates and increased costs in other areas, a safer limit is no more than one-and-three-quarters times the annual income. The matter is necessarily one that must be decided by each family. It is wise to stay closer to the lower end of the bracket if family operating expenses are high, if one is saving to give children a college education, if the down payment on the house will be small, and if chances for increased income are slight. On the other hand, if one can afford a sizable down payment, if his income will probably increase, if present living expenses are relatively light, and if he has few

serious financial responsibilities for the future of the family, he can probably afford to pay more for housing.

Shelter costs should be calculated to include *all* the expenses relative to maintaining a home. If one rents a house or an apartment his costs are rather fixed. If it seems desirable to buy a home, the following expenses must be included:

Payments on the mortgage plus interest charges.
Taxes.
Insurance.
Expenses for heating, lighting, and water.
Services for garbage removal.
Maintenance of house and yard.
Costs of repairs and remodeling.

The initial price of a house should also have added to it some of the fees that will probably be levied against the buyer. The advice and appraisals of trained people will cost money. The actual purchase may involve legal documents, a search of previous history, and certain permits that require fees.

The person with a realistic approach to homeownership is prepared for seasonal expenses and also for those that are unexpected. Mowing the lawn in the summer, removing the snow in the winter, a leak in the roof, or a broken pipe can all be expensive projects. Also, certain equipment may not be included in the initial cost of the house—for example, storm windows, screens, lawn mower, garbage cans, and so on.

Few families can afford to buy a house outright with a full payment of cash money, nor would it always be advisable to do so. In some cases there are advantages to partial financing of the purchase of a home. However, a down payment is required and this should be as large as the family can afford while still retaining reserve funds. The balance of the cost of the house is covered by a *mortgage*, which is, in effect, a loan. Various types of institutions negotiate mortgage loans—including savings banks, commercial banks, insurance companies, mortgage bankers, savings and loan associations, and special associations.

The Federal Housing Authority insures loans made by approved lending agencies when they meet with certain regulations that include some specifications for the type of home that can be insured. The Veterans Administration also guarantees up to $12,500 of a loan made to a serviceman borrowing from qualified agencies. On loans made with FHA or VA approval, charges and fees are regulated by the government. It is important, however, for the consumer to shop around for suitable terms when financing the purchase of a home. Interest rates on the amount of money borrowed will vary and the mortgage may run for different periods of time. Of course, the larger the down payment, the less money one will have to borrow, and interest charges will be less. Also, if the mortgage can be paid off in a shorter period, the total interest will be less. It is to the advantage of the purchaser, therefore, to set up a small mortgage and pay it off as quickly as possible, even though the monthly payments are larger.

There are several other aspects of the mortgage that should be of concern to the prospective buyer. Some include prepayment allowances so that the mortgage may be paid up sooner than anticipated if the homeowner is able to do so. Others give the owner the right to borrow additional money for remodeling.

In addition to the payments on the mortgage, one should remember that expenses for owning a home will include other items listed earlier. It is important to estimate *all* of these expenses in a realistic calculation of the cost of buying a home.

2

Where to Start

It is interesting to note the dictionary definitions of words such as *shelter*, *dwelling*, *house*, and *home*. Most of these words emphasize the physical aspects of protection, but the word *home* has more inclusive implications. One dictionary defines home as "a place or abode of affection, peace and rest; a congenial abiding place." It also uses this word to distinguish between "denote" and "connote" as follows: ". . . thus home *denotes* the place where one lives with one's family, but it usually *connotes* comfort, intimacy, and privacy." The ideas suggested indicate an atmosphere and a pattern of relationships that are more than a physical environment. This is a good beginning, but a home should also be a place that enriches the spirit, stimulates the mind, and encourages creative growth.

No matter what the physical environment may be, the atmosphere of the home expresses something about the people who live in it. The first visit to a person's home may be quite a revelation and may explain certain facets of a particular personality. We almost always feel as though we know a person better after having visited his home. When we travel to other areas or foreign lands we are usually grateful for an opportunity to visit homes because they tell us so much about people and their way of life.

Beyond creating the spirit or the atmosphere of the home, the homemaker is also faced with the problem of establishing a household that is truly functional. Today the homemaker is also a wage earner in many cases. Electrification and automation have changed our way of life and there are those who would have us think that various appliances and prepared foods have freed the homemaker to do little more than push buttons and open packages. Such is not the case. If anything, modern life makes greater demands upon the homemaker but in a different way. True, new conveniences have released her from much of the drudgery of managing a household. Although she no longer needs to scrub clothes on a washboard, new methods and new ideas have brought with them a host of new responsibilities and new chores.

Improved standards of living have brought more demands on family income and the wider consumer market makes each choice more difficult. The intelligent use of income and the other business of homemaking not only take time and energy but also require a background of consumer information. As just one example, in the realm of textiles a homemaker at the turn of the century had to choose between cotton, linen, silk, or wool, all of which had been used for centuries and which presented no new problems. Today the homemaker is faced with a myriad of fibers, fabrics, and finishes that require careful selection and special handling.

The modern family needs a special kind of household, which is planned and equipped to meet its needs. In view of the importance of the task and the problems involved, it is wise to work on some kind of plan, which is based on certain goals and objectives.

Almost everyone approaches the problem of setting up a new household with limitations of one sort or another—space, money, time, or location, to mention only a few. The project usually requires energy and imagination, but it is a creative experience that should be fun and it should be exciting. Above all, it requires an appreciation of the fact that the decisions that must be made will have a keen influence on personal and family life.

The relationship between the individual and his home carries with it important implications for the future structure and character of our society. These brief observations on the meaning of *home* should make it clear that the goals and objectives that people establish when setting up a home are important factors in patterns of family and community relationships.

The Six Basic Questions

One can begin to formulate a plan by asking six basic questions. Frequently the answers to these questions will be interdependent, or one will pose more of a problem than another. Yet a bit of clear analysis of each one will help the homemaker to embark on this important project with a feeling of reassurance.

1. Who will live in the home?
2. Where will the home be?
3. Will this home be a permanent or a temporary residence?
4. What should the home look like?
5. How much will it cost?
6. Where and how should one shop for the best values?

WHO WILL LIVE IN THE HOME? Of course if one plans to live alone, his own tastes, needs, interests, and activities are the chief concern; but when one plans to share a home, it must be everyone's home. Each person may have to compromise or sacrifice in some respects, but it is only through mutual consideration that there can be any satisfactory solution to this problem.

Individual tastes, likes, and dislikes must be carefully discussed. There may also be certain needs that should be considered. For example, if one member of a family has the kind of career that requires bringing work home from the office, the home must be planned to provide adequate space and equipment.

A young couple about to be married would probably have common interests in certain things, such as music, reading, and watching television. However, each one may have individual interests for which special provisions should be made. A young man with an interest in a hobby or in a collection of some kind and a young woman with another hobby of her own should each have the necessary space and facilities to maintain their interests. Hobbies such as photography, crafts, sewing, or music may require special areas in the home.

How one plans to entertain should also be considered. Some people prefer small, intimate groups whereas others prefer large parties. The provision for both kinds of entertaining would probably make some difference in planning. Relatives or friends who live out of town may require plans for overnight guests.

At the beginning a young couple might not be influenced by long-range plans for a family, but they would certainly want to discuss this matter in terms of planning a home. If they hoped to have children as soon as possible it would probably make a difference in their needs for space.

WHERE WILL THE HOME BE? One may be able to make some plans before he has an actual place to live. If he is fairly sure about the type of home he wants, he might begin to collect some silverware, china, and linens before he even starts to look for a home. Before he does much more than that, however, he should know where he will live.

The actual geographical location may make a difference in the kind of home one establishes. It may determine whether or not he will live in a private house or in an apartment.

The architectural style of a house may be an important factor in how it is to be furnished. Although it is not always necessary to follow an obvious line, the structural features of the home, especially in a private house, may lend themselves better to one style or another.

With an actual floor plan of the house or apartment drawn according to scale one can plan for the most efficient use of space and map out the areas of activity. It is important to know the actual measurements of doorways and windows, the height of ceilings and the size of closets. It is also important to know the exposures and to see the rooms at different times during the day to study the kind and amount of natural light that each one gets.

As soon as one knows where he will live, he should find out exactly what is provided by the landlord or agent. For example, many new houses are not equipped with a refrigerator, window shades or blinds, and some lighting fixtures. Screens, storm windows, and landscaping must also be considered.

Some apartment houses have restrictions on the use of certain appliances, such as washing machines and air conditioners. There may also be provisions in the contract concerning the use of wallpaper, colored paint, and pictures and mirrors. Frequently in such contracts the wall must be restored to its original condition if any of these means of decoration have been used.

WILL THIS HOME BE A PERMANENT OR A TEMPORARY RESIDENCE? One's plans for the future will certainly influence the way he furnishes his home. Many young people plan to rent houses or apartments until they can afford to buy their own. Some start in small homes or apartments with the idea of moving to larger quarters in the future. In any event, whether the home is to be con-sidered temporary or permanent will make a difference in some decisions. In furnishing a temporary home, each major investment should be considered with a view toward how the item might be used under other circumstances. For example, it would be unwise to invest in wall-to-wall carpeting for the living room of an apartment in which one expects to live for a short period. He might, however, want to purchase a good-quality room-sized rug that could be cut down to fit a smaller room later on. A folding table or a card table might serve as a dining table in a small apartment. If one knew that eventually he would want to furnish a dining room, it might be wiser to wait rather than buy an extension table for use in the apartment. Items such as upholstered chairs, tables, lamps, accessories, and beds could probably be used in either a temporary or a permanent home. Floor coverings, curtains, and draperies present more of a problem.

It is usually a mistake to buy cheap things for a temporary home with the idea of selling them or throwing them away when one moves. Corners can be cut on some needs, but it is more sensible to invest in good furnishings that will be adaptable to different situations. This requires careful evaluation and good judgment.

WHAT SHOULD THE HOME LOOK LIKE? A home reflects many things about the personalities of the people who live in it. Naturally it should be interesting, but homes, like clothes, should provide a background; they should never submerge people. Sometimes a very unusual home becomes such a fetish that it absorbs the people who live in it and becomes the object of all their interests, activities, money and—unfortunately—their conversation.

A home should be functional as well as beautiful. It is important to keep purposes in mind when making each decision. The manner in which the home works for those who live in it as well as the aesthetic satisfactions derived from it will provide the yardstick for measuring success.

Depending on the type of furnishings selected, the colors chosen, and the way the furniture and accessories are arranged, a home will express some theme or mood. As one thinks of possible adjectives that might be used, some may be more appealing than others.

Such a list might include *formal*, *sophisticated*, *elegant*, *gay*, *casual*, *exotic*, *exciting*, *restful*, *quaint*, *cheerful*. A room may have more than one of these characteristics. It may be formal and elegant or sophisticated and exotic.

Although some people have very definite preferences for a particular style and know exactly what they want, others are somewhat more vague about their ideas. Often they find that several themes are appealing and that it is difficult to select those that will blend well. Is it possible to plan a room that is both formal and casual or one that is both exciting and restful? Discretion should be used, because trying to express too many ideas in one room may result in a disturbing hodge-podge that spells nothing except confusion. A considerable amount of money, time, and energy is invested in furnishing a home. If it is to be thoroughly satisfying some preliminary efforts must be made to avoid mistakes.

If one's ideas about what he really wants are indefinite, he can sharpen his tastes by a little analysis of his likes and dislikes. Certainly some styles and colors are more appealing than others. One can begin by clipping pictures from magazines, including definitely disliked qualities as well as the preferred ones. The pictures should be separated into "yes," "no," and "maybe" categories. With a fairly large collection, one should go through each group and make a list of the desirable characteristics and another of those that are not desirable, applying as many adjectives as possible to each illustration. A list should also be made of the colors and textures preferred. Special little notes should be made about particular features such as furniture arrangements, window treatments, or accessories. Then one should visit a few department stores and even museum exhibits with a notebook in hand, and jot down special observations.

Putting ideas in writing helps to clarify them. On sifting through all these notes, one will begin to find the common denominators of all the ideas that are appealing. The pictures and notes in the "yes" category will undoubtedly have certain points in common. Possibly they will have a simplicity or an elegance or a certain type of gay charm. There may be particular colors and types of patterns that keep recurring. The "no" group will also have common characteristics. Are they mostly cluttered or garish or perhaps too formal?

This procedure will make one far more observing and much more discriminating.

When tastes are somewhat narrowed down, one should begin to probe those styles that he likes. It helps to know something about all the styles. The survey presented later in this text will help the student get started, but further research and a deeper understanding of two or three styles should prove to be very useful.

Once the purpose is clearly in mind it is time to formulate more definite plans for a budget, room arrangements, and color schemes. This book is aimed toward the preparation for these steps.

When one is actually about to furnish a home, the tasks will be much easier if all the floor plans, measurements, swatches, color chips, pamphlets, and specifications are well organized in a notebook and some sort of filing portfolio or loose-leaf arrangement of large envelopes.

HOW MUCH WILL IT COST? It is, of course, impossible to name a certain amount of money necessary for establishing a home. Nor is it possible to propose any one budget formula that will suit all needs. It is possible, however, to point out certain principles and guides that will help to set up a financial plan.

How much money one will need depends on his plans and his tastes. When people are planning to buy a house, it is usually recommended that they shop in a price range that does not exceed two-and-a-half times the annual income. Thus a family with an income of $8,000 a year would not want to purchase a house costing more than $20,000. Some authorities believe that two-and-a-half times the annual income is far too high an amount, especially if the family has an unsteady income or if they have long-range financial goals, such as sending children to college. The maintenance costs of financing the house would depend on the size of the down payment. If the down payment were relatively small, the carrying costs of the house might be a heavy drain on the income. Rent for a house or an apartment should be no more than 25 per cent of the monthly income.

Costs of shelter must be considered in conjunction with various other costs that may or may not be included in regular payments. Taxes, insurance, heating, and lighting may be high in some areas and may have to be added to the basic costs of shelter. The expenses of commuting or of owning a car will also be influenced by where one lives and should be considered in conjunction with the costs of the home. Maintenance is another expense that should not be disregarded.

Income is also used as a guide for determining how much one will need for furnishing a home. An amount equal to one half the annual family income is usually recommended. The young couple with the $8,000 income should have saved $4,000 for furnishing their home. This means that the cost of furnishings would be about one fourth the cost of a house if they were to buy one.

Realism points out that many young people start out with far less than a desirable amount of money. Some depend in part on relatives and wedding presents to furnish their homes. Others buy furnishings on the installment plan. Still others buy some essentials—a table, chairs, a bed, and a few utensils—and plan to furnish as they can afford to do so. But one young couple with about $600 spent $300 for a dinette set, a bed, and a chest of drawers, and the other $300 for sterling-silver place settings, though there was not one stick of furniture in the living room!

Naturally it is better to have an adequate amount of money saved before one begins to buy furnishings. It means having the kind of a home that will meet needs and be a source of satisfaction. Depending on relatives and friends to furnish a home has serious disadvantages. Many young brides receive six or eight salad bowls as wedding presents. While it is nice to have a variety, this is not the primary concern in setting up a household. In other words, one can't always depend on receiving the necessary items.

Spending plans and the financial aspects of furnishing a home are discussed in more detail in Chapter 19.

WHERE AND HOW SHOULD ONE SHOP FOR THE BEST VALUES? Because even a very modest home requires the investment of a considerable amount of money, it is important to use the available money wisely and to the best advantage.

Perhaps the first caution should be to deal with reliable merchants. A store or a company that takes pride in the goodwill it establishes with the public caters to satisfied customers. In many areas of furnishings it is extremely difficult to judge quality and one must rely on the honesty of the dealer for information about the products. For example, if a salesman insists that an upholstered chair has a hardwood frame, there is no way of checking this fact.

It is not always easy to determine how reliable a business concern is until one has had some experience in dealing with it. Usually stores and manufacturers that spend large sums of money promoting their names are interested in maintaining good public relations and will stand behind faulty merchandise, but this generality is no true guarantee for the consumer. Besides, there are many small business concerns that are thoroughly dependable though they do not invest in wide advertising campaigns.

The decision about where to shop must rest with the buyer. One should have a feeling of confidence in the dealer, who may even be a most helpful adviser. The buyer ought to avoid merchants who make a practice of pressuring their customers into buying things. A good merchant will want a customer to take time to think over his decisions before he actually makes purchases. One should beware of any dealer who makes all sorts of verbal claims but who refuses to put them in writing or to make any notations on the sales receipts about the information he gives.

Actual guarantees of durability present many difficulties. An item of furnishing may stand up very well under normal, proper use and care but not if it is mistreated. Just as the consumer has a right to expect honest information about merchandise he must also be reasonable in his demands for guarantees. The family that allows the children to roller skate on the carpeting can hardly expect the manufacturer to be responsible for signs of wear and tear, unless of course he makes the claim that his product can withstand such violent treatment.

A price policy that is very flexible does not tend to inspire confidence. Price tags that are not clearly marked or a salesman who keeps reducing the price while the customer is hesitating should make one immediately skeptical. Bargains are always exciting, but unless one is sure that he has really found one, he should be very wary.

The wide choice available in today's market is a blessing, but it also presents many problems for the consumer. Intelligent buying requires study and planning. Because a home is such an individual matter, there is no one source that can answer all questions or give all the necessary information. It is to one's advantage to qualify himself to make the best choices for his needs. The following sources of information may be useful:

1. *Newspapers and Magazines.* Most newspapers feature new and interesting ideas on home decoration during the week and in Sunday supplements, and many family-type magazines have monthly decorating articles. Some of the magazines have excellent bulletin services that offer useful information.

Certain magazines specialize in the decorative arts and provide a wealth of information and ideas. These, too, frequently have bulletin services and facilities for handling special requests for readers. Special magazines published for brides contain particularly useful material on establishing homes.

2. *Extension Services.* Most states have an agricultural extension service that publishes a variety of pamphlets and booklets. Some of these will be helpful in establishing and maintaining a home. One should check the list of offerings in his state and request the material that might be helpful.

3. *Local Libraries.* There is a wide variety of books on many phases of home planning, building, and decoration. One should find out what the local library has to offer. It may not have a complete selection, but the range of available information may be pleasantly surprising.

4. *The National Design Center (415 East 53rd Street, New York City 10022).* This institution maintains exhibits related to decoration and displays products of many leading manufacturers of home furnishings. Its information bureau has an extensive file of information about products and distributors and will answer questions about these by mail if one cannot visit the center.

5. *Retail Stores.* Many stores that handle home furnishings maintain trained consultants. Large stores have interior designers on their staffs. There may be no charge to customers for some of the services; in other instances, there may be a flat fee or charges based on a prorated scale. One should find out all he can about the stores in his locality and what they have to offer.

6. *Decorating Services.* An interior designer is not required to have a license, but a good one who meets a high standard of professional

training will probably belong to a professional group that limits its membership to qualified people. There are two such groups:

American Institute of Interior Designers (AID)
673 Fifth Avenue, N.Y.C. 10022
National Society of Interior Designers (NSID)
157 West 57th Street, N.Y.C. 10019

Both organizations have local chapters throughout the country.

Professionals use different methods for charging fees. In consulting a decorator, one must be sure to work with a reliable person and to understand fully all the terms of the contract. Both professional organizations listed will provide names of their members upon request.

The intelligent consumer should become acquainted with the publications of two organizations that attempt to provide unbiased information and evaluations of products currently available. Both of these organizations strive to assist consumers in making wise decisions and both operate independent of industry, business, or government. They are

Consumers Union
256 Washington Street
Mount Vernon, N.Y. 10550
Consumers' Research, Inc.
Washington, N.J., 07882

Local libraries usually subscribe to the publications of these organizations.

Furnishing as a Continuing Process

It must be pointed out that although our discussion up to this point has been concerned mainly with the problems of establishing a new household, furnishing and maintaining a home is actually a continuing process. Even the first home is not always completely furnished all at once, and plans often provide for additions over periods of a few years. By the time furnishing is completed, some replacements may be necessary or the homeowner may be ready to revise a color scheme or a special area. Eventually he may want to replace some or all of the major items. Sometimes, when children have grown and moved to homes of their own, parents find it more suitable to move to smaller quarters or to redesign or redecorate their homes.

One doesn't usually get rid of everything all at once in refurnishing. In many instances there are sentimental attachments to certain objects or there may be others that are still too good or too useful to sell or to give away.

The basic principles of furnishing apply to refurnishing and redecorating. Having a plan is equally important, if not more so, because of the possessions that you already have. It is not always easy to create a new setting that will make them look as if they really belong. The plan should be worked around the things to be kept. If possible, these should be separated from the items to be replaced and then visualized in a new setting. New colors in slipcovers or upholstery, new wall colors, different arrangements, different accessories, and a creative imagination will all help the situation. Sometimes upholstered furniture can be redesigned and rugs can be cut down. A problem often makes the project more interesting if it is approached with a creative attitude. One woman who wanted to refurnish her living room in the modern style also wanted to keep a beautiful oriental rug that had been chosen to blend with her traditional-style furnishings. She selected her new furnishings with careful attention to colors and textures. She planned her color scheme and chose her accessories with equal care. The final result was a magnificent modern room in which the rug was perfectly at home.

All new additions and replacements must be chosen with great care and skill. New fashions and fads in furnishings may be enticing. With some of them it may be possible to create exciting new effects, but with others the lovely existing effects may be spoiled. One has to exercise a discriminating taste to use the fashions that are just right.

Section II
Design

Perception and the ability to enjoy expression depend, to a large extent, on the degree to which we have developed a sensitivity to people, ideas, and physical surroundings. Quite probably, the home atmosphere in which we began to notice sensations was an important factor in determining our early reactions. In the process of growing up, as our interests, attitudes, likes, and dislikes became more firmly established, our personalities also became more individual. Consequently, we obviously have different ideas about beauty, and it isn't possible for one person to impose his values on others.

Learning in the field of the arts, therefore, is not a matter of accepting standards set up by other people. It is instead a process of becoming more perceptive and of developing one's own ability for expression.

A study of history shows that we have high esteem for any society that has shown sensitivity to beauty in daily living. Much primitive art intrigues connoisseurs and collectors because it represents honest and uninhibited expression in simple objects. We admire the appreciation of beauty that permeates daily living in many areas of the Orient. The ability of the Japanese to create exquisite compositions with a few simple flowers, or even weeds, reflects an inherent appreciation that has been developed over many years. In the Orient one pauses a moment during the day to admire the form and texture of a teacup. Or a "sand garden," merely a pile of sand that is formed to create lovely effects with light and shadow, may grace an empty courtyard. The Oriental child is frequently trained to appreciate beauty in simple objects and so enriches his daily life.

In the Western world we have been accused not only of separating true art appreciation from the simple experiences of everyday living, but also of using ineffectual methods of teaching the enjoyment of art. The ubiquitous coloring books and crayons that are so often

3
Design
Expression

given to young children have been berated as stifling to natural expression. Certainly most of them do very little to develop an appreciation of true beauty.

There is little doubt that we are becoming more aware of the importance of design in all phases of our daily life. Automobiles, type-writers, and telephones as well as kitchen appliances and numerous other articles have undergone radical changes in the past few years. Not all of the changes show true artistic progress, but the trend indicates that we want the more mundane objects to be pleasing to the eye as well as functional.

What Is Design?

The term *design* is used in many ways to convey different meanings. We might speak of the design of a salad bowl or the design of a city. In a broad sense, the word implies selec-tion and organization for some specific pur-pose or intention. Thus we might also think of the design of a musical composition, in which notes and tones are selected and arranged to create a pattern of sounds that will have a particular effect on the listener.

In the visual arts the designer works with lines, forms, colors, and textures. He selects and arranges these elements to suit his pur-pose, which might be to create something that is purely functional, or purely ornamental, or both functional and beautiful. In doing so he expresses various ideas, moods, or values, and his expressions evoke some response in the viewer.

Unity must be a basic factor in any con-sideration of design. As we look at the salad bowl, we see it as a whole or a unit. The rela-tionship of form, color, and texture produce the design. We look at the design of a house in terms of its relation to the terrain. We also look at each room in relation to the whole house. But we also see the design of the room itself as a unit. Thus, the meaning of the word *design* depends upon what we are talking about, but we might say that design refers to a com-position produced by the integrating of various elements.

Because we are individuals and react to the expressions of others in such different ways, any attempt to define good design is indeed an extremely risky business. The very expres-siveness of all forms of art is, in itself, a matter of beauty. But not every individual is percep-tive to all kinds of expression. Another very broad term, *taste*, represents what one accepts or rejects. Over the centuries, the popular tastes in what represents true beauty have varied and fluctuated, and different cultures have accepted certain modes of expression as representative. Some have emphasized the spiritual expression afforded through art; others have emphasized craftsmanship and techniques. Functionalism, which is such an important factor in contemporary design, represents a philosophy of art. There is prob-ably no universal appreciation and acceptance of any one form of beauty. Neither are there any simple, basic formulas or rigid rules en-compassing all design. We could not, nor would we want to, regulate expression in such a way.

It would be difficult to compile a list of one hundred examples of perfect designs, in-cluding buildings, paintings, sculptures, tex-tiles, and ceramics, that would be acceptable to all art connoisseurs and critics. Many master-pieces have survived centuries of general ac-claim and appreciation, yet almost every one has also had its adversaries. But popular ac-claim cannot be considered a criterion. We have innumerable examples of artistic expres-sion that were rejected by contemporaries of the artist but that are generally accepted as masterpieces today. We also have many exam-ples of "art" that were widely accepted by the populace but that are considered atrocities in this era.

Authorities disagree with each other on al-most every aspect of art, and certainly they will disagree on any analysis of it. How do we decide for ourselves what art forms we like or dislike? Perhaps we admire the same quali-ties in artistic expression that we do in people —sincerity, honesty, courage, and a bit of mysticism. We do not admire those who flaunt tradition for the sake of change, but we accept changes. Intelligent people are open-minded and eager for ideas that represent con-structive and creative thinking. Expressions of such qualities are more likely to be accepted as art and survive the tests of time.

There are certain facts that would be diffi-cult to deny—for example, the concept of optical illusion, the emotional impact of color, and the expressive qualities of textures. But when one begins to analyze the plan or the organization of these elements, it is difficult to draw a sharp dividing line between fact and opinion. No one, therefore, can tell anyone else what he should accept or what he should reject. A design that appeals to one person may be distasteful to his neighbor. But the more familiar one becomes with the language of design, the more pleasure he will gain from those expressions that are honest and sincere. There is a basic truth in something that is really beautiful, but one must develop his own powers of observation and discrimination to appreciate the message that the artist attempts to convey.

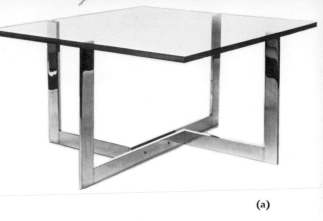

(a)

Types of Design

There can be no meaningful classification that would be useful in helping us to evaluate all designs. We must learn to judge the expressiveness of any design by the way all of the elements are blended to create the total effect. It is not possible to study line without color and texture. Neither is it possible to ignore the effects that color and texture have on each other. A small area in a bright color and a shiny texture will appear quite different in another, dull color and rough texture. Therefore, the overall design effects result from the intermingling of the elements, and we must learn to understand the effects these elements have upon one another.

We may be more aware of the inspiration of a design if we understand the methods a designer uses to express his ideas. In a very general way we might divide designs into five broad categories: structural, naturalistic, stylized, geometric, abstract. Within these categories there is much overlapping and it is frequently impossible to draw a hairline mark of division.

(b)

STRUCTURAL DESIGNS. In this type of design the structure determines the form of the design, and enrichment comes from the materials used. Much of our modern design is of this type, with form dictated by function. There is little, if any, applied ornament.

FIGURE 3-1 Structural designs with emphasis on form, texture, and color. (a) (*Courtesy of Jens Risom Design, Inc.*) **(b)** (*Courtesy of Dunbar/Dux. Designed by Roger L. Sprunger. Photo by Wesley Pusey*) **(c)** (*Courtesy of Thayer Coggin, Inc. Designed by Milo Baughman*)

(c)

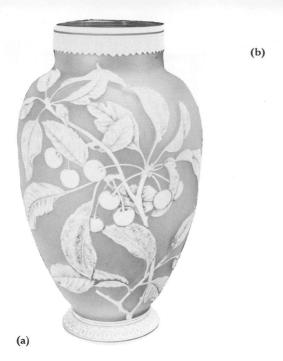

(b)

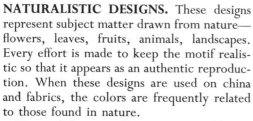

(a)

NATURALISTIC DESIGNS.

NATURALISTIC DESIGNS. These designs represent subject matter drawn from nature—flowers, leaves, fruits, animals, landscapes. Every effort is made to keep the motif realistic so that it appears as an authentic reproduction. When these designs are used on china and fabrics, the colors are frequently related to those found in nature.

Many different effects are possible in naturalistic design. Pastoral scenes or landscapes are useful for creating perspectives. Some motifs are arranged to form stripes, blocks, or medallions. The designs lend themselves to either formal or informal themes. But one must use discretion about how and where to use naturalistic motifs. Roses splashed all over the bedroom draperies may be charming, but it is quite another matter to have them on one's dinner plate as a background for steak and vegetables, even though the plate itself may be very attractive.

STYLIZED DESIGNS.

STYLIZED DESIGNS. One can recognize the natural sources of a stylized motif, but the design makes no pretense at actual representation. Flowers, leaves, animals, and figures are favorite themes. They are simplified, exaggerated, rearranged, or even distorted to achieve the purposes of the design. Certain natural aspects may be emphasized out of proportion to make those particular features more pronounced. The coloring of stylized designs may also be unconventional.

FIGURE 3-2   Naturalistic designs attempt true representations in different ways. (a) Vase. (*Courtesy of Cooper-Hewitt Museum of Design, Smithsonian Institute*) **(b) "Wild Rose" wallpaper.** (*Courtesy of Scalamandrè*) **(c) Wallpaper.** (*Courtesy of Cooper-Hewitt Museum of Design, Smithsonian Institute*)

(c)

(a)

(b)

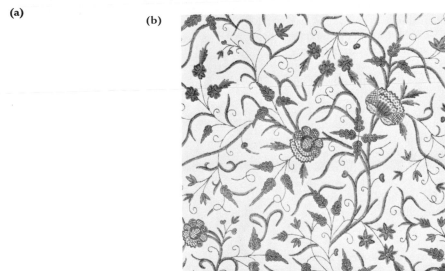

FIGURE 3-3 Stylized designs are old and new. (a) "Pop Art" area rug. (*Designed by Dorothy Liebes for Bigelow Sanford, Inc.*) (b) Crewel bedspread. (*Courtesy of Scalamandrè*)

GEOMETRIC DESIGNS. Ancient civilizations realized the design values of purely geometric forms, including circles, triangles, and rectangles. Stripes, plaids, and polka dots, as well as the intricate lacy patterns of the Muhammadans, are all based on geometric forms. Moorish designs used the geometric theme with a high degree of skill and refinement. The Greeks were also skillful in the use of this type of design, but more in border patterns than in all-over patterns.

ABSTRACT DESIGNS. Many abstract patterns are based on geometric forms, and some writers do not distinguish between geometric and abstract designs. Yet *abstract* implies an element of impressionism and a greater freedom than is found in most geometric designs. The shapes and patterns, although derived from geometry, are less rigid and formal than in the popular conception of a geometrical design.

(a)

(b)

What Price Design?

Fortunately the gap between cost and good design in home furnishings is becoming narrower. Of course one must expect differences in styling and in quality between very-low-cost merchandise and high-priced items, but that does not mean that it is impossible to find both good design and good quality in the less expensive categories. Many manufacturers of furnishings in the low and medium-price ranges have made sincere efforts to improve both design and quality. Some have hired well-known designers who are interested in improving the general level of design in mass-produced articles for the home. We have seen the results of these efforts in many areas—especially in fabrics, glassware, flatware, and dinnerware.

It is interesting to compare designs at different price levels by browsing in all types of shops, ranging from the low-cost variety and five-and-ten-cent stores to the more exclusive department stores. There is quite a difference in the general types of design, but it is possible to create very interesting effects on a low budget by choosing carefully from the less expensive items.

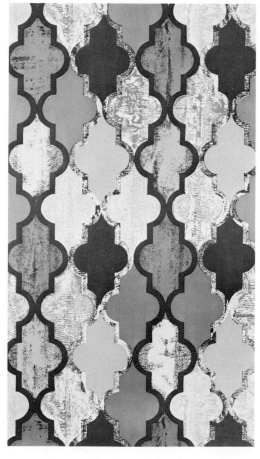

FIGURE 3-4 Geometrics coordinate with current interests in Mediterranean influences. (a) Floor covering. (*Courtesy of Robbins Floor Products, Inc.*) (b) "Almeria Grille." (*Courtesy of Scalamandrè*)

FIGURE 3-5 An abstract design makes less rigid use of geometric forms. Room setting designed by Tom Woods, A.I.D., features a Dorothy Liebes rug, "Blue Moon." (*Courtesy of Bigelow-Sanford, Inc.*)

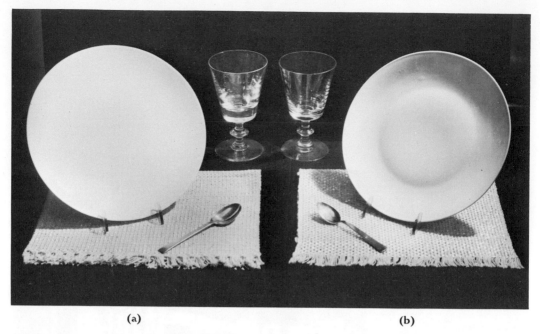

(a)   (b)

FIGURE 3-6 Designs at different price levels may be similar but not identical. Both plates are plain white; both placemats are pink and silver. The total cost of the four items in group A was $17.99. The less expensive items in group B cost $7.54. Differences in craftsmanship are responsible for differences in cost.

Figure 3-6 shows table appointments that are similar in theme. Both groups have plain white china, pink-and-silver place mats, and simple designs in both glassware and flatware. In group A the total cost of the four items shown was $17.99; in group B the total cost was $7.54. If the place settings were completed and the tables set for eight people there would be a difference of several hundred dollars. Of course in the more expensive group there are the fine textures and beauty that often come with very fine quality—for instance, the lovely gleam of the crystal and the beautiful patina of the silverware. But the less expensive setting does not represent cheap ostentation, nor is it obviously of poor quality and design. Neither does it seem to imitate a skill beyond its reach.

It is easier to find good design at budget prices in styles that are simple and free of excessive ornamentation. The pretense of elaborate elegance on a low budget will often achieve only pathetic effects. Differences in quality become more obvious in the wide variety of cheap imitations. There are some things that are expensive to produce and there is no way to copy them exactly at a lower cost, though many attempts are made to do just that. A cheap imitation of a fine, hand-cut crystal bowl, a beautiful silk brocade fabric, or a fine Oriental rug will not usually satisfy the discriminating taste.

Shopping for good design on a budget means that one must be particularly conscious of quality construction, and it is important to invest in durability. Some inexpensive furniture and floor coverings may have excellent designs, but if quality has been sacrificed for styling the investment will yield poor returns. Serviceability of some articles depends on high-quality materials and high standards of construction. It is especially important to give design and quality equal emphasis in selecting such items.

It has been pointed out that the relationships between the components of a design give it an individuality. It is therefore impossible to look at any particular design as a unit or a whole without considering the pattern of interrelationships between lines, forms, colors, and textures. However, because each of these elements contributes something in its own way to the overall effect, a discussion of them separately may help one to understand the total effect.

Line

Although most designs are composed of many lines, there is often a predominance of one type that contributes to the character of the design. Lines compel our eyes to follow them. Strangely enough, simple lines also evoke an emotional response and we associate certain feelings with different types of line. This is an important point to remember when trying to create a theme or a mood in any room.

The basic lines include:

VERTICAL. An erect, upward line expresses a forcefulness or a rigidity. It is likely to be formal and austere. A predominance of vertical lines is often found in churches and cathedrals.

HORIZONTAL. The sideways line suggests repose and relaxation. In a landscape or a calm seascape, the restful mood of the painting may be set by predominating horizontal lines.

DIAGONAL. Because the angle or the direction of the oblique line may take on many variations, this type of line is more dynamic in that it directs the eye more forcefully. Compare diagonal lines that approach the

4

Elements

of Design

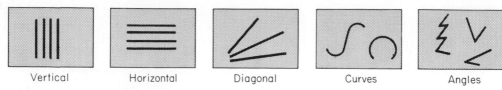

| Vertical | Horizontal | Diagonal | Curves | Angles |

FIGURE 4-1 Basic lines express different ideas or moods.

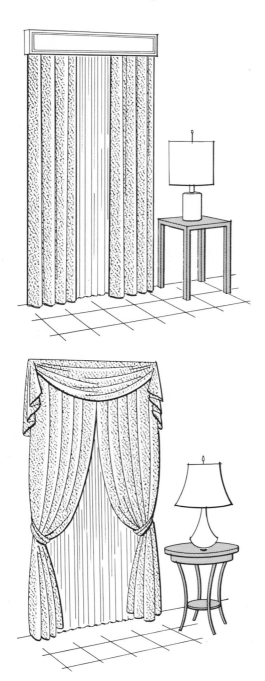

FIGURE 4-2 Different effects are achieved by straight and curved lines.

vertical and the horizontal. They tend to take on the characteristics of each. Or compare the right and left diagonals. They seem to suggest forces pushing upward or downward.

CURVES. The infinite variety of curved lines makes them useful in expressing many different moods or ideas. The circle, or any full, voluptuous curve, may give a feeling of gaiety or buoyancy as, for example, in a wallpaper with a motif of light, iridescent bubbles or a circus scene with balloons and clowns wearing polka dots and pompons. However, baroque designs in dark colors and heavy textures may give the effect of elegance or even opulence.

A softer type of curved line is found in the S curve, which is more likely to express gracefulness and refinement. These curves provide interest without being too dynamic or too energetic.

ANGLES. Here again, a wide variety of angular lines may be used for different effects. They are likely to be forceful, dynamic, and sometimes disturbing. They may also lend an exotic quality. The angular diagonal has an air of excitement.

Line combinations in the structural features of a room, the furniture designs, the accessories, and the patterns must be carefully considered to achieve the effects you desire. A composition with too much of any one type of line may become uninteresting or unpleasant, but emphasis on one type helps to promote the theme. Thus, in a room meant for relaxation and repose, horizontal lines should predominate.

One may want to emphasize certain structural lines in a room—such as doorways, archways, dados, panels, and moldings. Windows that are long and narrow will, of course, emphasize vertical lines unless a planned treatment is used to produce a different effect.

Both structural and decorative lines in interior design contribute to the theme. Some

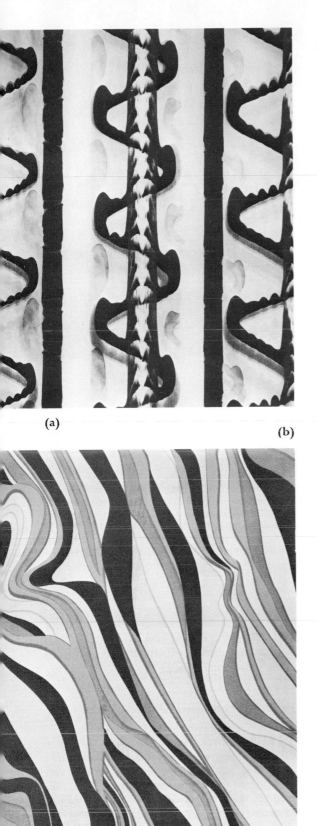

(a)

(b)

(c)

FIGURE 4-3 Fabric designs emphasize lines to create moods. (a) "Bolero." (*Designed by Timo Sarpaneva for Jack Lenor Larsen, Inc.*); (b) "Bojangles." (*Designed by Larsen Design Studio for Jack Lenor Larsen, Inc.*); (c) "Happiness." (*Designed by Larsen Design Studio for Jack Lenor Larsen, Inc.*)

(a)

FIGURE 4-4   (a) The DuPont-A.I.D. room for the Cooper Union Museum of Decorative Arts designed by Eugene Bell, A.I.D., uses various lines to blend the old and the new. The Early American heritage of the furniture is shown against a bold blue and white flamestitch print by Brunschwig and Fils and snowy white nylon carpeting. (*Courtesy of DuPont Textile Fibers*); (b) A masculine appearance is achieved by emphasis on straight lines. (*Courtesy of DuPont Textile Fibers*); (c) Diagonal lines emphasize a wall and lend a vibrant note to a room that uses line as an important element of design. (*Courtesy of Monsanto Company*)

furniture is composed all of straight lines; other types combine straight and curved lines. Curves in furniture design range from soft, graceful lines to full and voluptuous lines. Frequently, straight pieces seem to spell formality; softer curves introduce gracefulness; whereas fuller curves are more exuberant.

Patterned fabrics may be used to introduce emphatic lines. Stripes, plaids, and geometrics might be used for a severe or dramatic effect that would be difficult to achieve with a graceful floral scroll pattern.

Sometimes the mood of a room can be varied by very simple changes in important lines. One should experiment with draperies hang-ing straight at the windows, or try tying them back to form graceful, curved lines. Drum-shaped or bell-shaped lampshades may also make quite a difference.

Form, Area, and Shape

In a very broad sense, the form, area, or shape of a design refers to space relationships. Of course the forms are defined by lines and the preceding discussion of lines will also apply to those lines that mark off the divisions of spaces. One should remember also that the elements of color and texture will influence

(b)

(c)

area and must always be considered in relationship to it.

The first mass or area to be considered is the enclosure of the whole house or apartment. Interesting concepts of spatial relationships are evident in modern residential architecture where there is a conscious effort to design the house in terms of the geographical terrain. The desire to relate the interior to the exterior has led to the extensive use of window walls and huge picture windows. This trend has found disfavor among another group of architects, who decry the lack of privacy. One answer has been the use of lacy grille patterns in façades to let in light and air. Those on the inside can see out, but outsiders cannot see in. Apparently there is a need for a feeling of enclosure without one of confinement.

The room itself, the height of the ceiling, the placement of the windows, doorways, and the other structural features—for example, a fireplace—will determine to a large extent how the area is to be utilized. Every form and shape will introduce new area relationships. Furniture groups, pictures on the wall, draperies at the windows, floor coverings, and accessories will all contribute to the space divisions.

It may be desirable to divide a long, narrow room into different functional spaces, such as a living area and a dining area or a study area. Some rooms have alcoves that will determine such area division. One may separate areas from one another in many ways. Furniture placement, room dividers, "area" rugs, color, pattern, and texture may all be used to mark certain areas.

The more areas and divisions that are introduced, the less will be the feeling of spaciousness. To preserve a spacious airy atmosphere, one would divide the available space as little as possible. It would be important to use the minimum amount of furniture, widely spaced furniture groups, no sharp color division for large areas, and few accessories. Furniture on legs will contribute to a more spacious appearance than furniture bases that extend to the floor, because one is more conscious of floor area under the piece with legs. We shall consider the problem of spaciousness again in later chapters, but the area divisions and shape relationships in a room are extremely important factors in creating or destroying the idea of space.

Color

Although the phenomenon of color has fascinated man for centuries, it is only in recent years that we have begun to appreciate its true importance in daily living. Not too long ago it would have been unthinkable to paint schoolrooms and hospital rooms in bright, cheerful colors. Automobiles were always painted in a few standardized, dark colors. Telephones, typewriters, and sewing machines were black; refrigerators and ranges were white. In a very short period of time we have come a long way toward revising our thinking about the use of color. We are only beginning to investigate and to understand the emotional and physical effects of color. Research in the field is still meager compared to what must be done, but various studies have shown among other things that color plays a very important role in safety and accident prevention. In factories that house dangerous machinery, specific hazards, such as cutting edges and hot or acid-carrying pipes, are marked with high-visibility colors as a safety measure. (The American Standards Association has set up a Standard on Safety Colors.) Certain colors are better for traffic signs and road markings because they are easier to see at night or during stormy weather. We have come to believe that children learn more easily in gay surroundings and sick people recover more rapidly in rooms that are restful and pleasant.

Studies of the effects of color on the digestive system have led to some interesting experiments. One of these even involved mashed potatoes colored blue—not a very appetizing prospect. Although we like colorful food in general, blue food does not generally seem to stimulate the palate. However, the colors on plates and other table appointments, as well as the coloring used in the dining room, all seem to have an effect in making food more or less appealing.

Market research has revealed the value of color in promoting sales. The color of the product, the package, and the display counters will influence one's decision to buy or to reject, even though he may not be aware of it.

These facts are cited simply to point out that color probably plays a more important role in our lives than most of us realize. The matter of color in the home is discussed more thoroughly in Chapter 14.

(a)

FIGURE 4-5 **Architectural features, furniture, and decorative accents determine space relation-ships.** (*Designed by Patricia Harvey, A.I.D. Photo by Henry S. Fullerton*)

(b)

(a)

(b)

(c)

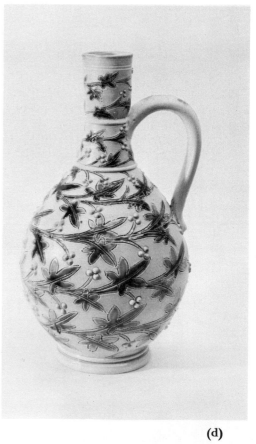

(d)

FIGURE 4-6 Texture adds to form and contributes to the idea that the design suggests. **(a)** *(Courtesy of Design-Technics)*; **(b)** *(Courtesy of Cooper-Hewitt Museum of Design, Smithsonian Institute)*; **(c)** *(Courtesy of New York Antiques Fair. Photo by Helga Studio)*; **(d)** *(Courtesy of Cooper-Hewitt Museum of Design, Smithsonian Institute)*; **(e)** *(Designed by Dennis Parks. Photo by Clayton J. Price)*

(e)

FIGURE 4-7 (below) This room emphasizes textures and contrasts in lines, forms, and colors to produce a warm atmosphere. *(Courtesy of Interior Design Studio, B. Altman & Co.)*

Texture

When we mention the word *texture* we immediately think of touching something. But texture is visual as well as tactile, because we associate past tactile sensations when we look at objects that are smooth or rough, hard or soft. The artist depicts textures on canvas as he paints a woman wearing a beautiful satin dress with glowing folds, or a bowl of flowers with lovely soft petals. The textures he portrays give character to his work and help to express ideas.

Just as lines, shapes, and colors convey messages, so do textures. Those that are rough and coarse have a rugged, sturdy quality. Handcrafts often owe their charm to texture that is not pretentious. Textures that are smooth and fine are more likely to suggest formality and elegance.

Rich textures that represent luxury, expert ornamentation, and highly skilled craftsmanship do not, as a rule, combine well with those of a more homespun nature. Although remembering that we must never say "never," we should realize that certain qualities seem to be incongruous when used together. A room furnished with elegant traditional pieces upholstered in brocades and velvets would undoubtedly have a peculiar character if the accessories included modern metal lamps, rough pottery ashtrays, hooked rugs, abstract paintings, and a dash of Spanish wrought iron.

Woods vary in texture and quality to such an extent that they must be selected and combined with great care. Those that are fine-grained or exotic in grain pattern are not likely to harmonize easily with those that are of a coarser open grain. A lovely figured walnut, therefore, would probably look uncomfortable in the company of rough, sturdy oak.

There are no hard and fast rules about the relationships of color and texture. Certain textural qualities are easier to emphasize with particular colors. Dark red, emerald green, purple, and gold suggest luxury and elegance of texture. The earthy colors of brown, mustard yellow, burnt orange, and yellow-green seem to be more suitable with less refined textures. But one should not feel restricted by any definite rules in reference to texture and color. The overall effect is the most important consideration.

harmony; on the other hand, Early Colonial and mid-Victorian styles had few common purposes, materials, or conditions of birth. It would be far more difficult to unite these styles, although the experienced decorator might very well do it through a judicious choice of elements.

Contrast is frequently employed to lend interest to a design, but here again, unless the contrasting elements are chosen with great discretion, it is easy to introduce a discordant note. Using contrasting colors is a relatively simple way of adding interest, providing the textures are somewhat similar. It is not quite so easy, however, to contrast textures, because those that are crude and rough suggest an idea that does not blend easily with those that are highly refined as a result of skilled, delicate craftsmanship.

Strong contrast of line and form is sometimes used very successfully to create a startling or an exciting design. We have ample evidence of the effectiveness of this type of contrast in modern art. But in good modern designs, the colors and textures are skillfully selected so that the final result has the unity that comes with the fine blending of the ingredients.

We look at a house, or any building, in conjunction with the surrounding terrain, or with the landscaping. Good architectural designers plan the building in terms of the site and the background. The areas within the building must also be planned in relation to the overall theme or mood. Thus it would be difficult to imagine a harmonious combination of a Cape Cod saltbox type of house with very formal, elegant furnishings set in a garden of Oriental style. The contrast would probably be not only confusing but disturbing. Yet a startling contrast planned with skill is often exciting. The unexpected note is stimulating because it defies the stereotype and we like this bit of change if it is not discordant.

Similarity with variance is, then, the keynote of harmony, but no one can dictate when and how to vary. This is the way one expresses himself in any design that he creates, and it will reflect his own perception, taste, and imagination.

Proportion

The untrained person often has an inherent sense of good proportion. The sofa is almost automatically placed against the long wall in the living room. The tiny woman avoids a huge hat and handbag that will overpower her. A letter typed without regard for margins on the paper is disturbing to the eye. These examples represent space divisions that are either pleasing or disturbing. Proportion and scale refer to the relationships of various parts of the design to one another and to the whole. In everyday life we are constantly aware of scale and proportion, and we are often applying this principle of design even though we are not always aware of doing so.

Ancient Greek designers were masters of proportions, and their art and architecture have for centuries been considered the epitome of perfection in space divisions. The scholars who have attempted to study these beautiful works realized that Greek proportions were derived from mathematical ratios that have been called the Golden Section. These ratios were based on a series of numbers that progressed by the sum of the two previous numbers. The ratio for a proportion was formed as follows: $2:3$; $3:5$; $5:8$; $8:13$. Compare in Figure 5-2 the areas formed on the Greek basis with the areas formed using other proportions. Are the basic relationships of the Greeks more pleasing to the eye than other spatial proportions?

Of course, many artists have experimented with more unusual proportions, and we find in the modern style a desire to depart from traditional space relationships. Some designers have produced results that are not only pleasing, but stimulating and exciting. Others with less keen perception have used proportions that seem interesting at first but soon lose their appeal.

Most of us do not measure areas in our homes to divide the spaces according to mathematical ratios, but our eyes soon tell us whether or not the proportions are interesting and the scale is pleasing.

Different-sized objects and areas in relationship to one another determine scale. We are constantly applying our sense of proportion when we select and arrange the objects in a room; a rug on the floor, a sofa against a wall, a picture or group of pictures over the sofa, a table and lamp next to a chair. The size and shape of the room will certainly determine the amount of furniture and the size of each piece. A very small room crowded with heavy, massive pieces is not likely to be either pleasing or

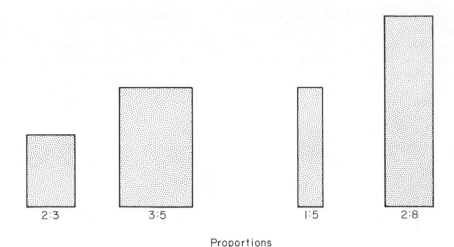

Proportions

FIGURE 5-2 Proportion—are traditional relationships more pleasing?

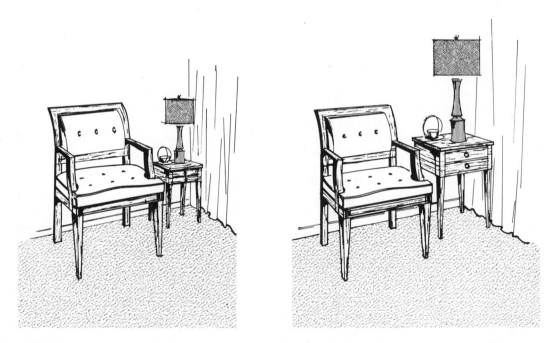

FIGURE 5-3 Pleasing proportions are established when all pieces in a group are in proper scale.

functional. In modern rooms we tend to use a few pieces of rather small-scale furniture to preserve an airy, spacious look. But again the design of the room must be carefully considered so that the furniture may not seem lost and insignificant.

Color and texture play a significant part in establishing proportions. Strong, brilliant colors advance and will therefore make a particular area more obvious. Textures that reflect light or patterned areas will also tend to increase the importance of an area. Strong contrasts of color and texture will emphasize lines and forms. Proportions, therefore, are subject to the types and amounts of color and texture in different areas. This interrelationship of the elements may be used in many ways to emphasize desirable space divisions or to minimize those that are not so pleasing, for example, the different effects created by the use of draperies that match the wall color and draperies that form a strong contrast (Fig. 5-6). We are not so aware of the window as a separate area when the drapery color matches the wall. On the other hand, contrasting draperies create a different space division.

Balance

The principle of balance in design appeals to our sense of equilibrium. It is more pleasing to the eye when weights are so adjusted around a central focal point that they appear to be in a state of repose. A feeling of unbalance is almost always disturbing and unpleasant.

The "weights" of the furniture and other objects in a room are determined by size, shape, color, and texture. All of these elements must be considered in adjusting the balance. The seesaw is, of course, a perfect example of physical balance, and the basic laws affecting a seesaw may be applied to artistic balance. When two objects of equal weight are placed at opposite ends of the board, they must be equidistant from the central point to balance each other. If one object is replaced by a heavier one, it must be moved closer to the center to balance the lighter one at the other end of the board.

When applying this principle to design, one should remember that similar areas will seem lighter or heavier in different colors and textures. On the visual seesaw, therefore, if two objects are the same size but one is bright yellow and the other gray, the brighter one will appear heavier.

FORMAL AND INFORMAL BALANCE. When objects on each side of the center point are alike in every respect, there is no problem in balancing them. The type of balance is called *formal* or *symmetrical balance*. However, when objects that are not similar are grouped around a focal point to create a feeling of equilibrium, the balance is *informal*, *occult*, or *asymmetrical*.

Frequently, the size, shape, and other architectural features of a room will influence the way furniture must be placed and where it will be desirable to use formal or informal balance. On a wall that has identical windows symmetrically placed it would seem logical, although not always necessary, to place furniture in a formally balanced arrangement. When the structural features of the room are asymmetrical, an informal arrangement of balance is usually more attractive.

The theme of the room will also influence the type of balance that should predominate. A large, elegant room that is formal in character could well stand several groups of furniture arranged in formal balance. Having all the groups arranged this way, however, would be monotonous and would, in addition, lend an air of rigidity that might be unpleasant. A predominance of occult arrangements produces a more casual atmosphere in a room, but one must be careful to avoid a feeling of confusion through the excessive use of informal balance.

Although formal balance has more static and stable qualities, it does not need to be dull and uninteresting. This type of balance may be achieved through arrangements in which the objects on either side of the central line are not identical but are of equal weight and importance.

Occult, or informal, arrangements are more difficult, but when they are well balanced they add interest and variety. There are some excellent examples in the work of many Japanese artists, who were masters of the technique of producing fine occult balance.

Large pieces of furniture must usually be distributed around a room so that the walls and various areas of the room balance one another. All heavy pieces at one end and all lightweight pieces at the other would certainly produce an unbalanced design. If function or some other reason dictates such an arrangement, color and texture can be employed to reestablish a more pleasing equilibrium. For example, a dining area at one end of a living room would probably have furniture that is lighter in weight than the heavier upholstered pieces at the other end. In such a case one might use a different wall color, bright accents of color on chair seats, or some emphatic center of interest to add importance to the dining area.

(a)

FIGURE 5-4 An asymmetrical arrangement (a) requires careful consideration of lines, shapes, and colors to achieve balance. Formal balance (b) is more easily achieved by symmetrical placement of furniture and accessories.

(b)

FIGURE 5-5 **Examples of formal and informal balance.** (*Courtesy of Dunbar/Dux. Photo by Wesley Pusey*)

Rhythm

When the elements of a design are arranged to make the eye travel from one part to another, the design has movement. If the eye moves smoothly and easily, the motion is rhythmic. This principle of rhythm is extremely important in producing unity, because it makes the eye sweep over the whole design before it rests at any particular focal point.

The principle of rhythm is an exciting one to work with because the effects are interesting and dramatic. A few simple tricks of decorating will provide an easy, graceful motion. If the eye jumps from one spot to another, the result may be most disturbing.

There are several methods of producing rhythm in a design. These include:

1. Continuous line.
2. Repetition.
3. Gradation.
4. Radiation.

CONTINUOUS LINE. We have already discussed the way lines compel the eye to follow the directions they take. This powerful quality may be employed in various ways to control the movement of the eye. Of course the design of a room is usually composed of many different lines, but a predominance of one type will cause the eye to move in that direction.

Moldings, borders, and chair rails are simple ways to introduce continuous lines. Wallpapers, fabrics, and rugs frequently have dominant line directions that can be employed to create rhythmic movement.

REPETITION. Some very interesting, simple experiments can be performed in any room of the home to show the power of repetition in creating movement. Through the repeti-

(a) Continuous Line

FIGURE 5-6 Rhythm produced in various ways.

(b) Repetition

tion of line, color, shape, or texture one can control the movement of the eye so that it will move in any desired direction.

Although it has been pointed out that vertical lines carry the eye up and down, a series of vertical lines that are horizontally arranged and evenly spaced can carry the eye from side to side. Various border designs, such as the familiar egg-and-dart and fret motifs, illustrate this principle. Repetition of shape will also cause the eye to move in various directions. For example, a series of pictures mounted in frames of similar shape will cause the eye to travel from one point to another.

Color provides an excellent means of producing rhythm. To experiment, one can take any two objects of a bright color that will contrast with the other colors in a room, or use two pieces of bright fabric, and place them at different spots in the room. When the effects are viewed from the doorway, the eye goes from one to the other. This experiment should be tried with different locations so that the movement is easy and graceful. Try the same experiment with a patterned fabric.

GRADATION. A progression through a series of intermediate steps will carry the eye from one end of the scale to the other. This principle may be applied to line, shape, or color. It is perhaps more easily used with accessories than with large pieces of furniture.

Gradations of color are used in some fabrics. The eye will travel from the more dominant tone to the more subdued.

RADIATION. Although diverging lines do not tend to carry the eye *smoothly* from one part of a design to another, they are sometimes useful in creating a particular effect. Radiation is frequently employed as a basis of design in lighting fixtures, structural elements, and many decorative objects.

(c) Radiation

(d) Gradation

FIGURE 5-7 Repetition creates a feeling of movement in this room setting designed by Tom Woods, **A.I.D.** (*Courtesy of Bigelow-Sanford, Inc.*)

FIGURE 5-8 The principle of gradation is used in a rug designed by Marie Creamer of new "Source" fibers and titled *Infinite*. The deep gold color of the rug is repeated on one wall. Textural interest is added by a clear lucite stand and an etagere with tortoise shell finish. (*Courtesy of Allied Chemical Corporation*)

(a)

(b)

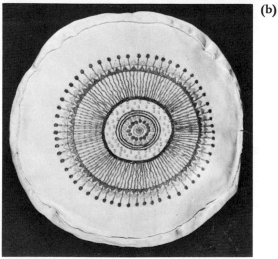

FIGURE 5-9 (a) An area rug with a radial design might serve to make a small area appear larger. (*Courtesy of Allied Chemical Corporation, Caprolan nylon*); (b) This embroidered pillow cover has a feeling of movement. (*Courtesy of Cooper-Hewitt Museum of Design, Smithsonian Institute*)

Emphasis

A good design needs leadership or some particular note that attracts the interest. Other components of the design enhance the focal point, but they are subdued to it.

There may be more than one center of interest in a room, but too many points of emphasis will produce a confused effect.

What one chooses to emphasize as the focal point of an arrangement depends on the type and purpose of the room. Occasionally some structural feature of the room will almost automatically become a center of interest—for example, a fireplace or a large window. When there is no built-in center of attention, it is a simple matter to create one. A particular furniture grouping or even one piece of furniture can be a focal-point. In a bedroom, for example, the bed is often the center of interest with all other furnishings subordinate. In a living room the point of emphasis may be the conversation area. However, a large area of pattern might provide a center of interest. An Oriental rug, or any rug with an outstanding pattern or design, may become a focal point when other furnishings are simple and subdued. A scenic wallpaper or a painting might serve the same purpose.

Sometimes a special interest or hobby provides individuality when it serves as the dominant note in a room. For example, in one den, a collection of figures of giraffes was displayed on wall shelves. The owner had started the collection quite by accident, but as her friends traveled around the world they delighted in finding unusual figures to add to it. Soon there were giraffes of various sizes made of wood, straw, glass, metals, ivory, pottery, and so on. The display provided quite a whimsical touch as well as a conversation piece—quite definitely a center of interest that might not appeal to many other people. Yet such a personalized touch does add interest if it is displayed with imagination and good taste.

FIGURE 5-10 Emphasis is achieved in this dining area designed by Tom Woods, A.I.D. with two framed motto rugs by Dorothy Liebes. An integral part of the geometric pattern in the rug on the left is the word *Hope*, and on the right, the word *Love*. (*Courtesy of Bigelow-Sanford, Inc.*)

(a)

(b)

FIGURE 5-11 Emphasis may be produced by arrangement of furniture as indicated in the two room settings shown here. (*Designed by Barbara D'Arcy, A.I.D., Bloomingdale's, N.Y. Photo by Richard Averill Smith*)

FIGURE 5-12   A small room designed by Lawrence Peabody, A.I.D., illustrates how various principles of design may be employed to create a feeling of harmony. Emphasis is achieved through arrangement, contrast, and repetition. (*Courtesy of The Upholstery Leather Group*)

EMPHASIS THROUGH ARRANGEMENT.   As one walks into an empty room, certain areas will strike his attention first. Therefore, the shape and the structural features will determine to some extent where the centers of interest should be placed. It is important to choose a dominant area rather than some obscure corner of the room. The background and surrounding areas must be carefully planned to recede rather than advance.

EMPHASIS THROUGH CONTRAST. When a white object is held against a black background, the white seems whiter and the black takes on added depth. Whenever two extremes are used together they intensify each other. The principle of emphasis through contrast has numerous applications. Draperies

in strong contrast to the wall color will emphasize a window treatment.

EMPHASIS THROUGH REPETITION. Another simple experiment will clearly show how repetition can be used for emphasis. A patterned fabric that has several colors may be held next to various samples of solid colors that repeat those in the print. If the pattern has both blue and green, the green color in the design will be more prominent when the fabric is held next to a solid green fabric. Next to a blue fabric, the blue in the design will become more pronounced.

Repetition of color, line, shape, or texture can be used to give added emphasis to any element you choose to stress. But repetition should be used in a subtle fashion. Too much is likely to become monotonous.

Principles of Design **67**

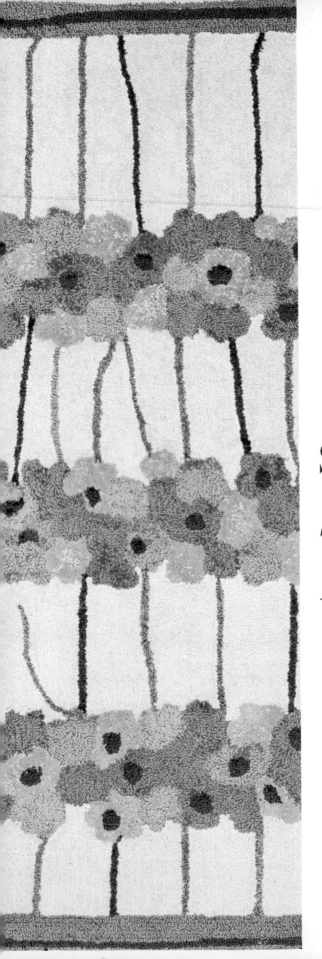

Section III
Styles of Furniture

The consumer today is faced with a wide variety of choices in the area of furnishings. The many styles and types available make it possible to create almost any atmosphere that one desires. This bountiful market, however, may be a paradoxical blessing because it makes decisions more difficult.

Terminology

The terminology relating to furniture styles has become somewhat confusing. Not many years ago one might have asked, "Shall I use 'period' or 'modern'?" Now we are more likely to hear the terms *traditional* and *contemporary*. *Modern* is often used with some qualifying word, such as *Danish* or *organic*. These terms are rather difficult to define, because there is an overlapping of connotation and meaning. Individuals give them different interpretations and there is no agency for establishing definitions that clearly mark the differences.

TRADITIONAL. *Traditional* refers to furniture designs that have come to us from past generations. The words *period* and *style* are often used interchangeably with reference to traditional furnishings. Some authorities prefer to use the term *period* to define a particular time, and the term *style* to define the work of a particular individual. Thus, Chippendale and Hepplewhite would be two styles of the Georgian period. This distinction is by no means a hard and fast rule. We often see references to Queen Anne "style" rather than "period," though the queen did not design furniture.

In the true sense, a period piece would be either the original or an exact reproduction. Very few pieces of furniture made today are exact copies of original designs. Styles have been adapted to present-day living and the

6

Choosing a Style

71

current methods of production. Changes can be made in scale and in ornamentation without destroying the characteristics of the style. We have a variety of furniture that is called *traditional*. The design retains enough characteristics to make its origin clear and unmistakable, yet it is not usually an exact reproduction of any one specific original piece.

However, because of our current interest in restorations there are several manufacturers who do reproduce traditional designs in the most authentic manner possible and many of these are available to the consumer who desires the more exact copies.

It should be mentioned here that the popular, and sometimes indiscriminate, use of the word *antique* has given it a variety of meanings. An Act of Congress stipulates that ". . . Artistic antiquity and objects of art of ornamental character or educational value which shall have been produced prior to the year 1830" may be admitted to the country duty free. Reputable antique dealers, however, reject any theory that something is good simply because it is old. They want examples of the best designs and craftsmanship and accept or reject antiques on the basis of artistic merit as well as age. The government has upheld this view in a decision qualifying the use of the word *artistic* and the phrase *objects of art* and does not allow items to enter duty free merely because they are old.

CONTEMPORARY. *Contemporary* refers to a rather broad category of current designs. Many of these draw upon traditional styling for inspiration without actually reproducing any one style in particular. Much of this furniture cannot be identified with any previous design nor can it be associated with the new concepts of the modern style.

In another category, current designers have created various hybrid styles that seem to have popular appeal. Some influences of the past are quite evident but the designs are modified and simplified to produce a flavor rather than a true representation. Examples of this type of contemporary design might include Italian Provincial, Mediterranean, and the more recent adaptations of early English styles, such as Tudor.

A considerable amount of contemporary furniture is designed for mass production. At the present time there is a growing interest in the use of molded plastic components to develop this new transitional type of design. Some authorities view with horror the simulating of wood carving with plastic. Others seem to find a challenge in adapting new techniques and new methods to bridge the transition between the past and the present. It is probably too early to evaluate these modern methods in terms of design, but there can be little doubt that in the future plastics will become more important in the contemporary style.

FIGURE 6-1   A traditional setting with reproductions of English Georgian Furniture. (*Courtesy of Kittinger Company. Photographed in Williamsburg, Virginia*)

FIGURE 6-2   This living-dining room combines several traditional styles of furniture. (*Designed by Patricia Harvey, A.I.D. Photo by Henry S. Fullerton*)

FIGURE 6-3   A traditional atmosphere with suggestions of contemporary design is expressed in this living room. (*Designed by Patricia Harvey, A.I.D. Photo by Doris Jacoby*)

FIGURE 6-4   Accessories reflecting "mod" tastes include a blown-up wall poster and primitive Indian and Eskimo artifacts. (*Courtesy of Allied Chemical Corporation*, Source *fiber*)

FIGURE 6-5 An Early American theme is introduced into an unusual family room with separate nooks. (*Designed by Edmund Motyka, A.I.D.*)

FIGURE 6-6 A contemporary room that represents no authentic period style is given an Oriental feeling by the use of accessories in a setting designed by Lois Kelley, N.S.I.D. (*"Trend East" Room Group by Stratford. Courtesy of Futorian Mfg. Corp.*)

MODERN. The modern style which has been developing since the early part of the twentieth century, breaks all ties with previous designs. New forms, unusual proportions, and modern materials characterize furnishings that bear little, if any, suggestion of past heritage. This style has gone through periods of growing pains, with abundant examples of poor design that were rejected shortly after they were born. However, the classic examples of the modern style have reached a high level of artistic refinement and have recognized the relationship between modern technology and beauty of line, form, color, and texture.

Which Style?

A family will usually have to live with furnishings for many years because a considerable amount of money is involved in establishing a home. Before any selections are made, therefore, it is desirable to investigate the various possibilities so that the final selections will provide lasting satisfaction.

Many factors will influence buying decisions. In addition to the theme or the mood one wants to create, problems of space, functionalism, maintenance, and cost may have to be considered. The more familiar one becomes with different types of decoration, the easier it is to understand how certain styles can be used to achieve specific purposes.

Perhaps the first consideration should be the atmosphere of the home. Qualities such as formality, elegance, comfort, cheerfulness, gaiety, or simplicity may be more easily achieved through one style than another. It is important, therefore, to explore the characteristics of various modes of design in terms of such expressiveness.

Traditional designs have withstood the time test. The styles that are most popular today have been here for many years. They have grown, have developed, and have reached the ultimate in proving their worth. They have shown that they are easy to live with and that they are not likely to become boring or obnoxious because they are no longer fashionable. In furnishings, a truly good design is always in fashion. Living with traditional designs may give one a certain sense of security, and those who desire a calm relaxed atmosphere will probably lean

FIGURE 6-7   A truly modern room that emphasizes new forms and textures. There is little recognition of tradition in the design of this room. (*Designed by Barbara D'Arcy, A.I.D., Bloomingdale's, N.Y. Photo by Richard Averill Smith*)

FIGURE 6-8   This room is modern in mood with a hint of the traditional in chest and table. (*Courtesy of Bloomingdale's. Photo by Richard Averill Smith*)

toward traditional styles. This certainly does not mean that the home will be dull and monotonous. It can be as gay and cheerful as one wants, but there will still be that feeling of security that comes with time-tested design.

Some personalities may find this expression of security in their homes rather dull. People who react well to change and to new ideas will probably find the contemporary and the modern styles more stimulating and exciting. Because these styles have grown up with us, they are often more closely keyed to our requirements in modern living. They are designed to cope with the problems of space and care. The furniture is flexible so that it may be adapted to different conditions and situations. It must be remembered, however,

that these styles are more vulnerable to fashion changes. Each year new developments, new ideas, and new advances in technology threaten the current modes.

Of course, no one can be sure that his taste will not change in five years or even two years. The person who chooses traditional styles may become bored with them and suddenly find modern furnishings very exciting. Strangely enough, this sometimes happens to people in their middle years. There has been a trend toward modern furnishings among couples whose families have grown up and moved away from home. Frequently the parents move to smaller quarters and refurnish in the modern style after having lived with traditional furniture for many years. Simplicity and ease of care seem to be the influencing factors. As one woman pointed out, she had dusted bric-a-brac for twenty-five years and was tired of it. Now she wanted smooth, uncluttered surfaces. On the other hand, there has been a trend among young people to furnish in traditional styles. In an age where one must face stark reality and the pressures of daily living in a mechanized society, the repose of soft, graceful lines in a traditional-style home may be a real antidote.

From the economic standpoint one usually gets better value by selecting styles that have a minimum of ornamentation. Probably the two best values in this respect are modern and early American. In both styles the emphasis on simplicity, texture, and color make it possible to achieve various effects without

undue expense. It should be noted, however, that some manufacturers are experimenting with very new methods of constructing other types of furniture that can provide high quality at low cost. If the application of plastics continues to develop we may see a much wider variety of better quality furniture in the low-cost category.

Combining Styles

We are in an eclectic period and it is common practice to combine various styles of furnishings in the same room. The trained eye of an expert interior designer sees each choice in relation to the final effect. He may, therefore, combine furnishings in a most unorthodox manner with very pleasing results. Sometimes designs of widely different heritages blend well and complement each other in an exciting manner. An example of this might be the use of certain Oriental rugs with very modern furniture. Within recent years, several interior designers who have experimented with such combinations have initiated a trend that seems to have popular appeal. This is not exactly a new idea because the seafarers in the eighteenth century brought back rugs and accessories from the Orient and they blended beautifully with the formal Georgian designs, which were, of course, the "modern" of the time.

It is difficult to achieve a feeling of unity with indiscriminate combinations. The novice, therefore, may find it more difficult to combine the unusual without creating a feeling of confusion.

Components are more likely to blend well if they express similar ideas or if they have a common spirit. Furnishings that are formal in character may be quite compatible even though they represent different styles. It is not quite as easy to relate the quaint to the sophisticated or the elegant to the rustic. However, there can be no rigid rules about unusual combinations.

In simple terms, harmony refers to similarity with some variation for interest. Color, texture, and form must all be carefully considered. Although one or another might be used as the variant for the sake of unity there must also be some unifying concepts or elements to provide the similarity.

FIGURE 6-9 (top, left) Can one mix modern and traditional styles? The room above shows antique Georgian chairs, a modern painting, a steel and glass coffee table, and an Oriental rug in perfect harmony. A Jacobean print on the loveseat accents the blues and greens in the border of the rug which has an ivory background. The background is a subdued champagne color that serves the purposes of contrast in line and color accents. (*Courtesy of Oriental Rug Importers Association*)

FIGURE 6-10 (bottom, left) An unusual example of eclectic design is found in this room. French chairs combined with a bold plaid are in striking contrast, yet they seem to complement each other. The baroque designs of pattern on the sofa and on the base of the coffee table are additional unexpected elements. (*Designed by Patricia Harvey, A.I.D.*)

7

Development
of Furniture
Styles

Study of the decorative styles used by various groups in the development of civilization presents a fascinating approach to history. Throughout the ages, homes have represented a way of life. Customs, beliefs, political interests, economic conditions, new discoveries, and particular personalities have all been influential factors at one time or another in determining decorative modes. In more recent years, technological advances, the development of communications, and the expansion of travel facilities have had important effects on modern tastes.

As one studies the evolution of interior design it is rather entertaining to imagine what it might have been like to live with some historic style when it was the "modern" of the age. It is difficult to imagine living in a feudal castle with huge, dreary rooms. There would be no comfortable chairs, no telephone, and no electricity. Visualize a glamorous, but damp, house on a canal in Venice or a lovely formal Georgian mansion. With a good imagination it is hardly possible to become acquainted with any particular period without becoming more aware of the people who lived in such homes.

One approach to our heritage is through a bird's-eye view of the influences on current styles. Table 1 presents a synopsis of development. By reading both vertically and horizontally one can see the broad relationships between eras and cultures.

Ancient Designs

Although the inspiration for current furniture designs usually dates back only to about the fifteenth century, we have frequently borrowed ideas and motifs from the ancient Greeks, Romans, and Egyptians. Actually there is very little of their furniture still in existence, but from art and literature we know that they used certain basic forms that

(a)

(c)

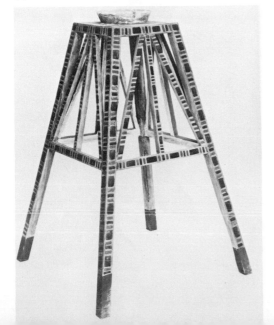

we are still using, such as couches, tables, chests, and stools. There was far less variety, however, because some of our more familiar furniture pieces did not develop until centuries later. Furniture of the ancient civilizations was, nevertheless, quite elegant. It was made of beautiful woods, marbles, and bronze. Decorative detail was supplied through carving, painting, inlay, and veneers.

It is interesting to note that many of the ancient tables were really tripods with tops mounted on three elaborate legs. There are some contemporary adaptations that seem to indicate a possible revival of interest in ancient designs.

Dark Ages

After the decline of the Roman Empire, the era known as the Dark Ages began. From an artistic standpoint we have little to draw upon from this long period. Most people lived in rather crude, simple cottages on feudal estates. There was little interest in the arts, nor were there many significant contributions. There seems to have been no interest in the "home" atmosphere as we know it today. Consequently, this is a long period during which there were few, if any, influences that are important today.

By the eleventh century, some of the nations of Europe had been established. As countries developed, so did national characteristics. Large buildings—chiefly castles, churches, and monasteries—slowly began to take on architectural styles that reflected the artistic environment.

Gothic Style

During the thirteenth and fourteenth centuries, Western Europe became somewhat

(b)

FIGURE 7-1 Ancient designs. (a) Replica of the "Princess Sitamun Chair" (c. 1400 B.C.) now in the Cairo Museum. The original is made of reddish tropical wood and ornamented with gold leaf. Pieces of this type often used designs representing protective spirits. (*Courtesy of The Baker Furniture Museum*); (b) King Tut's coffer, the ancestor of the modern chest of drawers. (*Courtesy of The Fine Hardwoods Association*); (c) Replica of an ancient painted stand (c. 1400 B.C.) has a circular cut-out hole in the top to receive a vase with rounded bottom. (*Courtesy of The Baker Furniture Museum*)

Development of Furniture Styles **81**

less rural. As towns grew, new buildings were needed and architecture became an important mode of expression. The Gothic style flourished and furniture followed the general theme. It was large and heavy, with extensive carving. Panels on chests assumed the lines of the tall pointed Gothic arch. The carved motifs included leaves, animals, and birds.

In France the Gothic style was somewhat more refined than it was in England. There was more expert carving and the decorative details were more intricate. In addition to foliage and animals, motifs included rosettes and fleurs-de-lis. France also produced many exquisite tapestries during this era.

Renaissance

A new way of life opened with the Renaissance or "rebirth." It was characterized by an interest in all phases of human activity. The spirit manifested itself in many ways. The new awareness of the individual tended to foster the development of artistic capabilities. The manner of life that evolved was creative, gay, witty, and intellectually stimulating. Social amenities and dress became more important. In such an atmosphere of activity, inquiry, and interest, the arts in particular flourished.

ITALY. The new era of appreciation began to develop in Italy during the fourteenth century and reached its height during the first half of the sixteenth century. During this "golden age," great artisans produced many of the finest art treasures the world has ever known. The Renaissance was most fruitful in Italy, but eventually its influence spread to other countries and inspired similar developments.

Furniture designs reflected the new interest in the arts. They became more refined in form and somewhat more graceful in proportion. As one would expect, the techniques of ornamentation followed the development of an appreciation of high levels of artistic achievement.

(a)

FIGURE 7-2 **Renaissance designs. (a) A walnut Sgabello chair from Italy, 16th century, shows both classical and Baroque influences.** (*Courtesy of The Brooklyn Museum, Gift of Frank L. Babbott*); **(b) Caryatids are used to ornament a French armoire in walnut, 16th century.** (*Courtesy of The Brooklyn Museum. Gift of Mrs. J. Fuller Feder*)

(b)

FRANCE. By the end of the fifteenth century there were many Renaissance influences in France, but the French were slow to give up their preference for Gothic forms. During the reign of Francois I (1515–1547), the court at Paris attracted many of the Italian artists and their influences continued during the reign of Henry II (1547–1559). However, religious strife in the succeeding years caused a decline in all the arts.

In 1589 the Bourbons took over and a new era began in the cultural progress of France. There was a very close relationship between the development of the arts and the government. There was no clear-cut style of art during the ensuing years because of the many different influences, but the prestige and dignity accorded to the artist laid the groundwork for the future development of French artistic achievement. During the reign of Louis XIII (1589–1643), French art showed many Flemish and Italian influences. Furniture was rather heavy with the prolific use of carving and turning. Although this period has not had great influence on present-day styles, it is important because the craftsmen in the decorative arts were accorded a prestige that made it possible for France to develop the glorious court styles that were to follow.

One must always bear in mind that the court furniture was quite different from the furniture used by the masses of people. Yet in an indirect manner the influences of the court seeped into French national design and provided the basis for styles that have become extremely popular in our current trends of decoration.

ENGLAND. The Renaissance influence was felt later in England than in other European countries. Feudalism had just about disappeared in England by the end of the fifteenth century, and the feudal lords gave way to a new class of wealthy English merchants who lived in manor houses. Magnificent houses with beautiful gardens became the prized possessions of this new strata of English aristocracy. England was becoming a sea power with a rapidly developing colonial empire. There were many forces at work in the development of English nationalism.

In the latter part of the fifteenth and the early part of the sixteenth centuries, art in England was dominated by a mixture of Gothic and Flemish influences. All during the Tudor era (1485–1558), the furniture was essentially Gothic in form; but after 1530, Renaissance themes became increasingly important. Furniture was carved and decorated with inlay, although the techniques were not as refined as those employed in other countries. During the reign of Elizabeth I (1559–1603), the Renaissance took hold in England and almost completely supplanted the Gothic style.

The Jacobean period, beginning with the reign of James I (1603–1625), ushered in an era of increasing wealth and expanding trade for England. Renaissance influences became more important during this period and by the middle of the seventeenth century they were very strong.

SPAIN. Prior to the Renaissance, almost all art in Spain had been influenced by the dominance of the Moors, who had ruled Spain for almost eight centuries. The Spanish Christians were influenced by the Moorish taste for geometrical designs. It was during the Renaissance that Spain went through her "golden age" in history. The sixteenth century marked a brilliant era of Spanish power in Europe: it included the reign of Ferdinand and Isabella, the Spanish discoveries in the New World, and flourishing commerce. By the end of the century, however, Spain was almost bankrupt and did not continue to exert important influences in world affairs. Today there is interest in travel to Spain, which seems to be encouraging a widespread revival of interest in Spanish art.

The central patio around which the Spanish home was built provided a setting for beautiful iron grillwork. The rooms in the house usually had stark, white, plastered walls, but the wide use of mosaic-tile work, wood-paneled ceilings, tooled leather, and magnificent fabrics for seat cushions and wall hangings gave the Spanish interior an exotic quality that was different from that of any other European country. The furniture was essentially simple in design and consisted of a few basic pieces, such as tables, benches, stools, chairs, chests, and cupboards. The ornamentation throughout the Renaissance reflected the Moorish taste for geometrical designs and vivid coloring, which gave a distinctly different flavor to the Spanish interpretation of the more conventional Renaissance motifs.

Table 1 Furniture Styles

Period	Egyptian (4500 B.C.–7th Century A.D.)	Greek (2000 B.C.–2nd Century B.C.)	Roman (8th Century B.C.–5th Century A.D.)
ANCIENT	High level of craftsmanship. Furniture carved and decorated with inlays of ivory and ebony, gold, enamel, and precious gems. Legs of chairs and couches carved to resemble dog leg with paw on small block of wood. Shaped seats and backs of chairs, sometimes covered with loose cushions. Used metal (gold, silver, bronze), glass, alabaster. Colorful fabrics; painted leather. Pottery used for tableware and personal accessories.	Furniture carved and decorated with painting. Legs were plain graceful curves with turning and animal forms for decoration. Used metals, marble, and beautiful woods. Wide use of tripods or three-legged tables. Exquisite urns and vases pictured daily life, history, beliefs, and customs.	Adapted and borrowed from Greeks but art was more ornate. Furniture quite heavy looking. Used more veneering, especially ebony. Much inlay done with exotic wood, gold, silver, ivory, and tortoise shell.
DARK AGES About 6th–11th centuries	Western Europe in a period of upheaval. Growth of Christian Church. Large buildings were monasteries, churches, feudal castles. People lived in crude cottages on feudal estates. Development of different religious orders; monks chiefly responsible for education. Romanesque style of architecture developed during the 11th century and showed strong Byzantine influences, especially in Italy, where there were principal trade routes between East and West. Long warfare between Christians in Western Europe and Muhammadans. Period has little significance for interior design.		

Period	England	France	Italy	Others
MIDDLE AGES	Norman conquest (1066 A.D.) brought influences of refinement. Large homes had a great hall, which was center of all activity. Gradually began to add more rooms. Gothic style of architecture. Stone walls and floors of earth or stone.	During 12th–14th centuries developed Gothic style of architecture, which reached its height in 14th century. Precise carving of foliage, fleurs-de-lis, rosettes, trefoil and cinquefoil, birds and animals. Art of tapestry weaving developed to height of excel-	Became center of trade routes which brought great wealth. Gothic style did not flourish to same degree that it did in other countries although Venice had some fine examples. During 14th century Renaissance began in Italy. New interest in artistic and scientific	**Spain** Centuries of Muhammadan domination resulted in intermingling of Moorish influences with art of Christian Spain. Wide variety of geometrical motifs used on furniture and in wrought-iron decorative work. **Dutch and Flemish** Pros-

RENAISSANCE

Few pieces of furniture in large, solid rectilinear forms. Mostly oak carved with Gothic motifs, panels, foliage, figures, and tracery work in somewhat crude manner. Used chests, trestle tables, benches, and cupboards. Wall hangings of rich, colorful tapestries and other fabrics.

lence during 14th century.

pursuits and interest in ancient Roman civilization. Palaces richly decorated and elegantly furnished. Ornate carving, magnificent fabrics, wide use of Venetian glass and lace.

Medici family encouraged cultural development and humanist ideas.

perous trade centers. People liked decorative objects. Highly skilled craftsmen produced exquisite work in metal, glass, ceramics, leather, fabrics, lace, and embroidery. Southern areas associated with Catholic art and architecture. Northern parts chiefly Protestant and did not mix religion and art to same extent.

Spain Wealthy, leading world power. Moorish influences in art but applied to Gothic forms. Rich decoration. Homes built around a central courtyard. Much built-in decoration—grille work, painted ceilings, tile in colorful mosaics. Moorish influences persisted throughout the Renaissance. At end of 16th century, furniture was more austere, but during 17th century followed Baroque style with more lavish decoration.

16th Century Height of Renaissance. Michaelangelo, Da Vinci, Raphael, and Titian contributed to "golden age" of Italian art. Furniture became more delicate. Various art centers had individual approaches to all phases of art, including furnishings. Designs became more excessively carved and more pretentious. Furniture mostly walnut. Baroque style developed in late 16th century. Pompous and luxurious; dramatic splendor. Many whirling curves.

17th Century Baroque influences continued with some influences of French Rococo styles.

15th–16th Centuries Fusion of French Gothic and Italian Renaissance styles. English and Italian influence on Gothic forms. Furniture simple and well constructed. Much of it imported from Italy, Spain, and the Netherlands.

Bourbon regime marked beginning of new emphasis on French artistic and cultural development. Carpet, tapestry, and silk industries encouraged. Paris became center of social and intellectual activities.

17th Century Strong Italian influences but characteristic French style developed. Baroque designs with short, stopped curves. Court styles with magnificent grandeur and stately elegance. Craftsmen in the decorative arts on a plane with painters, sculptors, and architects.

AGE OF OAK

Tudor Period (1485–1588) Gothic forms prevailed. Renaissance influences slow to develop. More towns; end of feudal system: Style of domestic architecture developed. Large rambling country houses with lawns and gardens instead of castles. More furniture used; gradually became more refined.

Elizabethan Period (1558–1603) Renaissance influences spread. Transitional period.

Jacobean Period (1603–1649) and Restoration (1660–1689) Furniture still heavy but new forms introduced. Used sofas, gate-leg tables, round tables; more upholstered pieces. Parquet floors, oriental rugs. Rich fabrics in brilliant colors. Fine embroidery included crewel and needlepoint.

Table 1 (*continued*)

Period	England	France	America	Others
18th CENTURY	AGE OF WALNUT **William and Mary (1687–1702)** Dutch influence. Design showed more refinement and simplicity. Graceful curves with little carving. Cabriole leg originated; highboy made its appearance. Use of lacquered furniture; wallpaper. **Queen Anne (1702–1714)** More emphasis on comfort, hominess. Shell carving, spoon foot. Small tables, lowboys, desks with simple, curved lines. Smaller-scale furniture. **Early Georgian (1714–1750)** Continued style of Queen Anne, but new influences toward middle of century made this a transitional period. Furniture became more elaborate and mahogany became more popular.	**Louis XIV (1643–1715)** Development of Rococo style with flowing serpentine curves. **Louis XV (1715–1774)** Rococo style flourished. Complete emphasis on curves. Ornamentation elaborate and luxurious. Chinese influences fostered by Madame de Pompadour. Wide use of gilt, lacquer, ormolu, fine silk fabrics. Furniture fine in scale, comfortable. Wide use of tables, commodes, writing desks.	**Colonial** **a) Early American (1608–1770)** Early homes had few pieces of furniture. Styles derived from familiar forms popular in native countries of settlers but executed in woods readily available in America and scaled to smaller rooms. At first, construction simple and crude with little ornamentation. By 1700 more skilled craftsmen and greater interest in comfort and beauty of the home. **b) American Georgian (1720–1790)** Growth of cities produced more elaborate homes and demand for furniture that followed prevailing styles in Europe. American interpretations of English designs became popular.	
18th CENTURY	AGE OF MAHOGANY **Middle Georgian (1750–1770)** French designs in Rococo mood more popular. Interiors formal and elaborate.	**Louis XVI (1774–1793)** Reaction to overuse of curves and emphasis on Neoclassicism; Refined, delicate designs; fine craftsmanship.		

Chippendale (1718–1779) Designed elegant furniture that showed French, Gothic, and oriental influences. Beautiful carving with emphasis on C curve. Solid and substantial proportions that give style "masculine" appearance.

AGE OF SATINWOOD
Late Georgian (1770–1810) Neoclassic period. Furniture design during this "golden age" was at its height with graceful lines and beautiful proportions. Architecture and interior design blended to produce lovely effects. Fine craftsmanship and appreciation for unusual woods provided exquisite designs.

Robert Adam (1728–1792) Architect who designed furniture to be made by other craftsmen. Designs were refined and noted for classical simplicity and architectural qualities. Used mahogany and satinwood.

French Provincial Styles that developed in provinces during late 17th, 18th, and early 19th centuries. Influences of court styles uneven. Furniture in cities followed spirit of elegance and splendor but in simplified manner. Country styles graceful but less elegant—used native materials with woods usually waxed or painted.

Directoire (1795–1799) (Political unrest influenced arts but new spirit of freedom combined with interest in classical forms and French heritage of fine design produced graceful style. In general, lines and proportions followed Louis XVI style.

Federal (1780–1830) Styles followed English designs, especially those of Sheraton and Hepplewhite. Excellent cabinet work in America but furniture less elaborate than in England.

Duncan Phyfe (1768–1854) Famous American cabinet maker. Used graceful, delicate proportions; adapted styles of Sheraton and others. Noted for use of lyre motif, cornucopia legs, and pedestal bases. His work continued into Victorian period.

Table 1 (*continued*)

Period	England	France	America	Others
	George Hepplewhite (?–1786) Delicate furniture that showed modified classical influence. Combined straight and curved lines in skillful manner. Best known for shield-back chairs. *Thomas Sheraton (1751–1806)* Known for beautiful proportions. Restrained designs on small-scaled slender lines. Extensive inlay. Secret compartments and dual-purpose furniture.			
19th CENTURY	**Regency (1810–1820)** French influences that showed interest in Greek, Roman, and Egyptian designs. Furniture gradually heavier and more elaborate. Eventually exaggerated and bizarre. Period marks end of "golden age" in English furniture design. **Victorian (1837–1901)** Long period marked by many diverse influences. Style generally characterized by exces-	**Empire (1799–1815)** Furniture heavier and more pretentious. Motifs reflected patriotic spirit and influences of Napoleon.	**American Directoire and Empire (1805–1830)** Some influences of French styles. Patriotic motifs, widespread use of eagle in all phases of design. **Regional Styles** Development in different parts of country of Pennsylvania "Dutch," Scandinavian, Shaker, and Spanish Colonial styles.	**Biedermeier (1815–1860)** Style developed in Germany and Austria. Interpreted designs from various sources, including French Empire and Sheraton. Characterized by heavy proportions with simple decorations.

sive ornamentation, mixture of unrelated themes and ideas, elaborate and exaggerated forms and motifs. However, amidst clutter, designs can be adapted to present-day living with appealing gracefulness.

Post-Federal Period After 1840, designs followed Victorian styles. Many influences; elaborate furniture. Decoration in general heavy and cluttered. However, some fine examples of American Victorian cabinetwork.

20th CENTURY

DEVELOPMENT OF THE MODERN STYLE

Late 19th Century Evidence of reaction to overelaborate decoration of Victorian era and to use of machines to imitate handcrafts. William Morris, Charles Eastlake, Jr., and E. W. Godwin promoted skilled craftsmanship in design.

19th–20th Centuries **L'art Nouveau** fostered a new style based on naturalistic themes but rejected traditional forms. Idea of functionalism manifested in work of Louis Sullivan.

Early 20th Century Formation of **Deutsche Werkbund**, group of craftsmen who attempted to design for machine age.
Formation of **The Bauhaus**, school led by Walter Gropius, Marcel Breuer, and Ludwig Mies Van der Rohe; continued to emphasize proper use of machines and materials to create good designs.
Work of Le Corbusier and Frank Lloyd Wright in architecture developed theme of functionalism and had important effects on residential design.

1925 **The Paris Exposition** awakened widespread interest in new ideas, forms, and materials.

CURRENT TRENDS

Wide variety of designs. Some top-level designers working on problems of mass production at various cost levels. Scandinavian designs have had major role in development of style; Italian designs becoming increasingly important. Modern movement has shown rapid progress in America since 1940.

General Features—Functional designs; fresh, new proportions; asymmetrical space divisions. Emphasis on beauty of color and texture; use of new materials. Production of modular furniture to meet individual needs at lowest possible costs.

FIGURE 7-3 The seventeenth century influences some of the designs produced today.
A stately poster bed in oak echoes the architectural motifs of the seventeenth century. (*Courtesy
of Globe Furniture Company*)

FIGURE 7-4 A chair-table adapted from a
seventeenth century design shows that dual-
purpose furniture is not a new idea. The back
flips down to rest on the arms and the piece
can serve as a small dining or serving table.
(*Courtesy of Globe Furniture Company*)

FIGURE 7-5 Baroque styling is introduced in a room created by Joseph Braswell, A.I.D. Antiques and an elegant window treatment are emphasized by luxurious carpeting in a vibrant spring green color. Accents in coral and pale apricot create a subtle contrast that avoids a heavy appearance. (*Courtesy of Allied Chemical Corporation*, Source *fiber*)

Baroque and Rococo

Styles have developed gradually over a long period of time and have reached different areas of the world at widely spaced intervals. Following the Renaissance, a style known as Baroque developed in Italy and eventually spread to other European countries. Although the word *baroque* is French, it comes from an Italian name for a pearl with an uneven shape. The style is characterized by complex curves that are full and vigorous. It developed in different ways in Italy, France, England, and Spain but the general characteristics were splendor, elegance, and glamor. The first application was in architecture, and the most notable example is St. Peter's Cathedral in Rome. This magnificent structure was begun in 1506 and completed 120 years later. All during this period and until about 1670, the Baroque style flourished in the Italian architecture of churches, palaces, and villas. Naturally the feeling of the style spread to interior design and furniture. Although the furniture was large and heavy, it was lavish and elaborately decorated with panels, inlay work, painting, and nailheads.

Even while the Baroque style was flourishing in Italy, another style known as Rococo began to appear. It became increasingly popular by the end of the seventeenth century, particularly in France, where it reached its height by the middle of the eighteenth century. France was aspiring toward leadership in the artistic world and there was close association between Italian and French artists.

The Rococo style developed the use of curved lines and shapes, but in a much lighter and more delicate manner than the Baroque style. The word *rococo* comes from two French words meaning "rock" and "cockle shells." These two motifs, along with delicate but elaborate scrolls and foliage, were widely used in wall paneling, woodwork, furniture design, textiles, and ceramics. The Rococo designs of the Louis XV period were characterized by the French creative genius and perfect techniques in craftsmanship. They did not reach the same degree of refinement in Italy, where the work was somewhat coarse and theatrical by comparison with the French. The best examples of Italian Rococo furniture were made in Venice, which was the center of artistic and social life in Italy during the eighteenth century. The Venetian furniture of this period was notable for its painted decoration, which was applied in a manner that produced exquisite texture. The furniture was extremely ornate, but it also had a delightfully graceful quality.

By the time the Renaissance came to England, the Baroque style had a strong foothold on the Continent. Eventually the English borrowed and adapted both the Baroque and the Rococo themes, but because of the general feeling of English interior designs, the styles were interpreted quite differently.

Post-Renaissance Styles

The furniture designs that developed after the Renaissance are the ones that have the most significance for current home furnishings. As each country went through various periods of affluence or strife, popular tastes were guided by many factors. We must remember, however, that communications were not nearly as advanced as they are today. Influences did spread from one area to another, but not as quickly as they might today. Nationalistic interests and immediate happenings were more potent forces in setting the various styles that developed.

The following chapters contain a brief analysis of the furniture styles we live with today. These chapters represent nothing more than a survey, which is presented with the hope that the student will find some areas that interest him in more intensive study.

It has been pointed out that Renaissance styles were accepted rather slowly in England. During the sixteenth century, furniture was dignified and solid. It was generally made of oak. Relatively few pieces were used, but these included large refectory tables with carved bulbous legs, straight chairs with high backs, benches, stools, cupboards, Welsh dressers, some chests on legs, and large, canopied beds.

There has been a revival of interest in early English styles interpreted by current designers. Of course the contemporary versions are adapted to current needs, proportions, and methods of manufacturing. The sturdy qualities, however, seem to be becoming increasingly popular.

Jacobean and Restoration

James I was an admirer of Renaissance trends, and he became a patron of Inigo Jones, a celebrated architect who promoted Renaissance influences in England. During the Jacobean period, which derives its name from the name James, furniture was still straight lined and heavily carved, but it became somewhat smaller in scale. Spiral turns and carved scrolls gradually replaced the heavy bulbous legs. New pieces were introduced including drop-leaf and gate-leg tables. Chairs and sofas became lighter in weight and began to have upholstered seats and backs nailed to the framework. Until about 1660, oak was still the most popular wood, though walnut had become popular on the Continent. Wood paneling was widely used on walls and some wallpaper was introduced. Fabrics became more elegant and more brightly colored.

In general, Jacobean trends continued during the reign of Charles I (1625–1649). However, the middle of the seventeenth century was a period of destruction and disorder

8

English Styles

in England. Charles I was executed in 1649; during the Cromwellian period that followed, neither industry nor the arts made significant progress.

The monarchy was restored in 1660 when Charles II took over the throne. He emulated the lavish French court, and although his reign was corrupt he encouraged the arts. Another new era began, and progress in the decorative arts was given new impetus by the interest of the court and the wealthy middle class.

Both French and Flemish influences were strong during the Restoration period. Furniture became more refined and more comfortable. The backs of some chairs were slanted and the wing chair was introduced. Spiral turning and Flemish curves became much more popular on legs, backs, arms, and stretchers. Some chairs were made with caning. Smaller tables, some of them round, became popular. Game tables and bookcases were introduced.

Oriental themes were popular and Oriental rugs were used. In accessories there was greater use of marble and ivory, rare woods in inlay work, framed mirrors, and crystal chandeliers.

William and Mary

James II succeeded Charles to the throne but was eventually ousted. Mary, the daughter of James II, and her husband William, Holland's Prince of Orange, were asked to rule.

This period (1689–1702) is significant because the Dutch influence put great emphasis on a happy, comfortable home life. The English people had reacted unfavorably to the extravagance and lavishness of the previous court and they welcomed the simple tastes of William.

Furniture became much more delicate and graceful. Walnut was used almost exclusively. This was the beginning of the "age of walnut" in English cabinetmaking. Veneers were used in decorative treatment, notably in panels and cross-bandings on borders, with the grain running perpendicular to the main section. In general there was far less carving of furniture than in the previous styles. Strong French and Dutch influences continued throughout this period. A number of outstanding artists and craftsmen had migrated to England, including Daniel Marot, a French designer, engraver, and architect. He had gone from France to Holland, where he had served William as chief architect. Marot came to England in 1694 and his background was instrumental in promoting both the Dutch and the French influences on the English design of the period. France under Louis XIV had become the leading center for all the arts. As a result, the French influences were widespread throughout Europe.

Turning, often in the form of an inverted cup or of a tapering trumpet, was a favorite mode of decoration for supports. Marquetry in the forms of floral patterns and rambling foliage was popular. Lacquered furniture was widely used.

Although the form of furniture was essentially rectilinear, more curves gradually appeared. This was seen in the hooded tops of chests, the aprons of tables, and the splats of chairs. In about 1700 the cabriole leg was introduced in England. This curved leg, which was a decorative adaptation of the foreleg of a four-footed animal, had been incorporated in French furniture design during the Louis XIV period.

During the reign of William and Mary many new types of furniture appeared. These included various cabinets, tall case clocks, writing desks, dressing tables, and—probably the most important—the tall chest or highboy, which was a chest of drawers supported on a table. Tea drinking as a social custom was popular and resulted in the need for many small tables. There was a much wider use of upholstered furniture, and some pieces were done in overall upholstery.

Queen Mary had a large collection of porcelain and Delftware. It became quite fashionable to collect china and to display it above doors and chimney pieces. Tiered shelves and china cabinets also became popular.

Needlework was a favorite pastime. Beautiful subtle coloring was used for crewelwork (wool embroidery on linen). Designs for tapestries and other forms of needlework were often based on Oriental themes.

Queen Anne

The period of prosperity and expansion that England was enjoying was to continue for some time. During the reign of Queen Anne (1702–1714), increased trading and the resulting

wealth brought new ways of living and new ideas. Social life developed and the aristocracy enjoyed lives of comfort and culture.

The queen's name has become associated with a style that really began to develop during the later part of the William and Mary period. It flourished during the reign of Queen Anne, although she personally was not responsible for it, and it found continued popularity well into the reign of the following ruler, George I. The Queen Anne style, therefore, is also characteristic of the Early Georgian period.

The Queen Anne period, which saw the flowering of the "age of walnut," ushered in a golden age in English furniture design. Although there was a fairly rapid succession of different styles, the eighteenth century is notable for the artistry and the exceptionally high standards of craftsmanship in cabinetwork.

The rapidly expanding economy during the early years of the century gave rise to widespread activity in building. Inigo Jones had promoted increased interest in the works of Palladio, the famous Italian architect of the Renaissance who had been particularly influenced by structures of ancient Rome. The Venetian influence in English architecture was quite evident in the many Palladian mansions built for the wealthy.

Part of the education of young English aristocrats included travel to the Continent for first-hand study of the arts in Paris, Rome, Florence, and Venice. The interest in the arts and in literature and the familiarity of the wealthy Englishmen with life on the Continent were to influence interior design. The vogue for collecting extended to books, statuary, and all objects of art. Homes were built to display prized possessions. This mixture of the English love of formality, the grandiose style of the Italian Baroque, and the more subtle French Rococo and Oriental influences resulted in a charming elegance in English mansions.

The style of furniture of the Queen Anne period is characterized by a graceful simplicity and excellent proportion. There was a continuation of the Dutch influence, and the trend toward curved contours developed and expanded. The result was a style that has been popular ever since.

Curves were particularly evident in chairs, with fiddle- and vase-shaped center splats, and in the widespread use of cabriole legs. On *early* Queen Anne pieces, the legs were quite plain and usually rested on club feet. H-form stretchers were often used but gradually disappeared. As the style developed, a carved shell-motif was added to the knee of the leg and in later adaptations the foot was carved as a ball and claw.

A spoon-shaped profile curved at the back of the chair made it more comfortable. Seats flared so that they were wider at the front than at the back. Perhaps one of the most notable of the chair designs of the period is the upholstered wing chair, which became very popular. It was often upholstered in needlework with a floral design, and it often had a loose seat-cushion. As the style developed, the legs became more heavily carved and more massive. The arms of the wing chair as well as of the other forms of easy chairs generally curved outward in a scroll form.

The period is also distinctive for the wider use of many newer pieces of furniture, including the tallboy and the lowboy. Various small tables, secretaries, writing desks, upholstered love seats, and Windsor chairs also became popular during this period.

The highboy, which had been an innovation during the William and Mary period, developed into a much more graceful piece of furniture with the addition of a hooded top and cabriole legs. Queen Anne style highboys are still popular. Of course, our present-day interpretations have been scaled and adapted to current needs, but the essential style features still remain.

The simple, graceful lines of Queen Anne furniture, combined with beautiful fabrics, exquisite needlework, rugs and exotic accessories from the Orient, and Dutch, English, and French *objets d'art*, produce an atmosphere or a flavor in interior design that has remained appealing for generations.

Georgian

The eighteenth century was a glorious period in English cabinetmaking. The period takes its name from the kings who succeeded Queen Anne, but they were not popular rulers and their immediate courts had little influence on the English way of life. The aristocracy and the wealthy class held the power and set the modes.

The style divisions of the period do not coincide with the reigns of the kings. For our purposes we may divide the period as follows:

Early Georgian: 1714–1750.
Middle Georgian: 1750–1770.
Late Georgian: 1770–1810.

EARLY GEORGIAN. Essentially the style of the Early Georgian period is that of Queen Anne, and frequently the two periods are treated as one. Much of the furniture that is referred to as Queen Anne was designed and made during the Early Georgian period. Although the furniture became somewhat heavier and was decorated with more elaborate carving, the designs actually improved because of their finer proportions and more subtle lines. Some of the more beautiful examples in the Queen Anne style were made during this period. Many of the fine English cabinetmakers continued to follow the Queen Anne style of furniture until almost the middle of the eighteenth century.

During this period, an architect named William Kent was exerting considerable influence in England both in architecture and in furniture design. He was particularly active from about 1725 until 1745, and he initiated several trends that were to be developed in later years. The furniture designs of Kent were done mostly in mahogany, and this period is generally considered the transitional one between England's "age of walnut" and "age of mahogany." His furniture had architectural features meant to harmonize with the doors, windows, walls, and pediments of the Palladian mansions that he designed. Kent's furniture showed strong influences of the Venetian Baroque style, with much carving, gilding, and heavy ornamentation.

Wood paneling on walls was used extensively during the early part of the eighteenth century. Toward the middle of the century it became fashionable to use fabric or paper on walls. Oriental rugs remained popular. Rich, elegant fabrics were still used, but prints gained in favor.

MIDDLE GEORGIAN. As stated above, the vogue for mahogany started in the Early Georgian period. The dates for the so-called age of mahogany are generally given as 1710 to 1770. By 1733, mahogany was used almost

MIDDLE GEORGIAN
CHIPPENDALE

exclusively. About 1740, a new style of furniture began to evolve. The fact that mahogany lends itself better than walnut to more elaborately carved detail was one contributing factor to the new style.

An important factor in the design of this period was the increasing popularity of French designs in England. Rococo was at the height of its popularity in France. In the beginning, English cabinetmakers adapted the Rococo decorative motifs to the typical English forms, but from about 1745 to 1765 the French influence was obvious in both form and ornamentation.

One must remember that there was a pronounced interest in architecture all during the Georgian periods, and that architects were held in very high esteem. Not only were architects interested in furniture designs, but cabinetmakers were serious students of architecture. From these varying influences evolved a style called *Chippendale*, named after the man who was not only the most famous designer of the period but perhaps of all time.

Thomas Chippendale. Much has been written about the genius of Thomas Chippendale (1718–1779). He is renowned as a furniture designer as well as a master craftsman, and his name is almost exclusively associated with the style of the Middle Georgian period. It seems only fair to point out that research by students of the Chippendale style has punctured some of the bubbles and exploded some of the myths that have created an aura of such greatness about the man himself. This is not meant in any way to discredit the elegance and magnificence of the Chippendale style, which is still popular, nor to underestimate the quality of furniture that came from his shop. The studies merely suggest that Mr. Chippendale was not personally responsible for a number of the accomplishments that have been attributed to him for many years.

Chippendale's father, also Thomas Chippendale, was a cabinetmaker and woodcarver who opened a shop in London in about 1727. The younger Chippendale opened his own shop in 1749. Four years later he moved his shop to 60 St. Martin's Lane, and for the rest of his life he headed a large firm that decorated a number of important English mansions.

Chippendale was a good businessman and enjoyed an admirable rapport with his clients. He maintained very high standards of workmanship and his staff included fine designers and craftsmen. In 1754 he published the "Gentleman's and Cabinet Maker's Directoire," the most impressive book on furniture design that had ever been produced in England.

A question has been raised as to whether or not all of the designs in the directory were those of Chippendale or whether some were done by members of his staff. It has also been pointed out that although Chippendale has been extolled as a master woodcarver, there is actually no evidence that he did any of the carving himself.

The book published by Chippendale invited many other cabinetmakers to copy his designs, which they did. Because the furniture was not signed or identified in any way, it is difficult now to determine exactly which pieces actually came from the Chippendale shop. There are relatively few authenticated pieces for which bills of sale or other corroborating evidence are available. Other editions of the directory were subsequently published. Although not all the designs were suitable for actual execution, they give us a good idea of the influences that prevailed.

Thomas Chippendale, Jr., carried on his father's business until 1804, when he went bankrupt; so for almost a century the name was esteemed in the circles of British cabinetmaking. Although Chippendale has been questioned as a "leader" in style trends, the fact remains that during the Middle Georgian period, the style of furniture that was made bears his name and it has been extremely popular ever since.

Basically, the Chippendale style has a masculine quality combined with a graceful elegance. Probably this is why it has been so widely used for over two hundred years. The curves, such as the typical "camel back," are strong and forthright, yet gentle. The proportions are comfortable, and the design is sturdy without being too heavy.

Three important influences have been associated with Chippendale design: French, Oriental, and Gothic.

FIGURE 8-1 Some excellent reproductions of Georgian furniture are produced by today's craftsmen. (a) Queen Anne Coffee Table; (b) Chippendale Pie Crust Table; (c) Hepplewhite Bookcase Desk; (d) Chippendale Blockfront Secretary. (*Courtesy of Biggs Antique Company*)

(a)

(b)

(c)

(d)

The Rococo mode, fashionable in France from about 1720 until 1760, was interpreted in English furniture design by the combination of broken curves and straight lines in basic forms and by the carved ornamentation of flowers, foliage, and fruit. Rococo themes were used in heavily carved small tables, sconces, mirrors, and other small pieces. Though these motifs were also used to decorate larger pieces, the English could not quite equal the skill of the French designers in combining form and decorative features to express the Rococo spirit in larger pieces. Nevertheless, the Chippendale designs in the Rococo style are excellent examples of graceful elegance, representing the rather unusual blending of a somewhat solid quality with the fanciful lightness of Rococo themes.

Perhaps some of the best examples of the French Rococo influence in Chippendale designs are in the openwork backs of chairs and settees. These have been copied, adapted, and modified in countless ways. The ribband back is perhaps the best-known Chippendale chair design.

The vogue for Chinese motifs and ideas was very much evidenced in French design during this period. It is not surprising that the interest spread to England, nor that the English designers produced furniture intended to satisfy the British "Chinese tastes." Although the basic forms were still typically mid-Georgian English, they were carved with Oriental motifs such as pagodas and Chinese figures. Fretwork was widely used in moldings and panels as well as for the arms and backs of chairs. The interest in lacquered furniture, which had been so popular earlier in the century, was renewed. Chinoiseries, somewhat whimsical motifs or scenes showing make-believe Chinese figures, were popular decorative themes in lacquered furniture, fabrics, and accessories. Chinese wallpaper was widely used as were Oriental accessories.

The Gothic influences in Chippendale's work have been somewhat discredited as his merely yielding to the whims of clients during a phase of interest in the Gothic revival. Straight legs, resembling columns, carved details of trefoil and cinquefoil, and tracery work gave the designs a Gothic flavor but that was about all. There was no attempt to adapt or emulate basic Gothic form and proportion. Certainly the Gothic influence was not responsible for Chippendale's best designs. It is generally recognized that the French influences were by far the most important.

It should be pointed out that although Chippendale's work was mostly in mahogany and his style is best known for the mahogany pieces that came from his shop, during his later years he did produce some furniture in other woods and in designs that were typical of Robert Adam. For almost ten years, from 1770 to 1779, he worked with woods other than mahogany and in a style that was quite different from the one usually associated with his name.

LATE GEORGIAN. The later part of the eighteenth century and the early part of the nineteenth century was a period of intense interest in classicism, brought about by archaeological discoveries in Pompeii. The site of this ancient Roman city was discovered in 1748 and excavations were begun of the ruins. Pompeii had been a flourishing city that was also a resort for wealthy Romans. In 79 A.D. it was buried under ashes by an eruption of Vesuvius. The preservation of the complete city, including works of art, during the following centuries was somewhat amazing. When the excavations were underway it was possible to reconstruct an unprecedented picture of the life of the ancient Romans. The publication of numerous books on the findings of these studies led to a revival of interest in the classics, and this interest led to a Neoclassic movement that permeated the arts. Although the discovery of the Pompeiian ruins served as the trigger for the classic revival, it has been suggested that the movement was certainly fostered by a weary reaction to the Renaissance and the Rococo art forms. The time was ripe for new themes and the interest in classics provided a suitable basis for new ideas.

The Late Georgian period probably represents the zenith of the "golden age" of English interior design. There was a keen awareness of a room as a blending of furnishings and architectural features. Plaster walls painted in soft colors replaced the wood paneling that had been popular earlier in the century. Plasterwork festoons, garlands, panels, and medallions gave a lightness to the architectural composition.

The Neoclassic mode brought with it a revolt against curves and heavy proportions.

Although elegance was still a key theme, it was expressed in a much more formal, restrained type of grandeur than the Rococo themes had produced.

This era is sometimes referred to as the ''age of satinwood.'' Mahogany was still used, but the trend toward lighter colors and more exotic grain patterns resulted in the use of a wide variety of woods, such as satinwood, rosewood, harewood, tulipwood, and holly. Instead of an emphasis on carving as a decorative medium, contrasting veneers were used in many ways. Grain patterns were selected and arranged to lend their intrinsic beauty. Inlay, gilding, and painted decorations were

also favored means of decoration.

Although Chippendale's name is more closely associated with designs of the mid-Georgian period, his shop did produce some excellent furniture in the characteristic mode of the earlier years of the Late Georgian period. The names associated with these later years of the eighteenth century include such famous peers in furniture design as Robert Adam, George Hepplewhite, and Thomas Sheraton.

Robert Adam. Probably the strongest force in the application of classical themes to furniture design was an architect named Robert Adam (1728–1792). He and his three brothers received early training from their

FIGURE 8-2 A typical Georgian dining room adapted to one of today's more luxurious homes. (*Designed by Barbara D'Arcy*, *A.I.D.*, *Bloomingdale's N.Y.*)

LATE GEORGIAN,
ADAM

LATE GEORGIAN
HEPPLEWHITE

father, a Scottish architect. Robert enjoyed a most successful career as an architect in London. He and his brother James worked together, designing many public buildings and private homes for wealthy clients. The Adam brothers published their architectural designs and included designs for furnishings. They were not cabinetmakers and the actual construction of the furniture was done by other firms, including Chippendale.

Although there were many fine architects during the Georgian period, Robert Adam was probably the best known. He was held in high esteem and served as architect for the king for several years. Because Adam was so concerned with final effects, he considered every detail important. The furniture that he designed to blend with his interiors clearly reflected his architectural styles and the work of Adam is noted for classic simplicity. He had a remarkable ability to use the motifs and themes found in Roman stuccowork in light and delicate ornamentation. He also used festoons, garlands, and trails of vine.

Adam's work, with its fine proportions and delicate ornamentation, was a source of inspiration for other designers. He catered to the wealthy who could afford large, sumptuous homes, but his work was widely copied and adapted for smaller homes by other architects and designers. Because Adam emphasized the importance of proper scaling and the use of harmonious detail, the modifications and adaptations of his designs for smaller homes produced many interesting effects.

George Hepplewhite. Not very much is known about the personal life of Hepplewhite (d. 1786). He was both a cabinetmaker and a furniture designer, and his shop in London was responsible for a style of furniture that was extremely popular in the latter part of the eighteenth century. His designs have been widely copied and adapted ever since.

The catalog of Hepplewhite's shop, the *Cabinetmaker and Upholsterer's Guide*, was published two years after his death by his widow, Alice. She had continued to conduct the business and two more editions were published later.

As in the case of Chippendale, it is difficult to tell exactly which pieces were the work of Hepplewhite himself, because only a few of the several hundred designs were actually signed by him. It is reasonable to assume that most of these signed designs were done under his supervision or were approved by him. In the preface to the catalog there is a statement that "we designedly followed the latest or most prevailing fashion." The esteem accorded Hepplewhite has been based on his ability to translate the prevailing tastes for the Neoclassic style into furniture designs that were both elegant and useful.

Probably some of the furniture designed by Robert Adam was made in the Hepplewhite shop. The influences of the Adam brothers and the contemporary French Louis XVI style are clearly seen in the work of Hepplewhite. The style is delicate, light, and refined. The contours of the style are essentially rectilinear, but Hepplewhite used more curved lines in the basic forms than did other designers of the time.

The best examples of Hepplewhite designs were chairs and small pieces, such as pier tables, dressing tables, commodes, and screens. The open backs of the chairs and the settees were almost always shaped in curves to form shields, hearts, or ovals. The famous shield back with which Hepplewhite is always associated was also used by Adam, but Hepplewhite used it more constantly and more successfully. Many of the chair backs were intricate compositions of curving lines. Some of the heart-shaped backs give a rather sentimental, feminine flavor to the designs. The arm supports for the chairs were usually curved. The chests of drawers and sideboards sometimes had bow or serpentine fronts. Curved lines were also introduced in oval table tops and semicircular commodes. Although some cabriole legs were shown in the catalog, the style favored straight, tapered legs. These were either quadrangular or cylindrical and were frequently fluted or reeded.

The furniture was usually mahogany or satinwood, but other woods such as tulipwood, sycamore, harewood, and rosewood were used for decoration. Beautiful colors and grains were carefully selected for use in bands or for exquisite inlay work. Some designs were painted, but gilding was also used for decoration.

A wide variety of decorative motifs is to be found in Hepplewhite designs. Of course the classic motifs favored by Adam were used. Acanthus leaves, scrolls, husks, ribbons, bowknots, rosettes, fans, wreaths, vines, garlands, and festoons were all employed in a refined, elegant manner to give the designs their graceful delicacy. Hepplewhite is credited with introducing the Prince of Wales feather as a decorative motif. Basic designs of the chair backs often centered around this feather emblem, but wheat stalks, vines, and urns were also used. Sometimes the furniture was decorated with lovely insets of Angelica Kaufman's painting or with medallions made by Josiah Wedgwood, a contemporary who was interpreting the Neoclassic spirit in the field of ceramics.

The fine proportions of the Hepplewhite style, and the lightness and simplicity of his design have made it a favorite with those who prefer a graceful style with a simple elegance.

Thomas Sheraton. Many people consider Thomas Sheraton (1751–1806) the greatest of all the designers in this "golden age" of English furniture. From what is known about him, it seems that he was a rather peculiar person who led a varied career in the fifty-five years of his life. Although he had some early training as a cabinetmaker, he was also a Baptist preacher, an author of religious works, a drawing teacher, an inventor, and a mechanic. Sheraton came from impoverished surroundings and never enjoyed any degree of financial success. When he settled in London in about 1790 he lived in a humble abode with his wife and two children. It has not been established that he actually carried on a business of cabinetmaking there, but he did publish a book in four parts entitled *Cabinet-maker and Upholsterer's Drawing Book*. The first part appeared in 1791. Later he published a dictionary of terms for cabinetmaking and upholstering and had plans for an encyclopedia, which he did not complete. A book of designs from these works was published posthumously in 1812.

Sheraton may have done some cabinetwork in his early life and perhaps supervised some of the construction of his designs, but his fame is certainly not based on actual cabinetmaking. His books were intended for use by other craftsmen and they were widely used in both England and America. The Sheraton style is based on the drawings in these publications.

Sheraton's designs interpreting the Neoclassic trends were unsurpassed for their excellent proportions, fine balance, and exquisite ornamentation. His early work showed many adaptations of the Adam, Hepplewhite, and Louis XVI styles. Later his work was undoubtedly influenced by French Directoire and Empire styles. Nevertheless, the designs showed originality and an unusually keen awareness of beautiful lines.

The basic forms were generally rectilinear with emphasis on the vertical line. Straight lines were favored, but lovely graceful curves were incorporated in a somewhat subtle manner with convex corners on sideboards, gently curved arms on chairs, elongated urns in chair backs, and festoons or garlands used as ornament. The rails across the backs of chairs were usually straight, however, and the legs were mostly straight and tapered.

Sheraton's mechanical ability manifested itself in furniture with secret compartments. He also designed several dual-purpose pieces and was probably the first furniture designer to show twin beds.

Satinwood and mahogany were used for much of the Sheraton-style furniture. Other woods, including tulipwood, harewood, ebony, and rosewood were frequently used for bands or panels. Techniques for veneering and inlay work were excellent by the late eighteenth century. Sheraton ornamented his designs with garlands, scrolls, festoons, trailing vines, rosettes, fans, and shells. Marquetry and painted decorations were also used. He also liked gilding. Sometimes painted medallions or panels showing classical motifs or figures were used as decoration. Although Sheraton adapted many of the favorite motifs and used all the tricks of reeding, turning, inlay, and painting, his designs never had a gingerbread appearance. His fame as a furniture designer probably stems from the restraint with which he used the techniques of ornamentation and his feeling for beautiful proportions and purity of line. The combination of these qualities produced some of the finest furniture designs ever known.

Regency

George III was declared mentally incompetent and the Prince of Wales acted as regent from 1810 to 1820, after which he became George IV. This ten-year period is known as the Regency, but the style trends associated with it started in about 1795 and lasted until almost 1837, when Victoria became Queen.

Political developments were shaping new styles in France and America. Both of these countries looked upon English designs with disfavor. The "golden age" had come to an end and furniture designers seemed to lack the creative inspiration that had marked the

LATE GEORGIAN
SHERATON

eighteenth century. Ideas were borrowed from the French Directoire and Empire styles, which reflected a revived interest in ancient Greek, Roman, and Egyptian art. In England, this revived interest was manifest in English adaptations of the Empire styles. With this revival of classicism, however, it was the heavier of the classical forms and motifs that were preferred to the more graceful and delicate themes.

Furniture gradually became heavier in scale and more massive in proportion. Attempts to reproduce and adapt the forms of Greek and Roman furniture resulted in arms with heavy outward scrolls and couches with scrolled headrests. Tripods and adaptations of the characteristic Greek side chair known as the *klismos* also appeared. In the early Regency furniture, these designs were executed with simplicity. The heritage of fine English design and expert workmanship gave them a dignified beauty. Although there are no great designers associated with the Regency period, it should be noted again that in his later years Sheraton showed the French Empire influences. This phase of his work is not closely associated with the so-called Sheraton style and is more representative of early Regency. Thomas Chippendale, Jr., was continuing the business of his father and made some excellent furniture in the Regency style.

A noted English architect, Henry Holland (1746–1806), designed some beautiful interiors and included designs for some lovely, graceful furniture in the Regency style. In addition, a wealthy art collector named Thomas Hope (1769–1831) published a book of furniture designs that reflected the French Empire influences and his own interest in archaeology.

In addition to Greek, Roman, and Egyptian motifs, Chinese and Gothic themes were found in ornamentation. Thus furniture was decorated with cornucopias, Egyptian figures, sphinxes, lotus flowers, and chinoiseries. Animal heads and paws were used in various ways. Furniture legs terminating in paws were popular.

Rosewood, mahogany, and satinwood were widely used. Brass and bronze were used extensively for inlay work and trellis insets in doors, moldings, and fretwork.

As the Regency style developed, it became bizarre. English designers showed a lack of discrimination and taste in applying ornament to form. Exaggerated curves and superfluous decorations marked the decline of the Regency furniture designs.

REGENCY

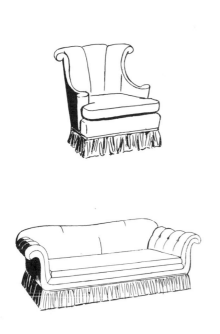

Victorian

Queen Victoria had the longest reign of any English monarch. The sixty-four years of the Victorian period, from 1837 to 1901, naturally saw many different influences and trends, so it is difficult to generalize about the characteristics of the style. When one must generalize, however, the adjectives usually used are *lavish*, *ostentatious*, *eclectic*, and *ugly*. The disdain that most aesthetic souls feel toward the Victorian style is somewhat understandable, because the decline that had started during the Regency period continued to a point where taste and the appreciation of beauty reached an incredibly low level. But it is unfortunate that there is a widespread trend to associate only the bad with Victoriana. It is true that not many of us would want to be confined to authentic Victorian surroundings today, but we should not dismiss the possibilities that various facets of the style have to offer. Some designers have recognized the elements of charm beneath the rather grotesque clutter of Victorian design and have managed to adapt the Victorian flavor to contemporary interiors. When this is done with taste and discrimination, the effects are not only lovely but livable. There are some basic qualities of the Victorian style that can be extremely appealing. It is something of a challenge to accept the "good" and discard the "bad" in order to create an atmosphere of beauty and functionalism.

The aesthetic sense of the English people reached a low ebb, and they eagerly accepted novelties, fakes, and imitations. The abundance of poor-quality merchandise on the market is often attributed to the inception of the technological age and the use of machines. Most of these inferior products were designed to represent lavish luxury at the lowest possible cost. This attempt produced some decorative horrors.

The Victorian period may be divided into three phases: the early period, which lasted until about 1850; the mid-Victorian period, from about 1850 to 1875; and the late Victorian period from about 1875 to 1901. There was much overlapping of trends in each of these phases, and because of the general borrowing of ideas from many different sources and the ready acceptance of novelties, it is difficult to define the trends at any particular time. The early period seems to have been most dominated by enthusiasm for Gothic styles. By the middle of the century the taste seems to have leaned toward Renaissance and Rococo forms, with excessive and exaggerated curves and overabundant ornament. The third phase shows some simplification with a rather poor adaptation of medieval themes. Throughout the period the eclectic mood was dominant. Ideas were borrowed from Greek, Gothic, French, Venetian, Turkish, Persian, and Egyptian sources. The adaptation of modes, forms, and motifs was carried out with no semblance of authenticity. Frequently a designer mixed several unrelated ideas and then added a bit of novelty of his own choosing.

By the middle of the nineteenth century the typical Victorian interior was confusing, heavy, and oppressive. Pattern and ornamentation were used everywhere. The motto seemed to be "never use a straight line," and the abundant curves were voluminous. The mania for bric-a-brac cluttered rooms with statuary, figurines, artificial flowers, and a wide variety of other such ornaments. The "what-not," a special shelf arrangement that displayed these possessions, was almost mandatory. Windows were covered with curtains and heavy draperies in intricate arrangements usually embellished with fringes or tassels—or both. Carpeting of many colors, often floral patterns, was popular. Walls were covered with patterned paper or fabric. The furniture, often poorly proportioned and massive in scale, was heavily carved and ornamented. Black walnut, rosewood, ebony, and mahogany were popular woods. Mother-of-pearl was often used for inlay work. Marble was used extensively for table tops. Even *papier mâché* was used for furniture.

Chairs, sofas, and love seats—which were especially popular—were upholstered with horsehair. Plush, velvet, satin, and brocade were used extensively and were often tufted. Tidies or antimacassars were small doilies used on the backs and arms of chairs to protect them from soil. Lambrequins or strips of cloth were draped over windows, man-

tels, and tables. These also were decorated with fringes and tassels. Elaborate chandeliers and sconces were fashionable. In some, gas jets replaced candles.

It seems incredible that we could adapt any part of this mélange of ostentation and poor taste to present-day living. Yet there were some very fine pieces of furniture made by expert craftsmen for wealthy Victorians. In addition, our contemporary designers have modified and adapted the styles to produce furniture that has the Victorian flavor without excessive ornament. These reproductions are often improvements on the originals from the standpoint of design and comfort.

Several men should be mentioned in connection with the Victorian period because of their efforts to instigate reforms. Sir Charles Eastlake (1793–1865) was an English architect and art critic who deplored the lavish designs of the Victorian era and urged a return to simplicity. He preferred the Gothic themes, and furniture manufacturers attempted to comply with demands for furniture in the Eastlake style.

William Morris (1834–1896) was a cabinetmaker, designer (mostly of textiles and wallpaper), weaver, printer, poet, and essayist. He wrote, "Have nothing in your home that you do not know to be useful and believe to be beautiful." Morris, along with John Ruskin and several other leaders, decried mechanization and attempted to revive both purity in design and pride in craftsmanship. The dissatisfactions voiced by these writers and their associates gave impetus to a renewed interest in skills. Their dislikes for machine-made designs could not, of course, stem the forces of mechanization, but they were instrumental in provoking a more discriminating level of taste and a more thoughtful approach to the role of the designer in a mechanized society.

The inspiration for the movement toward modern style might be indirectly traced back to Morris and his associates, though they had no direct relationship to it.

9

French Styles

For generations, France—and particularly Paris—held a unique position of world leadership in the development of the arts. There are probably many reasons for this, not the least of which is the inherent love of beauty so characteristic of the French people. The nationalistic appreciation of the joy and the art of living is sometimes exuberant and sometimes restrained, but it seems to be always present. Art is part of the French life and soul. The spirit of romanticism that pervades the French approach to the business of everyday living is witnessed by French excellence in the culinary arts and in the world of fashion. A close personal association with the arts seems to be a more intrinsic quality in the French people than in many other peoples.

In spite of the dark periods in France's history when creative activity reached low ebbs the country managed to survive with a certain position of prestige in the arts. Even as France's supremacy in some fields is being challenged today, we tend to harbor a certain sentimentalism for her leadership in design.

Economic, political, and social forces have fostered the interchange of artistic ideas among various countries. France has welcomed and encouraged artists. She has established an atmosphere of freedom for the creative spirit. When France has borrowed ideas from other countries, the results have usually had a distinctive French interpretation—the French "touch," as it has been called. Except in a few outstanding instances, other countries have not been as successful in adapting French ideas to their own particular styles. There have been some excellent designs based on French influences, but the flavor remains French rather than being absorbed in the way the French use foreign ideas.

The esteem accorded to artists and craftsmen in France may be traced back to the Renaissance. In the latter part of the sixteenth century, the French court began to look with envy at the splendor enjoyed by the Italian rulers. The Renaissance movement had been underway for some time in Italy. During the reign of Francis I (1515–1547), Italian artists, including Da Vinci and Cellini, had been invited to work at the French court. Catherine de Medici, the wife of Henry II (reigned 1547–1559), was Italian and continued to encourage this Italian influence in the French arts. It was not until the reign of Henry IV (1589–1610), however, that the government actively encouraged the development of the decorative arts. He wanted the personal glorification of a splendid court and made plans for the development of France as the artistic center of the world. These plans included various programs of sponsorship for artists and craftsmen as well as encouragement of the industries making tapestries, rugs, and fabrics.

During the reign of Louis XIII (1610–1643), Cardinal Richelieu was a potent factor in encouraging the development of the arts. He urged French artists to travel to other countries and invited foreign artists to work in Paris. The result was a mixture of many influences in French art during the first half of the seventeenth century—mostly Spanish, Flemish, and Italian.

The style of the Louis XIII period was confused by the various foreign influences. In general, the furniture was rectilinear in form and heavy in proportion. But the French craftsmen were learning and adapting new ideas. Gradually a French style was developing. In the characteristic French manner, the new ideas were modified with the stamp of good taste. By the middle of the seventeenth century, the Baroque style was popular and it continued to develop during the following years.

Louis XIV

When Louis XIV was proclaimed king he was only five years old. He reigned from 1643 to 1715, but his mother, Anne of Austria, acted as regent until 1651. Cardinal Mazarin, first minister until he died in 1661, was an enthusiastic patron of the arts. When Louis assumed the responsibilities of the throne he did so with a firm hand. He was an absolute monarch who chose the sun as his emblem—"*Le Roi Soleil.*"

He established a glittering, pompous court. Splendor and magnificence were the keynotes

of his reign. Louis XIV was intensely interested in establishing France as the world leader in the arts. His efforts in this direction gave France the position of supremacy that Italy had enjoyed since the Renaissance.

The palace at Versailles is a monument to the pompous splendor of the Sun King's court. The huge building was surrounded by formal gardens, lakes, temples, statues, and fountains. The project was the combined work of many great architects, painters, sculptors, designers, and craftsmen working under the direction of Charles Lebrun. He was a painter who viewed the decorative arts on a par with the fine arts, and though he had the ability to conceive and execute projects on a grandiose scale, he was cognizant of every detail in the design.

Throughout the building were great public rooms, salons, and private apartments that were works of magnificent architectural splendor. Walls and ceilings were decorated with carving, paintings, paneling, mirrors, and tapestries with an extravagance that had never been known before. The famous Hall of Mirrors, 240 feet long, has been the scene of many historic events since the building was made a museum. The beautiful windows, the magnificent ceilings decorated with paintings by Charles Lebrun, and the green marble columns provide an atmosphere of incomparable splendor that is characteristic of the whole palace. Because the walls and ceilings were such magnificent decorative features of each room, the furniture was somewhat secondary. However it was designed in the elaborate Baroque style to blend with the decor.

The style of furniture that developed during the reign of Louis XIV is important because it was the first of the truly French styles. It was massive, regal, and formal. Because it was so elaborate it was suitable only for the aristocracy. Rich carving, gilding, oriental lacquer, and marquetry were used to produce the elegant pieces. As the period progressed, the lines of the furniture became more curvaceous. Both S and C scrolls were widely used. The tables, usually placed against the walls, were quite large. Commodes became quite popular and various types of writing desks made their appearance. Armoires were widely used. Huge beds with much ornamentation and elaborate draperies were the vogue. These were often considered a status symbol. The more elaborate the bed the more desirable it was as a mark of distinction.

Rich carving, elaborate inlay, and metal mounts were used to produce the elegant pieces. Carved wood was often gilded and pieces were frequently topped with beautiful colored marble. The upholstery fabrics were richly colored velvets, damasks, satins, and brocades. Tapestries were used for both upholstery and wall hangings. Various types of needlework were also popular.

Although the Louis XIV period was inspired by the Italian Baroque style, the French artists handled the theme with refinement and restraint.

Perhaps the most famous cabinetmaker of the time was André Charles Boulle (1642–1732), the favorite of the king and of the aristocracy. He developed techniques that had been used before but not perfected. "Boulle work" refers to marquetry of tortoiseshell, ebony, and metal, including bronze, copper, silver, and brass. Boulle used bronze mounts and ormolu.

The enthusiasm for Chinese art during this period prompted the development of delightful chinoiseries. The French interpretation of the imaginary Chinese figures and scenes founded this whimsical form of decoration, which was to be copied and adapted in many different forms.

Regency

It must be pointed out that the period referred to as French Regency occurred about a century before the one known as English Regency. The intervening years were marked by technological advances due to the Industrial Revolution and the resultant sociological changes. The student must be careful not to associate these two periods because of the similarity in names.

Louis XIV died in 1715. The actual period when France was governed by Philippe, the Duke of Orléans, serving as regent for Louis XV, covers only the years 1715 to 1723. From the standpoint of style development, however, the period includes the transitional years from about 1700 to 1720. Many features of the Louis XIV style were disappearing and new ones associated with the Louis XV style were beginning to appear. Changes in style evolve over a period of years and one supersedes another in a very gradual process.

During the Louis XIV period, furniture had

been majestic and elegant. The trend during the Regency period was toward less formality and a lighter spirit. The heavy Baroque features of the earlier style were gradually replaced by the more graceful and exuberant forms of the newly developing Rococo theme. The spirit of gaiety and the preoccupation with fantasy were becoming more marked, although the Regency style managed to retain its dignity.

Architects and painters exerted a tremendous influence on interior designs. The work of Antoine Watteau (1684–1721) and his followers established a new school of painting and was largely responsible for the increasing popularity of the Rococo trend. Watteau, as well as many other great artists, delved into decorative design to produce compositions that were reproduced or executed by skilled craftsmen.

It was quite evident that during this transitional period a new spirit of vivacious gaiety was developing in France. The interest in the Orient continued and the new spirit stimulated the French imagination to produce compositions that were thoroughly delightful in their amusing fantasia. Turkish, Hindu, and Persian figures were also themes employed in all forms of decoration. Another favorite subject was the monkey in whimsical motifs known as *singeries*.

The furniture, although lighter in scale and softer in design, was still embellished with carving and marquetry. Much of the furniture was gilded, but beautifully colored woods were also employed. Bronze was popular for mounts and decorative hardware, but frequently it was chased and gilded.

Although chairs and tables became lighter in scale during the Regency period, commodes remained rather heavy. The *bombe* shape was introduced and was to become increasingly popular.

These trends initiated during the Regency were to develop during the reign of Louis XV to establish the style associated with his name.

Louis XV

Several factors contributed to the rather black period for the French monarchy during the reign of Louis XV (1723–1774). The king did not have a talent for ruling the country with a firm hand and instead conducted a court renowned for its frivolity, extravagance, and corrupt behavior. The aristocracy was indifferent to the people and the national problems.

A rather strong middle class had developed and had begun to resent the heavy burden of taxation coupled with the mismanagement of the government. France also fared badly in her efforts toward colonial domination. The general spirit of discontent was fired by the critical writings of French philosophers and economists. Although the seeds of revolution were germinating all during this era it was actually a period that saw the development of a wealthy upper-middle-class bourgeoisie composed of merchants, professional men, bankers, and prosperous farmers. The rise of this group created new demands for homes that were comfortable, refined, and representative of social position.

Most of the palaces and residences of the aristocracy were filled with extremely elaborate furniture that was impossible to reproduce in any large quantity. However, some of the pieces could be adapted or copied in a less sumptuous manner to meet the requirements of the bourgeoisie. This type of furniture, with its gracefulness, excellent proportions, and somewhat restrained elegance, was often more beautiful than its more elaborate royal counterpart.

The French Rococo style reached its height of perfection during this era. The skill of the French craftsmen was highly developed during this period. The manner of life with its emphasis on comfort and convenience resulted in a desire for smaller rooms designed for special purposes—music rooms, game rooms, sitting rooms, and—later on—dining rooms. Accordingly, furniture became smaller in scale and a wider variety of small pieces, especially tables, was used.

The prevailing characteristic of the Louis XV style was the emphasis on curved lines. Basic forms were curved whenever possible. *Bombe* and serpentine curves were widely used. Corners were rounded, legs were curved, and ornamentation was based on curved motifs. Asymmetrical balance was employed whenever possible. With all of these principles employed in one piece, the resulting beauty of design was indeed a tribute to the French artistic genius, good taste, and technical flare.

A wide variety of different colored woods was used for veneers and in marquetry work.

Chair

Commode

Much of the furniture was painted or gilded. Lacquered work was extremely popular both for panels and for whole pieces. Some of this work was imported from the Orient, but European craftsmen developed new lacquering techniques. Porcelain plaques or panels of mirrors were often used as embellishments.

Motifs were delicate and feminine. Exquisite floral bouquets were depicted in inlaid panels. Garland and trellis patterns were widely used, as were cupids, hearts, doves, bowknots, ribbons, and musical instruments. Pastoral scenes and motifs were also popular. Leaves and the cockleshell were extensively used.

This was an era of intrigue, and much of the furniture was designed with mechanical devices that transformed the piece in some way or opened up secret compartments.

Madame de Pompadour, favorite mistress of the king, was instrumental in setting many style trends during the period. Her interest in the Orient added impetus to the vogue for Chinese decoration. She is credited with having exquisite taste, which is probably responsible in part, at any rate, for some of the restraints found in design toward the latter part of the reign of Louis XV.

Several eminent architects and artists opposed the Rococo style during the Louis XV period. Derisive publications appeared criticizing the exaggerations of the style, and as the criticism was mounting the importance of the archaeological excavations at Pompeii was beginning to have an impact on all the arts. In about 1760 the classical influences were beginning to appear in furniture design, and the next decade was a period of transition from the Rococo style to the Neoclassical. The exaggerated curves gradually became softer and more restrained, until a new style evolved with emphasis on rectilinear shapes and straight lines. Although these Neoclassical trends are not usually associated with the Louis XV period, the new style was firmly established by the time the king died in 1774.

Louis XVI

The designs that are associated with the Louis XVI style represent classical beauty interpreted with the exquisite taste of the French. The style embodies graceful lines, perfect proportions, and restrained ornamentation. The principles of the style, executed with the superior skill of the French craftsmen, produced the acme in French furniture design. By the time Louis XVI ascended the throne in 1774, the style was well established and it remained popular until the Revolution in 1789.

The aristocracy during this era continued to live lives of ease and luxurious comfort. It had become the vogue, however, to profess simplicity and to admire the noble virtues of a humble life. It was fashionable to be interested in antiquity, and the inspiration for the decorative arts was drawn from Roman architectural form. The French designers and craftsmen incorporated the Greek and Roman ideas with grace and delicacy. Although the basic forms were rectangular and the emphasis was on the straight line, they avoided severity and heaviness by skillful incorporation of graceful curves. The wide variety of ornamental motifs included bouquets of flowers, garlands, flags, wreaths, and festoons. Classical motifs such as the Greek fret, vases, and mythological figures were used, especially in panel moldings and for mounts. The pastoral scenes were used in various forms of decoration and some motifs had an agricultural flavor. The romantic cupids and cherubs continued to find favor. Panels were often used for decoration and sometimes the panel corners were indented and embellished with rosettes.

Marie Antoinette had several favorite cabinetmakers—notably Jean Henri Riesener (1734–1806), one of the outstanding craftsmen of the time. His work typified the finer qualities of Louis XVI style and is notable for exquisite floral marquetry and bronze mounts. Riesener also excelled in making furniture with mechanical devices and secret compartments, which were still popular.

Mahogany was a very popular wood, although woods such as walnut, satinwood, and sycamore continued to be used. Much of the furniture was painted, usually in tones of ivory or soft gray. Small tables and commodes often had marble tops, but writing desks and tables frequently had tooled leather tops.

Although the beautiful French silk fabrics continued to be used for upholstery, there was widespread use of hand-blocked cottons and linens. The well-known *Toile de Jouy* cottons with pastoral scenic motifs were especially favored. Needlework was also used extensively.

Soft color tones on walls and ceilings and in Oriental, Aubusson, and Savonnerie rugs were the general rule. Delicate shades of blue, gray, green, and pink were popular, and walls were often painted in one of these soft colors or off-white. Panels of painted fabric or scenic wallpaper were also used.

Accessories included mirrors, crystal chandeliers, lusters, candlesticks, clocks (usually ormolu), statues, and an almost infinite variety of vases and objects in the famous French ceramics.

During this period the interest of the upper middle classes in home decoration continued to spread. This was partly because of the changes in production methods, with more widespread use of machines and the introduction of new materials that could be used as substitutes for those previously available only to the wealthy. More people began to enjoy the pleasures of homes that were simple but artistically decorated.

Directoire

Although *Directoire*—the revolutionary government—existed in France for only four years (from 1792 to 1795), the name is given to a style that represents a transition from the Louis XVI style to that of the Empire under Napoleon. Actually the Directoire style began to take form before the Revolution, and some elements continued to exist after the rise of Napoleon. One cannot assign specific dates to style trends, which tend to evolve slowly, but the Directoire period might be considered as lasting from about 1789 to 1804.

Naturally the political upheaval in France during and after the Revolution had its impact on the arts. Many craftsmen were forced to turn to other types of work, and the apprenticeship system—which had been responsible for the development of great skills—was disrupted.

However, the designers and craftsmen who did continue their work developed during this rather short period a style that has found widespread appeal. The furniture retained the graceful lines and beautiful proportions of the Louis XVI style. The classical influences not only continued but developed to the point where structural forms were adopted. The Directoire style employed Greek curves in chairs and sofas. Many chairs took direct in-

spiration from the Greek *klismos*. Chairbacks were often concave and showed a slight roll backward. The legs had gently flowing curves, and the arms on sofas curved outward. Daybeds with both ends of equal height and curved-outward scrolls became very popular.

Egyptian motifs were freely borrowed. In addition to human figures, designs included lotus flowers, sphinxes, papyrus, date palms, and lion heads.

Anything reminiscent of the monarchy was carefully avoided. The spirit of equality, democracy, and freedom prevailed in all modes of life. Ornamental motifs were based on military, revolutionary, and agricultural themes —drums, spears, stars, wheat, and farm tools. Fabric motifs followed these principles but stripes were also very popular. Color schemes became stronger and were often related to the new flag colors—white was often used with accents of bright red and blue.

Empire

In 1804 Napoleon became Emperor of France. The widespread changes in the political, economic, and social life of France during this era were naturally reflected in the Empire style, which remained very popular while Napoleon was in power—until 1814. The style continued to be fashionable during the succeeding years until about 1830. However, these later years witnessed the decline of French furniture design.

The style associated with this era reflected many facets of Napoleon's personality and career. It was inspired by militaristic ideas.

The use of Greek, Roman, and Egyptian motifs was fostered by Napoleon's interest and by his successful campaigns. The love of power, grandeur, splendor, and pomp that was characteristic of Napoleon resulted in designs that became heavy and imposing.

Two architects, Pierre Fontaine (1762–1853) and Charles Percier (1764–1838), were largely responsible for establishing the Empire style. Their admiration for the styles of antiquity and their fervent devotion to the authentic reproduction of its principles resulted in designs that were austere and formal. Curved lines were almost completely eliminated, except in chairs and sofas. A severe angularity developed and was sharpened by the use of highly polished flat surfaces, usually

(a)

(c)

(b)

FIGURE 9-1 Current adaptations of French furniture reproduce the basic forms and motifs with elegance. Note the emphasis on curves in the Louis XV chairs shown in (a). The Louis XVI chairs in (b) follow straighter lines. In (c) a Regency mirror complements an Empire chest and a Louis XVI chair. (*Courtesy of Brunovan, Inc.*)

French Styles 115

unrelieved by any form of carving, paneling, or marquetry. Sometimes carving was used on chairs or sofas, or bands of contrasting woods were used for inlay, but for the most part the decoration of furniture was achieved by the use of gilded bronze appliqués and mounts.

Supports of gilded metals or woods frequently took the form of fantastic figures. Horns, winged lions, the sphinx, a lion's head extending down to a single paw, and various forms of weird figures were combined to produce these decorations. When other motifs were employed they were chosen to represent military power. Napoleon's initial, often encircled by a wreath, was also a favorite motif.

Mahogany was the favorite wood but marble was widely used for table tops and fireplaces. Other woods used included ebony, rosewood, yew, elm, pear, and apple. These were usually highly polished to emphasize the grain.

Striped fabrics were very popular. Rich brocades, damasks, and velvets often had small conventional motifs. *Toiles de Jouy* with pastoral scenes were also used. Rich, vibrant colors were used, including wine red, purple, bright blue, emerald green, and gold.

Accessories included procelain vases and urns, and marble and bronze clocks. Candelabra often had caryatid supports (tall, slender figures). Also used were busts and statues on pedestals or in niches, and mirrors in beautiful Empire frames.

The severity and richness of this style depict the spirit of the Roman Empire translated into the mode of nineteenth-century French living. The emphasis on symmetry gives it a feeling of formality; the large proportions make it a masculine style. However, in the early phases, which reflect some of the Directoire trends, the formality is both graceful and unpretentious. Present-day adaptations of the traditional Empire style have scaled down the proportions to provide a style that can be most appealing and suitable to current needs.

In the early part of the nineteenth century the Industrial Revolution was responsible for many changes in France. The country had been essentially agricultural, so the factory system took hold more slowly than it did in England; however, by the middle of the century the use of machines had become somewhat widespread, and the guild system of training fine craftsmen had disappeared. The glorious age of French furniture design had passed and there was neither the inspiration, the creative genius, nor the skilled craftsmanship to produce another historic style.

French Provincial

Only the nobility and the wealthy class could afford furniture in the French "court" styles described in the preceding sections. Nevertheless, these styles did influence, to a great extent, the furniture used throughout the country. However, geographical position, cultural and economic development, and local customs all influenced the development of furniture styles in the provinces.

Until the seventeenth century, the houses in rural districts, populated chiefly by peasant farmers, were simple cottages that were sparsely furnished with rather crude furniture. Tables, stools, chests, and beds were often built by the people themselves. Where towns and cities had developed, local cabinetmakers with varying degrees of skill met the demands. At about the beginning of the seventeenth century, furniture from Italy and the Netherlands started coming into France. It was also during the early half of the seventeenth century that local cabinetmakers became more skillful in adapting the prevailing styles to local modes. The middle class was becoming larger and the farmers were becoming more prosperous. As the various provinces developed economically and culturally, the homes became more completely furnished.

Quite naturally the changes in home furnishings took place much more slowly in rural areas than they did in larger cities. In addition, countryfolk used the materials at hand and whatever native craftsmanship was available. The wealthier bourgeoisie, especially in the cities, could begin to emulate the court styles but in a highly simplified version. The very fine craftsmen worked in Paris and their

FIGURE 9-2 Current adaptations of French styles feature graceful curves and elegant fabrics. In this setting the colors of muted rose and apple green in the taffeta stripe are repeated in the chintz on the sofa and in the colors of the rug in a Savonnerie design. (*Courtesy of Globe Furniture Company*)

labors and the materials with which they worked were available only to the wealthy nobility. As the interest in home surroundings mounted during the seventeenth century, local craftsmen became more skillful and more aware of the changing fashions in furnishings.

The innate French artistry adapted the court styles to a simple manner of living. The result embodied the exquisite proportions and graceful lines of French furniture design at its best. It had the feeling of elegance that comes with the use of beautiful fabrics and woods, and the unpretentious simplicity that is appealing to so many people today. Perhaps no other style of furniture has ever been so successful in combining grace, elegance, and simplicity. No doubt this is why it enjoys phenomenal popularity today.

From this very brief introduction to French Provincial furniture, it should be evident that there are wide diversifications in the style. The crude type made and used by the rural peasants is somewhat akin to our own Early American. The stress was on utility, but with the characteristic French taste and beauty it was charming and even graceful in its sturdiness. The border provinces showed influences from neighboring countries—Germany, Italy, and the Netherlands. Different regions fostered individual customs or wares, but there is a distinctive French touch in the rural French Provincial style. The woods—mostly the fruit woods, walnut, and oak—were usually waxed. Some furniture was painted, but it was rarely gilded. The fabrics of wool, linen, and cotton, were gay and colorful. Toiles, checks, prints, and many forms of needlework were used. The accessories of copper, pewter, and pottery were often useful as well as decorative. Tole candlesticks and *Quimperware*, a pottery with colorful local scenes, were popular.

The furniture made by local cabinetmakers for the wealthier merchants and lesser nobility showed more of the influences of court styles. This type could not be as elaborate as the actual court furniture, but its simplification was an improvement. It was characterized by the elegance that comes with the use of fine materials and the refinement of skilled craftsmanship. This is the style we are likely to associate with the description "French Provincial" and it is the style we frequently use in our homes today. It adapted mostly the Louis XV style, with its graceful

curves and excellent proportions, but it eliminated the excessive ornamentation. It represents an interpretation of the Rococo style—which reached its height during the Louis XV period—in a beautifully subdued and restrained version.

Some Louis XVI forms were used, but very few of the Directoire or the Empire themes influenced the Provincial style. Carving and marquetry were used moderately, as were gilding and metal mounts.

Silk fabrics in damask or satin added to the richness and elegance. Whereas in the rural-type furniture loose cushions of a rough-textured fabric might be merely tied on, this more refined Provincial furniture was beautifully upholstered.

The larger pieces, such as armoires, cupboards, and sideboards, were often decorated with Louis XV type paneling. The beds were fitted into alcoves, which were curtained with draperies or shut off by paneled doors. Our contemporary version of the Provincial style frequently makes use of upholstered headboards.

The accessories used with the more elaborate type of French Provincial furniture were more in keeping with the feeling of elegance. Crystal, silver, and fine porcelain were popular and added accents to the theme of elegance.

10

American Styles

To understand and appreciate the development of American art, one must remember that many different factors and influences enter the picture. It is hardly possible to present a simple and concise story, because different sections of the country were developed at widely spaced intervals. The settlers came from different countries; in some cases they brought with them strong heritages that significantly influenced their modes of living, and in other cases influences of previous roots yielded to the new life and the new country.

The very early settlers were, of course, concerned with clearing the land and establishing their farms. The hardships and tremendous physical labors left them little time to do much more than build houses that were habitable and utilitarian. Because space on the sailing vessels was extremely limited, they brought very few possessions and very little furniture with them. The homes that they managed to establish were sparsely furnished with bare essentials that were crudely made.

Gradually the industry and the fortitude of the pioneers began to reap dividends. As agriculture flourished, the towns and then the cities began to develop. The growing and expanding colonies attracted new settlers with different financial backgrounds as well as groups of different national origins. However, the majority of the American settlers were English, and ties to the English culture have always predominated in the evolution of the American pattern. No one can deny the important contributions made by other national groups to the development of America; the very philosophy upon which the American structure is based was certainly influenced by the desires of these groups to find a haven that would transcend nationalistic boundaries. Yet we find that the Dutch tended to settle in New York and Pennsylvania, the Spanish in Florida, the French in Louisiana, and the Germans in Pennsylvania. Their tendencies to preserve nationalistic roots, while at the same time they absorbed a new way of life, is one of the phenomena of the American scene. In later years, particularly in the nineteenth century, immigration from Ireland, Italy, Russia, and the Balkans had important effects on the economic and industrial conditions in America. From a cultural standpoint, however, these groups have been more or less absorbed by the English tradition in America. In view of the rich aesthetic backgrounds of some of these nationalistic groups, this fact is somewhat paradoxical.

As the American pattern evolved, the wealthier settlers, who received their land by royal grants, tended to settle in the South. They built up huge plantations with luxurious homes and imported the furnishings. They adopted a way of life that was in sharp contrast to that in New England, where the settlers who had been attracted to America for political and religious reasons lived a comparatively simple life. In the small New England town the church was the center of activity. In addition, geographical conditions and the nature of the settlers made large estates impractical and undesirable.

The development of the western part of the country was accompanied by strong Spanish and Oriental influences. It is interesting to travel through the United States today to observe how traditions have maintained certain flavors in many areas. Despite a rapidly changing world and speedy communications, which should tend to dissolve and obliterate such characteristics, we still find something of an austerity in New England, the gracious hospitality of luxurious living in the South, the quaintness of the Pennsylvania Dutch, and the modernized Latin atmosphere of the Spaniards in Florida and the West. Somehow these influences have managed to persevere throughout the more than three hundred years of American history.

As the country developed, cities grew and various industries became concentrated in different localities. Philadelphia eventually became the center for cabinetwork, and other industries were more or less localized in other sections.

As one studies trends in America, he should bear in mind that the different regions of the country were developed by many different groups of people. It should also be remembered that the new ideas and styles that prevailed in

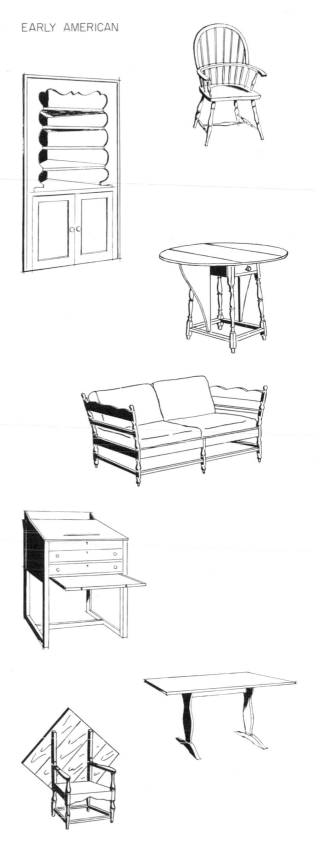

other parts of the world were somewhat slow in reaching America. It often took several years for foreign trends to become effective here.

For our purposes, we may divide the American styles of furniture as follows:

1. *Colonial:* The period up to the establishment of the Federal Government.
   (a) Early American; 1608–1770.
   (b) American Georgian; 1720–1790.
2. *Federal:* 1790–1830.
3. *Regional Styles.*
4. *Post-Federal:* American Victorian; 1840–1880.

Colonial

The Colonial period covers over 160 years when the colonies were growing. According to present-day standards, the changes were not rapid, but this was an era of growth and development. The mosaic of American culture was being formed and the foundations for an American way of life were taking shape. The heritage of America, so different from that of other countries, was formed in a relatively short span of time.

EARLY AMERICAN (1608–1770). The term *Early American* is used rather indiscriminately today to refer to a style that we associate with colonial life. Charming as the modern interpretation is, it is not authentic in its portrayal of the furnishings actually used in the very early days of the colonies.

Since most of the early settlers were from the English middle class, the furnishings with which they were familiar were of the Gothic-Renaissance forms used in the cottages in provincial England. The few simple items of furnishings that they produced here were based on the general lines of Elizabethan and Jacobean forms and those of the period of William and Mary.

Even in the native lands there was not yet a widespread interest in beautifying home surroundings. Because of the struggles and hardships that faced the newcomers in an undeveloped land, it is not surprising that homes were furnished with only the bare essentials and that there was little concern for beauty or comfort.

The first houses had one room that served all purposes. The fireplace was used for both heating and cooking. Gradually this gave way to the two-room house and eventually to more complex plans with two chimneys. Sometimes the expansions were made by the addition of wings, and the "saltbox" style of architecture evolved.

The furniture for these houses was sparse. The bare essentials—chests and cupboards, tables, stools, chairs, and beds—followed, in general, the Jacobean style. When local carpenters were called upon to produce furniture, they had neither the talent nor the tools to do fine cabinetmaking. They could only copy, to the best of their ability, the furniture that had been imported or that they remembered from their homelands. They worked with the woods that were readily available, mostly pine, beech, cherry, maple, ash, elm, and cedar. Because the American houses tended to be smaller, the American furniture also assumed smaller proportions. Ornamentation was simple and crude. Carving, turning, and painting were usually done by amateurs trying to pass long winter evenings.

Wooden chests played an important role in Early American furnishings. Many of these had been brought over by the settlers in lieu of trunks. They were copied and reproduced in various forms and served as seats as well as storage space. Soon they were made with legs and then with drawers. One type, called a desk-box, was made to hold writing materials and had a slanted top. This was the prototype of the familiar slant-top desk.

Because the houses were small, many pieces of furniture were designed to conserve space or to serve dual purposes. Drop-leaf tables were popular and were made in different sizes and forms such as the butterfly and gate-leg types.

The proportions of the early chairs were heavy. They had turned legs, stretchers to support the construction, and either plain wood or rush seats. By the middle of the seventeenth century loose cushions were used for comfort, and upholstered chairs were later introduced.

The chair-table was also used. This was a grotesque arrangement of a chair with a table-top back. Although this contrivance has historical interest, it has not found popular favor in modern interpretations of the Early American style.

By the beginning of the eighteenth century

trained cabinetmakers had come to the new country and were making furniture in the William and Mary style. Shaped aprons, bun feet, and bell turnings on legs appeared in furniture designs. By 1700 a greater interest in beauty and comfort in the home had gradually developed.

AMERICAN GEORGIAN (1720–1790).

As the wealthier group in the colonies grew there was a greater demand for more elaborate houses. More formal architectural design was applied to the interiors as well as to the exteriors. Moldings were used to trim doors, windows, and mantels. Wood paneling became popular in the larger homes, and in the smaller houses walls were often decorated with stenciled designs, murals, or wallpaper.

A more social way of life had developed and entertaining in the home required more furniture. There was a demand for more tables,

especially ones that could be used for serving tea and playing parlor games. Upholstered furniture, desks and secretaries, consoles, pier tables, and roundabout chairs were all very popular. There was greater interest in decorative accessories, including china, mirrors, and tall case clocks.

Those who could afford to import furniture eagerly followed the style trends prevalent in England and on the Continent. However, a large number of skilled craftsmen had emigrated to America in the early years of the eighteenth century, and they began to reproduce the English styles by copying imported models. They avidly used the design books published by the well-known English designers.

Many pieces were accurate reproductions of original designs, but soon the American craftsmen began to vary their interpretations. They made changes in the details and in the

FIGURE 10-1 **Many interpretations of colonial furniture are popular today. The room below adapts some modern ideas to an Early American theme.** (*Designed by Barbara D'Arcy, A.I.D., Bloomingdale's, N.Y.*)

FIGURE 10-2 A revival of interest in colonial styles and in Oriental rugs is shown in this corner of a living room that is keyed to contemporary color schemes. An unusual modern Sarouk has an ivory ground with turquoise, rose, gold, blue, and green in the stylized design. The rich wood tones of the Early American adaptations blend well with these colors. (*Courtesy of Oriental Rug Importers Association. Designed by Duke Piner and Harvey Barnett, A.I.D.*)

proportions. It is common practice now to refer to "American Queen Anne" or "American Chippendale" when discussing this furniture made in America but based on English styles.

Many fine cabinetmakers were located in Philadelphia. Beautiful examples of American furniture in the Early Georgian style were produced in that city. The Philadelphia craftsmen followed the Queen Anne, Chippendale, Hepplewhite, and Sheraton styles as each became popular in England.

Two cabinetmakers in Newport, Rhode Island, became well known for furniture with block-front designs. During the second half of the eighteenth century John Goddard and John Townsend made chests, cabinets, and desks with the fronts divided into three panels decorated with shell motifs. The central panel was usually concave and the outer ones convex.

By the middle of the eighteenth century,

the Windsor chair had become extremely popular and has remained so ever since. Although the design originated in England, the American adaptations produced a variety of types. The distinctive characteristics of the chair included a shaped seat and legs slanting outward. Stretchers were always used, and both the legs and the supports were usually decorated with turning. The various forms of the back were made of spindles placed in the rear of the seat. The loop back, one of the more popular versions, had a bent frame. The fan back with a straight or curved top rail sometimes had an additional section resembling a ladies' comb. The chairs were often made of several different woods and were painted. Black, red, and green were popular colors.

Rocking chairs were widely used during this period. Of the many different rocking chairs, the Windsor rocker was the most commonly used.

Federal

In the period following the Revolutionary War there was an increased awakening of interest in the arts. The prevailing spirit of freedom and democracy fostered interest in the classics. Inspiration drawn from Greece and Rome during this period permeated all phases of activity. The politically important figures—Washington, Jefferson, Franklin, and Hamilton—were all men with highly developed cultural tastes and they undoubtedly influenced artistic standards.

The political spirit strengthened the bonds of understanding between France and America. Also, after the French Revolution, French styles influenced English designs, and these English designs were, in turn, important factors in American production.

During the Federal period (1780–1830) both the Hepplewhite and Sheraton styles were popular in America. When the war ended, the Hepplewhite style was widely accepted in England; as normal relations between the two countries were resumed, the style was adopted by American cabinetmakers. A little later, the Sheraton style became popular in England; it also was adopted in America. Because the pattern books of both Hepplewhite and Sheraton were extensively used by American cabinetmakers, there was a period at the end of the eighteenth century when much of the furniture combined the characteristics of both styles. By this time cabinetmaking in America had reached a high level and the Federal era saw the production of many fine pieces of furniture.

The American interpretations of the English styles were notable for their delicacy, refinement, and excellent proportions. However, the furniture was not as elaborate as that made for the aristocracy in England. Philadelphia was the center of activity during the Federal era and assumed a position of leadership in setting the fashions; but the great American fortunes had not yet been built up and there were not many Americans of tremendous wealth, so there was no great demand for sumptuous homes and interiors such as Adam was designing for his very wealthy clients in England. Adam's influences in American design were seen in some decorative work and were important insofar as they were interpreted through Hepplewhite's designs. Although the style never really flourished in

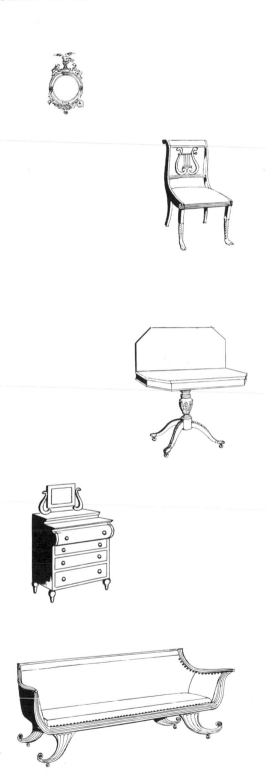

America, it was of considerable influence in the work of Samuel McIntire (1757–1811), an architect and a craftsman of Salem, Massachusetts, during the Federal period. He created beautiful interiors with expert wood carving and paneling. His carved mantels, cornices, dadoes, and stairways were beautifully proportioned and exquisite in detail. McIntire designed and made excellent furniture, and his interiors represent a high level of artistic achievement in the Federal style.

The American designs patterned after those of Hepplewhite and Sheraton reflected the graceful elegance of the originals. Chests of drawers, sideboards, dining tables, secretaries, card tables, shield-back chairs, and settees were all made to follow the styles. Veneer work was carefully done and the pieces were decorated with carving, inlay work, reeding, and fluting.

From 1805 to 1815, a style of furniture often referred to as American Directoire was popular. It is characterized by Greek and Roman influences. Chairs were derived from the Grecian *klismos*, with the tops showing a backward sweep. The legs were frequently concave. Sofas and settees were also inspired by Greek and Roman designs.

The period from 1810 to 1830 marks the American Empire period. It should be noted that the Directoire and Empire styles overlapped. The style of this period did not closely follow the French Empire style, though there were some similarities.

The theme of American ornamentation was patriotic. It glorified the abundance of the land with motifs of fruits, flowers, leaves, and the horn of plenty. The eagle had been adopted as the national emblem and was so widely used as a decorative motif that this era is sometimes referred to as the "American Eagle Period." Brass eagles were imported; others were carved and gilded. They were used as finishes on wall mirrors and clocks and they were painted on glassware and chinaware. They were used in every conceivable way and there can be little doubt that this was a period when Americans were proud of their insignia.

DUNCAN PHYFE (1768–1854). Probably the most famous name in the decorative arts of this period is Duncan Phyfe. He came from Scotland to America as a young man, and after learning cabinetmaking in Albany he moved to New York in the early 1790's. He operated a very successful shop until 1847.

Contrary to the popular conception, Phyfe did not originate a style of furniture. He designed in the Sheraton, Directoire, and Empire styles, although he gave the designs his own interpretation. He was an expert cabinetmaker but he was also a good businessman. While his great ability is generally recognized, his superiority to all other cabinetmakers of the era is questioned by some authorities. Many believe that his eminence is partly due to his long career and his good business sense. There were many other fine craftsmen working in the decorative arts during the Colonial and Federal periods. Nevertheless, for the first twenth-five or thirty years of his career, Phyfe made furniture that was graceful and delicate, beautifully proportioned, and exquisite in detail. Sheraton was a strong and distinct influence in the work of this period. The lyre motif that Sheraton had used was extremely popular with Phyfe, and he continued to use it on much of the furniture that he made in the Directoire style. He also used acanthus leaves, swags, cornucopias, and sheaves of wheat. The carving and reeding were expertly done, mostly on beautiful mahogany. His most famous designs in chairs, sofas, sideboards, and tables with tripod bases reflect the Greek and Roman influence in the Empire style. The refined curves, excellent proportions, and delicacy of detail gave the pieces an elegance that has kept these designs popular in contemporary interpretations.

After about 1820, the proportions of Phyfe's designs gradually became heavier and more cumbersome. The decorative details were coarser and overdone. In all probability much of this work was done to meet the popular demand. It is reported that Phyfe was unhappy enough about such designs to refer to them as "butcher furniture."

Regional Styles

As America grew and developed, there was a tendency for certain groups of people to settle in particular areas. Frequently the previous customs and traditions were eventually blended into or absorbed by a new American way of life. In other instances, however, past associations and patterns remained dominant with the result that we have several styles in the American decorative arts that are referred to as "regional." Although some of these styles have spread far beyond their specific regions, and some of them have been very popular, they have not had any great influence on general styles. Their contributions have been so important, however, that they must not be overlooked in any discussion of American styles.

PENNSYLVANIA "DUTCH." The Mennonites, who settled in Pennsylvania toward the end of the seventeenth century, were mostly Germans who were eager to establish themselves in a land where they could find the freedom to follow their religious beliefs. They formed isolated communities where they clung rigidly to their customs and language. Even today these people resist change and have managed to preserve their old ways of life. The Mennonites are a simple and industrious people with an inherent love for beauty and gaiety. They decorate their homes in a delightfully colorful style that is light and cheerful.

The furniture forms followed the simple lines of the country furniture used throughout the colonies, but the severe sturdiness is relieved by a greater use of curves. They used ladder-back chairs, drop-leaf tables, sawbuck tables, and many different types of chests, cabinets, and cupboards. The style has merited great popularity, chiefly because of the distinctive painted or stenciled decorations.

Symbolic motifs, such as tulips, hearts, birds, leaves, and hex signs, were painted on furniture and walls in bright gay colors. These designs were often combined with German script and included decorative scrolls showing family histories of births and weddings.

Fabrics and rugs followed a similar colorful pattern. Textile designs were often embroidered or appliquéd. Added to this joyful and pleasant atmosphere were the copper, iron, and decorated wooden kitchen equipment.

This simple style has been readily accepted by many people who delight in the gay informality and who welcome its sturdy practicality.

SCANDINAVIAN. Many immigrants from Norway, Finland, and Sweden established communities in the Midwest—particularly in Minnesota and Wisconsin. The blending of their heritage with the factors that inspired

PENNSYLVANIA DUTCH

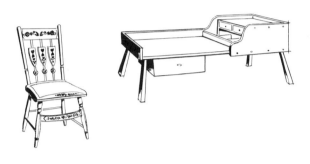

SHAKER

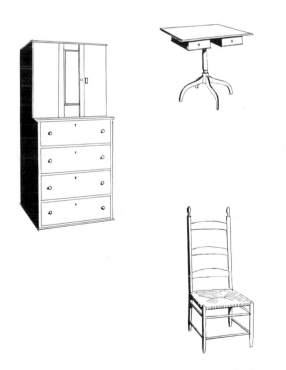

Colonial furniture produced another regional style that was somewhat similar to the Pennsylvania Dutch.

The furniture was simple and sturdy and it too was painted with designs that were bright and gay. Flowers and leaves decorated the furniture, but there was a tendency to use more animal and human figures than were used in the Pennsylvania Dutch style. Also, these designs were more realistic than the stylized German designs. Possibly for that reason they have not had the same widespread popular appeal in current times.

SHAKER. An interesting style of furniture was developed by a religious group known as the Shakers (or sometimes as the "Shaking Quakers") because of their physical manifestations during worship. The first group came from England in 1776 and settled in New York State. Other groups were formed later in New England, Kentucky, Ohio, and Indiana. Shakerism began to decline in 1860, but during their active period the Shakers were well known for excellence in agriculture and crafts.

Shaker life was based on communal "families" of thirty to ninety people. The members donated possessions and services to the group. They were dedicated to a community life in which men and women shared equal responsibilities although they lived and worked separately. They were also dedicated to pacifism, separation from the world, celibacy, and consecrated work.

Their rigid beliefs necessitated furnishings that were functional and completely devoid of ornamentation. They used built-in storage areas and multipurpose pieces. The simple chairs, tables, chests, beds, and candle stands were light in scale so that they could be moved easily, but the sturdy construction was testimony to the skilled craftsmanship of the Shakers. The lines were pure and uncomplicated. The natural grains of the woods were emphasized by light stains and polishing. The result of all this is a refined simplicity that lends a strange air of modernism and contemporary elegance to what is in reality a country style. Many modern designs find their inspiration in Shaker furniture, which was neither modeled after nor openly influenced by preceding styles.

SPANISH COLONIAL. The Spanish influence in America is widespread from the standpoint of both distance and time. From the seventeenth century to the present time and in various locations ranging from Florida to California there have been important Spanish contributions to the development of regional styles.

The nature of the Spanish styles made them a natural background for the preservation of much American Indian art. There are considerable regional differences throughout Texas, New Mexico, Arizona, California, and Florida, but there are some general themes in the character of the Spanish styles.

Architectural forms as seen in houses made of thick walls and built around a patio became common. The interior walls were whitewashed and the rooms were furnished with a few essential pieces that were heavy and crudely carved.

Some bright colors were used in accessories, but modern interpretations of the Spanish colonial styles have assigned larger areas of more garish colors than were actually used.

Decorative motifs blended Indian symbols with Moorish geometrics. Some Mexican influences were also seen. Favorite themes included flowers, leaves, and animals such as birds, deer, lambs, and goats.

In the Southwest, particularly in Texas and California, some Spanish influence was evident in the missions, the chapels and other buildings that were erected by inexpert craftsmen who worked with a few crude tools. The mixture of Mexican, Indian, and Spanish influences did not, in a true sense, represent authentic Spanish detail in either the architecture or the furniture. The crude, heavily proportioned, rectilinear cabinets, chests, tables, and chairs were sturdy and simple. They were made from woods that were readily available. This type of furniture is sometimes associated with designs that developed during the early stages of the modern movement and were known as Mission style.

Post-Federal

The nineteenth century was marked by periods of rapid expansion. The physical frontiers of the country were broadening through the acquisition of new territories. The new wonders of the machine were fostering an industrial development that had extensive social as well as economic implications. By the middle of the century this pattern had developed to the point where the huge fortunes of America's wealthy class were being built up. The period was also marked by the popular love for ostentation and display, with a resulting disregard for intrinsic artistic merit. It has been pointed out that there is no sharp dividing line between one period and another in furniture styles. The period of 1815 to 1830, generally referred to as American Empire, has already been discussed. The following decade, 1830–1840, is often spoken of as late Empire. The furniture of this era began to assume heavy proportions and cumbersome lines. There had been a gradual decline in taste for fine art and this was reflected in the concurrent decline of American furniture styles.

AMERICAN VICTORIAN. After 1840, American designs followed the Victorian style. As in the case of the English Victorian, much of the furniture was heavily proportioned and far too elaborate. There was much borrowing from Gothic, Turkish, Egyptian, and French Rococo themes. The excessive ornamentation was often inspired by a mixture of unrelated influences that served only to clutter the designs.

The elaborate upholstered furniture was decorated with fringes, cords, tassels, and buttons. The excessively ornamented wood pieces were frequently machine inspired and were decorated with whatever could be produced by the new machine methods. Omnipresent bric-a-brac was displayed on mantels, tables, shelves, and special "what-nots" made for the purpose. Needlework was also displayed everywhere, in framed mottos, and embroidered pictures, on chairs in the form of tidies, and draped on windows, tables, and mantels in the form of antimacassars. All of this in the setting of patterned floor coverings, heavy draperies, and gas lighting gives the picture of the Victorian room. Yet it has been pointed out that in the midst of the clutter and the ugly, ostentatious designs there was furniture that merits respect. In America, as in England, some cabinetmakers maintained high standards of workmanship. They worked in the prevailing style but they managed to produce many pieces that had charm and appeal.

In New York during the middle of the nineteenth century, a cabinetmaker named John H. Belter made a considerable amount of outstanding furniture in the Victorian style from about 1844 to 1860. Belter was an expert craftsman who worked with several kinds of

FIGURE 10-3   An asymmetrical Belter sofa with tufting and intricately carved frame. (*Courtesy of Cooper-Hewitt Museum of Design, Smithsonian Institute*)

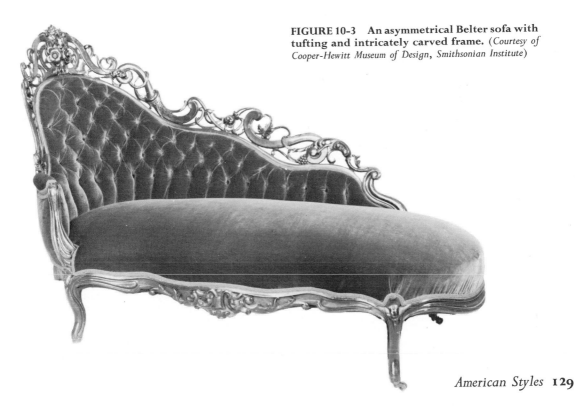

FIGURE 10-4 The parlor in a New York brownstone house built in the middle of the nine- teenth century is graced by Belter sofa and chairs. *(Photo by John T. Hill)*

wood, but he is best known for pieces made of fine-quality rosewood. He is noted for using a process of building up several layers of thin wood with the grain of each layer at right angles to the grain of the next layer. This type of lamination is commonly used today, but Belter was probably one of the first cabinet- makers to employ the process. The veneers were carved or pierced in lacy openwork patterns and ornamented with motifs of leaves, fruits, and flowers.

Another eminent cabinetmaker was Daniel Pabst, who made some excellent furniture in his Philadelphia shop during the 1860's. Much of his best work was executed in black walnut and showed distinct French influences.

It is interesting to note that certain Victor- ian accessories hold an appeal for the modern collector who may have no general interest in Victoriana. Popular in this respect is much of the Victorian glassware and ceramic work, as well as bronze statuary, notably that of John Rogers, who was active in this field around the middle of the century.

Currier and Ives prints were made in New York, also around the middle of the century. The originals of these colored lithographs were the work of several artists and they covered a wide range of subjects. The prints were inexpensive and were widely used. It was also about this time that daguerreotypes became very popular, shortly after Louis Daguerre had discovered this process of photography in France.

The end of the nineteenth century brought more leisure and wealth and an awakened interest in culture and the arts. Increased travel to Europe created a demand for an- tiques and reproductions of foreign furniture styles. Art publications and the establishment of several art schools indicated the growing interest. In 1870, the Metropolitan Museum of Art was founded.

Reactions to the debased forms of art were giving rise to the rumblings of the modern movement. By the turn of the century this was in the developmental stages. This period is discussed in another section.

Various countries throughout the world have played more or less important roles in influencing our homes today. The arts of different cultures have provided rich inspiration for decorative motifs and accessories. Furniture forms, however, have not been as affected as one might expect. For example, the vogues for Oriental design during the eighteenth and nineteenth centuries were manifest chiefly in ornamentation. There was some adaptation of Oriental design, but the basic furniture forms drew little from outside sources.

Some reference has been made to earlier contributions of the Scandinavian countries as well as to those of Spain and Italy. Germany and Austria have also contributed to the decorative arts in various ways. Some of these have already been referred to in the brief survey of decorative styles and it is not within our scope here to elaborate on all of them. Perhaps it will suffice to point out that modern interior designers are turning to some of these less well-known areas for inspiration and the results have been quite exciting. We have seen in recent years a growing interest in blending Oriental and Near Eastern themes with contemporary styles. When the arts of more primitive cultures are used to add interest and accent to modern styles, the effects can be intriguing and enchanting. The potentials of combining the new with the ancient have had tremendous popular appeal. The growing interest in these somewhat neglected sources has been stimulated by increased travel, especially among the less wealthy classes, and by the growing emphasis on cultural interchange as a factor in promoting world peace.

Some of the areas that bear investigation are the arts of the Oriental and Near Eastern cultures and those of the European peasants. The art of the American Indian should not be overlooked.

For our purposes here we shall consider

11

Miscellaneous Styles

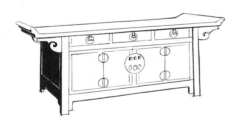

several miscellaneous styles that have been popular during recent years:

Biedermeier
Oriental
Italian
Spanish

Biedermeier

A style that has found rather popular favor during recent years developed in Germany and Austria during the nineteenth century. The name was taken from a popular fictional character named "Papa Biedermeier," a humorous, corpulent figure who did not hesitate to express his views on any subject.

The furniture was popular from about 1815 to 1860. It was a naïve interpretation of the French Empire style, although it also drew from other sources, such as Sheraton, Regency, Directoire, and even some German peasant styles. In spite of somewhat heavy proportions and unrefined curves, the style had a simple, comfortable appeal. The furniture was neither luxurious nor extravagant. It eliminated the excessive decorative detail of the French Empire mode.

The chair backs were carved in various designs, but the carving was never elaborate; the legs were rarely turned or carved. Decorative detail included simple moldings; some marquetry, often in border designs of contrasting wood; brass ornaments; and painted or stenciled designs. Motifs included simple classical themes, flowers, and human or animal figures. The character of the ornament sometimes introduced a gay, playful note that gave the furniture a spirit of humor and informality.

The typical Empire forms were executed in light woods, usually cherry, birch, walnut, and fruit woods. Some furniture was painted black and decorated with simple gilding.

Favorite fabric patterns were small, flowered designs and stripes. Silk, satin, and taffeta were sometimes trimmed with fringe, but in general the materials were of plain, sturdy varieties. The strong Empire colors of yellow, green, red, purple, and blue were popular. Wallpaper in bold patterns and figured Brussels carpeting were used extensively.

Some authorities seem to look upon Biedermeier with an ill-concealed disdain because it was imitative of several styles and did not attain perfection in proportion or purity of line. Yet its appeal for others is understandable, because it does express a down-to-earth feeling of comfort and simplicity. It mixes easily with several other styles, notably some of our contemporary designs. It seems to be the answer for those who would prefer the French Empire design in a simplified version.

Oriental

The term *Oriental* covers a vast geographical territory and a long period of time, and it would be impossible within the confines of this text to include an adequate analysis of the complex histories and philosophies of Eastern art. But neither may we overlook the Oriental styles, because they are of such importance today. We must, therefore, limit the discussion to a few significant points. The student should bear in mind that a more realistic approach would cover many different cultures over a broad period of time.

For our purposes we may divide the Orient into the Near East and the Far East. The troubled conditions in this part of the world make it difficult to identify areas by geographical boundaries, but India, Pakistan, Iran, and Israel compose most of the Near East, and China and Japan are considered the Far East.

The art styles of the Eastern countries have always been characterized by great beauty and purity of design. Oriental artists have shown an amazing ability of expression in every medium, and the arts reflect the deep appreciation of Oriental culture for all facets of physical and spiritual life. Concepts based on religion, mysticism, and philosophy give the art an intellectual appeal. The imagination and spirit of the Oriental mind, combined with the excellence of expression and execution, lend tremendous emotional appeal.

The expert skills of the Oriental peoples have been evident in long, glorious histories of architecture, sculpture, painting, textiles, ceramics, and metalwork. In recent years we have also come to appreciate more fully their excellence in cabinetmaking.

Architects and interior designers have drawn heavily from Oriental themes and concepts in the past few years. Eastern influences on our modern furniture are discussed in the section on modern style. Yet apart from these influences we have developed a deeper appreciation for the intrinsic qualities of the Oriental styles. We have not only drawn inspiration from them in modern design, but we are adapting some of their basic concepts to our way of living. This is understandable, because perhaps no other style of art is so successful in combining the practical with the exotic. The combination of functionalism and beauty, inherent characteristics of much Oriental art, satisfies modern requirements and taste. For example, current trends in modern architecture show Islamic influences in façades using geometric patterns. Many of these are designed to let in light and air, at the same time protecting interiors from strong sunlight and visibility from outside.

The Western world is becoming more aware of the true art of China and Japan as a source of inspiration for interior design. Although references have been made to the Oriental "mania" in French and English styles of the eighteenth and nineteenth centuries, it must be pointed out here that these adaptations did not represent the true spirit of the Far East. By the time trade relations between the East and the West began to flourish, the art of China had reached a decadent level. Oriental merchants, only too eager to meet a demand for their wares, produced quantities of horrendous items that completely violated their artistic heritage. In the past few years we have had a somewhat analogous situation with the Japanese endeavor to build up native industry. They have been willing to apply their skills to the imitation of almost anything and everything, including German china and Venetian glass. Some astute advisers are urging the Japanese to end this debasing practice and to promote their own designs, in the belief that eventually this will prove to be economically sound. There can be little quarrel with the fact that Japan would certainly benefit from the artistic standpoint.

Chinese history dates back several thousand years B.C., but the arts went through a period of active development during the Han dynasty (206 B.C.–220 A.D.). They flourished during the "golden age" of the Tang (618–906 A.D.) and Sung (960–1279) dynasties. Strength, vigor, and originality continued during the Ming dynasty (1368–1644), but during the Ching dynasty (1644–1912) art gradually became more imitative. The technical skills and craftsmanship were still superb, but there was a lack of the spontaneity and freshness that were characteristic of Chinese art during the high periods.

Students of Oriental culture have long recognized the fine talents of the Chinese in ceramics, textiles, carving, and lacquerwork. It is only recently, however, that the excellence of Chinese cabinetwork has been truly appreciated. This may be partly because the Chinese themselves have never held the same same regard for cabinetmaking that they have had for other crafts. Also, it is safe to assume that much of the finest furniture was destroyed during several turbulent periods when dynasties were overthrown and great palaces were destroyed.

In recent years some of the ancient tombs of China have been opened as a result of rail-road construction. The custom of burying material objects with the dead is responsible for the discovery of numerous works of art. The furniture, household utensils, and decorative objects revealed in the tombs have enabled scholars to reconstruct ideas about ancient Chinese civilization.

At first mats and then low platforms were used in Chinese homes for sitting, eating, and sleeping. Stools and chairs were eventually introduced in most areas of China, but the Chinese adapted all furniture forms to their own distinctive way of life.

Some of the finest furniture was made during the fifteenth and sixteenth centuries during the Ming dynasty, when a classical simplicity pervaded all the arts. Pure and simple lines, restrained ornament, squared proportions, and elegant woods make this

FIGURE 11-1   A living-dining room completely decorated in the Oriental style. (*Designed by Patricia Harvey, A.I.D. Photo by Henry S. Fullerton*)

furniture refined and forceful. It is severe and formal, but it blends with many contemporary designs with amazing ease. The techniques of construction were superb. Unique methods of joinery dispensed with glue and dowels unless they were absolutely necessary, yet the furniture is sturdy and durable. Most of the woods have a beautiful satin finish that enhances the texture, color, and grain patterns. Metal decorations in hinges and handles were shaped to blend perfectly with the designs of the pieces. The luster of the metal, often an alloy of copper, zinc, and nickel, was always in perfect harmony with the wood finish. Large pieces of furniture were not generally lacquered, but stands made to hold exquisite sculptures and porcelains were frequently lacquered in red.

Ming furniture had a limited amount of carved detail. The Chinese are expert carvers, but during some periods excessive amounts of carved decoration detracted from the basic designs.

Decorative accessories included scrolls, paintings, jades, carved ivory figures, and beautiful porcelains. Richly embroidered silk cushions added to the exquisite blend of colors. All furniture and accessories were placed with a studied decorum that was both rigid and formal, but the Chinese interior reflects a high esteem for home and family life. Theirs is the gift of creating an atmosphere of simplicity with a note of elegance that is never pretentious.

During the seventh and eighth centuries, Japanese culture was in a formative stage and borrowed heavily from the Chinese. The practice of sitting on mats, or *tatami*, is still followed in Japan. It is the custom to remove one's shoes before stepping on the mats, which cover almost the entire floor. Almost every room has an *oshi-ire*, a built-in cabinet with sliding doors. Very little furniture is used in the Japanese home. There may be special cushions for guests to sit on and low tables of various shapes and sizes.

Ceramics and paintings decorate the Japanese interior. Of course, flowers play an important role in decoration, because flower-arranging is a highly regarded art. Many schools of flower arrangement in Japan have developed skills in and appreciation of this form of art.

Italian

Although Italy was the scene of the archaeological discoveries that prompted the classical revival in the decorative arts, it was not until the Neoclassic style was fairly well established in France and England that it was widely adopted in Italy. The new style was accepted by the Italians with enthusiasm. The interiors of old palaces and villas were redecorated in the classical manner. Large quantities of furniture and decorative accessories were made to interpret the idea. Most of the designs were borrowed from the French and the English styles, but the Italians interpreted them with individuality. They used different techniques and materials, but they incorporated the architectural motifs and the graceful classical curves. Because walnut was plentiful in Italy, it was used to a greater extent. Caned panels were popular for chairs and settees. Some furniture was painted and decorated with moderate amounts of gilt. Marquetry work was also used for decoration.

The Italians followed both the Directoire and Empire styles, modifying them to suit their needs and tastes. The results were charming and individual interpretations of the classical style, but with a dash of the Italian spirit. The craftsmanship in Italy at this time was inferior to that in France and England, but local cabinetmakers did copy and modify the

elaborate furniture used by the nobility and the wealthy classes in Venice, Rome, Milan, and Florence.

There is current interest in a mode referred to as "Italian Provincial." Many authorities object to the name because what we see today is not an authentic style but an adaptation of classic Italian furniture designed to meet popular tastes and the requirements of mass production. In the process of adapting the style, current designers have developed a type of furniture that retains a degree of elegance and refinement.

This furniture is somewhat severe in line, yet there is an element of dignity that seems to appeal to us today. It mixes easily with other designs of contemporary inspiration, and with our present eclectic trends this quality is important.

Spanish

The style of Spanish Renaissance furniture was briefly discussed in Chapter 7. However, the current interest in Spanish culture has given rise to a very popular mode that is sometimes referred to as "Spanish Provincial" or "Mediterranean." The latter term is becoming more widely accepted because this is not a pure style but a contemporary adaptation of designs from countries that were influenced by Spain many years ago. Just as Spanish Provincial is a misnomer, so is Mediterranean because the current mode includes characteristics that were found in both North and South America. At present, there is growing emphasis on some of the Mexican characteristics.

With little regard for authenticity, today's furniture designers have interpreted these designs to produce a style that blends well with hybrid architecture, modern decor, and the eclectic trend in furnishings.

Although the furniture is scaled to present-day needs, it is rectilinear in form and somewhat heavy in proportion. With emphases on geometric design, grillwork, tile, mosaics, leather, and rich colors in sturdy fabrics, the style seems to meet a need to combine the new and the functional with a flavor of the exotic past.

It would be impossible to fix the beginning of the modern movement with one date, name, or event. The inception of the modern style might be traced, in a very indirect manner, back to the Industrial Revolution and the beginning of the machine age. The use of machines in the early part of the nineteenth century gradually supplanted most of the fine craftsmanship. But man had not yet learned to cope with the machine nor to appreciate fully its potentialities. The attempts to imitate handmade products with machine methods resulted in a glut of poor design and poor construction.

The popular taste during the middle of the nineteenth century was at a low level that readily accepted imitation and ostentation. The pretentious, overelaborate Victorian style was at its height of popularity, and in its pendulum swing was reaching extremes of debased designs.

Development

The situation described was naturally repugnant to several souls who pleaded for a return to simplicity and refinement, with emphasis on good construction and beautiful materials. This group protested the vulgarities of the period by attempting to revive the principles of medieval art.

Writers such as John Ruskin, Goethe, Walter Scott, and Victor Hugo supported the cause. In the field of interior design, William Morris and Charles Eastlake, Jr., are notable for their rebellion against the indiscriminate use of the machine. A noted architect, E. W. Godwin, designed furniture in the Jacobean style but also became interested in Japanese art and promoted an Oriental theme in design. Morris worked with a group of skilled craftsmen who became known as "Pre-Raphaelites."

12

The Modern Style

Eventually their designs were also debased by cheap imitation.

Another movement originating in Europe near the end of the nineteenth century was known as *L'Art Nouveau*. Led by Henri Van de Velde, many craftsmen tried to create a new style based on ornament inspired by nature. Leaves, flowers, branches, and sweeping curves were used in a manner that protested traditional designs, but shortly after the turn of the century this style degenerated and lost its popularity.

In England the emphasis was on arts and crafts with a deliberate attempt to establish an individual but amateurish quality in design. This movement resulted in a comparable trend in America. One manifestation of this new art was an interest in what was called "Mission" furniture, a style that was crude, simple, and heavy in proportion. It became outdated shortly after the first decade of the twentieth century.

An important development in furniture construction was introduced in 1856 by Michael Thonet. He experimented with a process of steaming wood and bending it into curves. Various chairs that he designed following the success of this venture have become internationally famous. At present, Thonet Industries, Inc., still pioneers in modern design.

FIGURE 12-1 Rocking chair designed by Thonet shows intricate bentwood curves. (*Courtesy of Cooper-Hewitt Museum of Design, Smithsonian Institute*)

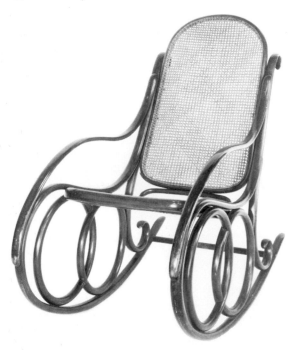

The theme of functionalism began to find favor toward the end of the nineteenth century. Earlier, in 1840, the American sculptor Horatio Greenough had decreed that function should determine design and that the beauty of any object should result from the form and the material. By the end of the century, this idea was being promoted in architecture by Louis Sullivan (1856–1924), who rejected all previous stylistic influences. The theme of his work was organic and the design of his Transportation Building at the Columbian Exposition in Chicago in 1893 received worldwide acclaim. He designed a number of commercial buildings in Chicago but he died before the public really accepted his ideas. His work was carried on by several followers, notably Frank Lloyd Wright (1869–1959), whose long career in architectural design won him international acclaim.

Several important developments in the modern movement took place in the early part of the twentieth century. Following the Art Nouveau a magazine known as *de Stijl* ("the style") was published in Holland in 1917. It represented new ideas of expression in painting, architecture, sculpture, and other forms of art with emphasis on the use of cubes, squares, and flat planes. Piet Mondrian was one of the famous painters associated with this group. Theo van Doesburg published the magazine and originated this movement, which had considerable influence on new styles of architecture.

In Germany, a group of craftsmen sought to reconcile machine production, good craftsmanship, and the proper use of materials by establishing the *Deutsche Werbund* in 1907. In 1919 one of the leaders of this group, Walter Gropius, organized a school known as the *Bauhaus* in Weimar. It moved to Dessau in 1925 and was housed in a famous building designed by Gropius.

The group involved in the Bauhaus pioneered in a creative approach to all the arts and had important influences on design in architecture and all home furnishings, including lighting fixtures, textiles, and ceramics.

Political conditions in Germany in the 1930's eventually caused the school to close. Gropius and many of his associates, including Marcel Breuer and Ludwig Mies van der Rohe left Germany and came to America, where they continued their work.

Another important development in the

modern movement was the work of Le Corbusier (the professional name of Charles E. Jeanneret, 1887–1965), a Swiss architect who designed residential buildings in the modern style. He designed structures supported by skeletons of columns that made his buildings seem to be off the ground. Le Corbusier preferred glass walls to allow maximum light and a closer relationship between the exterior and the interior. With many built-in features and only necessary movable furniture, he aimed to create homes that would make living simple. He emphasized the importance of surroundings that are easy to maintain, convenient to use, and healthy. Le Corbusier believed that the intrinsic qualities of the home could be spiritually satisfying. To meet this purpose, he advocated beauty through good proportions, the utilitarian aspects of materials, and the use of only a few accessories of superb quality.

The work of Frank Lloyd Wright also became very important in the progress of the modern movement. Although he designed public buildings, he applied many commercial techniques to residential structures with the result that his houses were innovations in design. Wright firmly believed in relating his structures to the geography of their settings, but he built from the inside out. The function of the building determined its form. He designed to take maximum advantage of sun, light, and view, but he rejected window walls when they violated privacy. He also made maximum use of the decorative qualities of building materials, both inexpensive and costly ones. He created a style of architecture that has been accepted throughout the world.

Wright's last public building received both acclaim and bitter criticism. The Guggenheim Museum in New York City was completed and opened shortly after his death in 1959. The unusual design of the building caused wide public interest and editorial comment. Some critics noted Wright's dislike for cities and implied that he had played a joke on New York. One referred to the building as an "upturned dish of oatmeal." Those who voiced acclaim hailed the structure as a milestone in modern architectural design. The only point of agreement seems to be that the building is certainly "different."

In Europe during the first quarter of the twentieth century, various new ideas for furnishings and home equipment were developed. By 1925, general interest in this new style was widespread. France sponsored an exposition in Paris to display and publicize the advanced ideas. Neither Germany nor the United States participated. After the exposition, many of the exhibits were sent to America, where they awakened public interest in the "international style." Designers and manufacturers were responsive, and the year 1926 marks a milestone in the development of the modern style in America.

Current Modern

At the present time the term *modern* evokes many different interpretations, and perhaps we are too close to the evolution of the style to evaluate it objectively. There is no doubt that much modern art is exciting, forceful, and expressive of our way of life.

The critics of modern style ask, "Must any change be one for the better?" and, "Is change without reason necessarily good?" The advocates ask, "Must we be chained to tradition?" and, "Are not current technologies and thinking geared to the new and the different?" The answers to such questions may not be simple "yes" or "no" replies, because true artistic expression has deeper implications.

The modern style has gone through a period of growing pains. We like to think, at this point, that it has reached fruition and is really meeting our needs and expressing our way of life. Whether or not it really is and will continue to do so are matters of conjecture. At the present writing there is considerable interest in styles of the past. Is there some need for association with the past that modern designers have overlooked? Do we need ornament and surface decoration to meet some spiritual need? Only time will tell. Perhaps we must find the meeting ground of the old and the new. Probably the best example of this point can be found in the architecture of Edward Stone, which has won popular acclaim in the last few years. Architecture has often dictated the styles of interior design. Stone's work has answered the need for the functional and the need for embellishment. His openwork façades in magnificent geometric patterns let in light and air but curb intense sunlight. One has privacy, yet the indoors is not alienated from the outdoors. Stone has incorporated this useful but ancient idea into buildings of the most modern design. They meet contemporary needs and tastes, they are functional in every respect, yet they also provide an atmosphere of elegance. In this architecture one senses a respect for tradition mingled with admiration for the present. Perhaps this is one answer to some of the questions about the modern style. Must it be totally and completely different to be effective? Is there not a blend, or a happy medium, of the old and the new that will meet all our current needs? Some will still say "no," that we must break with past tradition to make the new form of expression completely effective; others will say that we must use the experiences of the past in combination with current objectives.

Every style in the past was at one time "modern," and each one had both good and bad examples. So it is with the modern style today. Whether or not it is good design depends on the sensitivity of the designer to forms, proportions, and the materials with which he works. Success depends also on the designer's ability to appreciate true functionalism and modern production.

Although some of the critics of the modern style have felt that there is too much effort to be different without just cause, there are many examples of new ideas in design that now have classic value. There are others that have become tiresome, or even irritating, in just a few years. Much of the furniture manufactured ten years ago now appears terribly dated and out of fashion. Fortunately, most of the top-notch designers in the modern style are striving toward ideals that give some degree of permanency to their work.

Different influences and individual interpretations have produced a variety of designs at different price levels. In furniture and all household accessories, many manufacturers who produce on a national scale have hired competent designers to cope with the problem of designing low-cost items that are well constructed and in good taste. It should be borne in mind that not all expensive articles are necessarily of good design. Some are as grotesque and ostentatious as the worst examples of Victoriana, and in years to come they may be viewed with more horror.

However, modern designers would have the public educated to appreciate a more intrinsic type of beauty, one that is achieved through structure and substance. They admire hand craftsmanship, but they recognize that beauty of form and texture may be achieved even with mass production. We do not believe that contemporary design has reached its pinnacle, but where, how, and when it will must remain matters of conjecture for the time being.

Although American art and industry were rather late in accepting the modern movement, progress has been extremely rapid since 1940. Leaders in design and production have established America in a prominent position on the world scene. It is particularly encouraging that the bonds between art and industry have been steadily growing stronger, and there are many indications that the relationship will continue to grow and to develop. This closer association will no doubt strengthen American contemporary art, especially in the field of interior design.

The manner in which the Scandinavian countries have projected contemporary styles has been widely acclaimed. Keen appreciation for craftsmanship is not new to the Scandinavians, nor is the feeling for simplicity of line and form. This combination of values nurtured the development of the modern style, particularly in Sweden and Denmark. In many phases of the decorative arts, the Scandinavian countries have attained fashion leadership.

There has been a strong Oriental influence in modern decoration. The emphasis on simplicity and beauty of form that has marked so much Oriental art provides the basis for a happy association between modern and ancient styles. The similarity of purpose has been responsible for more supplementation of rather than direct influence on basic designs, but now that some of the Oriental countries are developing their industries to produce for a world market we shall probably see some interesting interpretations of the modern style.

The fashion world has felt the impact of a fresh, new spirit in Italian design, and the creative exuberance in Italy has spread to the decorative arts. The Italian interpretations of contemporary styles show signs of becoming increasingly important.

General Features

In our discussion of style terminology it was pointed out that it is difficult to draw a

FIGURE 12-2   Glass and metal lend themselves to new methods of construction. (a) *Courtesy of Laverne International Ltd., N.Y.*, (b) *Designed by Milo Baughman. Courtesy of Thayer Coggin, Inc.*

fine line of demarcation between "contemporary" and "modern." In the sense that contemporary designs recognize and often draw upon the ideas of the past we must remember that they are still part of the modern style in its broadest interpretation. The term *organic* is often used to distinguish modern designs that attempt to break with past tradition. Thus we have a variety of ideas represented by the term *modern*. Although the style has a unique character, it is almost impossible to generalize about characteristics. We may, however, point out some of the trends and ideas that seem to have won general favor.

A primary purpose of the modern style is to create beauty in a functional form. In this respect, many of the designs have been highly successful. We have furniture that is sturdy, durable, and well constructed. It is easy to care for, lightweight, and usually built on slim proportions. It is designed for modern tastes that lean toward a light, airy, spacious atmosphere. Much of the furniture, therefore, is up on legs and built with lines and proportions that suggest fluidity without making the pieces seem unstable.

PROPORTIONS. New shapes and forms have been introduced. In the past, forms were generally square, rectangular, oval, or circular, and certain proportions were generally accepted as being the most pleasing to the eye. Modern furniture has introduced the "free" form, which rejects geometrical stereotypes. Modern materials and technologies make it possible to mold chairs in which the seat, back, and arms are shaped from one piece of material (for example, the shell chair).

Modern styling has also accepted unusual proportions for standard forms. Until recently the emphasis was on "long" and "low" for the modern style. Newer fashions tend toward more unusual forms in designs for chair backs and some chests and cupboards.

Much modern furniture is still built on rectilinear lines, but the modern designer is becoming more at ease with the use of curved and sloping lines to create different effects.

Asymmetrical forms are not a new idea, but modern designs have given them fresh interpretations. Desks, sofas, and chests have been unleashed from perennial symmetry.

FIGURE 12-3   The Ribbon Lounge Chair designed by Pierre Paulin is covered with stretch fabric that lends itself to new forms in upholstered furniture. (*Manufactured by Artifort of Holland. Distributed by Turner T Ltd., N.Y.*)

FIGURE 12-4   The "Cognac" chair designed by Eero Aarnio of Finland is formed of white fiberglass on a swivel base. A recess in the "Eros" table can hold a bowl of snacks or a centerpiece. (*Courtesy of Stendig, Inc.*)

FIGURE 12-5   The "Gyro" chair designed by Eero Aarnio is a whimsical, eye-catching new design. It is made of reinforced molded fiberglass. (*Courtesy of Stendig, Inc.*)

FUNCTIONALISM. The idea of functionalism has been projected into the design of dual-purpose pieces intended to simplify living in small areas where each piece of furniture must earn its keep. Sofas, chairs, and ottomans that open to form beds have been particularly useful and popular. There are also tables that adjust to different heights so that they may be used as a coffee table or a dining table. Chests of drawers are made with tops that extend to form long tables or with "drawers" that open to form desk surfaces.

A few words of caution must be injected here with regard to dual-purpose pieces. Sofas that extend to beds must have space in front of them—or tables that are easily moved. A dual-height table cannot serve two purposes at once. If one were entertaining in a small apartment, would it be practical to use it first as a cocktail table, then raise it and use it for dining? Tiny desk surfaces are not useful for certain types of work. It is important to visualize such furniture in actual use and to evaluate the practical values.

NEW MATERIALS. Much of the furniture in the modern style has incorporated new materials or it has used old materials in new ways.

Wood is still the favorite substance, but glass, metal, and plastics are also used. Laminates and fiberglass have tremendous potentials for new design effects, and the exponents of the modern style are exercising their imagination to incorporate these materials into their creations. An intrinsic beauty of texture in a material that lends itself to the purpose and form of the object is basic to modern design. Leaders in the field have been willing and eager to use new scientific achievements to fulfill this purpose. However, they have not overlooked the fact that more familiar materials, such as wood, marble, glass, straw, and ceramic tile, may achieve the same purpose.

Urethane foam has become increasingly important in modern furniture. This is an extremely versatile man-made product that has found wide application in industry as well as in the home. The chemicals from which the foam is made can be varied in the early stages of production to provide a wide range of materials. Thus the manufacturer may vary the recipe to suit the end purposes. It can be produced in flexible, semirigid, or rigid forms and the degree of softness can be controlled. It resists many of the factors that tend to cause

FIGURE 12-6 Sides of amber plexiglass give this sofa designed by Milo Baughman a "floating effect." (*Courtesy of Thayer Coggin, Inc.*)

(a)

FIGURE 12-7 New wire furniture by designer-architect Warren Platner is akin to contemporary metal sculpture in appearance and intricacy. It took three years to perfect the complex technologies that made this furniture a commercial reality. (*Courtesy of Knoll International*)

(b)

(c)

FIGURE 12-8   A series of lightweight modular units made entirely of urethane foam may be interchanged to meet a variety of needs. (*Courtesy of Urethane Institute*)

FIGURE 12-9   A recent innovation in modern design is inflatable furniture made of a thick, vinyl-like fabric. Each chair is equipped with a foot pump and patches that can be used in case of puncture. (*Courtesy of Selig Manufacturing Co.*)

FIGURE 12-10   Clear plastic is used to mold "invisible" chairs that can add new dimensions to a room. (*Courtesy of Laverne International Ltd., N.Y.*)

deterioration in other materials and it is low in cost. The broad advantages of this substance will undoubtedly make it a very important element in future design, especially in the area of modular furniture.

Molded plastic components and impregnated plastic finishes on wood will certainly influence future designs in furniture. As these techniques develop, we may see some interesting ornamentation of contemporary designs and new adaptations of traditional styles. Let us hope, however, that the new technologies will be used with discretion. It is difficult to imagine a beautiful Hepplewhite chair reproduced in plastic. We may shudder at the thought but it might happen.

One of the most fascinating innovations in modern design has been the introduction of inflatable furniture. Chair kits, equipped with small pumps and repair patches, have captured our imaginations as to the advantages of this type of furniture. If one has to move rather frequently or very suddenly, the idea of letting out the air and packing the frame in a shoebox can be most intriguing.

It is too early to evaluate truly the advantages of this type of furniture. At this point it seems to have advantages for seasonal uses, such as for patios and swimming pools. It is comfortable and storage problems are minimal.

Paper is another material that is being explored for possible contributions in furnishings. Again, this development is too new to evaluate but rather rigid, inexpensive items have been produced to meet specific needs.

MODULAR FURNITURE. The production of a relatively few standardized units that may be combined in various ways has made it possible to achieve arrangements that will suit individual tastes and needs at a comparatively low cost. The idea of unit combinations has been popular for many years in unpainted furniture and in sectional sofas. It has also been applied to finished chest and shelf units that may be stacked or mounted on legs or bases. Small tables that lock together to form larger tables are also used.

Wall-hung furniture has become popular. With brackets mounted on walls it is possible to have a flexible arrangement of shelves and various storage units. This type of furniture has proven particularly appealing to those persons who live in small quarters and who desire to conserve floor space.

Designers in the Modern Style

Perhaps one of the most interesting features in the development of the modern style is the manner in which it has transcended nationalistic boundaries. Although the Scandinavian countries have assumed leadership in many areas, designers and manufacturers in other countries have accepted the challenge and there is an international exchange of ideas and methods. Several American concerns have employed foreign designers and have established showrooms throughout the world. On the other hand, foreign manufacturers have established factories in the United States and have drawn upon American technology to advance their ideas.

Because of this international scope, it would be impossible to name all the fine artists and craftsmen who have made major contributions to the special type of classicism that modern design has achieved. We have already discussed some of the earlier leaders, such as Marcel Breuer, who experimented with new chair forms using metal tubing and metal strips. The ''Barcelona'' chair, which Mies van der Rohe designed in 1929, has become a famous classic in the modern style.

A few other names must be mentioned because of the outstanding designs that have been associated with them.

Charles Eames is a versatile designer who has a background in architecture. His name has become associated with chair forms, though he designs other pieces as well. The famous Eames chair exhibited in New York in 1946 was a distinct departure from conventional chair construction and was one of the first widely accepted designs in the organic modern style. It was made of laminated plywood bent to provide comfortable contours. Eames has continued to experiment with new forms and new materials and his imaginative use of aluminum has won particular acclaim in recent years. He has designed many pieces that are in the line of Herman Miller, Inc.

Eero Saarinen (1911–1961) was another architect whose name is associated with innovations in chair design. He was particularly interested in the possibilities of molded plastics. His early ''womb'' chair (1945), the ''tulip'' chair, and the pedestal bases that he introduced in 1956 have sculptural qualities that introduced new dimensions in form. Knoll International, a group of outstanding

FIGURE 12-12 The "tulip" chair and pedestal base table by Eero Saarinen gave new dimensions to the modern style. (*Courtesy of Knoll International*)

FIGURE 12-13 The Eames Lounge Chair and Ottoman built on pedestal bases represent new refinement in line and form. (*Designed by Charles Eames for Herman Miller, Inc.*)

FIGURE 12-14 A famous innovation in modern design, the Eames chair was one of the first successful chair designs that broke with tradition and used new techniques of construction. (*Designed by Charles Eames for Herman Miller, Inc.*)

leaders in design, produces much of the furniture designed by Saarinen.

George Nelson has designed a considerable amount of furniture for Herman Miller, Inc., but he now operates his own firm in New York. Another very versatile designer with a background in architecture, Mr. Nelson has created a variety of storage units that indicate a superb ability to combine beauty of form with the highest degree of functionalism. However, his designs of other pieces are equally beautiful.

Harry Bertoia is a sculptor who has designed for Knoll International with an emphasis on airy metal construction. His work in furniture design reveals the sculptural approach as well as his appreciation of the adaptability of new materials to the creation of new forms.

It might be mentioned here that the firm of Knoll International continues to encourage new directions in the modern style. The wire furniture shown in Figure 12-7 and the pieces shown in Figure 12-14 indicate the high level of design that this group supports.

Edward Wormley has designed a great deal of furniture with emphasis on the beautiful colors and grain patterns of wood, although he is equally proficient in the use of other materials. Many of his designs, which indicate his fine appreciation of form and texture, are produced by The Dunbar Furniture Corporation.

George Nakashima has designed some furniture for Knoll International but in general his work is more closely associated with handcraft methods. He seems to have a particular ability to create very contemporary forms that have a certain flavor of the past. The slight suggestion of an Early American influence in his modern designs lends a very distinctive quality.

"See-through" furniture has become rather important in the modern style. Laverne International, Ltd., introduced a plexiglass chair in 1962 that became known as the "invisible chair." Transparent substances for furniture have provided a new dimension of lightness in modern design and they are being adapted in a variety of ways today. The Lavernes also design with great distinction in other areas, including fabrics and wall coverings.

Jens Risom is a designer-manufacturer who came to the United States from Denmark. He produces fine quality furniture with high standards of craftsmanship. Although Risom's designs are extremely suitable for the modern home, a considerable amount of his work is designed for institutional needs.

Isamu Noguchi is associated with several phases of the modern style. He is a sculptor who has designed furniture for Herman Miller, Inc. Noguchi has also done considerable work with lighting fixtures that reflect his interest in sculpture.

A leader in the field of designing good-quality furniture for mass production was Paul McCobb. He died in 1969 at the age of fifty-one but his designs have had significant influence, especially in the area of modular furniture and coordinated groupings.

Another designer who has shown interest in new methods for mass production is Milo Baughman. He has won several awards for furniture design and he is particularly cognizant of craftsmanship as it can be related to modern technology. His use of metals, such as steel and chrome, often combined with wood, his sensitivity to new materials, and his appreciation of vibrant colors and textures have established a new look in contemporary design.

Many foreign designers have either initiated trends or have influenced modern design on the international level. Again, it is not possible to cite all of the important leaders but a few must be mentioned.

A famous Finnish architect, Alvar Aalto, experimented with laminated wood and designed chairs and stacking stools that exploited the use of this material.

Hans Wegner is a Danish designer noted for exquisite simplicity. His chairs and storage units have qualities that combine comfort, functionalism, and a handcrafted appearance.

Finn Juhl, another Danish designer, has worked with The Baker Company in America. This association has been credited with being an important step in promoting the interest of American industry in developing the international style.

Contemporary furniture produced by Dunbar/Dux represents large-scale manufacturing of fine-quality modern furniture. This is a Swedish company that now has a factory in the United States.

Several other names must be mentioned in connection with Scandinavian design. Bruno Mathsson of Sweden experimented with

FIGURE 12-15 A classic storage unit designed by George Nelson. (*Courtesy of Herman Miller, Inc.*)

FIGURE 12-16 A sling sofa designed by George Nelson illustrates his command of line, form, and texture. Metal tubing is used in an ingenious manner for the framework. (*Courtesy of Herman Miller, Inc.*)

FIGURE 12-17 A new chair designed by Don Petitt has an easy elegance that results from what appears to be only three continuously carved wood pieces joined into a simple frame. (*Courtesy of Knoll International*)

(a)

(b)

FIGURE 12-18 (left)   A lightly scaled shell arm-chair rests on a dramatic cantilevered base of chrome plated steel. (*Courtesy of Jens Risom Design, Inc.*)

FIGURE 12-20 (right)   Frames of white tubular steel can be easily assembled into multi-unit sofas by means of a simple plastic clip device that secures bases firmly into place. The three-seater sofa with its foam seat cushions flipped over to make them level can serve as an extra bed. (*Furniture by Dunbar/Dux. Carpet by Bigelow*)

FIGURE 12-19 (below)   Milo Baughman uses a frame fence of steel tubing to support blocks of foam rubber covered in a textured fabric. (*Courtesy of Thayer Coggin, Inc.*)

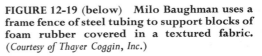

FIGURE 12-21 (below)   Swedish designer Bruno Mathsson uses a swivel base and neck cushions to insure comfort. (*Furniture by Dunbar/Dux. Vinyl flooring by Flintkote*)

FIGURE 12-22 "Astra", a Danish rya rug, provides a splash of bright color in a modern setting. (*Courtesy of Egetaepper, Inc.*)

laminated wood as did Alvar Aalto in Finland. Ib Kofol-Larson, Karl-Erik Ekselius, and Arne Jacobsen are other designers who have achieved distinction.

Italy has had a revival of spirit in various phases of design. Some authorities believe that the most exciting new ideas for interior design are now coming from Italy but that they are geared to avant-garde tastes and not yet ready for general acceptance.

In the realm of furniture design, Gio Ponti has had a significant influence as a purist. Carlo de Carli, Ico Parisi, and Franco Albini have also had considerable influence. There are a number of young Italian designers who will probably influence future designs because they seem to have a special awareness of beautiful form as it relates to functionalism in all aspects of daily living.

Our discussion up to this point has been concerned mostly with furniture, but in the field of textiles several designers have made outstanding contributions.

Dorothy Liebes pioneered in designing fabrics that combine unusual colors and textures in yarns. Much of her work is either handwoven or has similar effects. Her influences on modern textile design have been widespread. Since 1940, when she established her own firm, she has served more than twenty-five leading corporations in the textile and related industries as designer and color consultant.

Jack Lenor Larsen has had a background in architecture and interior design but chose to devote his talents to fabric design. With a perceptive appreciation for both handcrafts and the technical aspects of production, Larsen has managed to unite concepts that seem to represent widely divergent ideas. The firm of Jack Lenor Larsen, Inc., established in 1952, has been responsible for numerous innovations in textile design.

Another fabric designer with a background in architecture is Alexander Girard, who designs for Herman Miller, Inc. Girard draws upon a wide variety of sources from all over the world for design inspiration and some of his fabrics are actually woven in foreign countries.

Ben Rose is another textile designer who also designs wall coverings. He has been particularly known for excellence in printed fabrics, but he also designs plain fabrics with beautiful textures.

In other areas of modern interior design it is not quite as easy to name outstanding leaders. In various countries there are many designers who are striving to create lighting fixtures and accessories that combine innovations of form with functionalism. There have been important advances in this direction and several designers have won international recognition for their contributions. However, it is difficult to name leaders who should be cited in a brief survey such as this. In view of the fact that outstanding designers have had backgrounds in architecture, it seems odd that the challenging field of lighting has not attracted more attention. This is in no way meant to discredit those who have made significant contributions but merely to point out that there is an apparent need for more leadership in other areas of interior design.

Section IV
Decoration

Plan implies purpose, and the success of a home will depend upon how well one can keep purposes in mind when selecting and arranging *all* the furnishings. A comfortable, livable home that is also a joy to behold doesn't just happen; it must be developed with clearly defined goals. Most of us want our homes to be comfortable, convenient, and beautiful. It is essential, therefore, to consider very carefully how each area will be used and to integrate usefulness with beauty.

A room plan involves all aspects of furnishing. Colors, furniture, floor coverings, window treatments, and accessories must be chosen and used with certain objectives in mind. Although it is necessary to discuss these various factors in separate chapters, each one is vital to the final result. Here we shall be concerned chiefly with the selection and arrangement of furniture, but in succeeding chapters the other aspects of planning rooms will be discussed in greater detail.

Drawing a Floor Plan

Paper planning will prevent many of the serious pitfalls of furnishing a home. In Chapter 1 we discussed floor plans drawn to a specific scale; it is most useful to work with such a diagram when one is selecting and arranging furniture.

Graph paper is convenient to use if it is marked off in one-eighth- or one-quarter-inch squares. The most conventional scale for plotting the arrangement of each room is one-quarter inch to one foot. There are some kits on the market that use three-dimensional forms. These are usually done in a scale of one-half inch to one foot.

Almost all categories of furniture pieces are available in a wide variety of sizes, so one should have the exact measurements of any piece that he actually plans to use before

13

Room Plans and Furniture Arrangement

FURNITURE TEMPLATES

SCALE: 1/4"=1'

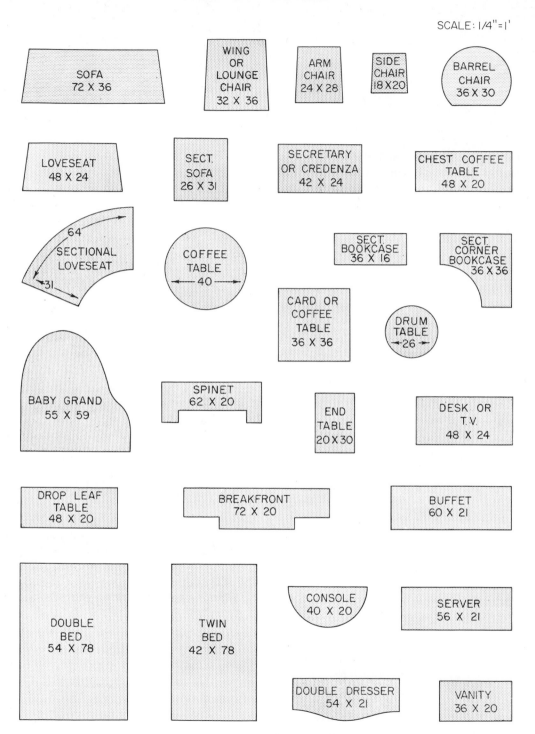

FIGURE 13-1 Furniture templates.

making a floor plan. Figure 13-1 shows templates of some basic design pieces drawn to scale. It should be noted that the sofa is represented as six feet long, but some sofas are shorter and many are longer. If an eight-foot-long sofa is to be used, a template should be made that will represent the accurate dimensions. Tables, chests, desks, and chairs also vary, so one should be sure to use accurate measurements.

Drawing should be traced or new ones made for the furniture to be used. Each piece should be cut from heavy construction paper or lightweight cardboard (a manila file folder is excellent). Each piece should then be labeled with name and measurements.

Now it is time to try various arrangements of furniture on the floor plan. Pieces may be easily moved around at will. When an arrangement seems satisfactory, each piece should be traced and labeled.

FUNCTIONAL PLANS. No matter how beautiful a room may be, if it does not perform well in actual use, it will soon lose its appeal. In planning a room, one must decide which pieces of furniture will be needed and then arrange them to best serve the purpose of the room.

What activities will be carried on in the area and what furniture will be required? Even in fairly large homes, each room may serve more than one purpose. In small quarters, the most efficient use of space will present a real challenge to the ingenuity.

For example, a living room in a small apartment must meet the needs for individual and group activities of the family; it must be adaptable for entertaining guests; and no doubt it will have to provide a certain amount of storage space. There may have to be areas for conversation, for music and television, for work or study, and even for dining. It is unlikely that all of these activities would be carried on at once, but the room must be planned so that it will function with ease for each purpose.

A small bedroom may be equipped for several purposes—sleeping, dressing, storage, and possibly work or study. Even an entrance hall may have to serve more than one function. In some small apartments the foyer may be used as a dining area or for storage units.

Selection of Furniture. The first step is to list the pieces that will be essential to each area. If the room is small, one will want to keep the number of pieces to a minimum and perhaps choose pieces that will serve more than one purpose. For example, in a small living area, a commode, a small chest, or a record cabinet might be used in place of a lamp table next to a chair.

In planning each area the scale of the room must be kept in mind. Areas must be kept in harmony with one another and must be designed to fulfill their particular functions. Chairs and sofas should be comfortable, storage units should be roomy and adaptable. When space is not precious, some furniture may be selected for purely decorative purposes; otherwise functionalism becomes more important.

Areas of Activity. Furniture must be grouped for the most efficient use. A sofa and chairs meant for relaxing conversation should be within easy distance of each other. Lounge chairs should have good light and tables nearby.

A desk should be equipped with a chair and good light. It is useful to have a desk with at least one file drawer for the storage of records and accounts. A cabinet for the storage of recordings should be near a record player. In addition to a table and chairs, the dining area might have a serving unit that will provide a storage space for linens and silver and a surface for trays.

Rarely is a piece of furniture useful by itself. It must be used in relation to other pieces, and a functional grouping of pieces allows for greater comfort and convenience.

It is sometimes advisable to divide a room into specific areas. Much modern planning provides for a large flexible area that can be subdivided by the manner in which the furniture is arranged. See-through room dividers have become popular for marking the division between the entrance foyer and the living room or between the dining area and the living area. Each area becomes a "room," but the absence of actual walls allows for an effect of greater spaciousness.

Traffic Lanes. Rooms have pathways from their entrances to their centers of activity. Obstructions in the way of normal movements should be avoided as much as possible. It becomes most annoying to walk around a piece of furniture to get from one place to another in a room or to have to move something everytime one wants to open a closet door or a bureau drawer. Extension tables should have

FIGURE 13-2 A well-planned living room provides a functional arrangement and recognizes architectural features.

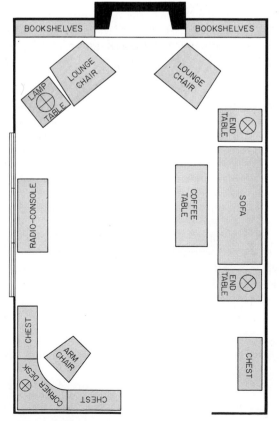

BOOKSHELVES   BOOKSHELVES

LOUNGE CHAIR

LOUNGE CHAIR

LAMP TABLE

END TABLE

END TABLE

RADIO-CONSOLE

COFFEE TABLE

SOFA

CHEST

ARM CHAIR

CHEST

CORNER DESK

CHEST

SCALE: $\frac{1}{4}'' = 1'$

PRIVATE PATIO

GARDEN

SHOWER

BOOK & T.V. CABT.

BATH AREA

DESK

BEDROOM

FIGURE 13-3 Rooms that serve a dual purpose are becoming increasingly important. A master bedroom with a small sitting-work area provides comfort and privacy.

165

FIGURE 13-4 One large room is divided into two with the aid of curtain poles. The living and dining areas are given different but coordinated window treatments. (*Courtesy of The Singer Company*)

enough room to really extend. Chairs around a dining table require enough space to be easily accessible.

Maintenance. Because most of us maintain our homes without staffs or servants, ease of care must be a major factor in planning each room. Modern materials that resist soil, and vacuum cleaners with attachments do simplify the problem of keeping the home clean. However, some locations have excessive amounts of dust and grime that will tax even the most carefree surfaces. Furniture should be easy to move and corners should be easy to reach.

In planning an easily maintained room, floor coverings need special attention. In an area of heavy traffic, a very light or a very dark wall-to-wall carpet installation can present real problems. An entrance hall, for example, may

look beautiful with a cream-colored carpet, but in stormy weather when people come in with muddy shoes, the carpet will soon lose its charm.

Accessories that are merely dust collectors should be avoided. Accents that require the minimum amount of care are the best choices.

AESTHETIC PLANS. A room can be both functional and beautiful, though there may be times when one aspect will have to be sacrificed for the other because of specific limitations. When such a problem does arise, creative ability can work out a happy solution. For example, radiators that are not concealed can really tax the imagination. One needs them for heating, yet they can mar the beauty of the room because of their appearance. One simple solution is to use bookcases on either side and a metal grill over the front of the radiator. With a shelf over the whole unit, the "problem" may become a very attractive adjunct to a room. Perhaps all problems won't be solved as easily as that, but is is more interesting at least to try some creative approach rather than just to ignore them.

The beauty of a home will depend on how well the principles of design are applied. As we have pointed out earlier, a design is a component of all the elements—line, form, color, and texture. Ability to command these elements can produce the desired effect.

To some extent, natural instincts dictate the placement of furniture in a room. Even people who are not well versed in the fundamentals of art place the sofa against the long wall in the living room because it seems to "look right" in that position. But a more refined awareness of design establishes the subtle aesthetics that make a room more beautiful. However, it should be remembered that one doesn't stand back and view a room the way he does a picture; when he is in it he is part of it. Once the room is put together, certain aspects of the composition become more important in a three-dimensional way.

Harmony. A room plan blends all the elements so that the whole area expresses a particular theme or mood. The old axiom that the "sum is greater than the total of the parts" can well be applied to the composition of a room. Each object and each element contributes to the whole, but the result must be a unit that has a charm and a personality of its own. The beauty of any room depends upon this interrelationship of all the components. The furnishings must look as though they belong in the room and in the company of one another.

FIGURE 13-5   A sleeping alcove in an L-shaped room is separated from the living area by a folding screen covered in a vividly striped fabric that matches the bedspread. (*Courtesy of The Englander Company, a Subsidiary of Union Carbide Corporation*)

Proportion. Because proportion is a matter of space relationships, the size of the room and the available wall space will determine the types of furniture and the amount of it that can be used. Furniture should be in scale with the room. A small room will usually appear to best advantage if it has small-scaled pieces and a minimum number of them; a large room can take the massive ones.

A wall area is broken by the outlines of the furniture and the accessories placed against it. Each wall arrangement must, therefore, be considered in terms of divisions that are pleasing to the eye. Pictures or other accessories that are hung on the wall should relate to both the furniture and the wall area.

Scale is also important in grouping pieces of furniture. A tiny, delicate table next to a massive chair becomes insignificant, although the table itself may be charming near a more delicate piece.

Balance. In almost every room there will be some pieces of furniture that are heavier than others. The larger, more important pieces should be distributed around the room in such a way that all areas will be in equilibrium. But the architectural features, such as windows or a fireplace, also bear "weight," and frequently these must be balanced by heavier pieces on opposite walls.

Frequently color can be employed to bring areas into balance. A small area of brilliant color or bold pattern takes on an added weight that can often balance a larger area of a more subdued nature. Thus a chair covered in a bright color might balance the more subdued draperies of a rather large window.

Balance within groupings of furniture is also important. In Chapter 5 we discussed the two principal types of balances—formal and informal, or occult. Most rooms need a bit of each, but in general, modern style and the more casual traditional styles lend themselves to occult balance. Elegance in a stately traditional room may be expressed by groups that are symmetrically arranged. The mood of the room will determine how much of each type of balance one may want to use. Too much asymmetry may lead to confusion and restlessness; too much symmetry may be stiff and forbidding.

Emphasis. Most rooms are more interesting if there are definite centers of interest that give leadership to their designs. A large room may have more than one dominant center,

but in a small room one or perhaps two centers will usually be sufficient.

One should study each room carefully to determine what or where the center of interest might be. Perhaps a fireplace, a large window, a pair of windows, or some other architectural feature can be used as the area of emphasis. One large wall area can be given importance by furniture, accessories, color, or pattern. For example, a wall treated with a mural, painted in a brighter color, or treated with a different texture, immediately becomes a dominant note. A large important piece of furniture, a large picture, or a picture grouping may lend added emphasis to an area.

Some special activity, hobby, or interest may provide an interesting basis for a dominant area in a room. A musical instrument or a collection of some sort can be emphasized by the manner in which it is placed or displayed. Such a center of interest frequently gives a room its individuality and may set the theme for the entire plan.

Rhythm. Lines, colors, and textures in the furnishings will cause the eye to move in certain directions. It is usually more pleasing for the eye to move in an easy, graceful manner rather than to move with a jumpy or jerky motion. We have discussed various ways of producing rhythmic sensations, and all of the techniques may be applied in developing a room plan. A pleasing rhythm depends on well-organized relationships of all the elements of design.

The lines of the more important furnishings are generally more attractive if they follow the structural lines of the room. Rectangular pieces will appear to better advantage when placed with the major line parallel to a wall or at right angles to it. Placing furniture on the diagonal, or catercornered, is often disturbing, except for pull-up chairs or even lounge chairs in some rooms.

Continuity of line helps the eye to travel smoothly. Thus tables that are the same height as the arm of a chair are not only more convenient to use but are usually more attractive in relation to the chair. Pictures and other accessories must be arranged to keep eye movements smooth and easy.

Repetition is an excellent means of providing a feeling of rhythm, but it must be employed with discretion. Too much may become dull or monotonous; some contrast is necessary for interest.

FIGURE 13-6 The fireplace in this room is a natural center of interest but another wall is emphasized by the use of a Baroque console and mirror. (*Designed by Patricia Harvey, A.I.D. Photo by Alexandre Georges*)

(a)

(b)

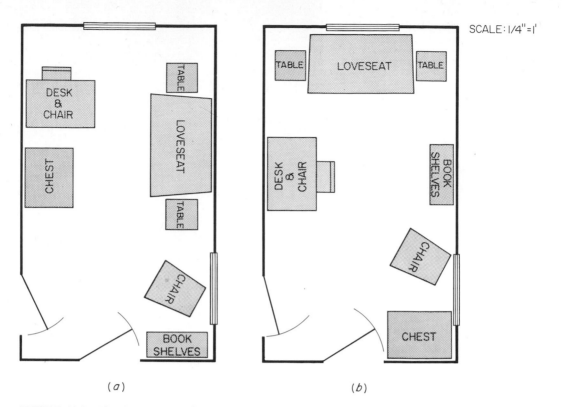

SCALE: 1/4"=1'

(a)

(b)

FIGURE 13-7 The arrangement in (a) decreases the size of the room. By rearranging the furniture as shown in (b), more floor area is visible as one enters the room. In this case, the love seat across the short wall gives the room better proportions.

FIGURE 13-8 Furniture in light scale and wall-to-wall carpeting make an area appear larger. (*Courtesy of DuPont Textile Fibers*)

The Spacious Look

In some rooms we tend to prefer a wide-open appearance to one that seems crowded and cluttered. Several tricks and devices may be employed to provide a feeling of spaciousness even in a small room. The use of color and pattern are, of course, very important, but these will be discussed later.

The type of furniture and the way it is arranged can do wonders to make a room seem more spacious. One should choose pieces that are small in scale and built on simple lines. Furniture up on legs or wall-hung units make us more aware of the expanse of floor space, whereas pieces that extend to the floor limit and define the area. Covering the entire floor with a solid color or a subtle texture rather than breaking up the area with rugs and borders will also increase the apparent size of the room.

In general it is wise to keep the center of the room clear. The more one breaks up the area with furniture projecting toward the center or actually placed in the middle of the room, the smaller the area will seem. When the room is large, however, some such arrangements may be necessary for convenience and interest.

The large pieces of furniture should be placed in the less conspicuous areas. As one walks into a room it will seem less spacious if the large pieces attract the attention first.

The Room as a Unit

A room is not usually furnished all at once. It evolves and develops, which is what makes preliminary planning especially important. Unless rooms grow according to well-organized plans, one may finish with a home that is neither as functional nor as attractive as it might be. But furnishing on the basis of a specific plan certainly does not mean that rooms must look stilted or "decorated." It does mean, however, that one must be able to visualize and define the way he wants his home to function and the particular type of charm that he wants it to express.

A plan makes it easier to keep objectives clearly in view as one makes each new addition. Awareness of the room as a whole or as a unit grows if one carefully evaluates each furniture group in terms of beauty and function.

14
Color

One of the most fascinating tools to work with in decorating is the element of color. Because it is relatively inexpensive, it can do wonders for low-level budgets, *if* it is used with imagination. On any cost level, color is often the decorator's pet element, probably because it is so important in establishing the mood and the personality of a home.

The homemaker who is unresponsive to color does not realize that colors and color combinations affect moods and attitudes. They can be depressing, irritating, disturbing; they can be restful and soothing; they can be stimulating and exciting. It is rather strange that so few people are aware of how much the colors that we live with day in and day out do influence our attitudes and moods.

WHAT IS COLOR? We see color only when there is light. When white light is passed through a suitable prism the wavelengths that compose the light are diffracted, or bent, at slightly different angles. This separates the wavelengths to form bands of colors collectively called the spectrum. Wavelengths slightly shorter than the violet part of the spectrum are called ultraviolet and are in-invisible; those slightly longer than the red end of the spectrum are called infrared, and are also invisible. If the wavelengths forming the spectrum are recombined by means of a lens, the white light is re-formed.

Objects exhibit color because of the selective manner in which their surfaces reflect and absorb light. As light strikes a colored surface, certain wavelengths are reflected to a greater extent than others, thus determining the color of the object. White surfaces reflect all wavelengths equally and absorb very little energy; thus white is a mixture of equal parts of all colored wavelengths. A black surface absorbs all wavelengths almost completely and is, therefore, the virtual absence of color.

As wavelengths strike the eye they stimulate receptor nerves in the retina and create the sensations of color. As children we learned to associate names with particular sensations.

Different groups of people are interested in color for various reasons. The physicist is concerned with wavelengths of light and the physical aspects; the chemist works with pigments and materials; the physiologist is interested in color as a stimulus of receptor nerves; the artist sees color as a medium of expression; the psychologist wants to understand the emotional factors involved in the use of color; the industrialist is interested in fashions of color that will sell his products.

COLOR TERMINOLOGY.

Color has various dimensions and characteristics that are given special names. We might point out here that there is a difference between working with colored lights and with colored pigments and dyestuffs. In discussing the spectrum, we noted that white light was the mixture of all wavelengths. Thus a suitable mixture of colored lights should produce white. Proper proportions of red, yellow, and blue will produce white light through additive mixture, and these colors are called the additive primaries. Similar mixtures of pigments and dyestuffs will not produce white because these colors work on a substractive principle, selectively absorbing portions of the white light incident upon them. Suitable mixtures of paints or dyes will produce neutral grays but will not produce white. Other pigments or dyes will absorb so much light that in proper mixtures they will produce black.

Hue is the term used for the name of any color. Yellow, green, red, violet are all hues.

Intensity refers to the brilliance or purity of the color. Other names for this quality are *chroma* and *saturation*. A color in its purest form has greatest brilliance. As we mix it with other hues, it approaches gray and loses some of its brilliance or its intensity. Thus we speak of "grayed green" or "grayed yellow."

Value refers to lightness and darkness of a color. If we mix white with a color, we produce a high value, or a "tint" of that color. Mixing black with a color will produce a low value or a "shade" of the color. We may produce tints and shades of all hues—both the intense ones and the grayed ones.

The terms *warm* and *cool* are frequently used in connection with color. The warm hues are those that we associate with fire, heat, and the sun: red, yellow, and orange. The cool hues are those that we associate with ice, shade, and water: blue and green. True purple, which is a mixture of blue and red, is neither warm nor cool; however, if there is a slight predominance of red, it will have a warm quality, and if it leans toward the blue, it might be quite cool. Because green is a mixture of blue and yellow, a predominance of either of these hues may change this characteristic of green. A yellow-green might have quite a bit of warmth, whereas a blue-green may be quite cool.

We also use the terms *advancing* and *receding* in connection with color. Several characteristics determine this color quality. The bright warm hues are more advancing than the bright cool hues. Yet any brilliant colors are more advancing than the grayed colors, which are said to recede.

COLOR SYSTEMS.

Various systems have been devised for working with colors, and some of these systems are more suitable than others for dealing with particular aspects of color. It would be beyond the province of this book to delve into all the color theories and unnecessary to present superfluous technical information that may only confuse the reader rather than clarify the subject of color. It is helpful, however, to understand color systems to develop one's own perception and ability to work with color schemes. We shall therefore briefly discuss two well-known color systems.

The Prang System. The simplest way to understand color relationships is to study a color wheel based on three primary colors—yellow, blue, and red. These three hues are called primary in the Prang system because they cannot be mixed from other pigments. Theoretically, starting with five cans or tubes of paint—the three primaries plus black and white—one could build an entire range of colors. This is not practically possible, however, because to get the exact gradations in color requires precise mixing of different pigments.

The color wheel indicates that a mixture

of yellow and blue produces green. Blue and red produce purple; yellow and red produce orange. Green, purple, and orange are secondary colors in this system. Each one is made by mixing two primary colors. By mixing a primary with a secondary color one will produce the tertiary or intermediate colors: yellow-green, blue-green, blue-purple, red-purple, red-orange, and yellow-orange. But there are infinite variations of each primary and secondary color. One might mix a small amount of yellow with a large amount of green, then add a bit more yellow, and then a bit more until he had more yellow than green in the mixture. If he took a sample of each mixture, he would have a variety of yellow-green hues ranging from one that was almost yellow to one that was almost green. One can produce a similar range of hues by mixing the other primary and secondary hues.

Colors that are opposite each other on the color wheel are called *complements*. By mixing any two colors that are opposite each other on the color wheel one is actually mixing the three primaries. If the hues are exact complements, the mixture will produce a gray. Mixing just a little of the complement with a hue will decrease the brilliance or intensity of that hue. Thus we produce the grayed colors However, in actually mixing colors it is more satisfactory to decrease brilliance by adding gray. Graying the yellow-oranges, orange, and the red-oranges will give various copper tones or the colors of saddle leather. *Burnt orange* is another name for a grayed orange. Naturally there are many gradations for each hue, depending on how much of its complement one mixes with it to decrease its intensity.

Now if we bring white and black into the picture we can produce the different values of each hue. A tint is produced by the mixing of white with any color. The various forms of beige would be the tints of the grayed yellows and yellow-oranges. Peach would be a tint of red-orange, and a pale lavender would be a tint of purple. A shade is produced by the mixing of black with a hue. A wide range of browns results from the mixture of black with grayed red-oranges, orange, and yellow-oranges. Although the beiges and browns are often referred to as "neutral" in the sense that they combine well with many other colors, in true color terminology only black, white, and gray are actually neutral.

The Munsell System. This color-order system describes and catalogs color in terms of the three visual attributes or dimensions mentioned earlier—hue, value, and chroma. These attributes are arranged into orderly scales of equal *visual* steps. The color solid so defined is an irregular spheroid, having a central vertical axis representing the neutral value scale, with white at the top, black at the bottom, and the intermediate steps of grays scaled between these two extremes.

There are no primary colors as in the pigment-mixture systems, but there are five principal hues—red, yellow, green, blue, and purple—spaced at equal visual intervals around the outside of the color solid. Spaced between the principal hues are five intermediate hues—yellow-red, green-yellow, blue-green, purple-blue, and red-purple. Radiating out at 90 degrees from the value axis are scales of chroma, or saturation, for each hue at each value level. The low-chroma colors, which are grayish, are near the gray axis, and the chroma increases until the most intense colors are reached on the surface of the solid.

Each of the ten hue families already listed is divided decimally as the hue gradually changes toward its neighbor, with the central hue in each family having the prefix 5. Numbers below 5 indicate hues inclining toward the hue family next in a counter-clockwise direction, whereas those above 5 approach the hue family in the opposite direction. Thus 5GY is middle green-yellow; 3GY is more yellow, while 7GY is more green.

On the vertical scale absolute black is N 0/ and absolute white is N 10/. The value notation is always followed by a slant line. The chroma attribute is written following the slant line and departs from the value axis, having a chroma of /0, through a series of visual saturation steps to the maximum that can be produced, in some cases as high as /14 or /16. Thus 5Y 8/4 is a middle yellow hue (5Y) at high value (8/) and low chroma (/4). It is a tint of a grayed yellow or beige.

Munsell notations are available for forty different hues, at the 2.5, 5, 7.5, and 10 positions of each of the ten hue families. Where possible, colors appear on each full value level from 2/ through 9/, and in some cases at half-value levels. Neutrals (white, grays, black) are available in eighteen steps (N 1/, N 1.5/, N 2/, . . . N 9/, N 9.5/). The Munsell notation is related to the internationally recognized CIE[1] system of color specifications by a series of translational diagrams, making it extremely useful in science and industry.

Factors That Influence Choice

This brief discussion of color indicates that one may choose from thousands of colors and that the possible combinations are infinite. The natural question, then, is where to start? Several factors will guide a selection of colors and some will be more important than others.

INDIVIDUAL PREFERENCES. The colors chosen should be those that the members of the family like to look at. Most of us lean at least a little toward one color or one group of colors. Even if one is not particularly color-conscious, there may be colors that he intensely dislikes. All colors that evoke unfavorable reactions should be avoided. The homemaker should get to know the color preferences of herself and her family. These are not always clearly defined, so this may take a bit of probing.

Living rooms, family rooms, and dining rooms should have colors that appeal to all members of the family. Strong preferences of any one individual can be limited to that person's bedroom.

THE STYLE AND PURPOSE OF THE ROOM. Although we need not be too restricted by style or purpose in choosing colors, a particular theme can be emphasized by the color scheme.

A gay, informal room calls for colors that are gay and bright; strong, stimulating contrasts are in order. A room that is meant for relaxation and repose should have colors that are quiet and restful. Children's rooms may have colors that are either gay or delicate.

Certain styles, such as Early American or Colonial, are best expressed by the authentic colors of the natural dyes that were used with the original furniture. Much of the French decor requires soft, delicate coloring. The luxurious themes of eighteenth-century Eng-

lish styles call for rich, elegant tones of claret red, emerald green, gold, and plum color. The modern style has made use of bold, brilliant colors, often in combination and often as accents against white or neutral backgrounds.

THE PHYSICAL CHARACTERISTICS OF THE ROOM. Certain aspects of the room itself may determine the choice of colors. These include:

Exposure. Both the amount and the type of natural light that enters a room may influence the choice of colors. If the room will be used mainly at night, exposure is not such an important consideration, but almost every room will sometimes be used during the day.

Light from the north has a bluish cast that shows colors in their most natural tones. This is the type of light that the artist prefers for his studio, because the light from a northern exposure has a cold quality that intensifies the characteristics of colors. In a home, however, we are more interested in a pleasant atmosphere than in seeing colors at their truest, and it is desirable to select colors that will blend with the natural light to provide the desired effects. To counteract the effects of harsh light, rooms with northern exposures are often decorated with warm colors. Yellow, orange, red, or warm pink may be used to produce a ''sunshine'' glow.

On the other hand, rooms with a southern or a southwestern exposure receive a warm light. Especially in areas that will be used a great deal during hot weather, these rooms are more pleasant when they are decorated with cool colors. Brilliant colors, especially in the warm group, will seem more intense if the room receives a large amount of natural sunlight.

Preferences for certain colors and the purposes for which a room is to be used may cause one to ignore these effects of exposure, but because colors vary so much under different conditions of light it is important that they be examined carefully in the natural setting of the room before they are selected.

Size. It isn't always necessary to make small rooms seem larger or large rooms seem smaller, but if one does want to change the apparent size of an area, color is a useful tool. In general, the light colors that are somewhat

[1] Commission Internationale de l'Eclairage.

(a)

(b)

FIGURE 14-1 Dark walls and floor make a room seem smaller.

grayed will make a room appear larger. Pale green, aqua, or pale blue—all cool colors—lend an airy quality that adds to spaciousness. These receding colors seem to push walls back, whereas brilliant colors and even some tints of the warm colors are more advancing. Dark tones define space and will make a room seem smaller.

Shape. The advancing and receding qualities of color may be used to emphasize or to counteract the shape of a room. A particular wall or an alcove becomes more important if it is decorated in an advancing hue while the other walls and areas are more subdued with colors that recede. Using different colors or textures is a handy technique for treating poorly shaped areas, but it need not be reserved for problem rooms. It is an effective way of adding emphasis or creating a center of interest. However, when a room does have poor proportions it can be made far more attractive by an imaginative use of color and texture. A high ceiling, for example, will seem lower if it is painted a dark color. A brilliant color would also be advancing, but it might serve to draw undue attention to the ceiling and defeat its own purpose.

The short wall in a long, narrow room can be made to advance while the others recede. Different values or different intensities of the same hue can be used; so can colors that contrast with each other. A room that seems too square can be given a more pleasing proportion by using different hues.

The Color Plan

Just as in plotting furniture arrangements, some preliminary paper work is important in working out color schemes. On the floor plans we were careful to work with scaled drawings so each piece of furniture was accurately represented in relation to the measurements of the room. With color plans, we cannot be quite so accurate about measurements of areas, but we must remember that the amount of each color used is important in the overall effect. It is important, therefore, to work with samples and swatches that are somewhat proportionate to the areas they will cover in the room.

A variety of colors and textures is used in each area of the home. The wood tones of the furniture also contribute to the color scheme. Certain areas, such as a bedroom or a dining room, may have larger areas of wood color. The living room will probably have a certain amount of wood, but the upholstered pieces and the draperies will form major color areas. In every room, the wall and floor areas are considerably larger than the other areas.

When planning a color scheme, one should list the areas of color that will contribute to the decor and mark off proportionate areas that approximate the amounts of space they will cover. This must of necessity be guesswork, but the important point is to keep the areas

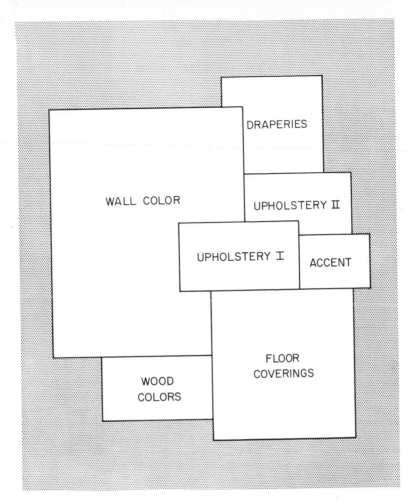

FIGURE 14-2 **Plan a color chart for each room. Try to keep areas in relative amounts.**

reasonably accurate relative to one another. The samples and swatches should be overlapped as they are arranged. This is important in showing the effects of having colors next to one another as they will actually be used. If the accent colors will be used in pillows on a sofa, the swatches of accent should be placed next to the swatch that represents the sofa to show the true effect.

Sometimes it is even more useful to draw a large-scale floor plan of the room. First we paint in the color of the floor covering and paste swatches of fabric in the places they will be used. This method is useful for showing the distribution of colors. Then we represent the wood tones with samples cut from magazines, or with bits of the adhesive backed plastic that comes in a variety of wood textures

and colors. The piece of paper used should be large enough for pasting generous samples of wall and drapery colors in the margin.

The purpose of either type of color plan is to help one visualize the finished room and to present some idea of how the colors will relate to one another. It is important to use actual swatches and colors, or else samples that are as close as possible.

Developing the Color Scheme

There are several ways of approaching a color scheme. Once the mood of the room has been decided upon, and all the factors involved have been considered, it is time to get down to selecting specific colors for each area.

The homemaker may work with the color wheel and develop her own color combinations, or she may choose some existing combination of colors that appeals to her and work from there.

Let us start with the color wheel. This is more fun and truly an exciting experience if one is equipped with a few jars of ordinary poster paint, a plastic egg container for mixing colors, a glass of water, and lots of white paper.

We start with the primary colors plus white and black, and follow the color wheel, mixing secondary and intermediate colors. Then we start graying colors by mixing them with bits of their complements. Tints and shades can be made by the use of the white and black. Samples of all the colors mixed should be kept. We are ready to work on color combinations.

COLOR HARMONIES. Actually, any colors can be combined with pleasing results if we are conscious of intensity and value. For example, one may not be partial to a brilliant red next to a brilliant orange, but in some primitive art this combination is used most effectively. But if we gray the orange and mix it with a little black we produce a rich chocolate brown. Now we mix some white with the red to produce a lovely pale pink. Brown and pink is not as shocking a combination as the brilliant orange and red. We have simply varied the intensity and the value of the two hues to produce a more acceptable combination of colors. In working with the color wheel, one must be particularly cognizant of variations in both intensity and value, remembering that black, white, and gray are neutrals that can be parts of any color scheme.

Monochromatic. *Mono* means one, and in working out a true monochromatic harmony, one hue must be the keynote of the whole scheme. The popular scheme of beige, brown, and orange is a truly monochromatic scheme, because the tans and browns are simply tints and shades of grayed orange. A brilliant form of orange may be used as an accent or even for larger areas, but if any other hue is introduced, it is no longer a monochromatic harmony. With monochromatic schemes, the key to success is to provide enough contrast through either hue or intensity to make it interesting.

Analogous. Colors that are next to each other on the color wheel frequently provide the basis of very pleasing combinations. Blue-violet, and violet have enjoyed tremendous popularity in recent years. A more standard analogous harmony combines yellow, yellow-green, and green. Once again, with different values and intensities, any adjacent colors may be used in combination with interesting effects.

Complementary. More contrast is provided by the use of colors that are opposite each other on the color wheel. A true complementary harmony uses colors that are directly opposite, such as orange and blue, red and green, or yellow and purple. When such colors are used in their fullest intensities, they emphasize each other. A brilliant red held next to a brilliant green will appear more intense than when viewed separately. Such combinations are common when a forceful use of color is desired. Note how often complements are used in advertising posters and flags. Although brilliant complements are frequently used in decoration, more interesting combinations of color result when the hues are varied a bit. A soft maize or pale yellow with a deep plum purple, for example, would probably have more appeal than a brilliant yellow and a brilliant purple used together. Instead of brilliant orange and blue, the grayed oranges or copper tones might be used with a blue that is also decreased in intensity. Using tints of each color would produce a combination of peach or apricot and light blue—still a complementary harmony but one that is easier to live with than the colors used in their most brilliant forms. Pink and dark green is also a softer combination than bright red and green.

Split-complementary. Instead of using colors that are opposite each other on the color wheel, one might select one hue and combine it with the colors that are on either side of its complement as though placing a narrow-angled Y on the color wheel. This provides three colors to work with, and by varying their intensities and values one can work out some interesting combinations. For example, if orange is chosen, the split complements are blue-green and blue-violet. It would be a good idea to experiment with various values and intensities of these three colors to see whether or not a pleasing combination can be worked out.

Double Complementary. If a narrow X is superimposed on the color wheel one has two sets of complementary colors with which to work. Four colors may be a bit confusing in a small area, but it is fun to test one's skill in combining such a variety. Use more of one and a tiny amount of another. Use a brilliant form of one in a small area as an accent. Just a touch of it will complete the scheme.

Triad. A triangle placed on the color wheel will point to three colors that form the triad. The primaries—yellow, blue, and red—might be used. In intense tones, such a combination might be suitable for a playroom or a kitchen because these are gay, dashing colors. But if the yellow is subdued to gold, and the red deepened to claret and the blue to indigo, the combination becomes one that is often found in elegant rooms with colors keyed to the jewel tones of an Oriental rug. Or if all the colors are softened to pastel tints of maize, rose, and light blue, a combination results that is often seen in prints and plaids that might be suitable to a gay but delicate scheme for a young girl's bedroom or for a dinette. This triad of the primary colors can lend itself to many adaptations, but triads of other hues can also be the basis of exciting combinations. For example, experiment with green, purple, and orange. In brilliant forms, the combinations may not be attractive, but with different values and intensities some fascinating combinations can be worked out.

Neutral. Black, white, and gray are the true neutral colors, and some modern rooms have been decorated in only these tones with amazing effectiveness. Yet we do seem to need a touch of color, and accented neutral harmonies are more popular. A neutral scheme with some areas in brilliant colors—orange, green, or red—makes an interesting combination.

READY-MADE COMBINATIONS. Another way to approach the planning of a color scheme is to choose some existing design or pattern and key the various color areas to it. One might select a vase, a picture, a rug, or a fabric with a combination of colors that is appealing. It is not necessary to match colors exactly, but the colors in other areas must be related to those in the design. Use different values and different intensities.

It should be remembered that a color can be emphasized by repetition or by the use of a contrast of value, intensity, or hue. For example, if a design has an interesting bright blue that calls for emphasis the exact color might be repeated in small areas or in a few accessories. Or one might use either a grayed tone of the same blue or a different value of the blue for larger areas, such as floor coverings, walls, or upholstery. Using the complement of the color will also emphasize it. A burnt orange (grayed tone) or apricot (a tint) will intensify the blue. One should study the color wheel to work out interesting combinations of complementary colors. Deep purple with a mustard gold (grayed yellow) may provide the basis for a most interesting color scheme depending on what amount of each color is used.

Practical Aspects of Color Schemes

For some rooms, the homemaker may want to keep in mind a few practical aspects of color planning. In anticipation of the possibility that she might someday want to change the color scheme, it is wise to see that the more durable furnishings such as rugs and upholstered pieces be of colors that lend themselves to a variety of color combinations. Walls can be refinished, and upholstered pieces can be slipcovered, but a floor covering is not as easy to change. This certainly does not mean that one must be limited to gray or some other neutral or so-called neutral, but if a sizable sum is to be invested in a floor covering, it is wise to think of its adaptability to various other color combinations.

In an area of heavy traffic, the maintenance problem should be considered too. A very light or a very dark color on the floor will show footprints and soil more readily than the medium values. In general, spots show up more readily on solid colors than they do on figured rugs and carpets. Upholstered furniture that will receive hard wear should have textures and colors that will not be soiled easily. The lovely light and bright colors are most appealing when they are fresh and clean looking. If one has to devote a great deal of time to keeping the home spick-and-span it will soon become a burden rather than a joy. But that doesn't mean that color schemes must be dreary. It's simply a matter of using interesting but practical colors in the right places. With a bit of forethought, a color scheme can be not only gay, elegant, exciting, or anything else that is wanted, but also very easy to maintain.

Color for the Spacious Look

The more an area is broken up with contrasts of colors, the smaller the area will appear. This is a good case for the use of a monochromatic harmony in a small area to make it look larger. But to keep a monochromatic harmony from becoming dull and monotonous, one must be sensitive to the values and intensities of the basic color. It is necessary to know also how to introduce the neutrals black, white, and gray most effectively. In some monochromatic schemes, they may be not wanted at all, but in others they can contribute a great deal to the interest of the color plan.

Let us consider the problem of working out a color scheme for a small living room. It doesn't necessarily have to be monochromatic harmony to make it appear larger. We shall use a complementary harmony of red-orange and blue-green.

Assume that this is rather a dismal room with little natural light and a northern exposure. We want to make the room light and bright; we also want it to seem larger than it really is. Our major color areas include:

Walls
Floor covering
Draperies
Sofa
Two upholstered chairs
Accents

Where shall we begin? Suppose we select a printed fabric that has a warm beige background (a tint of the red-orange) and a small geometric print in turquoise. The print may have a bit of cocoa brown (also related to the red-orange) and perhaps various shades of the turquoise.

Since this is a room with dull light, we shall choose the red-orange as the basic color for large areas. But because we do not want brilliant colors that will make the room seem smaller, we gray the red-orange and use a tint of the hue to produce a warm beige.

The color plan might evolve as follows:

Walls Beige to match the background of the print.
Floor covering Cocoa brown.
Draperies Printed fabric.
Sofa Beige slightly deeper than the walls.
Two chairs Turquoise or the printed fabric.
Accents (sofa pillows, ashtrays, and so on): Brilliant blue-green and a few small touches of red-orange.

How have we applied the theories to planning a color scheme for this room?

1. We do not have large areas of contrast. Although the drapery fabric is a print, the wall color *matches* the background of the fabric, unifying the wall and window areas. A solid-color drapery to match the walls would be better in this respect, but for this particular room we prefer a print for interest.
2. The large area of floor covering is a deeper tone of the wall color, which relates these two large areas. It is a medium value that will not readily show soil and footprints.
3. The sofa, which is a large color area, is not in strong contrast to the wall, so it will not be emphasized as a heavy piece of furniture.
4. The two chairs repeat the turquoise in the print, or the print itself, to provide a feeling of rhythm or unity.
5. The accents of brilliant color are used in small areas to emphasize the print and to provide interest.

It should be noted that no strong contrasts are used for large areas. Also, keeping the wall color closely related to the background of the print provides a unifying effect. A sharp contrast between the drapery and the wall would emphasize the window area by sharpening the vertical line where the drapery meets the wall.

To make a small room seem larger, the major color areas should melt into one another. Bright and more advancing colors may be used in smaller areas and in accessories.

Wood Tones in the Color Scheme

In popular writings we find a great deal about wood textures but very little about wood

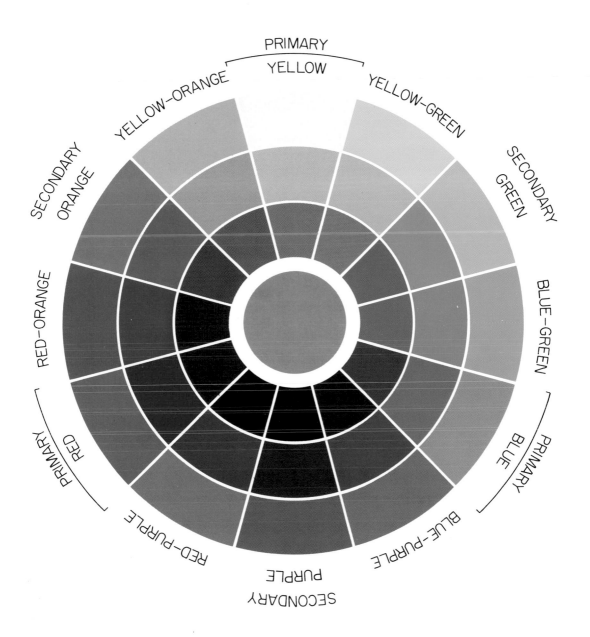

PLATE I The color wheel based on three primary colors.

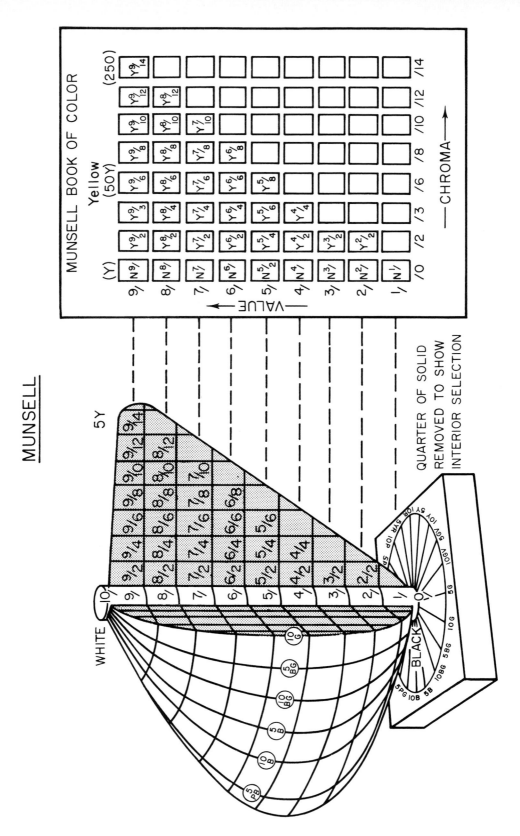

PLATE II **Chart of 2.5 YR in the Munsell System.** (*Courtesy of the Munsell Color Co., Inc.*)

HUE SYMBOL

2.5 YR

9.5/

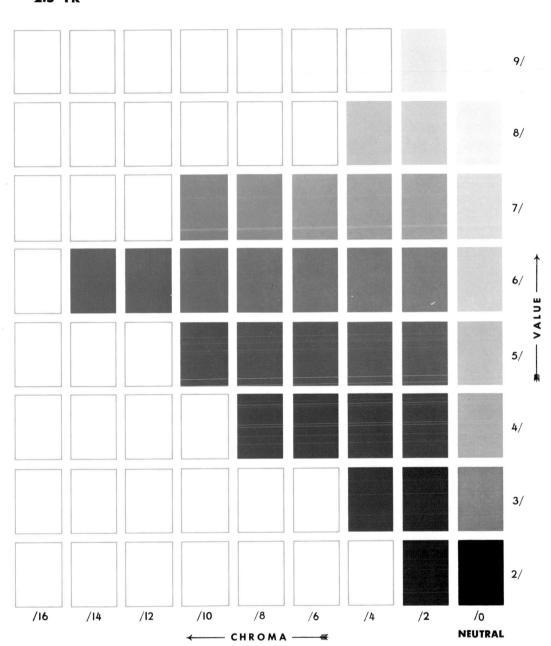

The nominal value notation 2.5/ should be used in making judgments with the chromatic color chips arranged on the 2/ value level of the charts on facing pages. The nominal notation 2/, as indicated on the charts, should be used for the Neutral color chip displayed in this position.

Munsell Color Co., Inc.

PLATE III The Munsell color-order system.

PLATE IV A monochromatic scheme lends an air of elegance to the drawing room in Celanese House. The Austrian valence combined with plaid shades dramatizes the window. Bamboo armchairs, light in scale, provide comfortable seating without adding heavy proportions to the rather narrow room. (*Courtesy of Celanese Corporation*)

PLATE V Strong color contrasts are used in a setting designed by Tom Woods, A.I.D. Repetition of the motifs in the area rug on the wall provides a feeling of unity. The Eames lounge chair suggests relaxation even in such a vibrant setting. (*Courtesy of Window Shade Manufacturers Association*)

PLATE VI Patterned carpeting used on the window seat, as well as on the floor, becomes the dominant note that unifies furnishings of different heritage. (*Courtesy of Monsanto Company*)

PLATE VII (above left) Warm, vibrant colors plus rugged textures and some variation in form contribute to a room that expresses comfort and relaxation. (*Courtesy of DuPont Textile Fibers*)

PLATE VIII (left) In a "Mini-Budget" apartment designer Emily Malino relies on color for interest. Everything was chosen with cost and practicality in mind for this project aimed at demonstrating the techniques of low-cost decorating. (*Courtesy of Monsanto Company*)

PLATE IX (above) An accented neutral scheme is used in a formal but restful living room. Note how the accents of red contribute to the unity. The graceful lines of the draperies are repeated in various ways. The atmosphere of the room is one of understated elegance. (*Designed by Patricia Harvey, A.I.D.*)

PLATE X Complementary colors of red and green take on new dimensions in the bedroom setting above. The sheer fabric lends itself to the balloon shades at the window as well as to the portiere treatment of the bed. (*Courtesy of The Singer Company*)

(a)   (b)

FIGURE 14-3 Large areas of pattern or strong contrasts make furniture seem more prominent and decrease the apparent size of the room.

colors. Yet woods do have important color tones that should harmonize with the decorative scheme if the furniture is to appear most attractive.

Woods can be bleached or stained to a wide variety of colors. Many of the bleached woods have decided yellow tones. Traditionally, mahogany has a distinct red color, but new finishes sometimes give it a nutmeg cast that reduces or eliminates the red color. Walnut, in its traditional color, is a grayish brown that blends well with many colors. The fruit woods may have distinct colors in grayed form.

A background should be chosen that will either relate or contrast with the tones of the woods used. A deep, rich, red mahogany is lovely against a sofe pale green or aqua, because the red and green are complementary colors. Against a soft, rose-beige background it will be equally attractive because the colors are related. Yet a bleached wood with yellow tones next to a light pinkish beige wall is not usually attractive, because the colors are neither related nor are they in contrast. Such a wood tone might be lovely against any dark or light contrasting color. Color harmonies can be applied to achieve interesting effects.

In some rooms there will be more exposed wood furniture than in others. Naturally, when the wood tones become a major color area in a room the background color is particularly important in the color scheme.

Color with Artificial Light

It was mentioned earlier that colors show up their truest characteristics in a northern exposure, which provides the most natural form of blue-white daylight. For artificial lighting we are likely to use electric light from incandescent or fluorescent globes, and these do not usually assume the harsh characteristics of a northern exposure. Some of them do simulate pure blue-white light, but they are not popular for living areas. We are more prone to select bulbs and tubes that cast soft yellow or pink glows. These are more flattering to people and seem to be more pleasing to live with. Candlelight casts a lovely yellow glow that is flattering to almost everyone. But we have gone beyond the candlelight stage in everyday living, and we want artificial lighting that is both useful and flattering.

Ordinary incandescent light bulbs cast a yellow glow, although in recent years bulbs have been manufactured with various other color tones. One can buy bulbs with pink, blue, green, or deep yellow tones. These are interesting for decorative effects in some areas, but so far as useful light is concerned, the colored light bulbs are not the most efficient sources.

Fluorescent tubes are also available in a variety of tones ranging from a true blue-white that simulates natural daylight to a soft pink.

The color and the amount of artificial light that is used will affect the colors in one's rooms. The yellow tones of the incandescent bulbs will emphasize any yellow that might be mixed with a color. For example, a yellow-green will appear more yellow under electric light than it will in true daylight. Pinks and reds will seem deeper or richer if the source of light is pink rather than yellow. Blue light will of course emphasize blue tones, but blue light is usually rather cool and may seem somewhat harsh.

Specific lighting needs are discussed in Chapter 17, but generally speaking light sources should be selected to emphasize the color scheme.

We think of windows as being essential for letting light and air into the home. Actually they are not necessary for either purpose, because we can control both light and ventilation in other ways. Yet it seems inconceivable that anyone would want to live with no windows at all. Natural light during the daytime and fresh air when the weather is pleasant provide a far more desirable indoor atmosphere than one controlled by artificial means.

Windows perform another major function in allowing for the indoor-outdoor relationship that is so important in modern living. A room with a view appeals to almost everyone, but even when a beautiful view is not possible we still need the psychological association with the outdoors that windows provide.

In many cases it is necessary to consider doors as well as windows in furnishing a room. The placement of these openings will influence the arrangement of furniture as well as the decoration of the room. When a door is part of a window wall or is in close proximity to a window, it may be a very important factor in determining how the window will be treated. The more usual situation, however, calls for a window treatment without any specific relationship to doorways.

In the modern planning of houses and apartment buildings there seems to be an increasing awareness of the importance of window design. In any building, the opening should be planned so that the proportions and space divisions are pleasing to the eye from both the exterior and the interior. The diversity of architectural styles has led to the use of many different types of window. Unfortunately, not all architects and designers are equally sensitive to the fine points of integrating the openings into the structural lines of the building and to keeping them functional. There has been an interesting variety of experiments and we find some rooms with small windows placed high in order to conserve useful wall space and other rooms

15

Window

Treatments

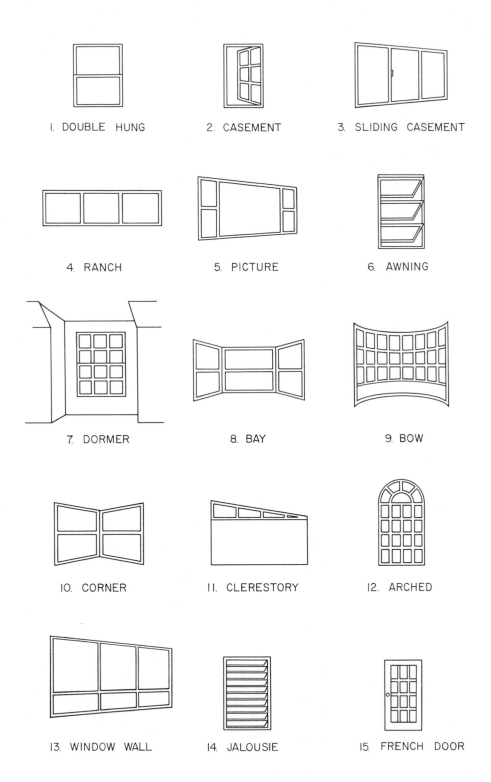

FIGURE 15-1 **Types of windows.** (*Courtesy of Kirsch Company*)

with whole window walls to allow for maximum light or to emphasize the relationship of the room to the outdoors. In between the two extremes there is considerable variety in the types, sizes, and shapes of windows.

Types of Windows

The treatment of windows may be determined to a large extent by the type as well as by the placement and size. Windows open in different ways. Some slide up and down or from side to side; others swing in or out; still others have panels that tilt to angles and project to both interior and exterior. There are also windows—or sometimes sections of windows—that do not open at all.

It is important to study each window in order to choose a treatment that will allow for maximum use and also emphasize the desirable features. Decoration should be planned to minimize any undesirable characteristics that the windows may have.

For most windows, a *casing* is built into the wall structure. This is a fixed part of the window and it is designed to hold the *sash*, which is the wood or metal frame that holds the glass and that is usually the movable part. On some windows there is a *sill*, or ledge at the bottom. An *apron* refers to a strip of casing below the sill.

The various types of windows include:

DOUBLE HUNG. Probably the most commonly used type of window, with sashes that slide up and down.

SWINGING CASEMENT. Window panels are hinged at the side and the full area of the window is opened when the panel is moved. Casement windows that swing out are relatively easy to decorate; those that swing into the room present problems. Some are operated by mechanical cranks whereas others are merely moved by hand.

SLIDING CASEMENT. Some window panels operate by sliding from side to side in horizontal sashes. These combine the interesting proportions usually found in casement windows with the weather tightness usually found in double-hung windows. However, to provide equal ventilation, they require more

lateral wall space than standard double-hung windows.

RANCH. Sometimes referred to as strip windows, this type is usually wide and placed high on the wall. They are popular because they allow for more usable wall space, but they do limit the easy view of the outdoors and they sometimes present problems of decoration. They may also be quite a safety hazard in case of fire, especially in children's rooms.

PICTURE. Various types of large windows are designed to allow for an increased view of the outdoors. The window may be one large pane of glass that remains fixed or it may have sections that slide or pivot. Movable sections might be placed at the sides, above or below the stationary panel of glass.

AWNING. These are wide horizontal panels that open outward from the bottom to any desired angle. Hopper windows are similar to awning windows, except that they are fixed at the bottom, and the top of the frame is pushed out to open the window.

DORMER. When a small alcove projects from the room a window is often placed at the end. This construction is frequently but not always found in attics. The window and walls of the dormer often require special treatment to integrate them into the room.

BAY. A group of three or more windows are set at angles projecting to the outside to form a recessed area in the room. A bay window usually provides a dominant architectural feature that must be treated as a center of interest.

BOW. This is somewhat similar to a bay window but built on a curve rather than with angled sections.

CORNER. Various types of window are designed to form the corners of rooms. These have the advantage of increased light and view, and such an arrangement may be an interesting architectural feature to emphasize in decoration. However, it may be difficult to provide a treatment that is both functional and attractive.

CLERESTORY. These are shallow windows that are set high on the wall, usually near the ceiling. Sometimes they are part of a slanted construction or the "cathedral" window popular in modern architecture. Such windows almost always present problems in decorating, though they do add interest and provide for additional light without reducing wall space.

ARCHED. A curved arch arrangement at the top of the window may have glass panes or be part of the design of the wall. In either case, the arch adds interest but also adds problems to treating the window.

WINDOW WALL. This is a favorite feature in modern architecture. An entire wall of glass may be sectioned in various ways so that some panels are stationary, others act as windows, and still others act as doors. A window wall is particularly desirable in areas where the indoor-outdoor relationship is important.

JALOUSIE. Narrow strips of glass mounted so that they can assume different angles have become popular. They may be used in ordinary windows, window walls, or even in all the walls of an indoor-outdoor room.

FRENCH DOORS. These can be used wherever ordinary doors can be used, and they also can serve as windows. They are useful when easy access to another area is important but when ordinary doors would cut off too much light. They allow for privacy, yet the separation of two rooms is less definitive with translucent doors than it is with other types.

Decorative Treatments

With all these factors in mind it is dangerous to state that one must "always do this" or "never do that." Nor is it possible to say that one method is correct and another is not if both are equally functional and pleasing to the eye. We have broken with tradition in many areas of furnishings. For example, many people now prefer to mount roller shades at the lower part of the window and draw them up rather than down. If they find this more functional and more attractive, who should decide that it is incorrect or not a proper treatment?

People also vary in their values about the exterior appearances of windows. Some consider uniformity from the outside extremely important and will choose shades, blinds, or curtains for the entire home on this basis. A uniform treatment often does add to the neatness of the exterior, but other factors may be more important for interior appearance.

The ultimate purposes of any window treatment should be to make the window functional and to make it attractive from both the outside and the inside. In most rooms control of the amounts of light and air that enter is important. At times one may want sunshine flooding the room, and at other times he may want to block out strong sunlight. Also, at times privacy may be particularly important.

SHADES AND VENETIAN BLINDS. For the reasons given above, some type of shade, Venetian blind, awning, shutter, or screen is usually considered desirable in treating a window. However, there are windows that may require no such treatment and some people prefer to leave these completely free from any suggestion of covering. This choice is often a matter of preference. For example, a strong natural light might appeal to one person whereas someone else would consider it glaring and hard on the eyes.

Because windows must be functional, any decorative treatment that is chosen should enhance rather than detract from their usefulness. Roller shades, Venetian blinds, or shutters may be used in many ways to integrate window design into the decorative scheme of a room and also to add to the functionalism of the windows. In addition, we sometimes use sliding panels, such as shoji screens, or grillwork to perform all the functions of shades or blinds and to add to the decorative theme. With the trend toward elegant interiors, Austrian shades have also become more popular. These are window coverings made of soft, drapable fabric mounted on tapes. As they are raised or lowered, the fabric falls in scalloped folds that lend graceful elegance to the window. They perform the function of shades and add the decorative qualities of the soft fabrics. With any of these window treatments, further decoration may be not only unnecessary but undesirable. Although a window should be an integral part of the decorative scheme, it should not overpower a room. Too much decoration can do just that, and it is usually better to understate rather than overemphasize.

FIGURE 15-2　In a problem room designed by Emily Malino, A.I.D., shade cloth vertical blinds are used to conceal radiators and air vents in the window wall. (*Courtesy of Window Shade Manufacturers Association*)

FIGURE 15-3 Edmund Motyka, A.I.D., used laminated window shades and open-framed shutters as a complete window-wall treatment in a small apartment. (*Courtesy of Window Shade Manufacturers Association*)

(a)

FIGURE 15-4 Shutters can be used in various ways to add interest. In (a) they provide the background for a more formal treatment. In (b) they blend with cafe curtains in an informal setting. (*Courtesy of Lord & Taylor*)

(b)

CURTAINS AND DRAPERIES. There are so many different types of curtains and draperies currently popular that these two terms have rather broad meanings. It is almost impossible to assign any concise, clear-cut definition to each one, nor is it possible to classify types in a consistent, well-organized fashion.

In general, we think of curtains as being made of sheer, semisheer, and lightweight fabrics, and of draperies as being made of heavier fabrics. Draperies may be used alone or over some type of curtain. Either curtains or draperies may be used with or without shades or Venetian blinds, but some windows have all three—shades or blinds, curtains, and overdraperies.

In general usage the term *curtain* refers to various types of fabric coverings that may extend over only part of the window, all of it, or from the top of the window to the floor; usually, we think of them as being hung next to the glass. On the other hand, *draperies* as a rule extend at least from the top of the window to the sill. More usually they extend below the sill to cover an apron if there is one, or they reach the floor. Both curtains and draperies can be designed to draw back and leave the window completely uncovered.

The broad coverage of these two terms indicates the wide variety of possible window treatments. Individual selections, therefore, will be guided by what the curtains and draperies are to do in the room. Some will be useful in controlling light and air and in providing privacy; others may be purely decorative. We sometimes use curtains and draperies only to add a feeling of warmth to a room. Draperies frequently do contribute to the actual insulation of a room, and some are lined with a special fabric that helps to keep interior temperatures at an even level. Nevertheless, whether or not they make any significant contribution to the actual heat control, fabrics at the window lend a softness to the atmosphere. They may also be useful for reducing noise in some areas.

Perhaps one of the most appealing arguments for using curtains and draperies lies in the fact that one can do so much with so little expense. Ready-mades are available in a wide variety of types, colors, and textures.

The woman who sews can achieve rich, elegant effects with comparatively little outlay of time or money. Making curtains and draperies that have a professional touch does not require a great deal of skill or practice. In view of the economy and the small amount of time involved, the saving is usually well worth the effort. The ready availability of fabrics and trimmings stimulates the imagination. The various types of fixtures, hooks, tapes, and pins that are currently on the market further simplify the process. Creating effects that are beautiful, functional, and economical can be a source of great pride and satisfaction. A few simple directions for making curtains and draperies are included in Chapter 26.

The style of curtains and draperies should be in keeping with the spirit of the room. However, texture, color, and pattern in the fabric play such an important role in determining the appearance of the window that once again it is difficult, if not impossible, to draw up any hard and fast rules that must be followed. For example, plain curtains that hang straight at the windows are suitable for many types of rooms. They may be gay and cheerful or they may be rich and elegant, depending on the fabric.

Different curtain styles suggest different degrees of formality. For example, short curtains tend to be more informal than those that extend to the floor. Also, some special treatment at the top of the window may provide a particular note of interest. A draped swag or a cornice might be used to emphasize the window, especially if some form of contrast is used. Frequently the top of the window is used for a concealed source of light. Fluorescent tubes inside a cornice may highlight the window and also contribute to the general illumination of a room.

Fixtures. There are so many different kinds of curtain and drapery rods on the market that it is important to plan the window treatment carefully and to choose the fixtures that are most suitable. Traverse rods allow one to draw curtains and draperies across the window. On a two-way draw rod, the curtains will meet at the center. However, for some openings—such as a corner window—one-way draw rods are more useful. There is also a wide selection of decorative fixtures that are attractive when the rod will be exposed.

FIGURE 15-5 Two patterned fabrics, a cornice, and concealed lighting emphasize an unusual window treatment in Celanese House. (*Courtesy of Celanese Corporation*)

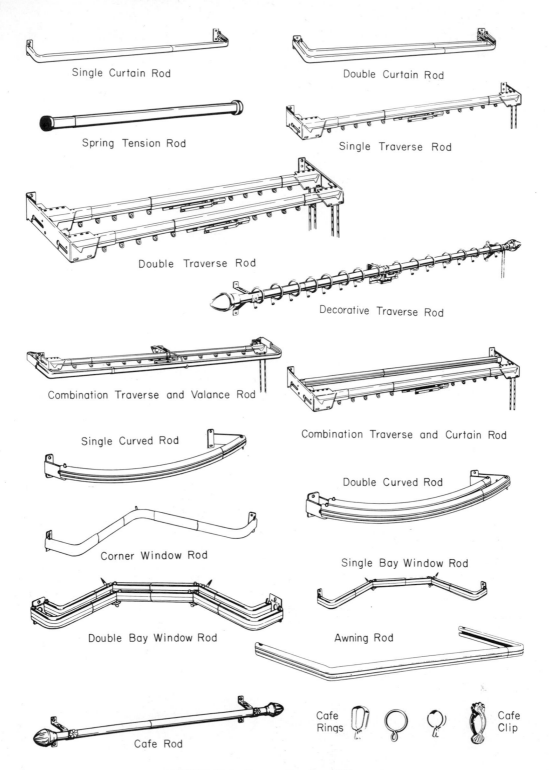

Single Curtain Rod

Double Curtain Rod

Spring Tension Rod

Single Traverse Rod

Double Traverse Rod

Decorative Traverse Rod

Combination Traverse and Valance Rod

Combination Traverse and Curtain Rod

Single Curved Rod

Double Curved Rod

Corner Window Rod

Single Bay Window Rod

Double Bay Window Rod

Awning Rod

Cafe Rod

Cafe Rings

Cafe Clip

FIGURE 15-6   Types of rods and fixtures.

Types of Curtains and Draperies. Some of the basic forms of window decoration include:

Glass curtains—Made of sheer fabric in simple straight lines. May be used alone or with draperies. Usually cover the whole window area. (Tailored.)

Tie-back curtains—Panels are draped aside and held to frame or wall with extra pieces of fabric or special fixtures. Tie-back curtains are often made of sheer fabric and decorated with ruffles.

Criss-cross curtains—Wide panels mounted so that they overlap and then tie back. Usually made of sheer fabric and trimmed with ruffles. (Pricilla.)

Draw curtains (or draw draperies)—Mounted on traverse rod so they can be drawn open or closed. Different types of traverse rods permit wide variety of treatments. Some draw curtain panels to meet at center of window (two-way draw); others draw one panel across entire window area (one-way draw). Curved traverse rods are also available.

Sash curtains—Similar to glass curtains, but mounted on rod attached to sash or frame. May cover only part of window. Sometimes held taut with rods at top and bottom.

Café curtains—Short curtains that cover portion of window. Often hung on decorative rods by means of rings, clips, loops, or hooks. Usually rather informal but with use of over-draperies may be adapted to more formal treatments.

Tier curtains—Two or more horizontal rows of short curtains mounted so that they overlap.

Valance—Decorative finish at top of window. May be gathered or pleated flounce of fabric.

Swag—Draped section of fabric at top of window. Usually used with short pieces at sides to form cascades. Suitable for more formal window treatments.

Cornice—Stiff boxlike treatment at top of window. May be wood, metal, or any other decorative material. Fabric-covered cornices are sometimes decorated with fringe or braid.

PROBLEM WINDOWS. The architectural deficiencies of windows that are poorly spaced or poorly shaped can often be easily camouflaged with curtains and draperies. Two windows separated by a narrow wall section might be treated as one with a unifying cornice or valance and draw draperies. Short windows may have to be given the effects of added height by the placement of fixtures above the actual window openings. Narrow windows will seem wider if the draperies extend beyond the sides. Various types of cornices and valances may be used to add height or width, the amount of dimension added depending on the manner in which these fixtures are mounted. Deep cornices and swags may be used to give tall, narrow windows more pleasing proportions.

Arched windows and slanting clerestory windows frequently present problems of decoration. Curved rods or flexible tapes can be used to mount curtains on curved frames. On clerestory windows, the rod can follow the slant of the frame. In this case, the curtain would have to be carefully measured, because it will be shorter on one side than on the other. With both these problems it is often more attractive to leave the unusually shaped area uncovered than to use a treatment that seems contrived or awkward.

Maintenance

Modern living seems to demand homes that are easy to maintain. Yet we do not always want to sacrifice warmth or a touch of elegance in decorating our homes. With modern materials and careful planning, we could easily furnish a home that required a minimum amount of care and we could make it both functional and attractive. If easy maintenance were the primary consideration, however, we would probably have homes with somewhat clinical appearances that would not appeal to most of us. The dilemma may be resolved in part, at least, by the choice of fabrics for interesting, glamorous windows. For example, simple, straight curtains in a lovely shimmering texture may add exactly the note of richness that a modern room needs. True, the curtains will have to be washed sometimes, but if the fabric is one that resists soil, can be washed in a machine, and needs no ironing, the problem is not serious. Without the curtains, the windows may be completely functional and reasonably attractive, but the

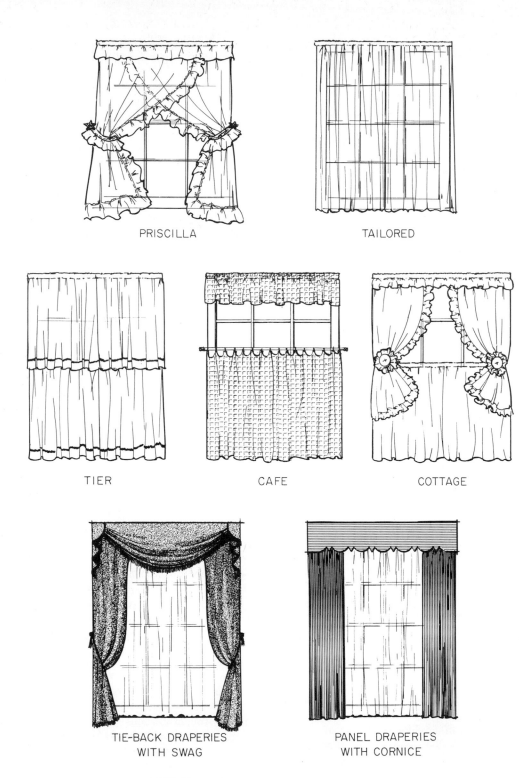

PRISCILLA

TAILORED

TIER

CAFE

COTTAGE

TIE-BACK DRAPERIES
WITH SWAG

PANEL DRAPERIES
WITH CORNICE

FIGURE 15-7 Basic window treatments.

room may lack that ingredient of warmth that woven fabrics seem to provide.

Fortunately, fabric manufacturers are providing materials that have rich textures and lovely colors but that require little care. Fabrics that can be washed without being ironed, finishes that resist soil, and metallic yarns that do not tarnish have all been combined to produce materials that are both elegant and easy to maintain.

It still takes careful shopping and a certain amount of knowledge to choose fabrics that meet all demands, but the results are well worth the effort. The beautiful effects and the little time required to maintain them will be most satisfying to the creative homemaker.

16

Accessories

Try to visualize a page of a book without capital letters or punctuation marks. It would be extremely difficult to read such a page and meanings would not be clear. A room without accessories would be equally uninteresting; we might consider accessories as the punctuation marks of decorating. They not only add meaning, they lend personality and individuality to a room that might otherwise be prosaic.

Because the choice of accessories is such an individual matter of expression, it is difficult to formulate rules about them. Each person's selection and arrangement will reflect his own interests and his sensitivity to good design. But accessories should follow the theme of the room. In a dainty bedroom they should be light and delicate; in a masculine room they may be heavier and more sturdy.

Too many little mementos or pieces of bric-a-brac placed indiscriminately around a room spell confusion and indecision. Accessories should represent interests and tastes, but they should also contribute to the unity of the room. Sometimes a collection, whatever it may be, grouped and displayed with a bit of flair can become a focal point. By all means, one should choose a few accessories that add to the expressiveness of a design rather than a conglomeration of objects dispersed here and there.

A logical question may be raised with regard to what constitute accessories. Some will have specific functions and others will be purely decorative. The functional group might include ashtrays, clocks, and lamps; decorative accessories might include pictures, sculptures, mirrors, flower arrangements, and bric-a-brac.

In the functional category, accessories should first of all be useful. Lamps should provide adequate light where it is needed. Clocks must keep time and have faces that are easy to read. In all cases, the line, shape, color, and texture should harmonize with the spirit of the room.

In selecting nonfunctional accessories, one should remember that a room is often more appealing if these pieces represent interests of the family. Otherwise the effects may seem forced or contrived and the interest will be considerably lessened.

Modern interiors have once again broken with tradition in the selection and placement of accessories. Almost any selection, combination, and arrangement is acceptable as long as it is pleasing to the eye. Thus we see modern paintings prominently displayed in rather traditional settings, or we find Oriental art completely at home in the most contemporary settings. The eclectic designs of modern homes preclude any rules: we live with the things we like to look at. Somehow, the most diverse and unauthorized extremes can become interesting companions that add interest and sparkle to one another. Yet an indiscriminate use of accessories can result in a hodge-podge of design. It takes a perceptive eye to combine the unusual in a pleasing manner.

Lamps

Well-chosen lamps and lighting fixtures are extremely important in determining the character of a room. Although the functional aspects should be the primary consideration in selecting them, it is no less important to choose designs that emphasize the spirit of the room. With the wide variety available today, it is possible to find useful lamps and fixtures that are suitable for any type of room.

Because they do play such a major role in lighting a room, lamps assume a special importance as accessories. The trend toward using tall lamps has also contributed to making them more important as accessories; either height or large scale can command attention. It is especially important to choose lamps carefully.

The style of the room and the spirit that it will express should suggest certain guides for selection. More formal rooms will usually require lamps with a certain amount of elegance. They may be extremely simple, but the colors and textures should have the richness that we associate with formal treatments. Fine china, glass, metals such as silver and brass, and ebony are all popular. Formal lamps often represent candelabra, graceful vases or urns, or simple columns mounted on heavy bases. Lamps with ornately painted designs or with elaborate figures may be suitable for certain rooms, but they must be chosen with discrimination.

Rooms furnished in the more informal styles should have lamps that are less suggestive of luxury. Materials with a more homespun character, such as wood, pottery, copper, and pewter, are usually suitable. Certain types of glass and some tole bases are also rather informal. Modern rooms may be either formal or informal in character, and the texture of the lamps should be selected accordingly. In either case, the lamps will probably be somewhat simple in design. Polished woods with lovely colors and grain patterns, metals, china, pottery, glass, and leather have all been used in modern lamps. Various types of pole lamps and wall lamps that allow for adjustable lighting often replace the more traditional forms of lighting in modern decoration. Some of these newer types have been adapted for use in traditional rooms.

When choosing several lamps for use in the same room, one should be sure that they harmonize with one another. It would probably be monotonous to have all lamps exactly alike, but there should be some similarity of expressiveness. It is usually advisable to have all the lampshades of similar color. For example, two white shades and one of rose-beige might not be attractive. However, a strong contrast may be of interest. A metallic paper shade on one lamp may blend very well with other types of shades.

Pictures

Whether or not one hangs pictures on the walls is purely a matter of taste. They are not necessary, but they can add considerably to the personality of the room if they are well chosen and well placed. However, some people prefer other types of wall decoration or even bare walls.

Choosing suitable pictures that one will enjoy living with is perhaps one of the most difficult problems in planning a room. The art chosen should certainly represent the owner's tastes, but it should also add interest to the room. It is usually safer to select themes and colors that are in keeping with the spirit of the

FIGURE 16-1 Paintings become the dominant note in a room designed by Renny B. Saltzman, A.I.D. The walls covered with fabric stretched from ceiling to floor provide a background that emphasizes the collection. (*Courtesy of DuPont Textile Fibers*)

FIGURE 16-2 A variety of pictures becomes a unit when they are carefully arranged. (*Courtesy of New York Antiques Fair*)

room. Although some people can violate this principle by electing to use the unexpected or the unusual, it is not easy to achieve happy results. For example, modern art in a traditional room may be interesting if it is used with discrimination.

Landscapes, seascapes, street scenes, flower prints, and still-life pictures are all popular choices for traditional rooms. They can be used in formal or informal settings, depending on their interpretation and color. Other types seem to be more appropriate for special rooms. For example, portraits are frequently quite formal, whereas pictures with animals are more likely to express informality. Oriental themes often lend themselves to a variety of backgrounds, including some traditional and many modern settings.

Personal taste again determines whether or not one will use only originals or include some reproductions. Good originals are likely to be quite expensive. Even reproductions are sometimes costly, but many of them are extremely well done. If the artistic qualities of a picture are appealing and suitable, whether it is an original or a copy should not be important.

The colors and textures of pictures should harmonize with those used in the room. Often a picture is useful for emphasizing some other element in a room either by repeating it or by providing a sharp contrast.

The size and shape of a picture must relate to the wall area on which it will be hung and also to the furniture placed against the wall. The outline of the picture will produce a space division that should establish pleasing proportions. It is frequently more interesting to group several pictures rather than to use just one. When pictures are exactly alike in shape and size, a group arrangement is usually symmetrical and presents few problems. It is far more difficult to assemble a group of unrelated sizes and shapes in a pleasing arrangement, but once this is accomplished it can be extremely interesting. In this case it is wise to experiment with the pictures to be used by trying different arrangements on the floor or on a large table in order to produce the most effective grouping.

The correct choice of frames and mats is vitally important for showing pictures to the best advantage. The textures and colors of both frame and mat should be chosen to emphasize the picture, but they should also be in harmony with the other elements in the room.

FIGURE 16-3 The two large panels of cork shown at the left make it possible to change and rearrange a collection without new nail holes in the wall. (*Courtesy of Directional Industries, Inc.*)

FIGURE 16-4 **One dominant abstract is the focal point in this setting designed by Albert Herbert, A.I.D.** (*Courtesy of Royal System of Denmark*)

Mirrors

In some areas, such as bedrooms and dressing rooms, mirrors are essential. They are also extremely useful in most entrance halls. In other rooms they are more decorative than functional. However, because mirrors increase the apparent spaciousness of an area they are particularly suitable for use in small rooms. Sometimes a whole wall is covered with a mirror for this purpose as well as for the decorative effect.

There is considerable variation in the quality of mirrors. The best grades are made of plate glass, whereas less expensive mirrors are made of window glass. The polishing and grinding of plate glass result in a smooth surface that prevents distortion and gives the glass more sparkle. In plate-glass mirrors of high quality, the silvered surface of the back is protected by a copper coating. It is then treated with a coat of shellac and another coat of protective paint. Copper backing renders the mirror more durable and prevents discoloration. High-quality mirrors also have the edges ground to an angle or beveled.

Various techniques are used for decorating mirrors. Some have designs cut or etched into the glass. Others are given an antique finish that provides a mottled, aged appearance. Although such mirrors have low reflective qualities they are highly decorative and are often used on large areas of a wall. A tint of some color in the mirror backing may also be used on decorative mirrors.

In modern decoration mirrors are often used without frames. Traditional styles usually have a frame of wood or metal in characteristic design. The girandole mirror, popular during the eighteenth century, has holders for candlesticks attached to the frame.

Mirrors should be selected with respect to wall area and furniture. Because a mirror is often placed over a mantel, a couch, a chest, or a table, the size and shape should be chosen to create a unified grouping that has pleasing space relationships.

Clocks

An interesting clock may be not only a major accessory but a real center of interest. In traditional homes, a tall-case or grandfather's clock is an elegant note, but another type used on the mantel or on the wall may be equally impressive. Clocks that chime have a special appeal for some people, although others find them bothersome. They should be used far enough from bedrooms so that they are not disturbing at night.

Some traditional clocks are extremely elaborate, with hand-painted panels and ornate cases. Modern clocks tend toward severe simplicity.

FIGURE 16-5 Wall units that provide storage space can also become an excellent means for highlighting accessories. (*Courtesy of Directional Industries, Inc.*)

Flower Arrangements

Plants, leaves, and flowers provide most effective and economical accessories for any type of decorative scheme. When used with taste and discretion, they add a warm, livable quality to almost any room. Just as with any other accessory, their overuse can defeat the purpose of accent and become monotonous. The selection of suitable arrangements that truly complement the spirit of the room is just as important here as it is with other accessories.

A few years ago we might have raised our eyebrows in horror at the suggestion of using artificial leaves and flowers. Now the practice is not only acceptable but quite chic. New techniques and materials have been used to produce arrangements that are actually quite lovely. Artificial arrangements have lost the stigma of the five-and-ten-cent store. They are popular now for both naturalistic and stylized effects. Nevertheless, with all the improvements in texture, color, and design, the artificial products cannot wholly win our love from growing plants and fresh flowers. Simulated leaves and flowers may be especially useful for some decoration, but they should not completely replace the real thing. One or two growing plants are not so very time-consuming to care for and they do add a touch of joy to the home. Even if the budget will not allow a steady supply of fresh flowers, special occasions become more festive when they are so honored. The flowers need not be the most expensive ones if they are carefully chosen and attractively arranged. Colors should blend with the colors of the room. The arrangement should be consistent with the container and vice versa so there is a unity to the whole design.

Techniques of arranging flowers should not be treated lightly. In the Orient this art is far more a part of the way of life than it is in Western cultures. Young women attend schools to develop their skills, and great emphasis is placed on flowers in the home. It should be noted here that the most interesting Oriental arrangements are composed of a few flowers strategically placed. The composition may include only simple stems or leaves. The beauty of the arrangement is often due to an artistic use of what we might consider weeds. In other words, we might learn a great deal from the Oriental art of creating interesting compositions with relatively little material. We tend to think more in terms of huge bouquets and elaborate arrangements. We also think of fresh flowers as an expensive whim. Neither attitude is necessary. Wild flowers picked from the side of the road or a few flowers purchased in season can be used with imagination and individuality to add a distinctive touch to the home.

Perhaps a few suggestions will open avenues of further interest. It is not our purpose here to delve into the fine techniques of flower arrangement, but to encourage the development of one's skill and imagination in this area.

1. A convenient place should be available for work with flowers. The laundry, kitchen, utility room, or bathroom may serve the purpose. A storage area should be planned for various pieces of simple equipment: shears, flower holders, wire, clay, and so on.
2. All sorts of containers should be experimented with—an old sugar bowl, a tiny pitcher, a beer glass, or anything else that strikes the fancy. Sometimes it is fun to shop in second-hand stores to find interesting and unusual containers that may not be useful for other purposes but that make ideal flower containers.
3. Flowers should be used in a thoughtful and imaginative manner. When one entertains, a flower arrangement in the entrance hall makes a delightful impression on guests as they arrive. In a guest room, even a tiny bouquet in a miniature holder seems to spell "welcome" to the visitor. At the dining table, fresh flowers or growing plants are usually more attractive than artificial arrangements. The centerpiece should be kept low so that it does not impede conversation.
4. A plant or a tiny bouquet of flowers in the bathroom may add an effective touch to an area that is otherwise difficult to decorate.

Miscellaneous Accessories

Various areas in the home will lend themselves to the use of other accessories. A hallway, living room, den, or bedroom may be suitable for shelves or cabinets. The lovely

FIGURE 16-6 Alternating panels of mirror and teakwood enrich and enlarge an entry hall designed by Albert Herbert, A.I.D., who used shelves and cabinets to display a collection of pre-Columbian sculpture. (*Courtesy of Royal System of Denmark*)

FIGURE 16-7 A few well-chosen accessories add interest to a small hallway. (*Designed by Patricia Harvey, A.I.D.*)

FIGURE 16-8   A tiny corner of a study-bedroom takes on an Early American atmosphere with a collection of tins, bins, and semi-antique pictures. (*Courtesy of Window Shade Manufacturers Association*)

FIGURE 16-9 Oriental pieces enhance the French theme in this room and emphasize the formal window treatment. (*Designed by Patricia Harvey, A.I.D. Photo by Henry S. Fullerton*)

FIGURE 16-10 Trophies, awards, newspaper clippings, prints, and photographs become decorative assets when displayed in this den-study-guest room designed by Mary Davis Gillies for a well-known sportsman. (*Courtesy of Allied Chemical Corporation*)

FIGURE 16-11 Variations in form, texture, and color relate to each other when shells are used for a wall treatment. (*Courtesy of Technika, Inc. Photo by Wesley Pusey*)

colors of book bindings and jackets may be utilized to form a mosaic that becomes an interesting accessory. As mentioned earlier, collections can become an integral part of a particular room.

Throw pillows can add a dramatic accent note to the color scheme in a living room, bedroom, or den.

A folding screen may serve a useful purpose as an area divider, or it may be used for purely decorative purposes. An inexpensive screen covered with wallpaper or fabric might be used as a background for some particular arrangement of furniture or accessories.

A fireplace in a room requires some equipment. The screen, andirons, poker, tongs, and shovel should all be considered as useful accessories.

A desk in any area of the home will need certain accessories. A lamp is probably the first requirement. The primary purpose is function but it should also blend with the decor of the room. Desk accessories can be attractive as well as useful.

We might add a word about trays as useful accessories. Serving trays have become popular with the trend toward informal meals. Many trays are now made to resist heat and alcohol. Sets of lap trays or tray-tables are extremely useful accessories for buffet meals. One interesting or unusual tray may well become part of the decorative scheme in either a living room or dining area. It may be mounted on the wall or placed on a desk or table. Frequently a beautiful tray is placed on a folding rack or stand and used as a permanent table.

Within the past few decades, lighting has developed as both an art and a science. Engineers have devoted a tremendous amount of effort to developing the aesthetic as well as the functional aspects of artificial lighting. We have seen the interesting results in many modern public buildings and in some homes of more progressive design. Unfortunately, most residential lighting has not kept pace with the advances made in industrial light. We still find many homes with inadequate or improper illumination, and frequently the potentials of decorating with light are sadly neglected. Even when there is an adequate amount, light is used in many homes in a rather stereotyped manner. Perhaps one reason for this is that we are a little bit afraid of using light as a decorating medium. The dramatic effects of valance and cove lighting make these methods seem complex to the average homemaker. However, with many new lighting fixtures and lamps, and with materials that have translucent or diffusing equalities, even the amateur can create beautiful effects.

In recent years, there has been considerable emphasis on adjustable lighting. Dimmer controls that are relatively easy to install make it possible to increase or decrease the amount of light as needed. Ceiling and wall fixtures that adjust to different heights or swing to different positions have also become popular. Lamp poles have several advantages in that they can be moved around, they take up little space, and they provide direct light where it is needed. Although these have been associated with a modern theme, they are now being designed to fit more easily into traditional rooms as well.

17
Lighting

The Characteristics of Light

We must understand a few basic facts about light before we can undertake any meaningful discussion of lighting the home. In the discussion of color it was pointed out that lighting is an important factor in planning color schemes. It should be remembered that without light, there is no color, and although we may feel textures in the dark, they have no visual significance unless there is some source of light.

As light rays strike a surface they are either absorbed or reflected. The color and the texture of the substance upon which the light rays fall determine the reflective qualities. A dull black surface will absorb all the rays of light; a shiny white surface will reflect all the rays of light.

We see color because of a pigment in the surface material. This surface will absorb some light rays and reflect others. Tints of colors, or the very light colors, reflect most of the light rays that strike the surface. Dark colors will absorb most of the light rays and reflect relatively few. Textures that are dull or uneven tend to reflect fewer light rays than those that are glossy and smooth.

Thus one element of practical lighting depends on how and where we see the light. For example, in a room with dark walls and all other areas in dark, dull textures, most of the light thrown from a light bulb would be absorbed. In a similar room decorated in white or light tints and glossy surfaces, most of the light from the same bulb would be reflected.

Therefore it would seem to emanate from about the room rather than from the bulb alone.

Another basic factor of lighting involves the color of the light itself. We are well aware of differences in natural daylight. In bright sunshine, daylight has a warm, yellow glow. Without the direct rays of the sun, natural daylight may have a gray or blue cast.

Artificial light also varies in color. Most of us are familiar with the soft glow of candlelight. The yellow-orange color of the light from candles is particularly flattering to skin tones and almost everyone looks more attractive in candlelight than in the harsh bluish tones of pure daylight. However beautiful candlelight might be, it would certainly be impractical to depend on it for lighting modern homes. We use two major sources of artificial light—incandescent bulbs and fluorescent tubes.

INCANDESCENCE AND FLUORESCENCE.
There are several major differences between incandescent and fluorescent lighting. In incandescent lighting a tungsten filament, sealed in a glass bulb, is heated to the point at which it glows. In fluorescent lighting a tube is filled with mercury vapor and the inside of the tube is coated with powder. When the cathodes at each end of the tube activate the vapors, they cause the fluorescent coating to produce light.

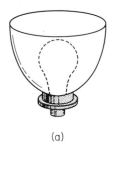

(a)

(b)

(c)

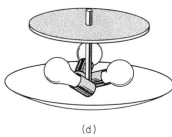

(d)

FIGURE 17-1 Ways of diffusing and softening light: (a) and (b) diffusing bowls; (c) frosted bulb in harp; (d) translucent and perforated shields.

Each type of lighting has certain advantages, which we might summarize as follows:

Incandescent bulbs
1. Are generally less expensive to install.
2. Produce more light from a smaller source.
3. Light immediately when activated.

Fluorescent tubes
1. Last longer than incandescent bulbs.
2. Produce more light on less current.
3. Produce little or no heat.

Both incandescent bulbs and fluorescent tubes have been produced in a variety of shapes, sizes, and colors.

Incandescent bulbs are generally available in clear or frosted glass. In addition, bulbs in definite colors of pink, blue, yellow, and green are available.

Fluorescent tubes are manufactured in various tones of white light, designated as follows:

1. Natural white—warm pink cast.
2. White—yellowish cast.
3. Warm white—beige cast; suitable for use with incandescent bulbs.
4. Deluxe warm white—warmer beige cast.
5. Soft white—pink cast.
6. Cool white—blue-gray cast; shows colors in true form.
7. Deluxe cool white—slightly warmer gray cast than cool white.
8. Daylight—blue cast similar to natural northern light.

Lighting Needs

Plans for home lighting should recognize three important factors:

1. *Function*. Certain specialized activities will require specific amounts and possibly certain kinds of light. Function, therefore, must be evaluated in terms of both quantity and quality of light. Reading, writing, playing a musical instrument, sewing, shaving, and applying makeup all demand proper illumination. Many activities, especially in the kitchen, laundry, and workroom, require special types of light. In all these instances, functional lighting will prevent eyestrain and make it possible to carry on the activities in the most comfortable and efficient manner.

2. *Safety*. In many respects safety is related to functionalism, but it is such an important factor that it should be given special consideration. Improper lighting is a particular hazard in several areas that may easily escape notice—for example, on stairways that lead to a basement or an attic, on patios that have different levels separated by steps, or at any doorway that requires a step up or a step down.

   Another safety aspect involves adequate wiring and sufficient outlets for all needs. It is dangerous as well as unattractive to use long extension cords. Electric wires should never be placed under rugs where traffic might cause wear on the insulation. A circuit should never be overloaded with equipment that makes excessive demands on the current.

3. *Beauty*. We begin to appreciate light as a decorative medium when we see a room bathed in a pleasing glow of illumination. A dim, dreary type of lighting is as bad if not worse than one that is harsh and glaring. There is also the close relationship between the type of light and the appearance of colors. With the wrong choice of lighting a well-planned scheme may lose its effectiveness.

New materials on the market should provoke the imagination with respect to decorative lighting. For example, translucent panels and grillwork may be used in a wide variety of ways. Several new developments that are still in somewhat experimental stages promise even more exciting uses of light. Luminescent panels for ceilings and walls and new structural materials that diffuse or filter light will probably be incorporated into many homes of the future. It is quite safe to assume that within a relatively short time, many of our so-called modern methods of lighting will seem as outmoded as gas lights and oil lamps appear to us.

The wide variety of lamps and fixtures currently available makes it possible to plan lighting effects that are consistent with the expressiveness of other furnishings. Neither the functional nor the decorative qualities of light need be sacrificed in choosing lamps and fixtures that will emphasize the theme of the room. Lighting for each area must be planned with the specific requirements in mind, but there are certain basic recommendations and principles that might serve as guides in planning.

PROVIDE FOR BOTH GENERAL AND LOCAL LIGHTING.

Concentrated light is essential in areas where the eyes will be used for close work, but there should also be a general overall illumination to prevent strong contrasts of light. It is poor policy to work with one bright lamp in a room that is otherwise very dark.

General lighting may be provided by various means. Lamps and fixtures may provide either direct or indirect lighting; many produce both types. Light is direct when it travels from the source to the area to be lighted. Indirect light is reflected from walls, ceilings, and other surfaces in the room.

Local lighting provides concentrated illumination in a particular area. Various types of portable lamps and wall or ceiling fixtures are now made with adjustable features. These allow considerable flexibility in producing the correct amount of light exactly where it is needed.

AVOID GLARE AND SHADOWS.

It is usually uncomfortable to have light shine directly from the source to the eye. Some means of diffusing light generally provides a better quality of illumination. Frosted bulbs rather than those made of clear glass, and diffusing bowls that shield the bulbs entirely are commonly used. Translucent lamp shades in light colors allow for considerable diffusion of light, whereas opaque shades such as those made of heavy paper allow none at all. Certain fixtures are equipped with various sorts of diffusing shields to protect the eye from the glare of the light source as well as to eliminate the shadows produced by concentrated light.

PLAN AN ADEQUATE AMOUNT OF LIGHT.

The actual light yield in any room or special area will be the product of many factors, including the location and the direction of the light sources, the reflective qualities of the colors and the textures, the number of lamps and fixtures, and, of course, the wattage of the light bulbs or tubes. With so many variable factors, it is difficult to prescribe for specific needs.

It is customary to recommend standards for adequate amounts of light in terms of foot-candles. This is a quantitative unit of measurement, one footcandle being the amount of illumination produced by a standard plumber's candle at a distance of one foot. With a light meter it is possible to measure the amount of light at any given point in terms of footcandles.

Experts seem to agree that for general illumination in most areas there should be at least ten footcandles of light; utility areas require twenty footcandles.

Specific activities require greater amounts of light:

	(Footcandles)
Reading	30–70
Desk work	40–70
Sewing	50–100
Sewing on dark fabrics	80–200
Shaving or applying makeup	50
Kitchen Activities	50–70
Ironing	50

When there will be prolonged periods of close eyework, the upper limits are recommended. Also, specific conditions will dictate requirements; for example, sewing on dark fabrics with matching thread and working on fine details would require more light than simple work on light-colored fabrics.

Because few families have a light meter to measure the amount of illumination, the above recommendations are not a very practical guide. They are presented merely to indicate the relative needs in specific areas. From a more practical standpoint, the homemaker is interested in knowing what size bulbs to provide in specific areas. In view of the variables mentioned above, this is a far more difficult problem. Light sources may be rated in terms of lumens, a quantitative unit for measuring light output. Manufacturers of light sources publish data about output on various products, but once again these figures have little meaning for the average consumer.

Much close work, such as reading, writing, and sewing, is done with portable lamps as the source of illumination. For functional use the single-socket lamp should have a bulb of 150 watts. Multiple-socket lamps would require three 60-watt bulbs to provide a comparable amount of light.

Work surfaces in the kitchen requiring 50 footcandles of light should have a light source that provides about 1380 lumens. A 30-watt (thirty-six-inch) fluorescent with a white enamel reflector, placed eighteen to twenty-two inches above the surface, provides the proper amount.

USE LIGHT FOR BEAUTY. Some types of lighting may be purely decorative, but there is no reason why functional lighting should not be attractive as well as useful.

It is important to remember the relationship of light and color in order to plan for the most beautiful lighting effects. One should bear in mind that light itself has color tones. We may use light bulbs and tubes that have very definite colors, such as deep pink, blue, green, or yellow. These have somewhat limited use in the home for creating special effects. They are not usually recommended for most of the functional requirements of lighting. The more usual sources of light include the standard incandescent bulbs and fluorescent tubes.

Incandescent bulbs vary a great deal in size, shape, and wattage. Some are clear and others are frosted. In general, the light from the commonly used incandescent bulbs has a yellow-orange tinge that has considerable warmth. The various color tones of fluorescent tubes have already been noted.

A quick review of the color wheel should explain some of the effects that different colors of light will produce. It has been noted that we can gray a color or decrease the intensity by mixing it with its complement. Colored light will produce similar effects. Therefore, light with pink, orange, or yellow tones will tend to decrease the brilliance of blues and greens. Light with a special color will deepen or intensify similar colors in the room. Pink or red areas viewed under a pink light will take on added depth and richness. Mixed colors will take on added color from light; for example, a yellowish light will emphasize the yellow element in yellow-green or yellow-orange.

It is often difficult to combine different colors of light in the same room. When both incandescent and fluorescent lighting are used, the warm white or deluxe warm white tube is recommended, because it combines pleasantly with the color of incandescent light.

Sources of Light

Several methods may be used to provide illumination. Frequently, more than one type of lighting is used in the same room.

LAMPS AND FIXTURES. The most commonly used sources of light are portable lamps and fixtures that are mounted on walls or ceilings.

Lamps provide a certain amount of flexibility in that they can be moved from one place to another. Both lamps and mounted fixtures may be useful in emphasizing a particular decorative theme or in adding some special note of individuality. Fixed lighting makes it possible to conserve table and floor space and to light areas where portable lamps seem impractical. Individual preferences and the requirements for functional light must therefore guide one's choice. There could be no rules about where to use lamps or mounted fixtures. The ultimate goals are to provide the type of light needed and to choose designs that are in keeping with the decorative scheme.

In choosing lamps the following points might be considered.

1. A sturdy base or one that is heavily weighted at the bottom prevents tipping. With the tall slender bases currently in vogue, this is an important factor.
2. A lamp that has a diffusing bowl will give less glare.

AVG. 40"

FIGURE 17-2   Choose proper lamp heights.

3. A harp makes it possible to adjust the height of the shade or to tilt the shade if necessary.
4. A table lamp intended for reading purposes should have the lower edge of the shade about forty to forty-two inches above the floor. The lower edge of the shade on a floor lamp should be from forty-seven to forty-nine inches from the floor.
5. Lampshades should be similar in color and texture or else they should contrast. One beige shade, one white shade, and one pink shade would probably be unattractive. On the other hand, two identical beige shades and one gold metallic-paper shade might provide an interesting combination.
6. For some areas, swing-arm or adjustable goose-neck lamps may be practical.

In choosing fixtures, these points may be important.

1. Adjustability of position often increases functionalism. Chandeliers that may be raised or lowered and wall units that swing provide a variety of lighting effects.
2. Diffused light is more pleasant. In many fixtures the bulbs may be exposed and present an irritating glare.

3. The design of the fixture should be in harmony with the character of the room.

ARCHITECTURAL LIGHTING. Glamorous effects for general lighting may be achieved by the mounting of simple fixtures in valances, cornices, or coves, or behind translucent panels. One may light a window area, wall, ceiling, floor, or any special area for emphasis. Fluorescent tubes are useful for such lighting because they provide an even line of light. Incandescent bulbs may be used for many similar effects, but one has to be careful to avoid a spotty appearance.

In *valance* lighting the light source is mounted so that some of the light is directed up toward the ceiling and some down over the draperies or the wall. A *cornice* is usually either mounted at the ceiling or enclosed at the top so that all the light is directed downward. *Cove* lighting implies a troughlike arrangement, usually near the ceiling, with the light directed upward.

Soffit refers to the underside panel of a built-in light source. It may be in the ceiling or under a cabinet. Soffit lighting is often used over a sink or other work area in a kitchen.

FIGURE 17-3 A well-designed table lamp can be useful in uniting an eclectic assortment of furniture and accessories. (*Courtesy of The Stiffel Company*)

FIGURE 17-4 Hanging lamps and chandeliers are useful in dining areas but they must be chosen to accent the decorative theme. (*Courtesy of The Stiffel Company*)

FIGURE 17-5 When space is a problem, hanging lamps in the bedroom may provide a solution. (*Courtesy of Monsanto Company, Photo by Lisanti, Inc.*)

(b)

FIGURE 17-6 Strip lighting is used in various ways for both efficiency and decorative effects. *(a) Courtesy of Monsanto Company. (b) Courtesy of 1969 Rooms of Tomorrow. (c) Courtesy of Royal Systems of Denmark.*

(a)

(c)

FIGURE 17-8 Light from the floor represents a new concept in illumination. (*Designed by Barbara D'Arcy, A.I.D., Bloomingdale's, N.Y.*)

FIGURE 17-9   Concealed sources in a modern room highlight wall panels. (*Designed by Barbara D'Arcy, A.I.D. Courtesy of Bloomingdale's, N.Y.*)

Outdoor Lighting

Outdoor living areas have become such an important part of our way of life that they should have special mention with respect to lighting. The requirements for outdoor lighting differ from those for interiors. We are not so likely to need light for close work, such as reading or sewing. We are, however, concerned with functional light that will enable us to cook outdoor meals at night and also with the decorative qualities of outdoor lighting.

Usually the lighting fixtures must be placed to enhance the rustic or informal character of the setting. On the patio or terrace we want all the advantages of artificial light without making it seem contrived or too obviously planned. Torches with large glowing flames may produce the desired atmosphere, but well-placed artificial lights are more useful and more dependable. Fixtures placed at ground level and hidden behind shrubs or bushes should light steps. Yellow bulbs in all outdoor lighting will repel insects.

FIGURE 17-10 (a) One style of profile light in garden fixtures calls attention to steps, paths, walkways, and low plants. (*Courtesy of Shalda Lighting Products, Burbank, Calif.*)

(b) Fixtures such as the type shown here spread light downward on flowers and pool while simultaneously giving an upward light to emphasize overhanging foliage. (*Courtesy of Shalda Lighting Products, Burbank, Calif.*)

18

Specific Rooms and Areas

Most rooms will have to be planned and equipped to meet a variety of needs. Every aspect of furnishing should be carefully considered to make the available space as functional and attractive as possible. Furniture must be chosen with respect to suitability as well as design; it must be arranged to make the space both useful and beautiful. Thus specific purposes of the area as well as the *mood* or *theme* to be expressed will influence the selection of furnishings.

When space is at a premium, planning for maximum efficiency is particularly important. It is not always possible to foresee little pitfalls that may arise until one actually lives in a home. But wise and careful planning of each area can prevent serious mistakes. Minor difficulties that may pop up in the "use test" can usually be easily remedied.

Hallways

A home may have several kinds of halls and some of them may do no more than provide a passageway from one area to another. Hallways can serve so many useful purposes that they should never be considered waste space. More and more we are looking at them from the functional as well as the decorative point of view. Storage cabinets and bookshelves are being designed for the narrow proportions of some hallways. Wallpapers, lighting, and carpeting may be used to provide various novelty effects. Imagine, for example, a long, narrow hallway papered with a scenic wall covering that suggests a glen or forest, carpeted in soft velvety green and illuminated to give a sunshine glow. Just walking through such a hallway could be a delightful experience.

ENTRANCE HALLS. It should be remembered that the front door and the entrance hall create the initial impression of a home. As

FIGURE 18-1 A narrow hallway can be furnished without furniture. In this case, accessories, a console shelf, a mirror used in a problem corner, and a distinctive floor covering all contribute to a welcoming atmosphere. (*Designed by Patricia Harvey, A.I.D. Photo by Dennis Purse*)

people leave, they also create the final impression. This area, therefore, should represent the spirit of a household but it should also be useful. When one arrives there may be packages, books, or mail to deposit. Is there a convenient surface? In stormy weather there is always the problem of wet clothing. Is the hallway equipped to stand the rough treatment of muddy overshoes and dripping umbrellas? Is there a place to hang clothes when guests arrive?

Space in the entrance hall must frequently be used for additional purposes. In private homes this problem may not be as vital, but in apartments the entrance hall might be used as a dining area, a den, or for storage. Then functionalism becomes a major concern and requires a most careful utilization of space. Dual-purpose furniture that is small in scale or wall-hung units may be very useful in this respect.

Living Rooms

There is a general trend to plan more than one area in the home for group living. The family room as a second living area has become increasingly popular in modern homes, as has an outdoor "living room." Also, we no longer cling to the idea that bedrooms are only for sleeping or that dining rooms are only for dining. Either room may be furnished to relieve some of the demands on the living room. For example, a bedroom may be furnished to double as a sitting room or as a quiet study area, and a dining room may be planned to function as a second living room. However, there are many homes in which it is not possible to use any other area for the purposes usually served by the living room. In a one-room apartment, for example, there must be provisions not only for sleeping, eating, and storage, but also for reading, watching television, entertaining, and any other activities that appeal to the occupants. Even in somewhat larger homes, an all-purpose living room is often a necessity.

How a living area is furnished will, of course, depend on how the room is to function and whether or not there will be other areas in the home that might be used for certain activities of the family.

In all probability, the living room will be

FIGURE 18-2 A front hallway is converted into a sewing area with the addition of a closet specifically fitted to hold sewing needs. (*Courtesy of The Singer Company. Photo by Lisanti, Inc.*)

FIGURE 18-3   A rather formal living room can provide for various types of activities. (*Photo by the makers of Armstrong Linoleum*)

used for entertaining. The considerate host or hostess plans for the comfort of guests. Furniture is arranged so that people can converse with one another. A table or some other surface convenient for refreshments is provided. Buffet service and informal entertaining have become so popular that there are all sorts of lap trays and small folding tables on the market to ease the problems of entertaining in the living room. The important point is to plan the living area so that it is possible to entertain graciously in whatever manner is chosen without disrupting the normal arrangements.

If the living room is planned to accommodate guests comfortably it will probably also take care of the usual family needs. These might include several comfortable chairs with good light for reading as well as the convenient table surfaces mentioned earlier. But there may also be other family demands upon the living area. The television set, for example, may be in the living room. In the early days of television, this was the logical place for it. Now many families find that either some other area is more to their liking or that two, or more, TV sets are desirable. Watching television, even if only for short periods, has become pretty much a part of our daily lives, and where there is only one set in the home its location will influence the pattern of family living.

Frequently the living room must also provide for a music center. Hi-fi or stereophonic systems are often combined with TV sets in handsome cabinets that become an important part of the furnishings and may even become major centers of interest. A piano or some other musical instrument may also be located in the living room. Aside from its merits, the grand or baby grand piano often does present a problem in arranging a room. Because this is a large, heavy piece of furniture, it should be balanced with another important piece or

FIGURE 18-4   The small living room in Celanese House has different areas of activity without appearing cluttered. (*Courtesy of Celanese Corporation*)

furniture grouping in another area. The music center will often require some type of storage facilities for records or sheet music. Good lighting is another important consideration when planning this area.

In many homes the living room must also provide a study or business area. A desk, a chair, and bookshelves may provide all the necessary equipment, but good lighting is also of utmost importance. To carry on the business of family living in modern society, some functional work center almost seems mandatory. A typewriter is a useful tool and a desk equipped with at least one file drawer is very helpful for organizing letters, bills, and so on. Some sort of unit that accommodates address books, stationery, ink, labels, string, scissors, and other necessities ought to be included in the family business center. Whether or not this area of activity is located in the living room will depend on the overall arrangement of the home, but no matter where it is, well-planned organization can do a great deal to relieve the frustrations of daily living.

PHYSICAL CHARACTERISTICS. Although the living room should be planned primarily for utmost functionalism, the aesthetic qualities are no less important. This should be a pleasant, congenial room that appeals to every member of the family. In a certain sense the living room is synonymous with *home*, because this is an important area that we associate with family life. In some homes, some other area may assume a more important function, but the living room should, nevertheless, contribute to the spirit of family life. It should be a place where members of the family like to gather and enjoy both group and individual interests.

We have discussed some of the functions that the living room must perform; we must also realize that there may be certain limiting factors. The room may be too small, or a peculiar shape. It may have architectural features that become problems even though they also add to the interest of the room.

Fireplaces. A fireplace appeals to many people because it connotes various ideas, such as warmth, elegance, friendliness, and so on. A fireplace seems to add a certain touch to a home even though it may be useless. Few homes today depend on a fireplace for heating purposes, yet many homes include one for other reasons. In some instances a fireplace may be used for cooking informal meals, thereby serving as an indoor barbecue.

However, when a fireplace is included in the living room or some other area of the home it almost naturally becomes a center of interest. It often determines the character of the room and how furniture will be arranged. Although a fireplace adds character and distinction to a room, it also presents limitations with respect to efficient use of wall space.

A built-in fireplace may cost anywhere from six hundred dollars up. Portable models may cost a bit less, but they are still expensive adjuncts in terms of actual contributions to the efficiency of the home.

Window Walls. Modern planning favors a relationship between the outdoors and the indoors, and the window wall has been a convenient means of achieving this purpose. Yet a whole wall of glass, however desirable it may be, will present certain problems of furniture arrangement. Large, heavy pieces will not be attractive when placed against such a wall. The open appearance of this area is one of its chief attractions, so it must be relatively free of furniture. When other walls are cut up with doors or architectural features, there may be little wall space left for placing furniture.

Dining Areas

Today a home with one large room devoted exclusively to dining is indeed a luxury. In recent years we have seen various space arrangements that attempt to cope with the problem of the dining area. L-shaped living rooms with the alcove accessible to the kitchen are widely used in both apartments and private homes. Both small houses and apartments are often planned with a breakfast room or dinette adjacent to the kitchen. Or the kitchen itself may be designed to provide space for table, chairs, and serving units. Some apartments utilize a foyer hall as the dining area. Somehow none of these arrangements seems to have really taken the place of the lovely old-fashioned dining room. In many large homes, as well as in small homes, that are designed for construction at medium-cost levels, the addition of an adaptable room that can be used as a family room or as an informal dining room is finding increasing favor. Frequently the room is furnished to serve several functions.

Even when a separate room for dining is feasible, there is a trend to furnish it in a more individual manner. We are no longer bound to using matching suites of furniture. Often the chairs don't match the table and they may not even match one another. Contrasting servers, cabinets, and other storage units are also used. In other words, dining-room decoration is following in the path of living-room decor, which long ago rejected the idea of conformity.

Although we tend to think of the living room as the center of group activities for the family, in actual practice the dining area may be a more important one in terms of family living. Isn't the dinner table the place where conversation really unites the family as a group? How many families actually sit in their living rooms to discuss the happenings of the day or to exchange ideas? At the table, the very physical setup, with each person at his or her place, unites the family group. In a living room or even a family room, the distractions of television and other activities preclude the sense of unity that one finds at the dinner table. Probably for these reasons we have felt the need for an area in the home that provides a pleasant, relaxed atmosphere that fosters a family spirit. Dining areas in the kitchen or closely attached to the kitchen don't seem to do it, although the practical advantages of such arrangements are obvious.

In view of the above comments it can be readily understood that the spirit of the dining area must be pleasant. It may be gay and cheerful or quiet and restful, but it should be conducive to happy relaxation. Soft lights, flowers, plants, and music usually contribute to such an atmosphere.

There is no reason why the dining table must always be placed in the center of the room. With the trends toward dual-purpose dining rooms and greater freedom of expression in decorating, many interesting arrangements have been developed with the table at one end of the room or even projecting from a wall. The important points to consider are appearance and comfort. The shape of the table should harmonize with the shape of the area and the design should express the theme of the room. There should be adequate space at the table for each person. About two feet is a comfortable minimum. The height of dining tables usually ranges from twenty-nine to thirty-one inches and the seats of chairs range from seventeen to eighteen inches from the floor. A free space of about three feet around the table allows for comfort in sitting and serving.

A serving table on wheels is often useful in the dining area. Some of these are made with surfaces that can be heated and some have storage units or extra shelves below. Cabinets and various types of cupboards are designed to hold silver, dishes, linens, and so on. Sometimes a closet in the dining room is very convenient for storing extra table appointments.

FIGURE 18-5 An elegant, formal dining room can be furnished with excellent reproductions of eighteenth-century furniture, wallpaper, and fabrics. (*Courtesy of The Kittinger Company*)

FIGURE 18-6   A dining area at one end of the living room must often take the place of a separate room. Here a specially designed corner unit and graceful chairs create a room within a room. (*Designed by John and Earline Brice, A.I.D. Courtesy of Harvey Probber, Inc.*)

(a)

FIGURE 18-7   A relatively small cabinet can serve as a dining area when space is a problem. (*Courtesy of Greatwood Products, Inc.*)

(b)

Bedrooms

Because we begin and end each day in the bedroom, this is an area that should certainly be furnished to suit individual tastes and needs. Above all, the bedroom should be comfortable and convenient to use, not only for sleeping but for dressing and all the other personal activities for which it is the haven. A comfortable chair with a table and lamp for reading or a desk for work and study may add considerably to the usefulness of the room. Sometimes a bedroom furnished as an extra sitting room is the solution for families in which teen-agers or elderly people require a "living room" of their own. The various types of daybeds and sofa beds that are available make it possible to plan such rooms so that they are both beautiful and functional.

The usual size of a twin bed is at least six feet long and about three feet, three inches wide. A full-sized bed may be five feet wide. However, headboards and footboards add to the dimensions. In addition, there is a growing trend toward oversized or "king"-sized beds that are longer and wider, so it is important to know the exact dimensions of the beds to be used before planning an arrangement. Some beds may require as much as seven-and-one-half by five feet of space. The clearance space for making a bed must be about two feet.

For small bedrooms, various youth beds, daybeds, and bunk beds, and convertible chairs, sofas, and ottomans may conserve space. However, for a bed that is to be used every night, some of these smaller units may not provide the same comfort or convenience that the more standard bed offers. For example, bunk beds are difficult to make and convertibles frequently require extra storage space for pillows and blankets.

Easy access to closets and chests of drawers is a major consideration in arranging bedroom furniture. Standing in front of a chest and opening the drawers requires about three feet of clearance space. A closet door on hinges should swing back freely. Sliding or folding doors on closets will often conserve space in a small room.

FIGURE 18-8   An air of elegance and relaxation is evident in this room. Commodes used as night tables increase storage space. (*Designed by Patricia Harvey, A.I.D.*)

Children's Rooms

Child may mean anything from infancy to teen-age, and during these years the individual goes through many stages of development. At each stage the requirements vary, so furnishings should not be static.

We might consider four stages of child development with respect to furnishings: infancy, preschool, school-age, and teen-age. At each of these levels the requirements of a practical, satisfying room will be quite different.

INFANCY. The young baby really doesn't care much about color and design. He is interested in food, sleep, and comfort. The frilly nursery, therefore, is mostly an extension of the parents' ideas of a suitable environment for their offspring. Naturally the room should be gay and cheerful, but the practical aspects should make it possible to take care of the baby's needs with minimum effort. A crib and a storage chest for clothes are essential. A bathinette or a high table will be necessary for changing the baby's clothes.

Any surfaces with which the baby might come in contact should be treated with lead-free paint and should be free from sharp edges and other safety hazards.

PRESCHOOL. The toddler has requirements that are quite different from those of the infant. At this stage the youngster is learning to appreciate spaces, shapes, and colors. In all probability, he has outgrown the crib and a new bed is required. A low table with suitable chairs, and low open shelves are of primary importance.

This is a period when the child is learning to coordinate. He is also learning colors and developing habits of neatness. A chest for toys, or shelves that he can reach, become extremely important.

All surfaces should be easily cleaned, because the youngster, in learning to coordinate, may spill beverages or paints. He should never be made to feel guilty about such accidents, and if his room is carefully planned to allow for his development, such accidents do no harm.

SCHOOL-AGE. At the school-age stage, as the child is becoming more of a person, there will be individual tastes that should be considered. A desk with a good light is important. Bookshelves and a convenient storage space for clothing become more important. The child's room becomes something of a haven for his own interests and activities; there may be pets such as goldfish or turtles that assume major importance. The wise parent recognizes and develops such interests.

When it is necessary or desirable for children to share a room, a plan might be developed to give each one his own special area. Narrow shelves or chests of drawers can be used as dividers or ''walls,'' even though they may be low. Each situation requires special planning, but it is usually desirable to try to provide some feeling of privacy for each child.

TEEN-AGE. The transition period between childhood and adulthood often requires a special living area away from the family group. The teen-ager's room may become a second living room. Couches and sofas that pull out to form beds along with other dual-purpose furniture may solve this problem as well as other problems of different family needs at different age levels. Of course the teen-ager's room should be furnished to provide for his interests and activities. It is particularly important at this stage to allow individual expression.

Dens and Study Areas

A special room equipped as the home office or as a place where one might go to read or study in quiet solitude is an ideal arrangement, but space limitations frequently preclude the use of an entire room for such purposes. How delightful it must be to have a library or a study, but most of us have to settle for a more economical use of space. The study area, therefore, may be part of the bedroom, the dining room, or the living room. Nevertheless, wise planning can make even a tiny area conducive to comfortable, efficient, and enjoyable work at home.

What are some of the essentials for this type of room or area? Perhaps a comfortable, restful atmosphere would be of prime importance. There must be a good working surface provided by a desk or table, a comfortable chair, and good light. Books might

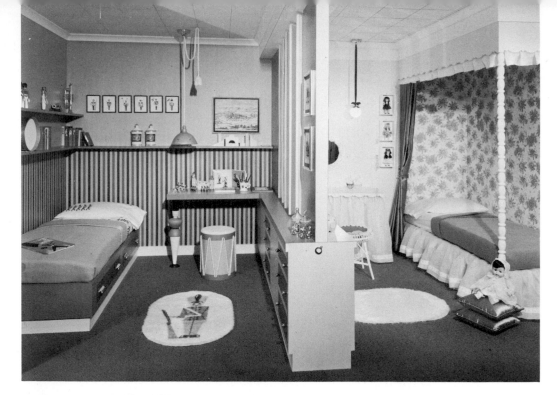

FIGURE 18-9 Brother and sister areas can be clearly defined in one large room. (*Courtesy of Creslan Acrylic Fiber*)

FIGURE 18-10 Private sleeping alcoves create a degree of privacy when two teen-agers must share a bedroom. (*Courtesy of The Englander Company, a Subsidiary of Union Carbide Corporation*)

be very important in such an area, so shelves in standing units or wall-hung brackets must also be provided. Storage facilities for records and various papers are essential. The "business of living" has prompted some manufacturers to make desks with file drawers, which can be a great asset to even the simplest household. Almost every family has a collection of bills, correspondence, and records that should be maintained in an organized, easy-to-reach manner. A typewriter has become an almost essential part of family equipment, and some of the cabinets designed for home use include storage compartments for a typewriter as well as file drawers.

The den or business area of the home is useful if it is equipped with stationery, stamps, and sundries such as paper clips, rubber bands, Scotch tape, a stapling machine, string, large scissors, and a letter opener. Because greeting cards have become part of our way of life, the den or study area might provide space for storing them as well as gift wrappings.

Whatever area is chosen as the business or study area of the home, the decor must be restful. Soft grayed colors along with comfortable, functional furniture provide the answer. Whether one lives in a small apartment or a huge house, the business of running a household must go on and life will be simpler if adequate provisions are made for it in some area of the home.

Family Rooms

A relatively new addition to the average household is the second living room, popularly referred to as the "family room." So many versions of such a room have been proposed that the term defies description. However, it connotes a less formal and more flexible room than the standard living room.

The added space for group living is especially desirable when there are several members of a family at different age levels. Teenagers or elderly people usually have needs that vary from the middle-age group. A home that provides two or more group-living areas helps to solve the problems that arise when several generations attempt to live with one another.

Once again, planning for the most efficient utilization of space is important. A second living room is not always possible. But should the situation require a second living area, a dining room, or even an extra bedroom furnished as a family room may provide some solution to the problem. In addition, kitchens may be planned to include living areas or to allow in some way for group activities.

In general, the family room or second living area usually has a more relaxed and casual atmosphere than the actual living room of the house. The less formal furnishings should provide for games and for various kinds of entertainment. It is convenient, therefore, to have this area near the kitchen or to make some provisions for serving meals and refreshments. In addition, it is useful to have family rooms accessible to outdoor terraces or patios.

The furniture should be comfortable, sturdy, and easy to move; the flooring and fabrics should be easy to maintain, and the color schemes should be bright and cheerful.

Kitchens

Perhaps more than any other area of the home, the kitchen has been the subject for intensive research by home economists, builders, and appliance manufacturers. This is understandable in view of the fact that kitchen activities require a considerable amount of the homemaker's time and energy. Also, the relative expense of kitchen equipment contributes to the importance of this area and must be considered as an investment that will satisfy demands for convenience and comfort over a period of years.

We must recognize that there is no one perfect kitchen that will meet the needs of all families. Homemakers differ in personal values concerning the needs that the area must serve. For example, although most families prefer some arrangement for food service in the kitchen, different families regard this area in various ways. Some have all their meals in the kitchen and also entertain guests in this room; others have only certain meals or light snacks in the kitchen and consider another area more desirable for the main meals. Also, homemakers place different amounts of emphasis on convenience and on aesthetics, although it is not always necessary to sacrifice one for the other.

The functionalism of the kitchen will be dependent to some extent upon the composition of the family. The needs, therefore, will vary not only with the type of family unit but also within each family as it goes through different cycles. We might outline four general categories in this respect:

1. The single individual, the young couple, or several adults who live together with no children in the home.
2. The "founding" family in which there are some children younger than eight years of age.
3. The "expanding" family with children between the ages of eight and eighteen.
4. The "contracting" family, in which the parents are older and children have grown and are probably leaving to establish homes of their own.

ACTIVITIES IN THE KITCHEN. In addition to the storage of foods and the preparation of meals, it is frequently desirable to plan the kitchen for other needs and activities. The service of meals in the kitchen has already been mentioned. In addition, the kitchen may include:

Planning Center. A writing surface with a convenient telephone and storage space for cookbooks, recipes, records, and bills.

Play Area. Mothers with young children sometimes like space for a playpen or a small table and chairs so that they can watch the youngsters while performing duties in the kitchen. Of course, the play area should be far enough away from the main centers of activity so that there is no safety hazard.

Laundry Area. It is sometimes desirable to provide space and equipment for laundering in the kitchen or very near it.

Hobby or Sewing Center. Other activities such as flower arranging, sewing and mending, photography, or some other hobby may require some space and equipment that can be conveniently located in or near the kitchen.

Needs for these areas will vary not only with each family but also at different stages of the family cycle. Some flexibility is desirable, therefore, to allow for the most efficient use of the space.

It is interesting to note that although different families vary in their needs and demands for a useful kitchen, there is a surprising similarity when the matter of storage space is considered. After extensive research, this statement was made:

The size of a household generally has no significant influence on the amount of space required for such items as groceries, baked goods, and dishes except in the case of such special items as bread, where there is an increase with an increase in the number of household members.[1]

In view of these comments, planning kitchens that are functional and adaptable to personal preferences and actual needs becomes a rather complex problem in mass-produced homes and apartments. Frequently we are forced to adapt to what is available or to what

[1] *The Cornell Kitchen*. Cornell University Agricultural Experiment Station and the New York State College of Home Economics (Ithaca, N.Y., Cornell University, 1955).

we can afford to have. Although an original design or even a remodeling project is not always possible, the astute homemaker who understands the basics of kitchen planning can frequently make simple arrangements that will improve conditions in poorly planned areas. Unfortunately, there is such a plethora of poor planning that one often has to accept the challenge of making the best of a bad situation. The only comforting note is that when the homemaker does figure out some way of making a seemingly impossible kitchen really work for her, it is a source of great satisfaction. Of course for some problem kitchens the only answer lies in either a partial or a complete remodeling project, but for others a few minor changes may make the room far more functional and more attractive.

LOCATIONS IN RELATION TO OTHER ROOMS. One basic consideration in evaluating any kitchen plan is how it relates to other areas of the home. Should it be at the front or at the back of the house? Should it be a prominent room where one might entertain guests or should it be relegated to the confines of private family living? Here again, there is no one set answer, because it depends on how one wants to use the home. There are some quite modern apartments where one steps into the entry hall to find himself in the kitchen area. There are also private homes where the first view is of the kitchen. True, the kitchen must be convenient to some entry, but is it the first area that one should see? Authorities agree that the kitchen must be located so that when foods and supplies are brought into the home they can be easily stored. For this reason, many kitchens in private homes have a doorway that connects with the garage or with a centrally located utility area. In apartments that have only one entrance the kitchen is often close to the entrance door.

The kitchen must also be convenient to the area for food service. This may be a tiny area in the kitchen itself, a dining room, or several areas, such as a dining room, a family room, and an outdoor living area. Nowadays we are likely to serve food in any one of several areas, depending upon the mood of the moment or the season of the year. Is it possible to have a kitchen that can service all areas of the home with equal convenience? Perhaps not, but it should be located so that it is convenient for most of the meal service in the home.

DOORS AND WINDOWS. The plan of the kitchen is often determined by the location of doors and windows in the room. Although the kitchen must be convenient for the delivery of foods and for the service of meals, more than two doorways may make the work area a through-passage traffic lane that will impede efficiency. One doorway convenient for delivery and the other convenient for service are usually sufficient.

Although in some modern apartment buildings the kitchens are being designed with no windows at all, for small private homes the window area is considered a major feature of the kitchen for both light and ventilation. In addition, homemakers with young children often prefer a kitchen window that allows them to watch the youngsters at play in the outdoors. Yet windows and doors do reduce the amount of available wall and floor space in the kitchen. The FHA specifies a minimum window area equal to 10 per cent of the floor area of the kitchen; the Small Homes Council recommends window space that is between 15 and 25 per cent for good light and ventilation.

AMOUNT OF SPACE. Kitchens range from tiny efficiency units to huge rooms, but it is not so much the amount of space as the planning for the use of space that determines how efficient the kitchen will be. A large kitchen that is poorly planned is as bad, if not worse, than one that is too small.

Any size kitchen will have three major pieces of equipment: the refrigerator, the sink, and the range. The work centers of activity in the kitchen are related to the placement of the equipment. An analysis of the work areas has shown that there are five major areas of activities:

1. Refrigerator.
2. Mix-preparation.
3. Sink.
4. Range.
5. Serve.

Time-and-motion studies have shown that for the various activities in each area of work there is a need for adequate storage and counter space. Also, the Small Homes Council recommends the following distance limits measuring from the center fronts of the equipment:

Refrigerator to sink: four to seven feet.
Sink to range: four to six feet.
Range to refrigerator: four to nine feet.

The distances between the three major pieces of equipment form the work triangle of the kitchen, and the sum of the distances should not exceed twenty-two feet.

BASIC PLANS. Depending upon the amount of available floor and wall space (determined by the overall size of the room and the locations of doors and windows), functional kitchens may be worked out on one of several basic plans:

A. The U-shaped kitchen utilizes three walls with corner cabinets and is designed to make the best possible use of space that is inconvenient to begin with.
B. The two-wall or H-shaped kitchen is frequently a corridor. Although there are no difficult corners, the center lane should be between forty-two and fifty-four inches wide for maximum efficiency.
C. The L-shaped kitchen uses two adjacent walls to free other wall space for dining or laundry areas.
D. One-wall kitchens are more suitable for small quarters and limited space.

There are a number of possible variations on these basic plans, including the peninsular or island versions, in which a unit either projects from one wall or is free-standing in the center.

GUIDES FOR PLANNING. Certain guides may be of great value in making a kitchen more functional. Each homemaker must study her own needs and evaluate her own situation, but whatever revisions may be indicated should be based on the following guides for better kitchen planning.

1. Kitchen design must be functional in the sense of minimizing reaching, stooping, and walking.
2. The limit of reaching height should be the height a woman can reach with bent fingers while standing in a comfortable working position with both feet flat on the floor.
3. Storage space should be arranged in such a way that items are located close to where the *first* operation involving them will take place.

4. Frequently used items should be stored where they can be taken down and put back without excessive strain.
5. Items should be stored so that they can be easily seen, reached, and grasped.
6. Storage space should be sufficiently flexible to permit its adjustment to varying sizes, amounts, and kinds of food, supplies, and utensils.
7. The work surfaces should not require an uncomfortable working posture.
8. The worker should be able to sit, if she wishes, while she does certain kitchen work, such as at the sink and the mix center.
9. The work surfaces of some counters should be adjustable to different heights.

Recommendations for adequate counter space and convenient heights and depths of storage units include the following:

COUNTER SPACE

Refrigerator Fifteen to eighteen inches at side where door opens.

Mixing area Thirty-six inches.

Sink Thirty to thirty-six inches to the left; thirty-six inches to the right.

Range Twenty-four inches on both sides.

CABINETS

Height Thirty-six inches counter height; thirty to thirty-two inches for mixing counter.

Wall cabinets Fifteen to eighteen inches above counter (first shelf fifty-two inches from floor).

Depth Twenty-five inches for base cabinets; thirteen inches for wall cabinets.

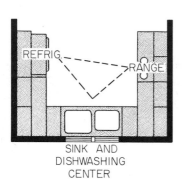

(a) U-Shaped Kitchen

(b) Two-wall Kitchen

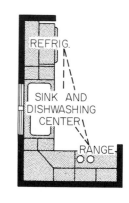

(c) L-Shaped Kitchen

FIGURE 18-13   Basic kitchen plans.

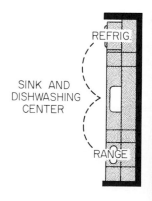

(d) One-wall Kitchen

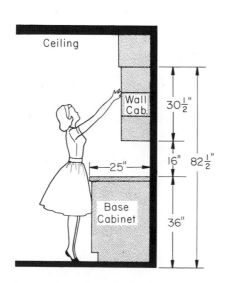

234

FIGURE 18-14   Cabinet heights.

PITFALLS OF PLANNING. Because of the difficulty of changing kitchen arrangements once they are made, it might be wise at this point to examine some of the common pitfalls of planning this area. Amateurs in the field of kitchen planning frequently make mistakes in the following major areas:

1. Use of space; improper coordination between appliances, work surfaces, and storage areas.
2. Provisions for changes in family patterns. Needs are different at various stages of family growth. The kitchen is not a static area and must be flexible enough to be adapted enough to different needs.
3. Actual use of facilities. On-paper measurements may vary considerably from the space required to open doors, pull out chairs, and so on.
4. Safety factors. Many activities in the kitchen affect health and safety. The range area must be large enough to allow pot handles to be turned away from the flame; storage areas for frequently used items must be convenient to reach; edges should be rounded and smooth to prevent injury.
5. Proper illumination, ventilation, and wiring are essential to a well-planned kitchen. Sufficient light over work areas, exhaust fans, and adequate outlets for small appliances all are items that the amateur may forget or overlook.

LIGHTING AND WIRING. The kitchen needs some form of general lighting, and it needs special lighting over counters—usually under wall cabinets—and at each center of activity. Wall outlets must be convenient for small appliances that will be used on counter tops.

DECORATION. There are trends toward using the kitchen for more family activities and even for entertaining guests. The concept of the kitchen-family room is not a new idea; kitchens in Colonial homes were often the centers of family life and they reflected the warmth that such a living area should have.

We have become accustomed to color in the kitchen, but now more sophisticated furniture design is being applied to both cabinets and appliances. With lovely textured woods treated for easy maintenance, more decorative hardware, and the growing use of carpeting, the kitchen is taking on an entirely new look. A French Provincial, Mediterranean, or Colonial theme is not unusual, and in some homes where the area is adjacent to another room, it is difficult to tell where the kitchen actually begins and ends.

The well-planned kitchens that look more like living rooms than scientific laboratories have not sacrificed functionalism. Plastic laminates, treated wall coverings, and new counter units that cook are easy to clean as well as attractive in appearance. New designs in utensils and accessories also make it possible to supplement the decorative theme without sacrificing efficiency.

FIGURE 18-15 New concepts in the kitchen include wall-to-wall carpeting. Constructed of easy-care fibers, these floor coverings lend a new dimension to decorating kitchen-dining areas. (*Courtesy of Hercules Olefin Fiber*)

FIGURE 18-16 A patterned kitchen carpet in a modern setting introduces a traditional theme. (*Couresy of DuPont Textile Fibers*)

FIGURE 18-17 Another new concept in designing kitchen appliances is the smooth-surfaced cooking counter that keeps electrical elements out of sight. (*Courtesy of Corning Glass Works*)

FIGURE 18-18 A tiny kitchen in a small apartment solves a problem with roller shades in place of doors on storage areas. (*Courtesy of Celanese Corporation*)

FIGURE 18-19 A small area can be planned for maximum efficiency in storage. (*Courtesy of Gas Appliance Manufacturers Association*)

The Laundry Area

There must be some provision for taking care of the family wash in every household. In many families the automatic washer is considered an essential piece of equipment and the automatic dryer is rapidly approaching the same status.

LOCATION. The laundry center is often planned as part of the kitchen or is placed adjacent to the kitchen with some form of division between the two areas. The basement has also been a favorite spot for the laundry, but some homes have special utility rooms on the main floor. Because most of the bulky items in the family wash come from the bedrooms and the bathrooms, there is an increasing trend to place the laundry center closer to these rooms. In other words, the most convenient and desirable location still has not been determined, and no doubt it will vary with the type of home and the preferences of the homemaker.

ACTIVITIES. Although automatic washers and dryers have simplified the task of doing the family wash, the myriad new fabrics that require special handling have also added something to the complexity of the problem. Some garments must be washed by hand, some respond better to drip-drying. New automatic machines are being developed to cope with the various types of fabrics, but so far they are still in a developmental stage.

All this means that the laundry center must be planned and equipped to keep the energy expenditure to the minimum. A large table or counter for sorting the soiled items and folding the clean laundry should be conveniently placed. The automatic equipment is best placed near a deep tub or sink for the hand-washables. Storage cabinets for soaps, detergents, and other supplies must be convenient. Some place to hang the drip-dry items is also an important part of the planning.

Many women find the task of ironing their most distasteful household chore. When this is the case, every effort should be made to lighten the burden. They should do the ironing in a pleasant atmosphere; use an adjustable ironing board so that they can sit and work in a comfortable position; and have a radio, television, or record player to provide some entertainment. They should also have a con-venient rack and table surface for finished items.

The laundry must have good light. Although a blue-white light is excellent for showing up spots and scorch marks, it is not a particularly pleasant form of illumination. The homemaker may want to sacrifice the functional for the aesthetic in this case if laundering is one of her "problem" chores.

Bathrooms

An extensive study of the bathroom was conducted by the Cornell University Center for Housing and Environmental Studies. The comprehensive report on the program indicates that little basic research has been done in the field of facilities for personal hygiene and that in general our bathrooms today are inadequate for the purposes they must serve. The report also suggests that if the needs for greater function and convenience are to be met there must be more direct contact between industry and the consumer.[2]

Although the bathroom is strictly a utility area and above all else must be functional, there is no reason why it cannot also be pleasant and attractive. Modern bathroom planning shows a recognition that this area is more functional if it is large enough and equipped to accommodate two people at once. There must be enough space so that a mother and a young child can move around with ease. When there is illness in the family, the patient may need assistance in the bathroom. Even in normal day-to-day family life, the bathroom is more functional if two people can use it at the the same time; yet privacy is also essential, so there is a trend toward bathroom compartments with separate areas for tub and/or shower, toilet, and basin. Two basins have become a popular feature of modern design, especially in homes where there is only one bathroom.

Although the equipment and the construction materials in the bathroom must necessarily be designed for cleanliness and easy maintenance, it does not follow that this room must have the clinical, scientific type of decoration to which it has been subjected in

[2] Alexander Kira, *The Bathroom*, *Criteria for Design*. Center for Housing and Environmental Studies Ithaca, N.Y., Cornell University, 1966.

FIGURE 18-20 Laundry equipment is concealed behind folding doors at one end of a dining area. (*Courtesy of American Gas Association and American Home Magazine*)

FIGURE 18-21 New developments in floor coverings have extended the use of wall-to-wall carpeting into the bathroom. (*Courtesy of Herculon Olefin Fiber*)

FIGURE 18-22 Compartments and more decorative accessories are being used in modern bathrooms. (*Courtesy of* Home Modernizing Guide)

the past. There seems to be a need for making this room a bit warmer and softer in appearance as evidenced by the interest in colored equipment, washable wall-to-wall floor coverings, and decorative fabrics. Pictures on the wall, growing plants, and other accessories also add to the decorative scheme. We really have not been very imaginative in exploring the possibilities of bathroom decoration nor of the use of possible storage space in the bathroom.

Storage Areas

Well-planned facilities for storage in the home have become almost as much of a status symbol as a swimming pool. So few families have adequate facilities that we are likely to regard a home that does have adequate, well-planned space for all the normal storage problems as something of a luxury.

Several factors will influence the needs of any family for storage space:

CLIMATE. A family that lives in a changing climate will have more complex storage needs than one living in a constant climate. Seasonal clothing that must be stored is an obvious problem. In addition, outdoor summer furniture, the lawn mower, garden equipment, snow shovels, children's sleds, and other large toys that can be used only at certain times of the year must be stored someplace. A home in a temperate climate will require storage space of a different nature because the equipment is more likely to have year-round use. For example, there will be no need for sleds and snow shovels, but the lawn mower is used all year round.

COMPOSITION OF THE FAMILY. The number of people in the family and their ages will influence the type and amount of storage space required. The expanding family with young children may need space for clothes, toys and play equipment, a carriage, a playpen, and a bathinette.

ACTIVITIES AND INTERESTS. Hobbies and interests demand varying amounts of space.

Sewing, photography, and collections of one type or another must have storage facilities. An interest in reading requires bookshelves; an interest in music will probably require record cabinets. Sports enthusiasts require space for both clothing and equipment.

The family that does a considerable amount of entertaining will also have special storage needs. Bridge tables, folding chairs, games, and records, and serving pieces such as punch bowls, large platters, extra dishes, large cooking utensils, and so on, may all be part of the standard equipment.

An adequate amount of space is important, but planning for the use of space is almost as important. So many homes with storage problems have not used available space in the most efficient manner. To be truly efficient, storage areas must make it possible to place every item within easy view and accessibility. Either deep, walk-in closets or narrow cabinets with adjustable shelves seem to be the most useful.

Storage walls are often an answer to special problems. Units that allow a certain amount of flexibility can be both functional and decorative.

Guest Rooms

Few homes today can boast of a special room reserved for guests. Space is at such a premium that it must be put to work for more than one purpose, but facilities for entertaining overnight guests are very important in some family patterns.

A guest room should provide for the comfort and convenience of anyone likely to use it. Various spots in the home may be equipped to fulfill a dual purpose. For example, a sewing room and extra sitting room may also be a guest room. A family room or even a dining room may be equipped to take care of overnight guests.

When planning a guest-room area, one should always put himself in the position of the visitor and try to make the arrangements as convenient as possible. If an extra room for guests cannot be provided, concern should be shown for the special little extras, such as a luggage rack, drawer space, a light for comfortable reading in bed, or a lounge chair. Within the limits of the available space, guests should be made as comfortable as possible.

A guest room should, if possible, be accessible to a bathroom or at least a half-bathroom. Guests should feel as though they have the complete freedom of the home and that they do not interfere with the normal functioning. The gracious hostess provides for as much comfort as possible within the limitations of her household.

Outdoor Living Areas

The terrace, patio, or porch has become another important living area in the home. The cookout for both family meals and for the entertainment of guests has a special appeal in our casual, relaxed, and informal pattern of living. When the weather is pleasant, so many of the family activities may be centered in this outdoor living space that it really must be considered as a room.

Various new pieces of equipment and new types of furniture have been developed to meet the needs of these outdoor activities. Portable barbecue grills range from very simple, inexpensive units to quite complex, luxurious, and of course more expensive arrangements for cooking and serving meals. We not only want outdoor furniture to be comfortable, attractive, and resistant to the elements; we also want it to be easy to maintain. Certain types of wood, such as cypress and redwood, have been popular, but metal, glass, and plastics, have also been favorite materials.

The outdoor living area, is, of course, unique, but some of the principles of room planning must be applied to the arrangement of furniture and to the decoration. Because the demands on this room for group living will probably be quite heavy, there should be several comfortable chairs arranged for easy conversation. Many people like to include at least one chaise longue for relaxation. Some sort of convenient table surface near each chair is usually desirable. Here the imagination may be used to include something different. A low retaining wall with a broad-surfaced top can provide a continuous ''end table'' around the whole area. A few bricks or cement blocks may be arranged to form convenient tables.

There are several types of folding tables that are useful when this area is used for large groups. Also, an ironing board with a plywood table top and an attractive cover can be used as a buffet table. Some families who entertain large groups of people at one time have several of these ironing-board tables scattered around the area for more convenient service of refreshments.

Accessories in the outdoor living room may not be necessary if the garden or surrounding landscaping provides enough interest. However, statuary, potted plants, or outdoor torchlights are sometimes used to provide interesting effects.

Homes for Elderly People

In recent years we have heard a great deal about the aging population and the special needs of our elderly citizens. People are living longer and retiring earlier. As children grow up and marry at an early age, the so-called senior citizens are often faced with the problem of maintaining a home that no longer meets their needs. Therefore, the demand for retirement homes is steadily increasing and the building industry is taking special note of designs that appeal to older people.

In actual fact, the types of homes that appeal to older people have many features that also appeal to younger people. It is a mistake to believe that retirement homes belong in some very special exclusive category. Older people want houses that are simple, sensible, easy to maintain, and safe to use. True, the retired couple may need less space than the expanding family, and certain other features of the home may be of greater importance in the later years than in the early stages of family life. For example, having all rooms on one level with no steps to climb is particularly important to older people, whereas the split-level or two-story house may have more appeal to younger people. Some other desires for convenience and ease of maintenance expressed by older people would certainly appeal to other age groups as well.

In situations where older people must live with other members of their families, every effort should be made to give them a sense of privacy and independence. In small homes this is sometimes difficult, but often a simple structural change can provide a happy solution. If adding a separate wing to the house is inadvisable, a bedroom might be converted to suitable quarters. Whenever possible, older people should have a private bathroom and kitchen. Even a tiny kitchenette unit that is relatively easy to install may simplify some of the problems that arise when several generations attempt to live together. A bed-sitting room that is both comfortable and attractive might be equipped with a private television set and any other equipment that can make it possible for older people to live independent of the rest of the family. Such arrangements should in no sense isolate or exclude older people from the family group, but merely make it possible for them to have a certain amount of privacy and independence when they prefer it.

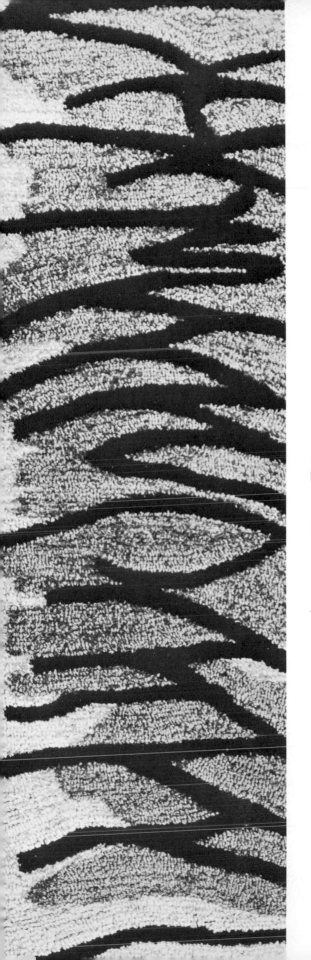

Section V
Consumer Buying

A budget is a plan for spending money. Probably no two individuals and no two families have identical situations with the same needs, the same resources, the same values, and the same tastes. It is impractical, therefore, to imply that there are specific formulas or budgets that can be applied to the costs of furnishing a home. Besides, most of the so-called furnishings budgets include allowances for furniture, floor coverings, draperies, and accessories, yet they ignore many of the expenses that can add considerably to the actual cost of establishing a household. Slipcovers, drapery fixtures, wall coverings, cleaning equipment, closet accessories, and telephone installation might be mentioned as examples of some of these "hidden" expenses.

Although there are certain things necessary for all homes, there are also items that might be considered essential by some people but superfluous by others. A piano or a stereo set could be very important to the person who likes music; in a private house landscaping and outdoor furniture might be big items in the budget. Appliances such as an electric mixer, an electric broiler, or a pressure cooker might be more important in one household than in another. If the homemaker plans to work, certain time- and labor-saving devices simplify the problem of a dual career, but they are not absolutely necessary.

The abundance of consumer goods on the market presents a constant challenge for people trying to live within the boundaries of their incomes. We all want to live as comfortably and as efficiently as possible but in establishing a household we should never lose sight of the importance of the spiritual values in the home. A family that goes overboard into financial debt for material items and is under constant economic pressure may find it difficult to keep those values in their proper perspective.

19

Spending Plans

Resources

With reference to resources we are likely to think of finances, but it should be noted that resources of time and ability are important factors in setting up a budget plan. The young man who is handy about the house and who has the time and the inclination to install fixtures and to build or refinish furniture adds considerably to the family resources. So does a young woman's ability and desire to make curtains and slipcovers. If such projects are not appealing, the cost of having them done by others makes a household more expensive to establish and to operate.

In the brief discussion of costs presented in Chapter 2, we mentioned that it is desirable to have adequate funds to pay cash for furnishings. Exactly how much money will be needed depends on many factors, such as personal tastes, the size and type of the home itself, family requirements, and so on. Also, in some instances gifts from relatives and friends may ease the financial demands to a considerable extent. Thus, the question of "How much does it cost?" is indeed a difficult one to answer. In an average situation, an amount equal to one half of the annual income usually provides a good beginning.

It should be borne in mind that buying furnishings on the installment plan has serious drawbacks. This is an expensive way to buy anything, because the service or interest charges must be added to the costs of purchases. Unfortunately, credit and loan experts are adept at concealing the actual dollar costs of buying in this manner.

If one buys a $400 couch, paying the service charge each month in addition to a $22 monthly payment, and the charge is one and one-half per cent of the unpaid balance, the payments in a year and a half will be those shown in Table 1. At the end of eighteen months the $400 couch would have cost $451.57. Some credit plans completely obscure the actual service charges. For example, one might pay a flat $22 a month for the couch. The one and one-half per cent service charge would be deducted from each payment, so the balance would decrease more slowly. In this case, it would take twenty-one months to complete the purchase and the actual cost for the $400 couch would be $462.05.

Buying the major portion of furnishings in

TABLE 1

Assume that you purchase a couch for $400 and pay $22 at the start. Your record of payments would be as follows.

Month	Unpaid Balance	Service Charge			Your Payment
1	$378	$5.67 +	$22.00	=	$27.67
2	356	5.34 +	22.00	=	27.34
3	334	5.01 +	22.00	=	27.01
4	312	4.68 +	22.00	=	26.68
5	290	4.35 +	22.00	=	26.35
6	268	4.02 +	22.00	=	26.02
7	246	3.69 +	22.00	=	25.69
8	224	3.36 +	22.00	=	25.36
9	202	3.03 +	22.00	=	25.03
10	180	2.70 +	22.00	=	24.70
11	158	2.37 +	22.00	=	24.37
12	136	2.04 +	22.00	=	24.04
13	114	1.71 +	22.00	=	23.71
14	92	1.38 +	22.00	=	23.38
15	70	1.05 +	22.00	=	23.05
16	48	.72 +	22.00	=	22.72
17	26	.39 +	22.00	=	22.39
18	4	.06 +	4.00	=	4.06
	Total $51.57				

this manner would be extremely expensive. However, not all installment buying must be frowned upon in such disapproving terms. There are situations in which it may be worth the cost to have the convenience of an article. For example, a mother with several young children may not be able to afford a washing machine, and by the time she saves enough money to buy one, the "period of crisis" may be over. The cost of buying a machine on the installment plan may be well worth the saving of her time and energy during the period when she has the problem of caring for young children. Nevertheless, it is important to know the cost of using credit plans. The Truth in Lending Law now makes it mandatory for the creditor to provide specific information about the conditions of a contract and the methods of calculating charges.

Investing in Furnishings

The money spent on furnishings should be considered as an investment. It is dangerous, and expensive in the long run, to assume that one will buy something for temporary use until there is money for something better.

Major items, such as upholstered furniture, mattresses, chests of drawers, cabinets, and floor coverings, are usually expensive even in the cheapest varieties. To decide, for instance, to buy a cheap living room rug to use for a year or two is not a wise investment. However, it is not always possible to invest in top quality for every item. There will be many factors influencing decisions about each major purchase, including cost, purpose, and appearance. In buying something with the idea of selling it later, it should be remembered that used furnishings usually have a low resale value. It is difficult, and often impossible, to receive a fair return on such an investment. Someone may even have to be paid to cart the article away when it is to be replaced.

The most interesting homes are not necessarily the ones that are the most expensive, but neither do they have masses of poor-quality furnishings. Imagination, taste, skill, and intelligence are the prime supports of a budget. One should use judgment about where to invest the major portion of his money.

It is wrong to assume that all low-cost furniture is of poor quality. There is some excellent furniture made in the low and medium price ranges, but the novice must be extremely cautious about judging value. In some items the quality features are hidden so that it is hardly possible to tell which offers the best value for the money. In mattresses and upholstered furniture, the "insides" are what count. It is difficult to judge the difference between a $30 mattress and an $80 one by looking at them.

Floor coverings are also difficult to judge. In carpets and rugs, the quality of material and construction is a hidden value. It takes years of practice to develop a sense of touch that can tell quality, and sometimes even the experts can be fooled.

Stretching the Budget

The current interest in the antipoverty program and the problems of the low-income family has prompted several well-known interior designers to apply their talents to creating attractive homes with the minimum amount of money. The ideas that have come out of the pilot projects and demonstrations are useful for any family that must cut corners on the budget.

In New York City, recipients of welfare who are relocated as a result of slum clearance projects are allowed $800 to furnish their new homes. Often these families have little, if any, furniture that is worth moving. It has become something of a challenge, therefore, for the interested leaders in the field to show how such a relatively small amount of money might be used to provide a home that is both functional and attractive.

Recently a "Mini-Budget Apartment" designed by Emily Malino was exhibited in New York City and received considerable attention in the press. The living room is shown in Figure 14–8. It was assumed that the hypothetical family did own some things that were useful but it was pointed out that even if they did not the apartment could have been furnished for about $1,000. Another such demonstration project was featured in a leading magazine.[1] Again it was assumed that the relocated family owned a few things that could be used but that they would have to provide most of the furnishings with a limited sum of money.

Both of the projects mentioned stressed imagination, simple do-it-yourself ideas, color, and functionalism. In both cases the intent was to suggest new ideas and to promote an interest in creating attractive homes even though funds are limited.

A number of manufacturers in the home furnishings field are devoting their attentions to sturdy, useful, attractive items that can be mass-produced at relatively low cost. Many of these are already widely available in stores throughout the country. The demonstration projects indicated some of the ways that modular units, shelving, self-adhesive trimmings, window shades, and printed sheets might be used.

There is also a new interest in rejuvenating good-quality second-hand furniture. Some of the new products, such as spray paints, antiquing kits, self-adhesive plastics, and a wide variety of hardware, make it possible to convert an old eyesore into an attractive and useful piece of furniture with relatively little effort.

[1] *American Home*, October, 1968, p. 70.

FIGURE 19-1 Director's chairs, roller shades laminated in a matching red and white print, and a wicker shelf painted to match the white Parsons table illustrate inexpensive ways to dramatize an area. (*Courtesy of Window Shade Manufacturers Association*)

FIGURE 19-2   The living-dining area in a low-cost decorating project features wicker furniture and a "do-it-yourself" room divider. Wooden poles painted in bright colors camouflage the steam pipe and take the place of draperies. (*Courtesy of* American Home Magazine)

FIGURE 19-3   Pillows hung on a curtain pole take the place of a headboard. Sheets used for bed cover and draperies give a coordinated effect. (*Courtesy of* American Home Magazine)

FIGURE 19-4   A home-made room divider is planned to provide a storage area as well as privacy in a small room shared by two children. (*Courtesy of* American Home Magazine)

FIGURE 19-5   Bright colors on a metal bunk bed and second-hand chairs, a plywood top fastened to a sturdy barrel, and a red rug add up to a gay but easily maintained room for children. (*Courtesy of Monsanto Company*)

Bargain hunting in secondhand stores and at auctions can be a fascinating hobby. Many young people are discovering the joy of making something out of nothing, and in some communities the ability to do this has become sort of a status symbol. Some projects are quick and easy, others require time and elbow grease, but sometimes the effort is worth the results. For example, one young couple found an old-fashioned icebox that they bought for two dollars. They removed numerous coats of paint and discovered a beautiful oak chest with interesting carved details on the front panels. They waxed and polished the wood, bought new brass hardware, and produced an interesting and useful cabinet, which is now a conversation piece in their living room. The total cost was about twelve dollars but the project has become their pride and joy and they had fun doing it.

Some tables, such as a coffee table, can be made at home for very little money. Sets of legs in various lengths can be easily attached to a piece of plywood covered with tile, adhesive-backed plastic, laminates, or veneer. Inexpensive bookshelves can be made from boards supported on bricks, blocks, glass tiles, or even tin cans filled with plaster.

Wallpaper, especially if one can apply it himself, is extremely useful in stretching a budget. The variety of patterns, colors, and textures can create almost any desired effect. Even when there are restrictions about applying paper directly to the walls, panels, screens, table tops, and accessories, decorated with wall coverings are effective ways of adding interest.

A new emphasis on window shades as an important element in decorating offers a multitude of possibilities for low-cost decorating. The self-adhesive motifs, fringes, braids, and plastics require imagination but very little time and skill to transform an ordinary shade into an attractive window treatment. There are also new products that make it possible to apply fabrics to window shades with relatively little time and expense.

Accessories in the minimum budget are a true challenge to creativity and imagination. Plants, huge paper flowers, collections—seashells, family pictures or memorabilia of one type or another—can all be used to provide individuality. In one of the demonstration projects an unusual doormat was hung on a wall. In another, a large piece of corrugated paper was painted and decorated. One's individual interests and skills can add the important ingredient in producing the necessary touch of emphasis.

Economy Styles

Some styles of furnishings lend themselves better than others to low budgets. The furnishing dollar will buy better value in those styles that represent a sturdy, functional kind of life. Simple lines and a minimum of expensive ornamentation make it possible for manufacturers to produce excellent quality at relatively low cost. There is some excellent furniture made in modern, Colonial, and provincial styles. The more austere and elegant styles require a certain amount of opulence. There are fine reproductions in all styles, but it is more difficult to furnish a luxurious room on a low budget. The furniture in the luxurious styles is usually more expensive to produce because of its more complicated styling and decoration. Woods that have beautiful textures, colors, and grain patterns add to the costs. Fabrics and other accessories in the elegant styles must also be more luxurious and are likely, therefore, to be more expensive. Simulated products, imitations, and makeshift projects do not usually portray elegance. A brave attempt at a theme that is obviously beyond one's means often becomes pretentious and insincere. However, if one shops carefully and is willing to invest time and energy almost any effect can be achieved.

Setting up a Budget

It was pointed out in Chapter 2 that one must know where he is going to live before he can draw up any detailed budget plan. An exact floor plan drawn according to scale and accurate measurements of windows, doors, and wall areas are necessary. Only then is it possible to know exactly what must be included in the budget. Also, one may or may not have to include flooring for the kitchen, shades or blinds for the windows, and certain appliances. Costs of paint and wallpaper may have to be included in the budget if one is expected to do this type of decorating himself.

One should try to foresee all the basic needs and make a list of the items to be included. From the floor plan, a list should be made of the pieces of furniture that appear there. Then for each room the items that do not appear on the plan should be added—such as draperies, fixtures, and accessories. Also, one may want to add certain items at a later time. The initial budget should include all the things considered essential at the beginning, but any furniture to be added later should also be indicated.

There are a number of less obvious costs that must be taken into account when preparing a budget. Large rugs and carpets should have padding underneath to make them wear better. Upholstered furniture, especially in light colors, will soil easily and slipcovers may be required. The maintenance of a home will require some equipment, particularly a vacuum cleaner if there is carpeting on the floors. The cost of a long traverse rod for heavy draperies may add almost $50 to a budget.

Lists should be drawn up of the items needed, with spaces provided for checking off items that might be received as gifts or for recording the costs of the items that will have to be bought.

Perhaps some basic items will be received as gifts. If one knows which ones, he may check these off and proceed to plan for the costs of the other items needed. He should shop around to determine the costs of the type of furnishings he wants. When he has a fairly good idea of the price ranges, he can begin to fill in the costs on the lists. Most of this paper work should be done before anything is actually bought.

For a small home these lists might include the following items:

Living-Dining Area
Couch
Upholstered chairs
Tables
Side chairs
Desk
Lamps
Accessories
Draperies and fixtures
Television and radio
Floor covering
Slipcovers

Each Bedroom
Beds, mattresses, and springs
Chests of drawers
Mirror

Bench or chair
Floor covering
Lamps
Accessories
Draperies and fixtures
Pillows
Bedspreads and blankets

Linens
Table linens
Bedding:
    Sheets
    Pillowcases
    Mattress pads
Towels:
    Large bath towels
    Hand towels
    Wash cloths
    Dish towels

Closet Accessories
Hangers
Shoe bags
Storage boxes

General Equipment
Vacuum
Mop
Broom
Pail
Basin
Tool kit
Curtain rods
Sewing kit
Light bulbs
Clocks
Iron and ironing board
Sewing machine—if you sew

Each homemaker develops her own methods of working in the kitchen. Certain utensils and gadgets will undoubtedly become more useful than others. The following list of food-preparation and service equipment is merely suggested as a basis, though not all of these pieces would be absolutely essential right at the beginning.

Dinnerware
Glassware
Flatware
Kettle
Saucepans (two small; one large)
Skillets
Roasting pan

Baking pans
Cookie sheets
Measuring cups
Measuring spoons
Mixing bowls
Colander
Strainer
Grater
Cutting board
Pitcher
Lemon juicer
Funnel
Carving set
Set of five utensils—large spoon, masher, pan-
cake turner, tonged fork, spatula
Food chopper
Can opener
Minute timer
Meat thermometer
Potholders
Canisters
Salt and pepper shakers
Toaster
Coffeemaker
Hand mixer
Trays

There are several other items that may be useful:

Dutch oven or pressure cooker
Electric fry pan
Electric blender
Muffin pans
Cookie cutters
Ring mold
Fluted mold
Baster
Tongs

The above lists are merely suggested. It is important to develop one's own lists designed to meet specific needs. For example, a spice rack, a chafing dish, a salad basket, and an egg poacher may also be important items in one person's kitchen, but they might be useless to someone else. The homemaker should decide which items are the most essential as basic equipment. The requirements will depend upon how she manages and operates her home.

20

Selection of Furniture

When one arrives at the point of actually purchasing furniture, the natural question is "How do you judge quality?" Unfortunately there is no simple, easy answer. The problem of the consumer is complicated in this respect by several factors. It takes time and effort to acquire the background knowledge that is essential if money is to be spent wisely.

The wide variety of furniture that is available ranges in quality from poor to excellent. Many of the features that determine quality depend upon how the manufacturer selects and handles his materials. There are many things the consumer cannot see or judge when shopping for a piece of furniture. These features are often referred to as "hidden" values. For example, wood must be properly aged or seasoned before it is used. It is impossible to tell just by looking at a piece of furniture whether or not this seasoning process has been done under carefully controlled conditions. In upholstered furniture it is particularly difficult to judge quality because the filling materials, framework, springs, and so on are completely obscured. Even if they could be seen, it would be difficult to determine whether or not the piece would really meet specific needs. In addition, the labels that do exist or any that are required by law are of little help because they often state information that has no meaning to the consumer who is questioning serviceability, durability, performance, and so on. Although many reliable stores try to maintain a sales staff that is both well informed and helpful, the word of the salesman is not always the most reassuring basis on which to buy. In absence of written guarantees, the consumer who returns to complain about merchandise that has not proved satisfactory only too often finds that the glib-talking salesclerk is too busy with other customers to show much interest or concern. Once one has the furniture in his own home and has used it, he is at the mercy of the dealer and the manufacturer as to whether or not they will stand behind their product. Reliable merchants will do this because they want to maintain the goodwill of their customers.

Although good materials and high standards of workmanship are costly, price is not always an indication of excellent serviceability. The mere fact that one bought the most expensive item does not mean that it will measure up to his needs in every way.

In spite of all these complications, the intelligent consumer who is well fortified with basic information and who is willing to do some comparative shopping will soon learn to be discriminating.

General Points to Consider

Before any piece of furniture is actually purchased, there are certain features that should be examined. These include:

DESIGN. The piece must harmonize with the other furnishings of the room. The lines, color, and texture should express the mood or theme of the room and blend well with all the other pieces.

COST. Is the price within the range of the budget? Almost all furniture should be purchased with the idea of using it over a long period of time. It must, therefore, be considered an investment.

SIZE. The scale of the piece should relate to the size of the room and the other furniture in the room. If the piece is to be placed against a wall, will it be in proportion to the wall area? With some very large pieces another practical problem may arise when it is time to deliver the piece to the home and the place where it is to be used. In an apartment house, delivering a ten-foot sofa, a large piano, or a huge breakfront may pose quite a problem.

FUNCTION. How is the piece to be used, and will it serve the purposes for which it is intended? A lounge chair should be comfortable. A table that will be used next to a chair should be about the same level as the arm of the chair. A dining table should be a comfortable height for the people who use it. Coffee tables should be large enough to be useful for

entertaining; storage units must be large enough to hold the items to be stored.

It has already been pointed out that many dual-purpose pieces are appealing at first, but in actual use they are not quite so practical.

Furniture may be divided into two general categories:

(a) Case goods. These include chests, desks, tables, bookcases, and chairs that have no upholstered parts. Most of this type of furniture is made of wood, although other materials are becoming increasingly popular.

(b) Upholstered pieces. Sofas and chairs that are wholly or partially upholstered and bedding would be in this category.

Case Goods

There are specific features that might be considered when case goods are bought. Some of these one can see for himself; others he will have to ask about. One should not hesitate to question the salesman about the parts that cannot be examined.

RIGIDITY. One should place a hand firmly on a table or a chest of drawers and try to rock it back and forth. It should be sturdy enough to withstand firm pressure; any piece that wobbles is poorly constructed.

UNEXPOSED PARTS. The finishing on the underneath parts of a table or the back panel of a chest is often a clue to the manufacturer's standards. It is quite natural that these areas will not be of the same quality as the exposed parts, but they should be sanded smooth and stained to match the rest of the piece. The back panel of a chest of drawers should match the frame precisely and be fitted in place in an inconspicuous fashion. On poor-quality furniture, these unexposed areas may have little finishing; the wood may be rough and uneven; there may have been only a careless attempt to match the color; and the back panels are often uneven and only roughly nailed in position.

CONSTRUCTION. The style and quality of any particular piece will determine how many steps are necessary for its production from beginning to end. Naturally, the more labor involved, the higher the production costs, and these are always reflected in the retail price.

Furniture construction is a complicated process. It is unnecessary for the consumer to delve in detail into techniques, but there are a few points that should be discussed because they influence quality and cost.

Shaping. For whole pieces that will be made of solid wood or for some parts such as pedestals and legs, the lumber is cut to the desired size by saws. A plane may then be used to shape the edges. If no decorative effects are required, the next step may be sanding. Much of this can be done by machine but some areas still require hand finishing.

Carving. Certain types of decorative cutting can also be done by machine, but the results are somewhat crude and this process is used on mass-produced inexpensive furniture only. For better qualities, the initial work may be done by machine, but hand labor is used for the finishing. Hand carving is found only on expensive furniture because the process is slow and laborious. It must be done by skilled craftsmen who are trained in the art.

Some carved effects are achieved by the use of a wood compound molded to the desired shape. The motif, often a beaded molding, is then glued in place on the piece of furniture.

Turning. Legs, posts, and bases may be shaped by a *turning lathe*, which cuts symmetrical indentations to form a design. The effect of a twisted rope is achieved when the block of wood is moved slowly along the cutting machine.

Fluting. Lengthwise grooves may be cut into posts, legs, and pedestals.

Reeding. The term *reeding* refers to a decorative process of applying parallel rows of beaded mountings that project from the surface. It is the opposite of fluting, and it too is used on legs and posts.

Joining. The various sections of a piece of furniture must be joined firmly and securely. Careful joinery is an art that is of utmost importance to the consumer, yet most of it is hidden from view in the finished piece. One must therefore rely on the words of the manufacturer that the piece has been joined with care and precision.

Nails, screws, and glue are also used to hold sections together at points of strain. Nails are the least desirable, but they are quick and cheap to use. Screws and bolts are more desirable when they are inconspicuous. They are frequently used for added security. A metal washer under the head prevents the screw from wearing away at the wood. Good-quality glue is also used to hold surfaces together. Old-fashioned glues would eventually dry out, but new developments have produced glues that are firm, durable bonding agents. They are resistant to the ordinary hazards of use, such as heat and moisture.

Various methods are used to join the frameworks of chairs, chests, tables, desks, and so on. On high-quality furniture the joinings are as near perfectly matched as possible, smooth and tight. One should beware of crevices and gaps that have been filled in with glue or other filler. These reflect a low standard of workmanship.

Butt. This is a simple joining made by nailing or gluing two ends together. It will not withstand much strain.

Miter. This is used on square corners. Each edge is cut on a 45-degree angle and the two are held together with glue, nails, or brads. Used on moldings, picture frames, and so on.

Lap. Two pieces have equal-sized grooves so that they are flush when placed together.

Tongue and Groove. A projection on one edge fits into a matching groove on the other edge. Used on drawer sections and wood panels used for wall coverings.

Dovetail. A series of projections fit into a series of grooves; the grooves are often fan-shaped. This is a secure joining that usually indicates good craftsmanship.

Dowel. A small peg of wood is used to join two edges. The dowel pins are used for various types of joining on chairs, frames for upholstered pieces, and so on. Double dowels provide added stability. Sometimes the dowels are grooved so that air can escape when the dowels are driven into place.

Mortise and Tenon. This is one of the strongest joinings for frames of chairs, and other case goods. A groove (mortise) on one edge is cut to fit a projection (tenon) on the other edge. The projection and the groove may be square or triangular. Sometimes glue or screws are added for extra reinforcement.

DRAWERS AND DOORS. If the piece in question has drawers, these are frequently a good indication of the general level of workmanship.

The drawer should glide back and forth easily. Those mounted on metal tracks often have wheels or ball bearings to ensure easy movement. A drawer-stop, or tiny lock on the back of the drawer, prevents it from pulling all the way out unless the lever is released.

The insides of the drawers on good-quality furniture are smoothly finished and treated with a coat of shellac or varnish. The top edges on the back and sides are rounded for smoother operation.

Drawer sections are joined by dovetailing on better-quality furniture. If the wood used in the drawer is good quality, this is a secure method of construction. However, if the wood is of poor quality, the tiny projections split away and the drawer will fall apart. This is another example in which quality is dependent on a combination of good material and good craftsmanship.

Drawer pulls also offer some indication of quality. All handles and hardware on any piece of furniture should be in keeping with the design of the piece. They should be firm and substantial enough to withstand strain over a long period of time. Drawer handles should be fastened in place by screws or bolts that go through the drawer panel. On some inferior furniture the hardware is merely nailed in place on the exterior.

On many well-made pieces a panel of plywood or fiber board is used to separate the drawer areas. This *dust partition* may serve a useful purpose in adding some rigidity to the frame. It protects articles placed in the drawer and helps to prevent the jamming of one drawer by material in another drawer.

Glass Doors. Cabinets and breakfronts often have doors made with panes of glass set into a wood frame. On high-quality furniture, the door might be composed of a rather intricate latticework of wood with each piece of glass set in place as an individual section. This process, called *muntin* or *mullion*, is expensive, especially if the glass sections are curved or bent. Less expensive copies of such design often use one panel of glass with a wooden lattice or fret superimposed on it.

Hardware. Naturally the design of the handles and drawer pulls should be in keeping with the style of the piece. Well-made metal hardware is heavy and substantial.

The hinges on doors and drop-leaf tables should be carefully examined. They must be sturdy and firm. Screws are usually more desirable than nails for holding hardware in place.

FIGURE 20-1

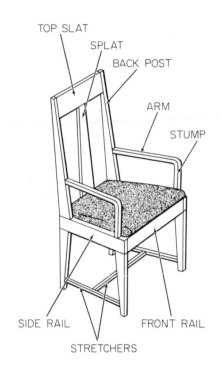

(a) Details of a chair.

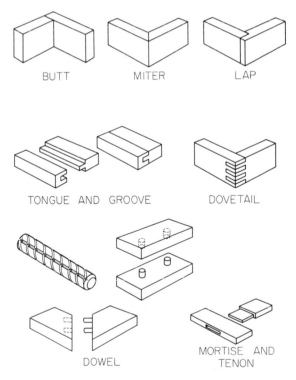

(b) Types of joints.

Supports. Tables and desks that open out often require some sort of support for the surface. In the case of desks, wooden brackets that may be pulled out to support the writing surface are desirable. Extension tables should usually have some sort of extra legs or braces to support the center section when the table is used with several leaves.

FINISHES. Manufacturers of fine-quality furniture take great pride in selecting materials. The surface of the wood is treated and polished to develop a beautiful color and patina—a mellowness or "glow" that comes from much rubbing and polishing. The grain pattern is carefully placed to enhance the design of the piece; sometimes panels are formed of matched sections to form an intricate design. On poor-quality furniture, the surface color and gloss may be applied in the cheapest and quickest manner possible, often a quick coat of varnish in which even the brush marks are evident. There is a hard shine rather than a subtle sheen.

The initial steps of finishing may be done by machine, but the final operations in high-quality furniture are usually done by hand. Several sandings and applications of stain develop a uniformity of color and bring out the beauty of the grain pattern. Some woods must have a "sealer" to close off the pores of the grain. Any special decorative effects, such as ebony finish or tortoiseshell, would be applied at this stage.

Wood finishes are applied for various reasons:

(a) To produce or develop color.
(b) To seal off the pores and produce a smooth, level surface.
(c) To protect the wood from heat, moisture, alcohol, and so on.
(d) To decorate the surface.

In fine finishing, several applications of stain, glaze, oil, or wax require sanding or rubbing in between. As these processes are repeated a richness and depth of tone develops. Naturally, the number of operations affects retail costs, but high-quality finish must be applied in a series of processes and can't be hurried.

Some manufacturers of fine furniture maintain that the lovely patina of the wood can be developed only by time-consuming hand methods and that machine polishing simply does not produce the same effects. They use hand rubbing of oil and wax finishes to produce sleek, satiny textures.

Distressing. This is a process used to give an old look to new woods. The surface is beaten and dented with light chains and then rubbed to develop a patina.

DECORATION. Those furniture styles that require some form of embellishment, such as inlay or stenciling, are naturally more expensive to produce than the plain, simple forms. Dollar-for-dollar one can expect better quality in furniture that is unadorned. In the more elaborate styles, one should be sure to buy furniture that has such decorative details executed with a high degree of skill. There can be elegance in simplicity, but it is difficult to achieve elaborate elegance on a low budget.

Fine carving and inlay work are expensive modes of decoration and they are rarely found in low-cost quality furniture. Cheap imitations that stimulate such skillful craftsmanship are usually crude and unattractive. In addition, they are done with poor-quality materials, which makes the situation worse. Here is one instance in which price is some indication of quality, and one can develop his powers of discrimination by carefully examining furniture in all price ranges from very low to very high. In the more expensive types, the decorative detail will be more refined and more tastefully executed. The crudeness of the cheap imitations will soon become obvious.

MATERIALS. Wood always has been and still is the favored material for furniture construction. However, metal, glass, plastic, and various fibers are also used, particularly for furniture in the modern style. Frequently, interesting effects are achieved by the use of these various materials in combinations.

Wood. The advantages of wood far outweigh any disadvantages of its use as a medium for creating beautiful furniture. The wide variety of natural color is further increased by the ability of wood to take stains and bleaches. Lovely textures and grain patterns are enhanced by polishing, which develops the mellow glow or patina. Because wood can be carved, it lends itself to a range of decorative effects. When properly treated and handled, most wood is sturdy and durable. The difficulties that arise in the use of wood result from the fact that it absorbs and loses moisture, which sometimes causes warping and splitting if it has not been properly *seasoned*. This process consists of drying the wood after the tree has been cut and it must be done under carefully controlled conditions to ensure excellence of quality. Wood has great strength across the grain, but it is relatively weak along the grain, which accounts for the splitting of improperly handled wood. Modern methods of kiln drying have made it possible to control carefully the moisture content of wood; the problems of warping and splitting are reduced to a minimum when wood is properly treated.

Wood is composed mainly of cellulose in the form of long fibers or cells. The characteristics and arrangement of these fibers are responsible for such qualities as the ability of wood to hold nails and screws and the ability to absorb paints, stains, and lacquers. As new fibers are formed during the growth of the tree, the grain pattern of wood develops. Various species of woods have different types of fibers that affect the texture. Maple and birch have a fine grain; oak has a coarse or open grain. Mahogany and walnut have a medium grain texture.

Fiber formation varies at different seasons of the year. A cross section of a tree trunk reveals the fibers arranged in annual rings or concentric circles. On some parts of the tree the fiber arrangement is distorted so that an interesting and unusual grain pattern develops. The familiar crotch figures occur at points where the trunk divides to form branches. Swirl patterns are often found just above the roots. Trees that form many small branches have knots that provide an interesting pattern, such as the familiar knotty pine. Abnormal growths on the tree trunk also produce unusual patterns. These growths, known as burls, are often responsible for beautifully figured grains. Other designs formed by fibers that have become twisted, curled, or wrinkled frequently have grain patterns that have lovely textural qualities.

Labeling. In December, 1963, The Federal Trade Commission promulgated Trade Practice Rules for the Household Furniture Industry. False and misleading representations of the wood and the wood imitations used in furniture are prohibited. The rules also cover leather and leather imitations, the outer coverings and the stuffing of upholstered furniture, as well as certain practices such as deceptive pricing and bait advertising. With regard to wood, the rules are quite specific in defining the practices that are considered unfair or misleading. In the future, the consumer will probably find more informative and more meaningful labels on furniture.

Hardwood and Softwood. A very broad and general classification of furniture woods divides them into hard and soft. This division refers to a botanical difference rather than to any definite degree of hardness that separates the two categories. Hardwood trees have broad, flat leaves that fall off after maturity. The softwood trees have needles or scalelike leaves that they retain all year; they are the evergreens. The two groups differ in cell structure, appearance, and general properties. Most hardwoods are stronger and less likely to dent than the softwoods; they also hold nails and screws more securely. But hardwoods range considerably in degree of hardness. There are some, such as basswood, aspen, and poplar, that are actually softer than some of the so-called softwoods. Pine, spruce, hemlock, redwood, and cedar are all classified as softwoods. Another softwood—yew—is often as hard as or harder than oak.

Solid Wood and Veneers. Some furniture is made entirely of solid wood. The logs of a tree are cut into boards of varying thicknesses, and wood sawn in this manner is called *lumber*. There are various ways of sawing the log to reveal the grain pattern in different ways.

Veneer refers to a thin slice of wood. Several layers of wood, usually three, five, or seven, are arranged with the lengthwise grain in alternate directions to form *plywood*. The top layer, or face veneer, is often cut from a log selected for beauty of grain, color, and texture; the other layers are made of good-quality wood that is strong and stable but less costly. The center layer, or core, is usually thicker than the others. All layers are glued together with synthetic resin that provides a very secure bond.

The principle of veneering dates back to ancient times. It was also used by the master cabinetmakers of the eighteenth century on exquisite tables and chests. Modern techniques provide plywood that is both stable and durable. Because of the plastic glues and alternating grains, plywood is equally strong lengthwise and crosswise and is therefore often more stable than solid wood. Plywood is used in

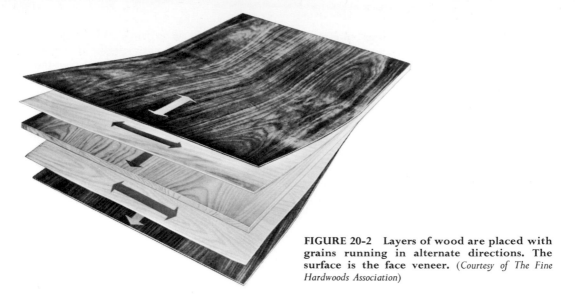

FIGURE 20-2 Layers of wood are placed with grains running in alternate directions. The surface is the face veneer. (*Courtesy of The Fine Hardwoods Association*)

much of the finest-quality furniture, both in the exposed parts and in the hidden areas. Rare and exotic woods are often used for the exposed surfaces.

Popular Furniture Woods. Use of various woods goes through fashion cycles. At the present time we use quite a variety of woods, and the designers in the modern style seem to be especially perceptive in choosing colors, textures, and grains that become an integral part of the design. This bond between form and material in contemporary design has served to further strengthen and deepen our appreciation of the beautiful qualities of wood as a medium for fine furniture.

In addition, new techniques for handling wood as a decorative medium are making it even more versatile. It is possible to inject dye into the living tree to obtain interesting color effects in the grain pattern. A relatively new process with the trade name of Fineline produces most unusual textural effects. Sheets of veneer are laminated into a solid block of wood, which is then sliced at right angles to the layers. In this manner it is possible to produce veneers with vertically striped patterns. Countless variations may be produced by alteration of the order and the species of veneers when laying up the block. Different methods of cutting the block also allow for a wide variety of pattern.

Mahogany. An excellent hardwood that is favored for fine furniture is mahogany. The best varieties grow in topical regions of Central America, the West Indies, South America, and Africa. Other woods are similar to genuine mahogany but not botanically related to it. Lauan, known also as Philippine mahogany, and primavera, known also as white mahogany, are both used for furniture but they are not true mahogany.

The master cabinetmakers of the past often preferred to use mahogany because of its strength, variety of beautiful grain figures, and workability. It has a uniform texture that is adaptable to many interesting finishes. Natural mahogany varies in color from a light golden brown to a deeper tone with a red cast. The traditional use of mahogany developed the reddish tones through applications of stains and finishes. This deep, rich purple or red came to be accepted as the natural color of the wood. In modern use mahogany is frequently finished to enhance its natural light brown color or it is bleached to an even lighter tone.

Walnut. Ever since the Renaissance, walnut has been an important wood for both furniture and interior architectural designs. This popularity is due to a combination of great beauty and practical characteristics.

The various species of walnut differ in color, so a range of tones is available. The native American walnut, or black walnut, is so named because of the color of the nut shells. The wood ranges from light to dark in rich grayish-brown tones. Butternut, another native American wood, is lighter in color and is often called white walnut. Circassian walnut from the regions near the Black Sea is a rich brown color. Its dramatic curly grain makes it ideal for decorative effects, but it is very rare and therefore expensive.

The American walnuts produce a wide variety of beautiful grain patterns. Crotch, burl, and stumpwood are all popular figures.

The wood is hard but not so hard that it cannot be worked easily. It has a natural resistance to shrinking and warping. Its high strength lends it to slim, tapered legs and other parts that must withstand strain. The medium grain is excellent for holding glue and it readily takes a wide variety of finishes, particularly the currently popular oiled finish.

Pecan. Increasing in popularity is pecan, a strong wood that is dense and hard. It is readily available in America but the seasoning requires special skill. The texture, grain, and natural light color of pecan lend themselves to a variety of stains and finishes with excellent results.

Oak. Many species of oak trees are found in North America, Asia, Europe, and Africa. About fifty varieties of oak are native to the United States, but the best known are white oak and red oak. The natural color ranges from a light yellow to amber-brown.

Oak is characterized by a coarse, open grain, which is particularly suited to various color effects and special finishes. A filler is sometimes rubbed into the wood to emphasize the coarse grain. This limed oak has enjoyed periods of considerable popularity in modern furniture.

The hard, durable qualities of oak plus its resistance to the vagaries of climate have resulted in its wide use for paneling and flooring as well as for furniture. From medieval times with elaborate methods of hand carving to the modern era with machine methods, the sturdy, versatile oak has appealed to craftsmen.

Maple. Although maple trees grow in many parts of the world, the sugar maple or rock maple of the northern United States was used so extensively for furniture during colonial times that its color and texture are closely associated with the style of that era. The close-grained wood is hard, strong, and durable. It resists splitting and is easy to shape. The fine texture takes a beautiful, smooth finish and the color ranges from almost white to a reddish brown.

Although most of the maple used in modern and Colonial-style furniture has a plain, straight grain, some varieties yield a curly, wavy grain figure that is on a par with other woods prized for lovely designs. Bird's-eye maple is quite rare, but it has an interesting grain pattern caused by an abnormal growth of buds that could not get through the bark of the tree. The resulting distortion of the annual rings produces a very interesting design in the wood.

Birch. Another strong, versatile hardwood with a close, even texture comes from the yellow birch tree, also known as the silver or swamp birch. The general characteristics of birch are similar to those of maple. Its durable qualities and relatively low cost make it a popular choice for doors, floors, wood trim, plywood, and the structural parts of furniture.

The natural color of birch is a pale golden brown, but it can be bleached or stained to resemble other woods, including maple, walnut, and mahogany. Most birch has a straight grain, but some varieties have curly figures that are usually reserved for veneers.

Birch takes paints and stains extremely well and can be polished to a lovely glowing luster.

Fruitwood. Consumers seem to have the misconception that this term refers to a particular species, but actually there is no *one* fruit wood. Cherry, apple, and pear woods are the most commonly used fruit woods. Other woods, such as birch and maple, are sometimes given a fruit-wood finish. They are colored in the delicate brown tones associated with much of the French Provincial furniture that was actually made of fruit wood. They are also frequently given a distressing treatment to make them simulate old, used, and time-worn woods.

The wild black cherry tree is the most widely used of the fruit woods in present-day furniture construction. Cherry has been used for many centuries in various countries, but we probably associate it most closely with Early American and Colonial furniture. It is strong, durable, and moderately hard. Much cherry has a natural reddish-brown color, but tones vary to amber and to a light yellow that may be almost white. The close grain is suited to a variety of finishes, and although the grain markings are not as dramatic as in some other woods, they do provide textural interest. Cherry furniture is likely to be expensive because there is much waste in cutting the logs.

Both apple and pear are smooth woods

(a) Mahogany

(b) Walnut

(c) Pecan

(d) Oak

(e) Maple

(g) Rosewood

(f) Cherry

(h) Zebrawood

that are fine-grained and light in color. They are rarely used today except for decorative trim and inlay work on fine furniture.

Teak. Furniture designers working in the modern style have favored teak, a wood native to India, Burma, and the surrounding areas. It is dense, durable, moderately hard, and easily worked. The natural color ranges from a light to a dark brown with fine black streaks. The wood darkens with age but it is often finished in a deep brown tone that is almost black. Some teak has a richly figured grain pattern, but most of it is plain.

Rosewood. Rosewood, an interesting wood ranges in color from light to dark reddish-brown. Various species come from India and Brazil. It is often figured with dark streaks that provide an interesting pattern. Rosewood polishes well and is popular for use in fine furniture and paneling.

Gum. Since the development of new methods of drying lumber, red gum has become an important addition to the family of furniture woods. If not seasoned under carefully controlled conditions, gumwood has a tendency to split and warp. However, if properly handled it is quite satisfactory and it has several advantages. It is readily available and relatively inexpensive. It is easy to work, and the close, smooth grain takes finishes extremely well. Gumwood is often used for framework, posts, and legs that must be made of solid wood. It can be finished to closely resemble other woods, such as walnut and mahogany used on veneered panels.

Ash. There are several varieties of ash used in furniture construction, mostly in frames and on unexposed parts. White ash is a hard, strong, durable wood with a grain that resembles oak. The natural color ranges from white to a light brown. Some varieties have pronounced grain patterns, especially the Japanese ash, which is also known as *tamo.*

Pine. Because pine is a softwood, its uses are not extensive in furniture construction. It is found in unpainted furniture, rustic designs, and some inexpensive cabinetwork. It is used on paneled walls.

Other woods that are used in furniture to a lesser extent are listed in Chart 1. Some of these are rare, exotic woods, used chiefly for decorative purposes; others are less expensive but for one reason or another have not achieved major importance in the furniture industry.

CHART 1 Other Woods

Acacia Hardwood from Australia and Africa. Used in ancient times for ecclesiastical purposes; also used in inlay work.

Amaranth A fine-grained hardwood that develops a red or purple color with age and exposure to air. Used for decorative work and inlay. Imported from Central and South America.

Amboyna Wood from the East Indies. Characterized by rich brown color with burls or mottled patterns in tones of yellow, orange, and red.

Aspen The white poplar of Europe. Simple figured grain; polishes to a satiny texture with high luster.

Avodire Gold or yellowish-white wood from western Africa. Grain is characterized by a rippled or mottled pattern in attractive designs.

Bamboo Treelike grass with woody stem that is smooth and lustrous. Yellowish tan in color. Characterized by knobby joints. Used for furniture and many decorative purposes.

Basswood Softwood with little or no figure. Used mostly for cores and for inexpensive furniture. Creamy white in color.

Beech A hard, strong wood that is dense in texture. Color ranges from white to slightly reddish tones. Must be carefully seasoned to prevent warping. Lends itself well to turning and polishing. Used in medium-priced furniture for frames, curved sections such as runners on rockers, drawer guides, and bent backs on chairs.

Cedar Various types that range in color from pale to dark reddish-brown. Pleasant natural odor repels moth larvae. Used for lining closets, storage chests; also for shingles and sidings.

Chestnut Gray-brown wood with coarse, open grain similar to oak. Not particularly durable although it resists warping. Used for core stock and for some less expensive furniture.

Circassian Walnut Highly figured wood from the Black Sea region. Brown color. Expensive. Used for paneling and furniture.

Cypress Light brown wood with close grain. Durable and extremely resistant to warping. Comes from southern and western states. Used for face veneers and for outdoor furniture.

Douglas Fir A strong, durable, creamy white or yellow wood from western United States. Similar to pine. Used for paneling, structural parts (and for exposed parts on inexpensive furniture), and for plywood.

Ebony A hard, heavy wood from Africa and tropical Asia. Dark brown or almost black in color; fine grain and smooth texture takes a high polish.

Elm Strong and tough wood from Europe and parts of United States. Color ranges from light to dark reddish-brown. Bends well, but it tends to warp and twist. Used for kitchen furniture, interior trim and frames, and decorative veneers.

Hackberry Light Colored wood that takes finishes well. Similar to elm.

Harewood (English Sycamore) A close-, fine-grained wood often dyed a silver-gray color. Figured grain in fiddle design used for veneer work.

Hemlock Similar to white pine. Lightweight and easy to work. Not used extensively for finishing.

Hickory Tough, heavy, and hard. Tree belongs to the walnut family. Not used extensively.

Holly Fine grain. Light in color, sometimes almost white. Used with other woods for marquetry.

Kingwood Used in fine cabinetwork because of dark brown color with streaks of black and yellow. Comes from South America and Sumatra.

Koa Figured wood that ranges from a medium tone of golden brown to dark shades. Comes from Hawaii and was formerly called Hawaiian mahogany.

Korina Light-colored wood from the Congo. Available in plain or figured grain patterns. Similar to Primavera.

Lacewood Durable wood from Australia. Polishes to high luster. Ranges in color from pinkish to light brown tones.

Laurel Highly figured with wavy grain pattern. Dark reddish-brown color can be bleached to lighter tones. Takes a high polish. Comes from India.

Limba Another name for Korina.

Linden Another name for Basswood.

Magnolia Similar to yellow poplar but harder and heavier. Smooth, fine grain that sometimes has a slight figure.

Makore African cherry. Similar to cherry.

Myrtle Usually light in color with a curly grain pattern. Used for veneers and panels. Comes from western United States.

Paldao Ranges in color from grayish to reddish brown. Interesting patterns. Comes from Philippines.

Poplar Several types that grow in eastern and southern United States range in color from white through yellow to light brown. Yellow poplar also known as whitewood. Easy to work, lightweight takes especially well to paints and finishes.

Primavera Light-colored wood with lovely grain pattern. Comes from Mexico. Sometimes called white mahogany. Takes well to high polish.

Purpleheart Same as Amaranth.

Rattan A vine rather than a wood. Used extensively for wicker furniture. Comes from Asia.

Redwood Durable, strong, and lightweight. Attractive red color. Resists weather and insects. Used extensively in western part of United States for outdoor furniture and some indoor work.

Sandalwood Close grain; yellow-brown, fragrant wood. Used in Oriental furniture and woodwork.

Satinwood Light-colored with lovely texture and grain pattern. Used in inlay work and border designs. Comes from India and West Indies.

Spruce Strong, lightweight wood; holds glue well. Sometimes used for core stock.

Sycamore Color is reddish to red-brown; may have interesting grain pattern. Dense and hard but some tendency to warp. Comes from eastern United States and England.

Tulipwood Light yellow streaked with red or purple stripes. Used for ornamental work.

Tupelo (Black Gum) Easily worked and may have intricate grain pattern. Tends to warp. Used for same purposes as other gumwoods.

Willow Rather soft wood not used extensively for solid construction. Flexible branches often used for wicker furniture.

Yew Hard and durable; close grained. European evergreen.

Zebrawood Characterized by brown or black stripes on light yellow background. Used mostly for ornamental work.

Other Materials. Although wood is still by far the favored material for furniture, other materials are becoming increasingly popular, especially in modern designs. Metals, plastics, and glass are favorites; caning is also used for panels and chair seats. Frequently these materials are combined with wood.

Metals. Brass, steel, and wrought iron are all used for legs, frames, and trim on various types of furniture. Copper and aluminum also find favor for certain designs.

Metal has a number of advantages as a furniture material. It is strong and durable, it is suitable for indoor and outdoor use; it can be easily molded and shaped. Joining by bolts, rivets, or welding is secure and sturdy. Aluminum outdoor furniture has been extremely popular because it withstands weather conditions; it is easily washed with soap and it is light in weight. However, surface finishes on metals will sometimes wear off and occasionally they are difficult to repair or replace.

Brass and brass finishes combine beautifully with interesting wood grains. The color and texture of this metal has appealed to designers in the modern style.

Plastics. Synthetics have become a vital part of the home furnishings field in many areas, including the actual construction of furniture. Molded chairs represent for modern design a complete break with traditional methods. Sturdy, durable, light in weight, interesting in texture, easily maintained, and relatively inexpensive, the plastics would seem to qualify for a major role in furniture construction. And so they have.

In previous chapters we have referred to periods such as the "age of walnut," the "age of mahogany." It is quite possible that in the future the twentieth century will be referred to as the "age of plastics" or the "age of the molecule." In Chapter 12 we discussed some of the plastics in connection with the modern style. They are becoming increasingly important in producing molded components and laminated surfaces for other styles as well. That the practical aspects of a surface impervious to moisture, resistant to heat, and easily cleaned with soap and water should appeal to the busy homemaker is understandable. There are numerous pieces that are made with wood as the basic material but finished off with a matching laminated surface to make it more serviceable and easier to maintain.

In a rather short period of time, man-made substances have permeated almost every phase of living, including medicine, construction, transportation, agriculture, and textiles. In spite of the impact that has been made, the plastics industry is still in a stage of infancy. It is difficult to imagine the innovations that will certainly influence our homes in the future but as one representative phrased it, "the best is yet to come."

Glass. For many years, the top surfaces of tables and chests were protected with glass, but the idea of a glass top has become rather old-fashioned. Glass has instead branched out into a more glamorous role in home furnishings. Thick plates of glass are used as tops for dining tables designed for both outdoor and indoor use.

FIGURE 20-4 **Molded components represent a new concept in furniture construction.** (*Courtesy of Shell Chemical Company*)

(a) A series of molds is necessary to produce simulated wood components.

(b) Wide design latitudes are possible with the new application of plastics. Chair backs are made of molded polymer.

(c) Testing in a research laboratory indicates high strength of molded components.

(d) Door panels molded of polymer indicate the versatility of this new technique.

Upholstered Furniture and Bedding

So much of the quality of any upholstered piece is hidden under the covering that it is extremely difficult for the consumer to judge value. There are some features that he can observe and test very carefully, but for the most part he must rely on the word of the dealer and the small amount of information that he may find on labels. This is certainly a case where the consumer should have confidence in both the dealer and the manufacturer before he invests any money.

CHAIRS AND SOFAS. Just as in the matter of case goods, the design of an upholstered chair or sofa must blend into the theme of the room and harmonize with other furnishings. The problem of slipcovering and reupholstering should also be considered. Slipcovers on upholstered furniture not only protect the fabric covering but allow a change of pace once in a while. As a matter of fact, some people prefer to buy furniture upholstered in muslin and keep two (or more) sets of slipcovers so they can change the color scheme for different seasons of the year. A removable slipcover reduces the problem of care, because it is easier to wash or dry-clean a cover than the actual upholstery. Although this is a matter of personal preference, furniture with simple, straight lines is easier and less expensive to cover or to reupholster. Intricate curves such as might be found in fan-back or tub chairs are difficult to fit with slipcovers. Upholstery that is tufted and held with buttons is usually more expensive to replace.

Some modern furniture has been designed with these problems in mind. The "upholstery" is really separate cushions, which are especially easy to recover.

Certain other specific points should be checked before the purchase of any upholstered pieces. These would include:

Comfort. We depend on upholstered pieces in our home for comfortable sitting and sleeping. It would be foolish, naturally, to buy a chair or a sofa without considering the people who will be using it most. A seat that slants a bit toward the back is usually more comfortable, but again this is a matter of personal preference. Some chairs that are very deep are uncomfortable for short people, whereas others that are too shallow are uncomfortable for tall people. Adequate support for legs, hips, and shoulders is necessary. The height, width, and slant of the seat and back should be tested carefully. The height of the arms will also affect comfort. One should try sitting in chairs and sofas with high sides, compare them with others that have lower arms or no arms at all, and then make a choice in terms of the purpose the piece will have to serve.

The firmness or softness of upholstery is another feature that must be considered for comfort. This too is a matter of personal choice.

Exposed Parts of Frame. If a piece has legs or a frame that is not covered, the finish should be examined very carefully. The workmanship here may be some indication of inside quality. Wood should have an even color tone and a rich texture. Carving or ornamental work should be refined and smooth.

Seams. The construction lines that are evident on the exterior should be firm, smooth, and even. A cording or welting is frequently used in the seams of upholstery for added strength and durability as well as for appearance. A firm clean finish with no projecting thread ends, bumps, or puckers is one sign of good workmanship.

On some designs decorative brass nailheads are used to emphasize a line. On better-quality furniture these are usually placed very close together.

Covering. It may be necessary to purchase a piece covered as it is, but more often the consumer will have a choice of upholstery fabric. If the sample swatches are small, it is not always easy to visualize the whole piece in its finished form, so one must be very careful about color, texture, and pattern. The chair or sofa may take on a completely different appearance when covered in another fabric.

Pieces that will receive hard use should of course be covered with a fabric that resists both soil and wear, especially if slipcovers will not be used all the time. Upholstery fabrics are discussed in Chapter 22, but we might point out here that a closely woven fabric in a medium color tone is a good choice for pieces that will receive hard wear. In many areas of the home the new plastic upholstery fabrics are becoming popular. The newer elegant styling of these easy-care coverings has increased their versatility and made them more generally acceptable. However, in some areas the warmer texture of the more traditional upholstery fabrics may be preferable.

Construction. It is important to know something about the way upholstered furniture is made so that it is possible to ask questions about any pieces being considered. The quality features concealed within the piece determine serviceability, durability, and comfort.

Framework. The basic frame of an upholstered piece must be carefully designed and constructed to withstand stress and strain over a long period of time. A hardwood that is free from imperfections and that has been kiln dried is most desirable. Ash, birch, maple, oak, and gumwood are commonly used. The frame must hold nails and screws securely and any wood that is soft or improperly seasoned will not be satisfactory in this respect.

The joints on good-quality frames are usually double-dowel constructions that employ kiln-dried, grooved pegs. Corners should be reinforced with triangular blocks carefully fitted and fastened with glue and screws. Metal plates are sometimes used for strengthening corners.

Springs. On most chairs and sofas, bands of webbing are interlaced and tacked to the frame. Woven jute is commonly used because it is strong, durable, and resilient. A steel and plastic combination is also used for webbing, and in some constructions plain steel bands form the base. The coil springs in better-quality furniture are made of tempered steel and are placed close together. Twelve coils for each seat area is best; there should be no less than eight. In high-quality construction the springs are tied in place with good-grade twine. Proper tying is important in keeping the springs firmly in place and in providing the correct degree of resiliency. It is desirable to have each spring hand-tied eight times. The coils are anchored to the webbing or to steel bands. In some high-quality pieces, the springs are covered with a muslin jacket. Then a piece of good-quality strong fabric is stretched over the springs and tacked to the frame. Heavy burlap is frequently used to support the filling material.

In some of the smaller-scaled upholstered pieces, flat springs of zigzag strips of steel are used instead of coil springs. These springs do not require the support of webbing nor do they have to be tied.

Filling. The material used for upholstery filling is as important as the way the piece is constructed. Well-made furniture will have an ample amount of filling selected and applied so that the piece will retain its shape for a long period of time. Poor quality and workmanship will be evident after a relatively short period of use. The filling will shift, mat, and lump to distort the shape of the piece in a most unattractive manner.

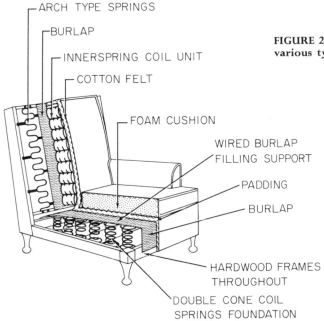

ARCH TYPE SPRINGS
BURLAP
INNERSPRING COIL UNIT
COTTON FELT
FOAM CUSHION
WIRED BURLAP
FILLING SUPPORT
PADDING
BURLAP
HARDWOOD FRAMES THROUGHOUT
DOUBLE CONE COIL SPRINGS FOUNDATION

FIGURE 20-5 An upholstered chair may have various types of springs and filling materials.

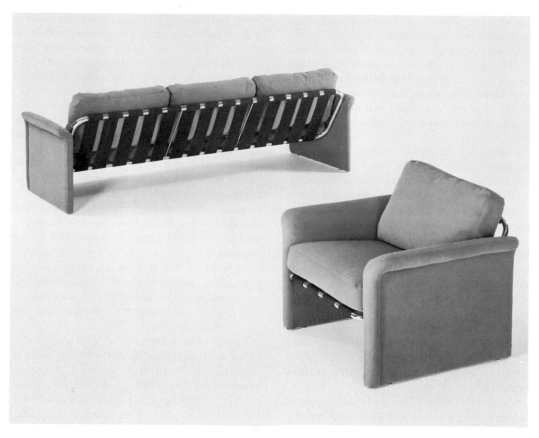

FIGURE 20-6   A new concept in construction is demonstrated here. Wide bands of black webbing on chrome plated tubular seat and back frames are used by George Mulhauser to integrate construction and design. (*Courtesy of Directional Industries, Inc.*)

Various filling materials are used for upholstered work, sometimes in combinations. Descriptive information about the filling used should be on a label permanently attached to the piece, but these labels usually do not indicate the grade or quality, which may vary considerably for each type.

Curled hair is a widely used filling because it is durable and resilient. Hair from horses, cattle, and hogs have varying degrees of body and also vary in cost. The most resilient and most expensive comes from the tails of horses. Frequently a mixture of several kinds is used.

Foam rubber has become a popular filling material for several reasons. It is durable, comfortable, and resilient. It retains its shape and is lightweight. Foam rubber may be used as a layer over a spring construction or it may be used alone.

Urethane foam is a test-tube product that has become popular as a filling material. It is resilient and lightweight, and impervious to water, perspiration, and cleaning fluids. Slabs of urethane may be sliced, cut, stitched, or glued. Because of its high tensile strength, urethane may be stretched around furniture frames without tearing. Its lightness is a desirable feature for mattresses. A twin-sized mattress of urethane foam weighs about eleven pounds as compared to thirty-five pounds for an innerspring mattress.

Dacron is a popular filling material made from polyester. It may be used by itself or with foam cores or innerspring constructions. Dacron is resilient, lightweight, odorless, and resistant to moths and mildew.

Rubberized hair or rubberized sisal may be used in medium- and low-cost furniture. The mixture is vulcanized and molded so that it has a fair degree of resiliency.

Cotton felt is sometimes used as a protective covering over springs and other filling materials. On medium- and low-priced furniture, cotton felt is often used without another more resilient filling.

Moss and shredded fibers are also used in furniture. Palm leaves, coconut husks, and sisal have some degree of resiliency but are usually found only in less expensive pieces.

The filling material is distributed over the surface of the chair. If the standards of workmanship are high, it is packed firmly and held in place to prevent lumping and shifting. This may be done by securing it to a layer of supporting burlap and placing a covering of cotton felt, foam rubber, or rubberized sisal over the filling at the top. On less expensive furniture, the upholstery fabric is the next layer, on better-quality furniture, a firm muslin is used to hold the filling in place and to serve as an interlining for the actual upholstery fabric.

Sometimes the price of an upholstered piece is quoted "in muslin." The cost of the upholstery fabric you select is then added to the retail price. It was mentioned earlier that some people prefer to buy furniture upholstered in muslin and cover it with removable slipcovers.

Tufting and Buttons. Sometimes the filling and the upholstery fabric are secured by decorative stitching or by buttons. There are advantages and disadvantages to this type of upholstering. The chief advantage is that the filling is less apt to shift out of position. If well done, it may add interest to the piece. However, it is more costly in the initial construction and also more expensive to reupholster when the piece needs recovering. If it is not used with discretion, the furniture may have a gingerbread appearance. Also, this type of upholstered piece is more difficult to keep clean because dust collects in the crevices.

Separate Cushions. Seats and sometimes backs may have separate cushions. When these are reversible, the wear can be distributed. Such chairs and sofas often seem more comfortable than those having "tight" construction in upholstery (without separate cushions).

The consumer is often given a choice of filling for cushions. Down, foam rubber, or spring constructions are used on better-quality furniture; inexpensive varieties may use cotton batting, cotton felt, kapok, or other fibers, all of which tend to become lumpy.

Down, the soft underfeathers of a goose or duck, provides a soft, luxurious filling. For added body, chopped feathers are mixed with the down. A fifty-fifty combination is commonly used. Seventy-five per cent down is softer and more expensive; less than 25 per cent down has little value so far as comfort is concerned. Many people prefer the luxurious comfort of down cushions, which have the disadvantage of having to be plumped up every time one sits on them. They depress and stay that way until fluffed up again.

Foam rubber cushions require no plumping, but the fabric covering must be firmly woven. Otherwise the covering will lose its shape and wrinkle on the cushion.

Some cushions are made with a spring construction covered with a layer of cotton felt or foam rubber. These are stable and comfortable, although they do not have the soft luxury of down cushions.

Other fillings for separate cushions include cotton, kapok, flax tow, or other fibers. None of these have the required resiliency for cushions that receive much use. They are found mostly on inexpensive furniture.

MATTRESSES AND BEDSPRINGS. Good beds are such a major item in furnishing a home that they should be selected with special care. Bargains are likely to be dangerous, because mattresses with poor construction and low-quality filling may begin to sag or become lumpy after a few months of use.

There is a wide variety of types available in different sizes and at different prices. The standard length is usually seventy-two inches; a single bed is usually thirty-nine inches wide and a double bed is fifty-four inches wide. However, longer and wider beds are becoming more popular and are readily available.

The popular types of high-quality mattresses include innerspring, foam rubber, and hair. Cotton felt is also used, but it is not likely to hold its shape as well as other materials.

Well-made innerspring mattresses have high-quality metal coils individually covered with heavy muslin. There may be several hundred small coils in one mattress. However, large coils may be satisfactory if they are made of best-quality metal and securely fastened together. A layer of filling material is placed over the springs for added comfort.

Foam rubber mattresses have become popular for a variety of reasons. They retain their shape well and are lightweight. However, there are different qualities available and one has to be sure to buy from a reliable dealer.

Hair is often used in high-quality mattresses. Layers of curled hair are used with cotton felt. Quality will vary with the type of hair and the amount. Curled horsehair is generally considered most desirable. Cattle hair and hog hair are sometimes mixed with horsehair.

Cotton felt used in layers is often found in less expensive mattresses and it may be of quite good quality. However, cotton batting or cotton fibers that have not been felted tend to mat and may cause the mattress to become lumpy.

Ticking is used as the outer cover of a mattress. It should be closely woven and strong.

Well-constructed mattresses are stitched through cover and filling to prevent the shifting of materials. This tufting is often secured by buttons. A sturdy reinforced edge will prevent the mattress from sagging at the sides. Firmly attached handles facilitate turning the mattress.

The bedspring used under a mattress provides support and is important for proper comfort. There are various types and qualities on the market, including the box spring, the open-coil spring, and several kinds of flat constructions made of bands and strips of wire.

Bedsprings are generally made of heavier gauge metal than innerspring coils. In the box spring, the coils are anchored to slats in the base and covered with ticking. Open coils are attached to metal slats and left uncovered. The box spring is usually more expensive, but it is more desirable because it is easier to clean and it has no rough areas to rub against the mattress or to tear sheets and blankets.

Springs with flat constructions do not provide as much support or resiliency as coil springs.

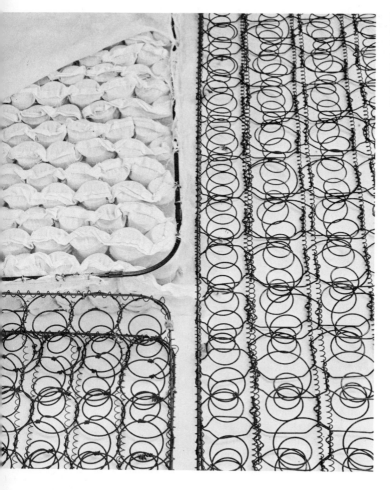

FIGURE 20-7 Of three types of coil construction tested, two proved consistently more durable than the other —the pocketed coil (upper left), and the open-end coil (right). The least durable type, the knotted-end coil, is shown at lower left. (*Courtesy of Consumers Union of U.S., Inc.*)

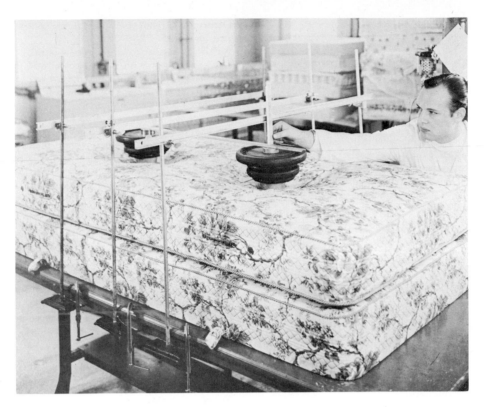

FIGURE 20-8 Various kinds of tests are performed to determine how well a mattress may be expected to conform to the body of a sleeper and to stand up under use. (*Courtesy of Consumers Union of U.S., Inc.*)

CHART 2 Furniture Types

Tables

Butler's Tray Table with hinged sides that fold up. Cut-out sections form handles.

Butterfly Small table with drop leaves that can be supported by wing brackets.

Cocktail Low table for use in front of a sofa.

Console Table made to be placed against a wall. Often made as an extension table. May have one top section that raises and rests against the wall.

Corner Square or triangular table. Often used with sectional furniture.

Dinette Small-scale dining table.

Dressing Used as vanity or powder table.

Drop-leaf Hinged sections on table drop down when not in use.

Drum Round or octagonal table with shelves, drawers, or compartments.

End Small table designed for use next to a chair or sofa.

Extension Dining table that can be enlarged by use of extra sections or leaves.

Game Top of table has game board in inlaid or painted design.

Gate-leg Has drop leaves that are supported by extra legs that are swung away from the base when the leaves are raised.

Harvest Long, narrow table with drop leaves.

Hunt Semicircular table. May have short drop leaves at both ends.

Lazy Susan Table with raised platform that revolves.

Library Long, narrow table sometimes used behind a sofa.

Nest of Tables Set of graduated tables made to form one unit.

Night Small table used next to a bed.

Parsons Usually a square table with straight legs. Often finished with high gloss enamel in bright colors.

Pembroke Small occasional table with short drop leaves.

Pie Crust Round table with edge raised and carved in fluted design.

Pier Similar to console table. Often used between two windows with mirror hung above.

Refectory Long, narrow table. May have leaves beneath it that can be pulled out.

Sawbuck Rectangular table top on X-shaped supports.

CHART 2 Furniture Types *(cont.)*

Tables (cont.)

Sewing Table designed with drawers or compartments to hold sewing equipment.

Step Table with two or more levels; adapted from library step-stools.

Table Chair Hinged top swings back so base can serve as a chair.

Tavern Small table of sturdy design.

Tea Wagon Table on wheels; often has one or more shelves below table top.

Tiered Small table with two or more levels.

Tilt-top Table top is hinged so that it may stand in vertical position.

Trestle Long table on sturdy bases.

Chairs

Barrel Chair with circular back; usually upholstered.

Bench Seat with no back; may or may not have arms.

Bergere Upholstered armchairs in the French style. Usually have exposed wood frames.

Boston Rocker Characterized by wide, decorated top rail and curved seat. Often painted black with gilt design.

Boudoir Small-scale upholstered chair designed for use in bedroom.

Captain Sturdy chair with rounded back, spindles and shaped seat.

Chaise Longue An elongated chair designed for reclining.

Club General term for a sturdy upholstered chair in simple lines and generous proportions.

Cobbler's Bench An adaptation of the old cobbler's worktable with a raised section at one end. May be used as a table or as a seat.

Cogswell Upholstered armchair with open arms and part of the wood frame exposed.

Contour Chair shaped for comfort; may adjust to different positions.

Corner Sometimes called *roundabout*. Diamond-shaped chair with one leg in the middle of the front.

Eames Seat and back of molded plywood; named after noted contemporary designer Charles Eames.

Fan-back Upholstered chair with rounded back.

Fireside Upholstered chair with recessed arms or no arms at all. Usually used in pairs.

Hassock Heavily upholstered stool. May have removable top so it can be used for storage.

Hitchcock American-type straight chair. Often painted and decorated with gilt stencil designs on top rail and crosswise splat.

Ladder-back Chair with horizontal rails or slats forming the back.

Lawson Sturdy upholstered chair in simple lines of English club furniture.

Lounge Upholstered chair with deep seat.

Occasional Small-scale chair usually used in living room.

Ottoman Upholstered bench or seat with no arms or back.

Pull-up Similar to an occasional chair.

Rocker Chair with curved runners at the base permitting the chair to tilt backward and forward. A platform rocker has a stationary base upon which the chair rocks back and forth.

Scissors (Savonarola) Slats form the side arms and base in an X-shaped arrangement.

Shell Side, back, and seat are molded from plastic or fiberglass.

Side Small chair without arms.

Stool Small seat with no arms or back. Usually mounted on legs.

Swivel Chair with seat that revolves.

Table Back of chair is hinged so that it can drop down to form a table top.

Thonet Chair with bent-wood frame.

Tub Chair with rounded back and sides.

Tubular Framework of chair is made of bent tubes, usually metal.

Wainscot Sturdy chair with panel back. Usually decorated with ornate carving.

Windsor May be side chair or arm chair. Various forms usually have bent-wood frames with spindles that form the backs. Seats are shaped; legs are attached directly to the bases of the seats and flare outward.

Wing Upholstered chair with high back- and side-sections.

Sofas and Settees

Camel-back Gracefully curved arch back.

Charles of London Upholstered sofa of sturdy club-type proportions. Usually has short, flat arms.

Lawson Sturdy upholstered club-type with square or key-shaped arms.

Love Seat Small sofa designed for seating two people.

Sectional Separate seating units designed to be used together to form a variety of arrangements.

Settee Lightweight sofa that may have open-work back and arms. Seat may or may not be upholstered.

Tete-a-tete Two-seat sofa designed so that seats face in opposite directions.

Tuxedo Sofa with slender proportions. Arms are same height as back.

Cabinets

Armoire Tall cupboard that may be used as a wardrobe or storage chest.

Bachelor Low chest of drawers with small proportions. Top may extend to form a table, or top "drawer" may open to form a desk.

Bookcase Any cabinet designed to hold books; may or may not have glass doors.

Breakfront Tall unit that usually has glass-enclosed shelves on top of drawer cabinet below. Center section usually protrudes from side sections.

Captains Sturdy wooden chest with hardware recessed so that surfaces are smooth.

Cassone   Long, low chest with elaborate ornamentation.

Cedar Chest   Long, low chest made entirely of cedar or lined with cedar for storage of household items with protection against moth damage.

Cellarette   Chest designed for storage of bottles and glasses.

Chest-on-Chest   Cabinet designed to appear as one chest placed on top of another. May have drawer or cupboard sections.

Chiffonier   Tall chest of drawers.

Chifforobe   Combination chest of drawers and wardrobe unit.

China Closet   Cabinet designed for display of china or glasses. Usually has glass front and sides.

Commode   Low cabinet with drawers and compartments. May be used against a wall or as an end table.

Corner   Any cabinet designed with a triangular back so that it can stand in a corner.

Credenza   Low cabinet with drawers or compartments. Designed to stand against a wall.

Curio   Cabinet with glass doors and sides for displaying various types of collections.

Dresser   Chest of drawers usually designed for use in a bedroom.

Etagere   Series of open shelves, supported by posts or columns.

Highboy   Tall chest that appears to be in two sections.

Hutch   A tall cupboard or sideboard that usually has open shelves on the top section and cabinets below.

Kas   Cabinet of Dutch origin. May be tall or short with compartments and drawers for storage. Sturdy, generous proportions with carved or painted decorations.

Lowboy   Low chest or table with drawers.

Room Divider   Various types of shelves and cabinets designed to separate one area from another.

Sideboard   Long, low cabinet designed to be placed against a wall. May have drawers, compartments, or a combination of both.

Wall-hung Units   Shelves and cabinets fastened to a wall with brackets.

Wardrobe   Free-standing cabinet made for storage of clothes.

Whatnot   Series of shelves designed for display of bric-a-brac. May hang on the wall or stand against a wall. Corner units often have graduated shelves.

Desks

Flat-top   Various desks having broad, flat surfaces.

Kidney-shaped   Desk with a curved top and curved drawer sections.

Kneehole   Any desk that has a flat top and drawer sections on one or both sides.

Rolltop   Desk with a flexible hood that can be drawn down over the writing surface and storage compartments.

Secretary   Desk with bookshelves above and storage compartments below. Writing surface is usually a drop-leaf panel.

Slant-top   Similar to the lower section of a secretary, with a drop-lid writing section and drawers in the base.

Tambour   Desk with flexible-slat shutters or doors that can be drawn closed to hide the storage compartments. Usually has one or more drawers below the writing surface.

Beds

Bunk   Two beds in a framework in which one bed is directly above the other.

Canopy   A drapery or hood decorates the head of the bed. It may be supported on posts or mounted on the wall or ceiling.

Cot   A small-scaled narrow bed.

Daybed   Various couches. Usually they have two ends of equal height and identical design.

Fourposter   Elongated corner posts at each corner of the bed.

Hi-riser   A single couch with an under section that can be pulled out and raised to form an extra bed.

Hollywood   A mattress and box spring supported on four or six legs. May be used with or without a headboard.

Sleigh   The headboard and footboard of the bed curve outward to resemble an old fashioned sleigh.

Sofa   Various sofas that convert into beds. Some pull out from under the seat section, others allow for the back of the sofa to drop down (jackknife).

Spool   Posts and spindles of headboard and footboard are turned in a spool design.

Studio Couch   A couch with loose pillows that rest against a wall. Some form single beds whereas others can be converted into double beds.

Tester (Field Bed)   A canopy or ruffled valance is supported on four posts to cover the top.

21
Floor
Coverings

Throughout the centuries, even in very primitive cultures, various types of floor covering have been used for very much the same reasons that we use them today: comfort, appearance, and warmth. Rugs and carpets as we know them were not generally used until after the Middle Ages, but in times past grasses, crushed leaves, branches, sand, stone, tile, clay, and animal skins have all been popular floor coverings. Strangely enough, the substance that we step on seems to have tactile as well as visual importance, even when we wear shoes.

The consumer today is faced with a wide range of possible floor coverings. In all probability, color, texture, and price will be the factors that have the strongest influence on one's choice. However, there are three chief reasons why selections should be made with care:

1. The floor is a large, important area. The design, color, and texture of the floor covering will therefore have considerable influence on the appearance of the room.
2. The floor is usually subjected to hard wear from abrasion, pressure, and soil. The surface should be both durable and easy to maintain.
3. Most floor coverings are relatively expensive and represent an investment of a fairly large proportion of the furnishing budget.

Personal likes and dislikes seem to be particularly strong with regard to floor coverings. Some people can't bear to live in a room without a soft rug; others enjoy the cool, clean feeling of a smooth, hard floor. Some people dislike having a floor become an accented area with brilliant color or design; others enjoy a feeling of luxury with a large area of brilliant color or interesting pattern underfoot. It's interesting to talk to people about Oriental rugs. They usually love them or they detest them; only a few are indifferent. Personal preferences in these matters certainly should, and will, influence one's choices.

Floor coverings may be divided into two general categories: the soft and the hard. Soft floor coverings include all types of rugs and carpets; hard floor coverings include tile, cork, linoleum, asphalt tile, rubber tile, and vinyl. The structural material of the floor is usually one with a hard surface, such as wood, concrete, or stone. Naturally the merits of each type are of major concern if the floor is to be left uncovered. But because floors are usually covered the advantages and disadvantages of the soft and hard coverings becomes increasingly important. Soft coverings provide warmth and comfort; they absorb sound; they are often more luxurious than hard coverings. They may, however, be more difficult to keep clean, especially over a long period of time. The hard-surfaced floor coverings are, in general, durable, cool, impervious to stains, and easily cleaned with soap and water. Most homes use both types, with the traditional tile or linoleum in bathroom and kitchen and the soft floor coverings in other areas for comfortable livability. But modern homes are tending to break with such traditions. We find people using the hard-surfaced floorings in many of the living areas and luxurious wall-to-wall washable carpeting in kitchens and bathrooms. New developments in both hard and soft floor coverings make it impossible to assign specific roles to each type. The hard-surfaced coverings are becoming more glamorous and more exotic; the soft coverings are becoming more durable and easier to maintain. Many people have resolved the dilemma of a choice by using both types on the same floor, with a background of a hard-surfaced covering accented with areas of a soft covering—a solution that has some obvious merits.

Rugs and Carpets

SIZE. Rugs are finished on all four sides and must be purchased in specific sizes and shapes. Standard sizes usually range from small scatter rugs two by three feet up to large rugs that may be twelve by eighteen feet or more. The recent popularity of "area" rugs has brought more unusual sizes and shapes, which include round, oval, and free-form.

Carpet comes by the roll and is available in widths that range from twenty-seven inches up to eighteen feet. A few types are made even wider but the twelve- and fifteen-foot widths are the most common. The term *broadloom* refers to carpeting fifty-four inches or wider and describes no other qualities or characteristics except width.

Room-sized rugs can be cut to fit any room. Any length of carpet can be purchased in the standard widths. For example, to cover the floor of a room eleven by sixteen feet a standard finished nine-by-twelve rug would be rather small; a twelve by fifteen would be too wide. One might, therefore, select a fifteen-foot-wide carpet and buy a ten-foot length of it. The rug would then have a six-inch border or floor showing around the edges. Because rugs usually stretch on the floor, it is always desirable to allow a small leeway when ordering such a rug.

How much of the floor should be covered? There is no one answer, but here are some of the factors to be considered. A solid, unbroken floor surface, even though there is a pattern or design in the covering, will add to the apparent size of the room. Wall-to-wall

FIGURE 21-1   Different effects are created by wall-to-wall carpeting, area rugs, and room size rugs.

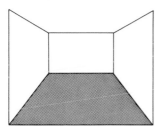 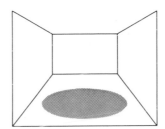 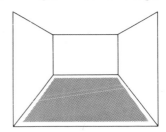

carpeting is a good choice for any room that one wants to appear larger. If the same carpeting is extended throughout adjoining areas and rooms, the effect of spaciousness is increased still further and the floor will provide a feeling of unity.

If a rug seems to be more desirable than wall-to-wall carpeting, it should be chosen in relation to the size of the room. It may extend almost to the walls for an effect that is similar to carpeting. When some of the floor will show around the edges of the rug, the border and the rug should be in pleasing proportion to each other. There are no hard and fast rules about this, but usually in a small room it is not attractive to have more than about eight inches of floor showing. In a large room, about a twelve-inch border of floor might be a good proportion. Of course, scatter rugs and area rugs are another matter. Or in a large room, several small Oriental rugs might be extremely attractive even with a fairly large proportion of the floor exposed. So it is impossible to make general rules that apply to all situations. But usually an ordinary nine-by-twelve rug sitting in the middle of a twelve-by-twenty-two room will seem sad and lost. Rugs should look as though they are at home on floors, and only when they are the correct size and shape for the room will they appear that way.

Because carpeting is sold by the square yard, there will sometimes be waste in cutting a length of carpet to fit a room. Sometimes one can reduce the amount of waste by using the *width* of the carpet lengthwise in the room. For example, if the area to be covered is seven and one-half by fourteen feet, purchasing a fifteen-foot width of carpet means that one foot would have to be cut off the width, and one would buy seven and one-half feet of it. Buying fifteen feet of a nine-foot width and having it cut to seven and a half feet wide would cause more waste.

To figure the amount of carpeting needed to cover an area, one multiplies length by width to obtain the number of square feet; for example, a room twelve by fifteen = 180 square feet. Because there are nine square feet in a square yard, one divides by nine (180 ÷ 9 = 20 square yards). Covering the floor with carpeting that costs $15 a square yard would cost $300 for the twenty square yards. In addition, there may be costs for binding the edges or installing the carpet wall-to-wall. A pad should usually be used under a rug or carpet and this will also add to the cost.

Certain areas in a room will receive more wear than others, so it is always an advantage to be able to reverse the position of the rug or carpet. Floor covering cut exactly to fit the shape of the room presents an attractive appearance but it does mean that the traffic lanes will show signs of wear more quickly. A rug that extends almost to the wall provides an effect similar to wall-to-wall carpeting and is more practical in that it can be turned to distribute the wear.

COLOR. Because the floor is a relatively large area of any room, the color decision is indeed an important one. Also the rug will probably remain longer than other color areas. One may change walls, draperies, and slipcovers before changing the floor covering. It is wise, therefore, to choose a versatile color that will lend itself to a variety of color combinations. This does not mean that the rug must be one of the ubiquitous neutrals, but some colors are definitely more limiting than others. In working with color samples, one will see that certain rug colors lend themselves to a wider range of color combinations than others. A deep, rich, cherry red, for example, combines beautifully with white, pale blue, pale green, beige, gray, or light pink. On the other hand, lavender or avocado green are somewhat more limited. Actually they can be used with a variety of colors in that they won't clash, but they need certain tones to bring out their true beauty. Color schemes should look as though they were meant to be. They should not merely be an inoffensive combination of colors. The choice of color may also be influenced by whether or not this will be the permanent place for the rug. For example, a young couple in a tiny apartment may have plans to move into a house at some future date. The current living-room rug may be purchased with the idea of using it in a bedroom or a guest room later on. Of course, the neutrals are always safe in a situation like this, but if they decide on a color with a strong

FIGURE 21-2 Plain wall-to-wall carpeting in a shimmering texture creates a mood of quiet elegance and makes an area appear larger than it actually is. (*Courtesy of Allied Chemical Corporation —Source fiber*)

character they must carefully consider its possibilities in other situations.

The practical aspects of color should also influence choice. Very light and very dark colors will show footmarks and soil more quickly than the medium tones. Any area that will receive heavy traffic can be a problem in this respect. A foyer hall, for instance, is bound to have many footprints on the floor covering. If it shows every one of them, it will soon become an irritating, bothersome eyesore.

Some people seem to live *for* their homes rather than *in* them. Consider the case of the young woman, mother of two children, who set her heart on a pale cream-colored carpet throughout her hallway, living room, and dining room even though she knew it was impractical. As soon as the carpeting was on the floor, she tore up a few old sheets and used them as runners on all the traffic lanes! The runners were always left in place, even for company. Of course, the carpeting was perfectly beautiful without the sheets, but no one ever saw it that way. Also, everyone felt rather uncomfortable. Those plastic runners

designed to protect carpets from footmarks have the same effect and are equally unattractive. It is more pleasant to have a home that does not present such problems. In all areas that receive heavy traffic one should choose floor covering that does not show soil and can be easily maintained.

PATTERN. Whether or not one wants to emphasize or dramatize the floor with pattern is purely a matter of personal preference, but there are some practical points that should be considered. Patterned rugs and carpets have advantages and disadvantages. Within the framework of personal likes and dislikes, pattern and texture should be considered in relation to the purpose and theme of the room.

Advantages of Using Pattern. Designs in floor coverings range from subdued, small, tone-on-tone texture to large, bold, colorful motifs. Any patterned rug usually has less tendency to show soil and foot marks; therefore, from a practical point of view, such a rug may be desirable for certain areas. The size of the pattern, the type, and the amount

FIGURE 21-3 An area rug designed by Dorothy Liebes introduces an exotic Polynesian note in a room furnished in the modern style and relates well to the Eames lounge chair in the foreground. (*Courtesy of Bigelow-Sanford, Inc.*)

FIGURE 21-4 A Zebra rug forms a base for the glass coffee table and emphasizes the primitive and modern art displayed on the wall. (*Courtesy of* 1969 Rooms of Tomorrow. *Designed by Roland Wm. Jutras, N.S.I.D.*)

of diversified coloring should certainly be in keeping with the room, but frequently a rug or carpet with some pattern lends character to a decorative scheme.

Some people feel that the design in a rug should have architectural qualities. They object to stepping on floral bouquets and delicate motifs, because a floor must be a support and any suggestion of delicacy seems incongruous. Yet floral designs may provide a charming atmosphere that is both interesting and tasteful.

The idea that only one pattern may be used in a room is old-fashioned. Many patterned fabrics blend with one another very nicely. It is a matter of selecting those that enhance one another rather than those that compete for attention. A small, all-over pattern will often blend beautifully with a large, bold design if other factors, such as color, texture, and theme, pull the two together. Sometimes even large designs harmonize extremely well. Elegant dining rooms have been decorated with scenic wallpaper or murals and Oriental rugs, certainly two large patterned areas but not at all disturbing if they are well chosen. However, large designs, especially in floor covering, are usually more attractive in large rooms.

Disadvantages of Using Pattern. Floor coverings with bold designs do tend to be more limiting than solid colors, although, as pointed out above, they are not as restricting as is commonly believed. Also, if the pattern establishes a particular mood, refurnishing the room becomes more of a problem. It is not impossible to completely change the character of the decoration, but it requires more careful planning and selection. In an earlier chapter we mentioned a traditional room with an Oriental rug that was retained when the owner refurnished in the modern style. Through careful choice of colors, textures, and accessories, the result was an extremely beautiful room that was altogether different from its predecessor. Some patterns will be more limiting than others in this respect. In choosing a design, one should consider how it might be used in other settings.

A good rug or carpet may last fifteen years or longer. There is always the possibility that a pattern that is most appealing in the beginning will become tiresome after a few years. Of course, one might also tire of a solid color, but there is a greater chance that a figured rug will become wearisome.

QUALITY. There is no one factor that is responsible for high quality in rugs and carpets; there must be a combination of good materials and excellent construction to assure durability and attractive appearance. The variety of materials used in rugs and the variety of constructions present a complex problem for the consumer who is anxious to receive maximum value for his dollars. Even after considerable study and careful comparative shopping it is important to purchase rugs from a reliable dealer who takes pride in the quality of his merchandise. There are some hidden values in rugs and carpets that even the most astute shopper cannot easily judge for himself.

The four chief factors that influence appearance and quality are

(1) Type and grade of fiber.
(2) Construction of yarn.
(3) Height of pile.
(4) Closeness of pile.

Fiber. New developments in synthetic fiber production have expanded the variety of soft floor coverings to the extent that they are now practical in every area of the home and in outdoor areas as well. The phenomenal changes in floor coverings within the past few years can be attributed chiefly to the recent developments in the man-made fiber industry.

The most commonly used fibers include wool, nylon, acrylics, and polypropylene-olefin, polyesters, cotton, and rayon. In 1968, the production of broadloom carpeting was divided into approximately the following percentages:

Wool	14%
Filament Nylon	36%
Staple Nylon	9%
Acrylics	25%
Polypropylenes	6%
Polyesters	9%
Cotton and Rayon	1%

It should be noted, however, that these figures will have little meaning in another year or two because the market is changing so rapidly. The polypropylenes are becoming increasingly important in the use of indoor-outdoor carpeting. Also, new fibers are appearing to challenge the existing ones. An example might be cited in a new biconstituent fiber produced by Allied Chemical Company under the trademark *Source*. It does not belong in any of the generic groups established by the Federal Trade Commission and has been assigned the temporary FTC symbol *AC-0001*. In all probability, other companies will develop new fibers that will require an updating of our current labeling legislation.

The fibers used in floor coverings must be either carefully selected or specially manufactured to withstand the rigors of wear. Resilience, the ability to retain color, and ease of maintenance are also extremely important factors.

Wool. The finest rugs in history have usually been made of wool, but only certain breeds of sheep produce a fiber that is coarse and wiry enough to be suitable for carpet. All carpet wool must be imported from the areas with rugged climates, chiefly the Middle East, New Zealand, South America, or Scotland. The fine, soft, clothing wools produced in America are not suitable.

A rug made of high-quality carpet wool is usually durable and beautiful because the manufacturer has selected and blended fibers to produce a yarn that has the desirable strength, resilience, and luster. Wool is resistant to abrasion and soil. There are many experienced manufacturers who still consider wool the queen of carpet fibers in spite of the economic difficulties of importing the material from the countries that produce the best sources. The production of natural fibers is subject to more pitfalls than the production of synthetics. The carpet industry has faced numerous problems, yet a large segment remains dedicated to wool as *the* fiber for superior carpets.

In addition to the qualities mentioned above, wool takes a wide range of dyes and retains color extremely well. Regular cleaning with a vacuum and a periodic dry cleaning will keep a wool rug attractive and in good condition. Although synthetic fibers have been developed to at least match some of the qualities of wool for fine carpets, many diehards of the industry, weighing all factors involved, still choose wool.

Nylon. All the wonderful properties of nylon would seem to make it an ideal fiber for carpets and indeed they do. The durability, resiliency, and easy cleanability of nylon contribute to a carpet even when the fiber is blended with another fiber. About 20 per cent nylon is necessary for significant results; a popular combination blends 70 per cent wool and 30 per cent nylon.

Polypropylene-olefin. High resistance to abrasion, stains, moisture, mildew, and rot have made olefin fibers particularly suitable for carpet use. In either pile or felted constructions they have been widely accepted for both home and institutional use. Weather resistance has made them dominant fibers for outdoor installations.

Polyesters. Strength, resiliency, the ability to take dyes well, and textural possibilities have made the polyesters important in many areas of the textile industry. They are becoming increasingly important in carpet production.

Acrylics. A significant contribution to the raw materials of carpets has been made by the acrylic fibers. Tests have shown these to be durable, very resilient, and extremely resistant to abrasion. They are, in addition, resistant to spots and stains as well as soil. Of all the synthetics, the acrylics most closely resemble wool. They are naturally mothproof and mildew-resistant.

Rayon and Acetate. Specially engineered rayon and acetates have proved to be a useful addition to the family of carpet fibers. From the standpoint of economy, the ability to take dyes, and cleanability, they measure up quite well. The chief problems are lack of resiliency

and low resistance to abrasion. However, it is possible to produce carpets of these fibers that will stand up fairly well.

Cotton. Although cotton has often been used as a backing for wool rugs, in recent years all-cotton rugs have gained in favor. Various types of cotton are blended to produce a yarn that has a desirable strength. Cotton is less expensive than wool, but it is not nearly as resilient. Unless a cotton rug is made with a firm, tight construction, there will be a tendency for the pile to crush and mat. Cotton fibers have the advantages of taking bright, clear colors and of being washable. Small cotton rugs can be laundered at home, but large ones of course need professional handling.

Yarn. The construction of the yarn may affect the durability of the carpet. It is a most important factor in determining styling and appearance. Many novelty textures can be created by the combination of the strands of two or more colors in a ply yarn. Tweed carpets are frequently made this way.

When fibers are given an additional crimp and used in a high-twist ply-yarn, the carpet takes on a textural quality that does not readily show marks and footprints. Popularly known as "twist" carpet, this construction has been widely used in recent years.

Yarns can be dyed before they are set in the weaving looms. Sometimes the fiber is dyed before it is spun into the yarn. However, many fine carpets are "piece-dyed" after construction. A reliable manufacturer will guarantee color fastness regardless of the method used for dyeing.

Construction. We might divide soft floor coverings into two categories: the pile weaves and the flat weaves. Either type can be made by machine or by hand, but our discussion here will concentrate mostly on machine-made rugs because these are the ones with which the majority of consumers are concerned. Most of the discussion will be concerned with methods of pile construction.

In past years the method of construction was a more reliable indication of quality than it is today. Now various grades are produced by each method, although to some extent construction processes will still affect costs.

Pile construction means that an extra set of yarns forms either loops or tufts on the surface of a background fabric. Loops, or an uncut pile, are generally more durable, but for appearance we seem to prefer tufts, or cut pile. This latter construction can be extremely durable if the quality of raw material is high, the yarns are tightly twisted, and the weave is close and tight. Flat weaving is just what the term implies.

Density of Pile. The terms *pitch* and *wires* are used to indicate the closeness of the weave in carpets or rugs with traditional pile construction. *Pitch* is the number of loops or tufts in a twenty-seven-inch width; *wires* refers to the rows of loops or tufts in one inch lengthwise. The latter term refers to the method of forming loops on the surface of a pile fabric. Extra warp yarns are strung over wires that are held across the warp and parallel to the filling yarns. As the backing yarns are interlaced, they hold the pile warp in place. Then the wires are withdrawn, leaving loops of the pile warp on the surface. Sometimes a knife is placed on the end of the wire. As the wire is withdrawn, the blade cuts each loop of the pile to form a tuft.

The closest construction has a pitch of 256 tufts or loops in a twenty-seven-inch width of carpet. A poor-quality carpet may have a pitch of 120. Some rugs may have as many as thirteen rows of tufts, or wires, in the lengthwise inch. It should be pointed out that the standards for pitch and wires will vary with the method of construction.

Height of Pile. Another factor that is important to both durability and appearance is the height of the pile, which can vary from about one-quarter to five-eighths inches or more. The higher pile will give greater serviceability, a richer appearance, and a more luxurious texture if all other factors are equal. However, unless the weave is also tight and close, a high pile adds none of these desirable qualities.

Backing Yarns. The underside or backing of a carpet is usually made of firm yarns that provide a sturdy foundation. They may be made of jute, cotton, rayon, or kraft cord (a special yarn made from wood pulp). These yarns serve to hold the pile in place as well as to form the backing of the carpet. On some carpets, the warp yarns of the backing may interloop in a chain effect. The crosswise or filling yarns, called *shot*, interlace with the warp yarns. Supplementary yarns called *stuffer warps* are frequently used to give added body to the foundation.

Much carpet is treated with a latex coating on the back. Because this seals the yarns in

position, the edges will not ravel and binding is not necessary. Worn or damaged areas of well-constructed pile rugs of this type can be replaced without conspicuous seams. Also, because sections of carpet can be joined without traditional seams it is possible to achieve special design effects with two or more colors.

TYPES OF CONSTRUCTION. We have already pointed out that quality in carpet depends on the combination of several factors. In the past the method of construction was a much more important indication of quality than it is today, yet it is still important for the consumer to know something about how carpets are made, because such knowledge simplifies comparative shopping.

Types of Pile Construction. Let us examine some of the types of pile construction:

Tufting. An entirely new process of carpet construction has made a significant contribution to the industry in recent years. Now it accounts for three fourths of the total production. The method of tufting represents a departure from traditional pile weaving in that the pile yarns are stitched to a woven cotton or jute backing by a multiple-needle machine. The process has the advantages of being relatively quick and inexpensive. Although it does not permit all types of design, it does permit a wide range of striped, rippled, and tweed patterns as well as various textured effects. All the major carpet fibers can be used in the tufting process. The backing of the carpet is always coated with latex to secure the yarns and to add body. Tufted carpeting is generally available in widths of nine, twelve, and fifteen feet.

As with other types of carpet, the tufted varieties differ in quality. With good-quality yarn, a thick, close pile, and a sturdy backing tufted rugs will be luxurious and durable.

Wilton. Wilton carpet is named after the town in England where it originated. It is woven on a special type of Jacquard loom that has a series of cards perforated to control the pattern. They regulate the way the different colors of yarn appear on the surface of the carpet. Each yarn is drawn to the surface as it is needed to form a loop, then it is carried along in the background of the carpet until it is needed again in the design. Wilton carpets have a considerable amount of the high-quality pile yarns actually buried beneath the surface.

(a)

(b)

FIGURE 21-5 The floor is an important area in every room. Texture of a carpet should be chosen with care. (a) Plush, (b) Short-pile shag, (c) Long-pile shag, (d) Three levels of loop-pile in a sculptured effect. (*Courtesy of Bigelow-Sanford, Inc.*)

(c)

(d)

This feature adds strength, body, and resilience, and because of it, Wilton is commonly known as the weave with "hidden value."

The yarns that form the pile are held in frames, so there is some limitation to the number of colors that can be used, but intricate patterns can be accurately reproduced. This method is also used for carpet in solid colors.

The pile in Wilton rugs may or may not be cut. The popular sculptured designs often combine both types of pile.

A good-quality Wilton is often made on a loom with five or six frames, and usually a fine, tightly twisted, woolen yarn forms the pile, although other fibers may also be used. In the better qualities, Wilton rugs have a dense, luxurious pile that is both durable and attractive.

Velvet. The simplest method of making carpet is with the velvet weave. Some striped and variegated color designs are possible, but the method is used mostly for solid colors. Many different texture effects are possible using various types of yarn. For example, a frieze surface is produced by the use of tightly twisted yarns in a cut pile, while a plush surface is produced by the use of straight yarns. Various pebble textures can be achieved by the use of tightly twisted yarns in an uncut pile. Tweed effects are achieved by the use of yarns of two or more colors in either a cut or an uncut pile. Further variations in surface texture are possible when both cut and uncut piles are combined to form a pattern; pile woven in different heights yields still another type of sculptured effect.

The velvet weave is used for carpet at all price levels. Because the method of construction is relatively inexpensive, it is possible to produce carpet that will be durable, serviceable, and attractive at a comparatively low cost.

The velvet method is also called a tapestry weave when it is used with a low uncut pile for a special effect.

Axminster. A special and very complex carpet loom is used to weave Axminster carpet, which also derives its name from a town in England. Its chief advantage is that almost any pattern can be woven into the carpet. The yarns are set in the loom so that each tuft in a crosswise row can be controlled individually for color. This allows for unlimited variety in both design and color. The

initial setting up of a pattern is a slow and expensive process, but once this is done the design may be repeated over and over again with relative ease.

It is easy to identify an Axminister rug because the crosswise backing yarns are stiff and heavy. Thus the rug will not roll crosswise, but it can be rolled lengthwise.

A standard-quality Axminster carpet has a pitch of 189 (seven tufts per inch crosswise) and at least seven wires or tufts per inch lengthwise. Better qualities have a closer weave. The pile, which is almost always cut, is deeper in the better qualities than it is in poor grades.

Chenille. There are actually two weaving processes required for the construction of chenille carpet. The first weaving process produces a "blanket," made with strong warp yarns widely spaced and softer wool yarns in the filling. The blanket is then cut into lengthwise strips, which are pressed into a V shape. These furry strips are responsible for the name *chenille*—the French word for "caterpillar." In the second weaving operation, the strips of chenille are placed over the background warp yarns of the carpet and each strip is held in place with several shots (filling yarns).

This method of construction is expensive, and today it is used mostly for custom-made carpeting. Any pattern or design can be woven into the rug. Naturally, special effects are expensive.

Finishing. Unlike other fabrics, carpets do not go through extensive finishings processes. The coating on the backs of rugs might be considered a finish. Dyeing or printing is sometimes done after the rug is woven, but the majority of carpets have color applied before the weaving stage.

A rug with a somewhat soft cotton backing may be washed in a chemical bath of caustic soda to impart a high sheen or luster finish to the pile yarns. Machine-made "Oriental" rugs are sometimes given this treatment to make them simulate the silky appearance of true handmade originals. The process must be carefully controlled to prevent loss of color and to develop a luxurious sheen rather than a hard, shiny gloss.

Carving or "sculpturing" a rug may be considered a finish when it is done by hand methods. A rug woven with a high pile may have a design applied by the shearing of parts of the surface. The hand-carving of pile results in beautiful textural effects that have been especially popular in area rugs in which the design is carefully related to the shape of the rug. However, carved or sculptured effects have also been produced in the weaving process by the combination of cut and uncut piles or by the use of loops or tufts of different heights. This is usually an all-over pattern, whereas the hand-carved rug will have a centralized motif and perhaps a border design.

ORIENTAL RUGS. The symbolism and mysticism of Oriental floor coverings hold an allure for many people who associate romance and tradition with the exquisite patterns and superb colors of the original rugs. The history and the implications of Oriental rugs are so intricate that it would require volumes to treat that subject adequately. Yet we hope that even a cursory introduction will open a few avenues of a fascinating study.

Perhaps in no other field of furnishings are people divided so clearly into two groups—those who thrill to the patterns, colors, and textures of Oriental rugs and those who are revolted by the thought of actually living with them even though they may enjoy seeing them in museums and exhibitions. We might point out here that Oriental rugs, like other forms or art, have been subject to the vicissitudes of fashion. At the moment, they are in the favor of not only the traditionalists in interior design but even a few modernists, who tend to reject the past or any association with it. Some of these forward-thinking artists have begun to sense a need for the "missing ingredient" of the modern style. The idea that "form follows function" may not be complete in its philosophy because of some human needs that are overlooked. At any rate, a few of the modernists have turned to the Orient for inspiration. As a result, we have seen various adaptations and combinations of modern style and Oriental design that have been most interesting.

Because it is only fair to state the other side of the story, a few more facts must be presented. The revulsion against Oriental rugs probably stems, in a large measure, from the fact that the originals were works of great beauty that are difficult to reproduce in mass quantities. The purists decry cheap imitations of any form of art that requires hand labor.

Today, even in the Orient, the production of rugs has become commercialized. Although Oriental rugs are still made by hand, machine-made yarns, synthetic dyes, and a flaunting of traditional designs have impaired the intrinsic beauty of the ancient rugs. The older rugs were usually made in the homes of families, with designs and methods passed down from one generation to the next. For some people, any attempt to commercialize or to mass-produce such products destroys the value.

The reaction to all of this discussion may be reduced to the question, "Does the end justify the means?" A few of the high-quality modern Oriental rugs simulate the lovely design and textures of the originals to such an extent that only experts can tell the difference. These won't suit the sort of person who must have an original work, regardless of the beauty of any copy. On the other hand, a *good* reproduction of a work of art will appeal to other people. Perhaps one answer lies in the fact that so many artistic reproductions are not of the best quality. Certainly this has been the case with Oriental rugs. Attempts to reproduce them for a mass market have resulted in many cheap imitations that revolt any discriminating taste. We therefore tend to reject any imitation, good or bad. Because the fine originals in Oriental rugs are beyond the economic means of most families, the question reduces to whether or not one will accept and enjoy a good reproduction. The cheap, poor-quality imitations are neither beautiful nor satisfying in any respect, and these should certainly be rejected.

Pile-surfaced Oriental rugs made by hand employ either the Ghiordes knot (Turkish) or the Senna knot (Persian). Rugs made with the Senna knot usually have a deeper, more uniform pile. Some of the fine old examples of Oriental rugs have as many as five-hundred knots per square inch, but a good-quality modern rug would have about two-hundred knots to the square inch.

Most Oriental rugs are made of wool, although camel's hair and silk are sometimes used.

Persian. Probably the most popular Oriental rugs are the various types of Persian rug, which are noted for expert craftsmanship, magnificent designs, and beautiful coloring. Rugs tend to differ in theme and interpretation depending on the town or province in which

(a) Sarouk

(c) Bokhara

(b) Kerman

(d) Chinese

FIGURE 21-6 (left) Some typical designs in Oriental rugs. (*Courtesy of Oriental Rug Importers Association*)

FIGURE 21-7 (above) An Oriental rug is a natural background for Georgian furniture. Many such rugs were brought back to the Western world by clipper ships during the seventeenth and eighteenth centuries. (*Courtesy of The Oriental Rug Importers Association*)

they are made. Some of the best known include:

Sarouk (Saruk, Sarook)—dark reds and blues with floral designs in lighter colors.
Kerman—light background of cream, rose, blue, with designs in other pastels.
Saraband—palm leaves on a rose or blue background.
Ispahan—intricate all-over design on deep red background.
Feraghan—small stylized flowers in rows on a deep blue ground.

In general, Persian rugs are covered with a variety of floral patterns, vines, and sometimes animals. Some types are characterized by large, geometric medallions in the center and stately borders. The designs are graceful and delicate.

Turkish. Designs in Turkish rugs tend to be more geometric in character, but they use floral patterns and adopt the botanical themes used in Persian rugs. In the small sizes used as prayer rugs by the Mohammedans, the design includes a *mihrab* or niche, which is always pointed toward Mecca when the owner kneels on the rug.

Turkoman. Tribes in Central Asia make these rugs with a short, close pile. The designs are geometric and the dominant color is a blood red, often combined with cream, brown, blue, or black. The best-known of these rugs are the Bokhara and those from Afghanistan and Beluchistan (now Pakistan).

Caucasian. Rugs from the Caucasus are bold in design and color. Elaborate geometric motifs are done in brilliant yellows, blues, greens, and reds, with some black. Characteristic patterns include the eight-pointed star, the swastika, crosses, and linear figures of both humans and animals. In some respects, the patterns of the rugs resemble those of the American Indians.

Chinese. Perhaps the outstanding difference between Chinese rugs and other Oriental rugs is the plainer background. The borders are usually narrow; the central medallions or small spaced motifs are almost always symbolic. The patterns include flowers—especially the peony—clouds, waves, and dragons. Soft yellow, gold, cream, and apricot are favorite colors, with designs frequently in blue. Modern copies of antique Chinese rugs often violate the traditions of the originals.

FRENCH RUGS. Several types of hand-loomed rugs originated in France and became so popular that they deserve special mention.

Aubusson. This type of rug bears the name of a small town in France where it is believed to have originated. It is made with a heavy tapestry weave in colors that are, in general, light and delicate with a somewhat faded tone.

The designs have followed the prevailing mode in France. The early patterns were probably all-over designs. Then, during the reign of Louis XIV, the motifs became more grandiose with the sunburst, acanthus scrolls, shells, and rosettes. The classical period brought more restraint, with daintier flowers, garlands, ribands, and latticework. The rugs followed also the Empire themes of the sphinx, drum, laurel wreath, and, of course, *N* for Napoleon. In modern times, Aubusson rugs have been reproduced in the best traditions of French design.

Savonnerie. The aristocrats of French rugs began in an abandoned soap factory (*savon* in French means "soap"). In the seventeenth century, the government took over ownership and in the early nineteenth century the looms were moved and the factory became part of Gobelins.

Large, luxurious rugs were usually made for the French palaces, but production was always at the discretion of the reigning king. Huge, elegant rugs with exquisite detail were made for the Louvre at the Savonnerie factory.

Throughout the years, the patterns followed French styles, and the colors were rich and deep. Lovely floral patterns in gold, turquoise, rose, blue, and green were often worked on a velvety black background. Frequently the pile around each motif was carved away so that the design would stand out in relief.

Moquette. This type of carpeting is not at all on a par with the Aubussons and Savonneries, which were made for the courts and palaces. Moquette was more widely used by the French people who could afford carpeting and it was woven on a twenty-seven-inch loom in a manner that was somewhat similar to the English Wilton.

Louis XVI sent a Moquette carpet to George

FIGURE 21-8 The old and the new are combined in a room designed by Paul Kraus, A.I.D. A modern chaise upholstered in scarlet seems at home with the precise geometric design of the Bokhara in black and red on an ivory background. (*Courtesy of The Oriental Rug Importers Association*)

Washington for the banquet room at Mount Vernon. This rug was in storage for a number of years, but has now been returned to its original place in Mount Vernon.

Modern methods of weaving Axminster rugs developed chiefly from the principles involved in the Moquette looms.

OTHER HANDMADE RUGS. Rug making as a handcraft has been practiced throughout the world by many groups of people with different materials, methods, and designs. As with any handcraft, the designs represent the artistic development of the people as well as their customs, beliefs, and values. Many rug designs that originated as handmade products are now reproduced by machine.

Hooked Rugs. A coarse fabric such as burlap or canvas is stretched on a frame and strips of cloth or yarn are drawn through it to form loops. Although the method has been used in various other countries, hooked rugs have become associated with New England, where they became extremely popular during the nineteenth century. The patterns varied considerably and included geometric, scenic, and floral motifs as well as mottoes and proverbs. In some rugs the looped pile was cut for a varied textural effect. Many of the more beautiful designs, especially floral patterns, have been reproduced on modern machines.

Braided Rugs. Strips of cloth were twisted and braided to form a thick strand that was stitched in a round or oval shape. Today, handmade braided rugs are also made from strips of felt. Design is introduced by the use of contrasting bands of color.

Needlepoint Rugs. The process of embroidering on heavy net or canvas with thick wool yarn has been used for some of the finest handmade rugs. Simple cross-stitches are used as the basis of construction, but the designs are often complex floral motifs with beautiful delicate shading.

Rag Rugs. Strips of twisted cloth were used as the filling yarn on a loom. Simple rag rugs were made in a plain weave with cotton or linen warp yarns.

Navajo Rugs. Blankets, mats, and rugs woven by the Navajo Indians are characterized by geometrical designs and symbolic figures in gray, white, and black, with accents in bright reds. Later, other brilliant colors were introduced. Modern reproductions use many strong color combinations.

Other Oriental Rugs. The term *Oriental rug* usually refers to the pile-weave constructions discussed earlier. However, there are several other types of hand-crafted rugs made in the Orient.

Khilims. Khilims are hand-loomed Oriental tapestries that are thin enough to be used as well decorations or table covers as well as durable enough to be used as rugs.

Soumaks. Soumaks, flat-surfaced rugs from the Caucasus, have a pattern woven in by means of an extra filling thread.

Numdahs. The numdah, a felted rug from India, is frequently made of cow's hair. The rugs are often embroidered with vines and floral designs in bright colors. They are familiar to us as the Indian druggets.

Modern Handmade Rugs. The high costs of labor naturally limit the production of handmade rugs, particularly in the Western world. However, there are a few in the luxury class that are being made in contemporary design. In the Scandinavian countries, the typical adaptation of native designs that has characterized other modern handicrafts has been evident in rug weaving. Both pile and flat weaves are used in modern handmade rugs. The current use of area rugs has encouraged modern designers to work on handcrafted products.

FLAT-WOVEN RUGS. A wide variety of flat-surfaced rugs is made by machine. In general, these tend to be less expensive than carpets made with pile construction. Although they are not usually as soft and luxurious as the pile rugs, they have been popular as cool, summer rugs or as starters where a low budget prohibits investment in costly carpet, but where some form of floor covering seems desirable.

Linen Rugs. Coarse, sturdy flax fibers have been used for a variety of textures and patterns. Linen rugs are usually reversible, durable, and inexpensive.

Fiber Rugs. Paper pulp, or "kraft" fiber, is twisted into yarn and used in plain, twill, or Jacquard weaves. Some fiber rugs combine fiber with cotton or sisal.

Natural-Strand Rugs. Sisal (related to hemp), coconut, and various other types of rush and grass are also used for rugs. They have been popular in rugs and in the form of squares, usually one foot, that can be sewn together to form a rug of the desired size and shape. The texture and color lend themselves to year-round use as an inexpensive floor covering in modern interiors. Full-sized rugs are also made from these natural fibers.

RUG CUSHIONS. Some sort of padding or underlay is usually desirable under a rug or carpet. Some of these are made of felted hair, others are made of rubber; a combination of rubber and hair is a popular type.

Paddings come in a variety of weights, designated in ounces per square yard. A forty-ounce cushion is usually suitable for normal home use.

Indoor-Outdoor Carpeting

A recent innovation in floor coverings has been the indoor-outdoor type of carpeting. This carpeting often has different textural qualities from the more conventional soft floor coverings, but it has opened up new concepts of decorating in various areas of the home. Terraces, swimming pools, playrooms, hallways, and kitchens are achieving an entirely new look with the introduction of a carpet that can withstand weather, stains, and wear. Several synthetic fibers, particularly the polypropylene-olefin and acrylic, are being used in either felted or tufted constructions that produce pile effects. Vinyl matting is also used.

There are advantages and disadvantages to these floor coverings. According to laboratory tests they have indicated high durability and

FIGURE 21-9 Indoor-outdoor carpeting dresses up a large terrace or a tiny porch. It can be cleaned with a garden hose or a vacuum. (*Courtesy of Herculon Olefin Fiber*)

easy maintenance. Most of them are rather easy to install. Because they are quite new, it is difficult to evaluate performance over long periods of actual use. One disadvantage that showed up in the laboratory tests, however, was that a number of samples showed a fairly high degree of flammability.[1] Undoubtedly, manufacturers will strive to overcome this drawback and in the future this type of carpeting will play an increasingly important role in home decoration.

Hard-Surfaced Floor Coverings

Hard floor coverings that can be applied to the structural flooring have taken on new glamour as well as more serviceable and durable qualities in the past few years. Floors are usually made of wood, cement, tile, or stone. When the flooring is attractive and easily maintained, it is usually desirable to leave it uncovered. However, in many instances, for either practical or decorative purposes, it is desirable to cover the flooring with something other than a rug or carpet. The hard-surfaced floor coverings offer several advantages in that they are durable, easily cleaned, and cool.

LINOLEUM. A mixture of flour, cork, and oil is applied to some sort of a backing, such as jute or fiber, to form linoleum. There are many different grades, ranging from a heavy inlaid quality to a printed variety in which the design wears off rather quickly. In inlaid linoleum, the pattern is impregnated through the thickness of the substance and will stand up under many years of hard wear. Thin linoleum with the pattern applied to the surface is, of course, much less expensive but cannot stand heavy use.

VINYL. Available in either rolls or tiles, vinyl floor coverings have branched out into the glamorous areas of interior design. To a large extent, they have removed the stigma of kitchen-and-laundry from hard-surfaced floor coverings, because luxurious vinyls in magnificent designs and colors are now used in the most elegant rooms.

Vinyl is a synthetic that resists abrasion, scratching, denting, and spotting from acids

and grease. Different types of vinyl flooring vary in durability as well as in cost; good quality and high style is not at all cheap, but the cost of vinyl compares favorably to other floor coverings of equal beauty and durability.

ASPHALT TILE. Asphalt tile is a serviceable and relatively inexpensive floor covering that is damage resistant and easy to maintain. It has been widely used in kitchens and other floor areas exposed to grease and oil. It is available in a wide range of colors and patterns, and is generally less expensive than lineoleum or rubber tile. However, it is more likely to crack or to show scratches.

RUBBER TILE. In general characteristics, rubber tile is somewhat similar to linoleum, but it is more resilient. It may be used on almost any type of floor and the range of color and design is practically unlimited. Often the colors are brighter than those in linoleum. It is extremely durable and attractive.

CORK. Shavings and granules of cork are compressed into sheets and treated with sealers to form a cork flooring. It may be colored, but it is usually used in various natural tones of light and dark brown. The chief advantages of cork are lovely texture, high resilience, and good sound absorption. Some types are difficult to maintain and need frequent waxing to preserve color and texture.

STONE. Marble, slate, and flagstone provide desirable flooring for some areas. The cost varies considerably, but these materials are usually expensive if they are at all attractive or unusual in appearance. They are extremely durable but also cold and uncomfortable to stand on for any length of time.

TERRAZZO. Terrazzo is a floor made of concrete with chips of stone or marble introduced. The surface is polished to a smooth finish for very elegant effects. It is durable and easy to maintain, but nonresilient and quite expensive.

TILE AND BRICK. Ceramic tiles and clay bricks are used for floors in certain areas. Various colors and effects are possible; durability is high. Both are easy to maintain, especially if they are glazed. They are, however, nonresilient, cold, and often expensive.

[1] "Indoor-Outdoor Carpeting," *Consumer Reports*, June, 1968, pp. 302–305.

Fabrics are an integral part of every room in the home, and they contribute so much to the general decorative atmosphere that they should be chosen carefully. Every note of texture and color, from the lowly dish towel hanging in the kitchen to the most elegant draperies in a formal living room, adds to the personality of a home. Thanks to textile designers and manufacturers, fabrics are available in a wide variety of colors, patterns, and types at all price levels. One should develop imagination and skill in using them effectively. Even that lowly dish towel isn't really lowly anymore, and there are colors and beautiful designs to perk up the chores in the kitchen. Pattern and color are found everywhere from rosebuds on the bed sheets to polka dots on the dust cloth.

The basic requirements for the various fabrics that are selected will differ, because each one will have to stand up under a different set of conditions. Curtains and draperies should be colorfast to light and perhaps washable; upholstery fabrics should resist abrasion and soil; towels should be absorbent and colorfast to laundering. Few if any fabrics have every desirable characteristic, so it is important to know how a fabric will be used to select one that has the most desirable properties.

The textile industry and most department stores tend to separate decorative fabrics from regular yard goods, but there is some overlapping. For example, gingham and percale are considered dress materials, but they are useful in several areas of the home; a few decorative fabrics may be used for certain articles of clothing. Sheeting, wide muslin, padding, and toweling are often sold by the yard in still another division of a store. It may be necessary to look in several departments to find exactly the right fabric for a specific purpose.

Widths vary considerably in fabrics. In

22

Decorative

Fabrics

general, decorative fabrics tend to be wider. Dress-weight cottons and linens are usually thirty-six inches wide, but in decorative fabrics forty-five to forty-eight inches is a more standard width. Of course it is important to know the width of a fabric when figuring yardage for anything one plans to make.

Terminology

Certainly we must be thankful for the new fibers and finishes that have improved the fabrics that we use in our homes today. But the rapid developments in the textile industry since World War II have been mixed blessings. The consumer is faced with a multitude of names and terms that provide little if any help in actually judging quality or serviceability.

Textile terminology has always been somewhat confusing for the novice. Now the widespread use of brand names and trademarks further complicates the picture. Very little labeling is required by law, and any labeling that does exist is in general rather inadequate from the consumer standpoint. But the manufacturer is not wholly to blame for this situation. Adequate labeling is a knotty problem. The more progressive manufacturers who have voluntarily attempted various methods of providing meaningful information have found that very few consumers have sufficient background to understand it. Manufacturers also complain that too few consumers actually read labels. There is an obvious need for more widespread consumer interest and broader programs of consumer education.

On the other hand, we must remember that the synthetics are relative newcomers to the textile world. Nylon, the first of the truly synthetic fibers, was introduced in 1938 and ushered in a new era of fiber development. In a rather short span of time, some of the new names have become household words. During such a period of rapid development and expansion, we must expect that education of the public will be a gradual process. It is also sporadic because consumers are more likely to become aware of those developments that have the greatest impact on daily living.

Some brief explanation of the terminology used on labels seems to be in order before we present a more detailed analysis of decorative fabrics. The Federal Trade Commission has promulgated Rules and Regulations under the Textile Fiber Products Identification Act effective March 3, 1960. In essence, these rules require the labeling of the textile fibers used in various products, including curtains, draperies, tablecloths, towels, floor coverings, and slipcovers. The outer coverings of furniture and stuffing materials are covered under another set of rules formulated by the FTC.

The act and the rules define certain terms and stipulate requirements with respect to the textile fiber products subject to this legislation. Fibers present in the amount of more than 5 per cent of the total fiber weight must be designated by their respective generic names except where another name is permitted under the act and regulations.

Generic names are established for manufactured fibers and each one is defined in specific terms. Chart 1 lists the classifications and definitions recognized by the FTC. Certain familiar names appear as trademarks owned by particular companies. The regulations stipulate that trademarks may be used on a label in conjunction with the generic name of the fiber to which it relates.

Quality

The characteristics and the quality of any fabric are determined by:

1. The fibers.
2. The construction of the yarns.
3. The construction of the fabric.
4. The finishes applied to the fabric.

Although no one of these factors will by itself be responsible for an excellent fabric, any one of them by itself may be responsible for unsatisfactory performance. The consumer therefore, should be familiar with these basic ingredients in order to judge quality in fabrics.

FIBERS. No one fiber has all the desirable qualities that would make it useful for every type of fabric used in the home. Raw materials may be selected on the basis of cost, availability, texture, strength, resilience, resistance to abrasion, ability to take dyes, resistance to soil, ease of care, and so on. In many cases the manufacturer finds that he can incorporate several desirable qualities into the fabric by blending two or more major fibers.

We may classify the major fibers used in decorative fabrics as follows:

Natural

Vegetable—fibers that come from plants (cotton, linen, jute, sisal, kapok).
Animal—fibers that come from animals (wool, mohair, silk).

Man-made.

Regenerated—fibers that are derived from materials found in nature (rayon, acetate).
Synthetic—fibers that are composed of new materials devised in the laboratory (nylon, polyester, acrylic, and so on).

The Natural Fibers. The position of the natural fibers has certainly been challenged by the synthetics, but natural fibers still play a major role in fabrics for home use. That natural fibers are still widely used is an indication that they have advantages for certain purposes.

Cotton. This versatile fiber from the seed of the cotton plant is used in fabrics that range from sheer, delicate textures to heavy industrial materials. The maximum length of the fiber is slightly over two inches in the best grades. The quality of the fiber varies with the type of cotton plant. Sea Island, Egyptian, and Pima (Egyptian cotton plants cultivated in the United States) are the finest kinds of cotton. These plants produce a long staple that is creamy white, strong, and glossy. Other varieties of cotton fiber are grown in the United States, India, China, South America, Mexico, and several other countries. There are many different grades of fiber depending on length, luster, and natural color. The poorer grades are short, dull, and creamy tan, a color frequently seen in unbleached muslin.

Cotton has the advantages of being relatively inexpensive and readily available. It can be laundered and bleached with little detriment. It takes dyes easily and retains color. On the negative side, the fiber has several disadvantages, but some of these can be overcome in processing and finishing. The length of the fiber, for example, presents problems. The shorter fibers produce a fuzzy yarn. To obtain a smooth yarn, the fibers must be of the longer variety and they must be combed or made more parallel before the spinning process. Mercerizing or treating the fibers with a caustic soda will increase strength and absorbency and will give the fibers a glossy appearance. Continuous exposure to light will cause cotton fiber to weaken and eventually disintegrate, but we still use it for draperies or curtains. Lack of resiliency is one of the chief problems of cotton as a carpet fiber, but to some extent this difficulty can be overcome by the use of a close, dense pile, which of course increases production costs.

Linen. The lovely textural qualities of real linen have never been equaled by the synthetics, although many valiant attempts have been made. The flax fiber has strength, luster, and a natural unevenness, which gives the "linen" appearance. Fibers average about eighteen inches in length and range from a deep grayish tan to creamy yellow. Qualities vary, and the best types require time and energy to produce. Linen has a natural body and crispness, but it is neither resilient nor elastic. It does not accept dyes readily, and the more interesting and expensive linen fabrics are usually printed by hand blocking. The natural color of linen can be bleached, but the process must be carefully controlled to prevent damage.

Wool. For centuries the excellent qualities of wool have made it a most important fiber for both decorative and clothing fabrics. Technically, *wool* refers to the hair of the sheep, but mohair from the Angora goat and fibers from various other animals, such as the alpaca, llama, and camel, are considered in the same category.

The various breeds of sheep produce fibers with different qualities. Some are softer and more resilient, others are coarser and more wiry. Even on one animal, the hair differs; thus fibers taken from the back and sides are quite different from those sheared from the head, neck, and undersides. If wool is sheared from a live, healthy sheep it has more desirable qualities than wool taken from a slaughtered sheep (known as *pulled wool*).

The desirable characteristics of wool vary considerably with the type and the grade of the fiber. Its length varies from one to eighteen inches. Resiliency and durability are two chief advantages that account for the use of the coarser types of wool in rugs and upholstery fabrics. The fiber takes dyes readily and holds color. The chief difficulties involve care. Most wool fabrics cannot be laundered easily. Strong alkalies damage the fiber. Processes involving heat and moisture may be used to advantage in making felted fabrics, but on other wool fabrics heat and moisture create an undesirable matted appearance.

Silk. The history of silk is steeped in tradition, romance, and legend. For centuries it has been used for so many luxurious and exquisite fabrics that we naturally associate silk with elegance.

The silk filament is produced by the silkworm to form a cocoon, but there are various grades of silk, depending upon the type of silkworm and several other factors. The finest qualities come from cultivated silkworms, which are reared with great care and fed on tender leaves of the mulberry tree. Filaments produced by these cultured silkworms are smooth, even in diameter, and creamy white. When the natural gum is removed the fiber has a beautiful luster. Wild silkworms, which feed on various types of trees, including oak, produce a fiber that is more coarse and uneven. Known as *tussah*, the wild silk has a natural grayish tan color. It is not usually bleached or degummed, so fabrics made from this type of silk have a texture that is rather dull and rough but not at all unattractive.

Minor Fibers. Several other natural fibers are used in the home to a more limited extent than the familiar ones mentioned above. *Jute* is a fiber that is in some ways similar to the coarser grades of linen. The natural color is grayish brown and because the fiber is weakened by chemical bleaches, it is usually used in its natural state or dyed in strong colors. It is used chiefly for twine, burlap, furniture webbing, and backings for rugs and carpets. *Hemp*, another coarse fiber, comes from various types of plants that grow in the temperate zone. It is strong and harsh; the natural color ranges from pale yellow to brown. It is used mainly in cord and to some extent for mats and fiber floor coverings. *Sisal* is closely related to hemp. *Coir* is obtained from the outer shell of the coconut. The hard, reddish-brown fibers are stiff and coarse. The chief use in the home is for mats. *Ramie* is sometimes used as a linen substitute. The fiber is coarse and durable. *Kapok* is a silky vegetable fiber that is not suitable for spinning into yarn but does have some advantages for use as a filling material in pillows, mattresses, and upholstery. It is not as durable nor as resilient as hair but it is much cheaper. *Grasses* and *rushes* from a variety of plants can be used in the form of thick ropes to make floor coverings.

Asbestos is an interesting mineral fiber that is difficult to spin into yarn unless it is mixed with some other fiber. Its chief advantage is that it is fireproof.

Man-made Fibers. There are many reasons why the synthetic fibers are becoming increasingly important in fabrics for the home. Because production can be carefully controlled it is possible to achieve uniform quality and to make fibers that are specifically designed for particular purposes. More uniform production costs are another important factor. At the present time some products made from synthetic fibers are more expensive than similar ones made from natural fibers; others are less expensive. It is difficult to equate products on this basis, because the fabrics will have different characteristics. However, it is expected that with an increased supply of some of the new synthetic fibers, the costs of production will decrease. It may well be that in the future differences in cost will become a more important factor.

Ease of care is an important advantage that many synthetics have over some of the natural fibers. In general, they tend to resist soil, spots, and stains, and damage from moths and mildew. Many of the washable fabrics need little if any ironing.

Synthetics offer a wide variety of textural possibilities. Because the diameter of the fiber can be controlled there is a wide range. Very fine fibers can have considerable strength, so delicate fabrics that are quite durable can be produced.

Length can also be controlled. Filaments can be as long as desired or cut into short pieces and spun in the same manner as the natural fibers. Different degrees of luster can be produced, which further increases the versatility.

The synthetics are finding their way at the present time. Some have shown themselves to be particularly suited to certain purposes, but the field is constantly expanding, with the well-established fibers finding new uses and new fibers being developed to enter the picture.

Rayon. Cellulose from wood chips or cotton linters is used to make the rayon fiber. Because the substance is not changed chemically, rayon is a regenerated cellulose fiber and has, therefore, many of the properties of cellulose. It is a versatile fiber in that it can be dull or bright, soft or crisp, smooth or rough. Rayon yarns can be made to resemble those made from other fibers. In the furnishing field, rayon is used for drapery and upholstery fabrics, as well as floor covering.

Acetate. Cellulose is changed chemically to produce cellulose acetate, the substance of the acetate fiber. Its properties are quite different from those of cellulose. Acetate fibers resist moisture and wrinkling; they also resist insects and mildew. The fibers are affected by high temperatures, however, and will fuse or even melt if an iron is too hot.

Triacetate is related to acetate but is more resistant to heat. It has excellent crease resistance.

Nylon. Nylon was produced in the laboratory from carbon, hydrogen, nitrogen, and oxygen by a process of polymerization, or building up giant molecules. When nylon was announced in 1938 it was hailed as the most significant textile discovery of the age because it opened up many new avenues of research.

Nylon is strong, durable, and easily cleaned. It is being used in curtains, draperies, upholstery fabrics, and carpets.

Polyesters. Dacron was the first of the polyester fibers, which are also polymers but of a different chemical nature.

Fibers in this group are strong and resilient. They resist damage from strong sunlight, moths, and mildew. When the fibers are crimped, they have a wool-like quality. Fabrics are easily cared for and do not tend to shrink or stretch out of shape.

Acrylics. Another group of polymer fibers are derived from basic materials, such as coal, air, water, petroleum, limestone, and natural gases. In addition to being strong and durable they have excellent bulking and insulating qualities, which has made them useful for blankets. They also have high resistance to outdoor exposure and strong sunlight.

Glass. Fibers made from glass have been particularly useful for curtains and draperies. They resist soil, but when necessary they are washed easily. They are nonflammable and nonabsorbent. However, fabrics made of glass fibers generally have poor resistance to abrasion. They should not be folded, crushed, or ironed.

YARNS. Fibers are spun into yarns in preparation for the weaving or knitting of fabrics.

The construction of the yarn influences the appearance, durability, and serviceability of the fabric. Shorter fibers need more twisting to form the yarn than do long filaments, and the way the fibers are twisted as well as the amount of twist will influence performance. In some cases a high twist is desirable for strength and durability, but because twisting decreases the luster of the yarn, the long, smooth fibers sometimes are given very little twist. Unless a strong, durable fiber is used, such low-twist yarns will quickly show signs of wear.

Ply. When two or more single yarns are twisted together in a *ply* construction, the resulting yarn usually has added strength and durability. However, a ply construction may also be used for producing a novelty effect.

Combed. Cotton fabrics are sometimes made with combed yarns. This means that only the longer cotton fibers are used, and they are made as nearly parallel as possible before the actual spinning process. Because there are fewer fiber ends projecting from the surface, a combed yarn will be smoother and usually more lustrous than one that is not combed.

Woolen and Worsted. In fabrics made of wool a distinction is frequently made between woolen and worsted. In woolen yarns the fibers are shorter and in a more random arrangement. Worsted yarns are made of longer fibers in a more parallel position. The cloths made from woolen and worsted yarns will, of course, have different characteristics. The soft woolen yarns will be fuzzy and lighter in weight. Little air-spaces trapped in the yarn have excellent insulating value, so this type of yarn is desirable for blankets, but it is not suitable for fabrics that will receive hard wear from abrasion. The smooth surface and the tighter twist of a worsted yarn will produce a more compact fiber and one that is geared to harder use.

Novelty. An infinite variety of textural effects can be produced in fabrics by the use of special yarns. A slub yarn that is thick in some spots and thin in others is frequently used. A ply yarn of one dull strand and one glossy strand, or perhaps two different colors will produce another effect. Sometimes the two strands are held at different tensions so that the looser one will form little curlicues on the surface for a bouclé texture. The possibilities are infinite, but the consumer must

CHART 1 Man-Made Fibers
(*adapted from "Modern Fibers and Fabrics," J. C. Penney Co., Inc.*)

Generic Term and Description*	Registered Trademarks
Acetate A manufactured fiber in which the fiber-forming substance is cellulose acetate. Where not less than 92% by weight of the cellulose is acetylated, the term *Triacetate* may be used as a generic description. (See Triacetate)	Acele† (du Pont) Celaloft ⎫ Celanese ⎬(Celanese Corp.) Celaperm†⎭ Chromspun† (Tenn. Eastman) Acele (du Pont) Estron (Tenn. Eastman) —and many in Canada, Europe, and Japan.
Acrylic A manufactured fiber in which the fiber-forming substance is any long-chain synthetic polymer composed of at least 85% by weight of acrylonitrile units.	Acrilan (Monsanto) Creslan (Amer. Cyanamid) Orlon (du Pont) Zefran (Dow Chemical) The acrylics are also being mass-produced under various trade names in Ireland, Belgium, Sweden, France, Italy, Holland, the Iron Curtain countries, and Japan.
Azlon A manufactured fiber in which the fiber-forming substance is composed of any regenerated naturally occurring proteins, as in corn (zein), milk (casein), peanuts, soy beans, and other natural products.	Ardil (England) Lanital (Belgium) Merinova (Italy) There is considerable Azlon production in Europe and Japan, but none is known of at present in the U.S., which formerly produced fibers known as Aralac and Vicara.
Glass A manufactured fiber in which the fiber-forming substance is glass. The special kind of glass used in making fibers is made by combining molten silica, stone, and certain chemicals and extruding filaments through a spinneret.	Aerocor Fiberglas (Owens-Corning) PPG Fiber Glass (Pittsburgh Plate Glass) Unifab Unirove (Ferro Corp.) Vitron (Libby-Owens-Ford)
Metallic A manufactured fiber composed of metal, plastic-coated metal, metal-coated plastic, or a core completely covered by metal.	Lurex (Dow Badische Co.) Metlon (Metlon Corp.) Reymet (Reynolds Metals)
Modacrylic A manufactured fiber in which the fiber-forming substance is any long-chain synthetic polymer composed of less than 85%, but more than 35%, by weight, of acrylonitrile units.	Dynel (Union Carbide) Verel (Tenn. Eastman) Modacrylics are also produced in Canada, Germany, Russia, and Japan.

Acetate comes in staple and filament form and produces fabrics of silklike hand and good draping quality. It is moderately hydrophobic (non-water-absorbing) and resistant to moths and mildew.

Acetate dyes are subject to atmospheric fading unless protected by a special finish. Solution-dyed acetates, marked by a dagger in the listing at left, are resistant to all kinds of fading.

Its pleasing texture and moderate cost make acetate desirable for wearing apparel and for household textiles.

Fabrics containing acetate should be dry-cleaned unless washability is specifically indicated. The fibers themselves are washable, but the finish may be vulnerable to water. Acetates must be ironed at a moderate temperature (325° F.). Contact with acetone (nail polish and remover) and other solvents should be avoided; they dissolve acetate fibers.

The acrylic fibers make light, bulky fabrics with a soft, resilient hand similar to wool. They retain pressed pleats and have good crease recovery, as well as being resistant to wrinkling. Acrylics take well to dyeing in bright colors.

The filament yarn is used for curtains; the staple in knitwear, blankets, rugs, and pile fabrics. Fabrics made of the acrylics are easy to wash and dry, but need moderate temperatures; heat is likely to cause yellowing. Rinse thoroughly; hard-water scum that adheres to the surface will cause graying. Ironing temperature should not exceed 325° F.

A resilient fiber that contributes a soft, wool-like hand and excellent draping qualities to fabrics.

It is naturally wrinkle resistant. In strength, however, it is so limited that its chief use is as a blend with other fibers used in making woven, knitted, and napped goods. It helps to retard pilling when combined with fibers that have this fault.

Glass fibers and the fabrics made from them are extremely strong, resistant to weather, water, and sunlight, and not combustible.

Its dimensional stability makes it excellent for curtains and draperies; it is also used to reinforce plastics in boat hulls, fishing rods, and golf clubs.

Glass curtains are hand washable, but they should not be rubbed, wrung, folded, or crushed. They drip dry quickly and smoothly and therefore need not be ironed.

Metallic yarns are usually made with clear polyester films, although acetate and butyrate films are also used. This depends on what the yarn is going to be used for.

Metallic yarns in merchandise that is normally washable, such as sheets and bath towels, do not affect the washability.

Modacrylics have a soft hand similar to that of the acrylics. They are resistant to chemicals and are non-flammable, but their heat resistance is poor; ironing temperature must be at 225° F. or lower. Principally used in synthetic furs and carpeting. Blended with cotton, the modacrylic fiber gives a luxurious cashmere-like hand to such knitted items as men's socks.

Generic Term and Description*	Registered Trademarks
Nylon Nylon is a manufactured fiber in which the fiber-forming substance is any long chain polyamide having recurring amide groups as an integral part of the polymer chain.	A.C.E. (Allied Chemical) Antron (du Pont) Caprolan (Allied Chemical) Nyloft (Hercules Powder) Nylon (du Pont, American Enka, Allied Chemical, Beaunit) Nylon, under various trademarks, is also produced in Mexico, South America, Europe, (including the Iron Curtain countries), Egypt, India, and Japan.
Nytril A manufactured fiber containing at least 85% of a long-chain polymer of vinylidene dinitrile, where the vinylidene dinitrile content is no less than that of any other unit in the polymer chain.	Not manufactured in U.S.
Olefin A manufactured fiber in which the fiber-forming substance is any long-chain synthetic polymer composed of at least 85% by weight of ethylene, propylene, or other olefin units.	Durel (Celanese Corp. [polypropylene]) Herculon (Hercules, Inc.) Marvess (Phillips Fibers Corp.) Vectra (Enjay Fibers and Laminates Company)
Polyester A manufactured fiber in which the fiber-forming substance is any long-chain synthetic polymer composed of at least 85% by weight of an ester of dihydric alcohol and terephthalic acid.	Dacron (du Pont) Fortrel (Celanese Fibers Co.) Kodel (Tenn. Eastman) Vycron (Beaunit Mills) Polyesters under various trade names are also produced in Holland, Germany, Italy, Russia, Israel, and Japan.
Rayon A manufactured fiber composed of regenerated cellulose, including that composed of regenerated cellulose in which substituents have replaced not more than 15% of the hydrogens of the hydroxyl groups.	Coloray (Courtaulds Alabama) Colorspun (Amer. Viscose) Cupioni (Beaunit Corp.) Bemberg (Beaunit Corp.) Cordura (du Pont) Fortisan (Celanese Corp.) Kolorbon‡ (American Euka Corp.) Avril (Amer. Viscose) Zantrel (American Euka Corp.). Also many foreign producers in Europe and Japan.
Rubber A manufactured fiber in which the fiber-forming substance is an elastomer composed of natural or synthetic rubber.	Contro (Firestone) Filatex (Filatex Co.) Lastex (U.S. Rubber)

Nylon is an extremely strong, abrasion-resistant fiber that washes and dries easily. It is thermoplastic; holds heat-set pleats. It has natural wrinkle resistance and crease recovery, and is both moth and mildew resistant. Stretch nylon yarns give elasticity to fabrics. Nylon is much used in blends with other fibers, imparting to the fabrics the strength and wash-and-wear characteristics of the nylon.

It should be laundered at moderate temperatures to avoid yellowing; thorough rinsing is essential.

Nylon scavenges color from even normally colorfast items, and white should be washed only with other white items. Low ironing setting is recommended, no more than 325° F.

Nytril is a soft, springy fiber with much of the feel of cashmere.

Fabrics of nytril are used for knitwear, fashion coatings, and for blending with worsted in men's suitings. Heat sensitive; must be laundered in warm water and ironed at no higher temperatures than 325° F.

A hydrophobic thermoplastic fiber somewhat like Dacron, but with a waxy feel. It is used for carpeting, blankets, robes, seat covers, upholstery fabrics, and marine cordage.

It is highly heat sensitive and should not be exposed to temperatures over 200° F.

This hydrophobic fiber is easy to launder and quick drying. It holds heat-set pleats, resists wrinkling, sunlight, mildew, and moths.

It may be produced in fabrics that resemble silk, worsted, wool, or cotton.

Some types are more resistant to pilling than others.

Garments made from the polyesters require little ironing because of this fiber's shape-retention properties.

Polyester fabrics need special handling in garment construction; for example, they cannot be shrunk for easing, as in putting a sleeve into an armhole.

Largest in volume of all man-made fibers; available in filament and staple. Characteristics similar to cotton. It is a hydrophilic fiber; loses some strength when wet, regains it on drying. Used in blends to produce a great variety of fabrics; lends itself well to special finishes.

When properly finished, rayon can be washed and ironed like cotton. Chlorine bleaches should be avoided on resin-finished rayons to prevent yellowing and tendering.

Rubber is produced neither in staple nor in tow; the yarn is extruded from the spinneret in the desired size. It is used in stretch fabrics, webbings, and rubber thread.

Fabrics containing rubber should not be subjected to heat, strong sunlight, oils (lotions, creams, body oils), or constant overstretching.

CHART 1 Man-Made Fibers (*Cont.*)
(*adapted from "Modern Fibers and Fabrics," J. C. Penney Co., Inc.*)

Generic Term and Description*	Registered Trademarks
Saran	
A manufactured fiber in which the fiber-forming substance is any long-chain synthetic polymer composed of at least 80% by weight of vinylidene chloride units.	National (National Plastics) Rovana (Dow Chemical) Saran (Dow Chemical) Velon (Firestone Plastic)
Spandex	
A manufactured fiber in which the fiber-forming substance is a long-chain synthetic polymer composed of at least 85% of a segmented polyurethane.	Curel (Reeves Bros.) Lycra (du Pont) Vyrene (U.S. Rubber)
Triacetate	
These are part of the acetate group. The designation *Triacetate* may be used where not less than 92% by weight of the cellulose is acetylated.	Arnel (Celanese Corp.)
Vinal	
A manufactured fiber in which the fiber-forming substance is any long-chain synthetic polymer composed of at least 50% by weight of vinyl alcohol units, and in which the total of the vinyl alcohol units and any one or more of the various acetal units is at least 85% by weight of the fiber.	Not currently produced in U.S.
Vinyon	
A manufactured fiber in which the fiber-forming substance is any long-chain synthetic polymer composed of at least 85% by weight of vinyl chloride units.	Vinyon HH (Amer. Viscose) Vinyon is also produced in Europe and Japan.

* According to the Federal Trade Commission.
† Solution-dyed acetates.
‡ Indicates solution-dyed.

always be sure that the use of a novelty yarn will not detract from the serviceability of the fabric. Frequently the durable qualities of a fabric are sacrificed for interesting texture. In drapery fabrics, this may not be so important, but in upholstery and slipcover fabrics it certainly should be a major consideration.

Metallic. Some of the most fascinating textiles in history were richly decorated with strands of real gold or silver, but these are impractical according to modern standards. We do have instead various metallic yarns that add a touch of luxury along with such practical characteristics as being washable and nontarnishable. And so we have glitter in towels and sheets that can go through the rigor of the washing machine; we also have lovely durable decorative fabrics that require no special care.

There are several ways of producing metallic yarns. Some employ a core yarn that is impregnated with a metallic film. Most of them have proved to be very satisfactory in service.

CONSTRUCTION OF CLOTH. There are various ways of constructing a fabric, and the method used will affect not only the appearance but also the purposes for which the cloth can be used. The major methods of construction include:

1. Weaving.
2. Knitting.
3. Netting.
4. Felting and bonding.

A tough, flexible fiber that resists stains, chemicals, insects, and flame. Its water repellency makes it useful for outdoor furniture; it is important in carpets, drapery, and upholstery fabrics.

It is highly heat sensitive and cannot be pressed. May be laundered or dry-cleaned depending on nature of material.

Combines light weight with good restoring force. The filament yarn is usually wrapped with another textile fiber or blend, but can be used bare. Makes foundation garments, swimsuits, and other items that demand high elongation, good flex recovery, and durability. It has better resistance than rubber to perspiration, body oils, and cosmetic oils.

Triacetate has excellent draping qualities, is wrinkle resistant, retains heat-set pleats even in high humidity. It is not as sensitive to heat nor to acetone as the acetates. Dyes well in strong colors but is also susceptible to atmospheric fading. Good wet strength.

An extremely strong fiber, resistant to abrasion and tearing. It is water resistant, but not as impervious to moisture as other synthetics. It is currently being used in rainwear and swimwear, but can be woven to look and feel like silk or wool. Because it is so easily wrinkled, its use in fashion fabrics is limited. It is heat sensitive and should not be exposed to heat over 250° F.

Vinyon is resistant to acids and alkalies, which makes it suitable for fishing nets and industrial uses. It is highly water repellent, strong, and has considerable resiliency. It is so heat sensitive that it melts at normal ironing temperatures.

Weaving. By far the most common method of producing cloth is by using a loom to interlace at least two sets of yarns. Some looms are quite simple, whereas others are complicated machines that are capable of weaving intricate patterns.

The lengthwise yarns, called *warps*, are wound on rollers and strung through some device that makes it possible to raise and lower the yarns. As certain warp yarns are raised, others remain in the lower position and a *shed* is formed. The crosswise yarn, called *weft* or *filling*, is carried through the shed. The raised warps are returned to the lowered position and another set of warp yarns is raised. The crosswise yarn is returned through the shed. Thus the weft passes over some warps and under others. The warp yarns at each side of the cloth are often thicker or closer together,

so in the finished fabric they appear as a narrow taped edge known as the *selvage*.

There are three basic weaves, and they are used singly or in various combinations to form patterns. There are also other methods of interlacing yarns, and these are known as *fancy* weaves.

The basic weaves include:

Plain Weave. The simplest way of interlacing the warp and weft yarns is an over-and-under arrangement of alternate warps crossing each line of the filling thread. A diagram of this weave would look like a checkerboard.

The plain weave is sturdy and durable if strong yarns are used in a compact construction, but not if weak yarns are used in a widely spaced, open construction.

Various effects can be achieved by using yarns of different colors or of different types,

Stripes, checks, and plaids are frequently woven in the plain weave. Ribbed effects are easily obtained by using a thick filling yarn.

The *basket* weave, a variation of the plain weave, uses two or more yarns as one in the same pattern of alternate interlacing.

Twill Weave. A wide variety of diagonal ridged effects can be produced by the twill weave. In the simplest pattern, the filling thread might in one line pass over one warp and under two, in the next line pass over and under different sets of warps, and so on. In some variations the filling may go over two and under three warps. As long as there is a progression at each crossing, the interlacing will provide the diagonal effect.

The *herringbone* weave is produced by reversing the direction of the twill at regular intervals.

Fabrics made with the twill weave can be extremely durable. Again, it depends on the type of yarn and the compactness of the cloth.

Satin Weave. In the true satin weave, the surface of the cloth is composed mostly of warp yarns. The crosswise threads are not usually visible on the right side of the finished fabric. The long sections of warp threads on the right side of the fabric are called *floats*. When glossy yarns are used for the warp, this weave produces the characteristic shiny texture of satin fabric. When the floats are exceptionally long and the warp yarns are not very sturdy, the surface of the fabric will tend to show signs of wear rather quickly. Some upholstery fabrics with designs in the satin weave may be a problem in this respect.

A variation of the satin weave reverses the positions of warp and filling so that long floats of the crosswise yarns appear on the surface. This is known as the *sateen* weave. It is frequently used with cotton yarns, and the resulting fabric is called *sateen*. However, cotton is sometimes used in the true satin construction, and this fabric is known as *warp-faced sateen*.

The fancy weaves are in general more complex than the basic weaves. Some of these include:

Dobby. An attachment to the loom makes it possible to weave a small all-over pattern in the cloth. The design and the background are, in effect, formed by combinations of the basic weaves.

Jacquard. Many decorative fabrics are made with rather complex designs woven in the cloth. In the Jacquard looms, each warp thread can be controlled individually so that it may appear on the surface of the cloth at any desired point. Raising the warp yarns is governed by a series of punched cards attached to the loom; there is a separate card for each crosswise thread of the design. As each card comes into place, certain warps are raised and the filling thread slides across the loom. The warps are returned to position and the next card moves into place to raise another set of warp yarns. In this manner, any desired design can be woven into the cloth.

Pile Weaves. In addition to the regular warp and weft yarns, a third set of yarns is used to form loops on the surface of the fabric. There are several methods of constructing pile fabrics, and in some of them the pile can be cut so that tiny tufts of yarn project from the surface instead of the uncut loops. Most pile-woven fabrics are constructed by the use of extra warp yarns to form the pile.

In good-quality fabrics, the pile construction often produces a rich, luxurious effect. If the weave is close and the pile is dense, this can be a durable construction, but serviceability will, of course, be influenced by fiber and yarn construction.

Leno Weave. For sheer, lightweight fabrics, the leno weave is sometimes used. Warp threads cross over one another between the filling threads. This construction, often seen in marquisette, prevents the yarns from sliding out of place and provides a more durable quality than that of similar sheer fabrics made with plain weaving.

Knitting. A series of interdependent loops of yarn form the basis of knitted fabrics, and there are no warp and filling threads in the same sense as in woven fabrics. Knitted fabrics have greater elasticity, but their uses are rather limited in home furnishings and very few decorative fabrics appear in this construction. Ready-made slipcovers are frequently made of knitted fabric to allow for better fit.

Nets and Laces. Various types of fabrics are made with a mesh construction in which yarns are knotted and twisted to form the cloth. Lace usually has a design worked into the mesh background. Net fabrics may have square, diamond, or hexagonal meshes.

Felting and Bonding. There are no yarns in fabrics that are felted or bonded. In felting, a mass of fibers is subjected to heat, moisture, and pressure, causing them to interlock and cling together. Wool fibers have excellent felting properties; cotton fibers can also be felted.

Bonded fabrics are made by the use of some other substance, a bonding agent, to hold a mass of fibers together. These nonwoven fabrics have improved in strength and durability in recent years. They have been used for such items as disposable napkins and towels, and for inexpensive draperies. Several companies have plans for further development of these fabrics for home furnishings, so more items may be available in the future.

FINISHES. A variety of finishes may be applied to fabrics to make them more attractive, more practical, or both. Some finishes are old standbys, but within recent years the textile industry has developed many new methods of making fabrics more serviceable. Not all of these finishes have been perfected to the point where they will last for the life of the fabric, but the situation is constantly becoming brighter as finishes become more useful and durable.

Dyeing and Printing. Color can be applied at any stage of manufacturing. Some of the synthetics have colorants added to them before the fibers are formed, a process which has been extremely successful with acetates. Natural fibers, especially wool, can be dyed before they are spun into yarns (stock dyeing). Other yarns are dyed before they are used on the loom (skein dyeing). In any of these methods, the cloth is, of course, colored when it comes from the loom. But many fabrics are piece-dyed after weaving, or they are printed. Stock dyeing and skein dyeing are often preferred for more uniform distribution and for deeper penetration of the color, which will, in general, make the fabric more colorfast. However, many factors influence the permanency of color and it is possible to produce highly desirable fabrics with both piece dyeing and printing.

Colorfastness is a difficult quality for the manufacturer to guarantee. Almost any fabric will eventually have some change in color. As consumers, we are concerned about perceptible changes during normal use, but who is to say what constitutes "normal" use? A drapery fabric might be perfectly satisfactory under most conditions, but suppose it is ex-posed to very strong sunlight for many hours each day and to excessive soil and fumes so that it needs frequent laundering. Such rigorous treatment could cause a color change faster than more normal conditions.

Rather than actually guaranteeing a fabric to be colorfast, the manufacturer will often merely assert that his fabric is vat dyed. The vat dyes are extremely colorfast; they are insoluble but can be made soluble for the process of dyeing the fabric. Once affixed to the fibers, they again become insoluble. They will not readily change color, but under extreme conditions they might.

Various methods can be used to print designs on fabrics, and each one has advantages as well as disadvantages.

Roller Printing. Most printed fabrics have the design applied by etched or engraved copper rollers. Each color in the pattern requires a separate roller. As a fabric runs through a series of rollers, each one applies the dye paste in the proper areas.

The initial expense of setting up the rollers is high, but once that is accomplished many yards of fabric can be printed very quickly. Also, the rollers can be used for different color combinations.

Screen Printing. A slower and more expensive method of printing fabrics is through the use of large screens, one for each color to be applied. The screen consists of a frame covered with a fine meshed fabric through which paste dye can be forced. Part of the screen fabric is covered with a film that will resist the dye. All parts of the design that will be applied in one color are left free. Each screen is placed on top of the fabric and the dye is forced through the open-mesh areas. The initial cost of screen printing is lower than for roller printing, but the actual process of applying the dye is slower and therefore more costly. This method is useful for more unique and unusual designs to be printed on limited amounts of fabric. It is also used for much custom work.

Resist Dyeing. Certain parts of the fabric can be treated in some way to make them resist dyes. An ancient method of coating certain areas with wax is called *batik* dyeing. *Tie dyeing*, in which sections of the fabric are knotted or twisted with cord, is another old hand-method. Any method that prevents dye from penetrating certain parts of the fabric might be called resist dyeing or printing.

Discharge Printing. This method is a reverse of the resist process. A cloth is dyed, after which parts of it have the color removed or lightened by the application of some chemical.

Block Printing. Wood or linoleum blocks are carved with a design and a paste dye is applied to the raised areas. When the blocks are placed against the fabric there is a direct application of color to specific areas. This method is used for printing some wallpapers as well as fabrics.

Blocking is a favorite method for printing linen fabrics because it allows for deeper and more uniform penetration of the dye. Linen does not absorb dyes readily, and when it is printed with the faster roller method, the color is more uneven.

Photoengraving. Interesting specialized designs can be transferred to fabrics through the use of photographic film. The photographed designs are transferred to rollers and printed on fabric.

Warp Printing. Although warp printing is somewhat out of favor at the present time, it occasionally appears in some very interesting fabrics. A design is printed only on the warp threads before the fabric is woven. A solid-color filling thread is used with the result that the design appears in the finished fabric in a rather shadowy or hazy form.

Sizing. A certain amoung of added substance is sometimes used to give fabrics body. In the past, excessive sizing was frequently used to make a sleazy fabric appear heavy. After one or two launderings, the consumer realized that it was a sleazy, loosely woven fabric. Today this malpractice is not quite as widespread. The sizing that disappears in laundering can often be replaced by starch to renew the original texture.

Napping. Some fabrics are made with low-twist yarns and the surface is brushed by rollers covered with tiny wires to produce a fuzzy nap. This finish is desirable in certain articles, such as blankets, because the fibers trap tiny air pockets that act as insulators, yet the weight of the fabric is not increased. When napped fabrics are subjected to abrasion, they tend to show signs of wear rather quickly.

Mercerization. Mercerization is often applied to cottons. The yarn or cloth is held under tension in a caustic soda bath, which makes the fiber more lustrous, more absorbent, and stronger.

Preshrinking. The familiar "Sanforized" label on cotton fabrics indicates that there is no more than one per cent residual shrinkage in the fabric. With other fabrics we have not been quite so successful in controlling shrinkage. Some won't shrink at all; others will shrink a considerable amount. With any washable fabric that does not have the Sanforized label, the consumer should make some allowance for possible shrinkage.

Glazing. A coating on the surface of the fabric produces a smooth glaze, which adds luster and stiffness to the fabric as well as resistance to soil. Chintz is the favorite fabric for glazing, and now we have glazed chintzes that will retain their finishes through repeated washings. The finishes do gradually disappear, however—even the "permanent" ones.

Starchless Finishes. Some fabrics, such as organdy, must have a crispness in order to retain the desired effect. In the past, these fabrics had to be starched each time they were laundered, but now a finish can be applied that keeps the fabrics stiff through several launderings. It may disappear gradually as the fabric is laundered many times, but soon we shall have fabrics that are truly starchless. Some of the synthetics and blends of synthetics and natural fibers have already achieved this.

Flocking. This is a purely decorative treatment that is applied to both fabrics and wall coverings. A pattern is applied to the surface with a form of glue; then short fibers are sprinkled over the area and embedded in the adhesive, often by an electromagnetic force. When insoluble adhesives are used, flocked fabrics are quite durable. The design is raised and has a felted appearance.

Special Finishes. One or more special finishes may be applied to fabrics to improve them in particular ways. Wool fabrics can be made moth repellent; cotton fabrics can be treated to resist mildew. It is possible to apply a finish that will make fabrics flame resistant, but there are still problems in this area, because the finish either affects the appearance or is not permanent. In buildings where fire-retardant fabrics are required, it has seemed more desirable to use fibres that are flame-proof rather than treated fabrics of other fibers.

Some special finishes have been developed to render fabrics resistant to soiling and staining. One of these has the trade name *Scotchgard*; another is called *Zepel*.

Plastic Film and Coated Fabrics

A whole group of materials in the plastics category is becoming more important for home use. Many of these are not fabrics in the true sense of the word. Some are sheets or films of plastic materials; others are made of traditional types of woven or knitted fabric with coatings of plastic on the surface.

The plastic-type materials range from thin, lightweight varieties that are particularly useful for shower curtains and table coverings to heavy upholstery fabrics. Coverings in the latter group are now widely used in the home on dinette chairs. New developments in this field have produced a wide variety of upholstery materials that are exciting and extremely practical. Beautiful colors and interesting textures are making these fabrics more suitable for other areas in the home. Up until the present time, such fabrics have been used mainly on modern furniture, but the elegance of the new designs is making them more adaptable to many different styles. Their great advantages lie in their being both very very durable and easy to maintain. The good-quality materials do not peel, crack, or chip, even with hard use. They may be easily washed with soap and water and they retain their original colors. There is little doubt that these fabrics will be used far more extensively in the home furnishings of the future.

The leather look has become very important in upholstery fabrics. It is now possible to make synthetic fabrics that closely resemble suede, doeskin, and other leathers. A particularly successful development in this area is a new polymer produced by Tenneco Chemicals, Inc., under the trade name *Frontera*. It is available in a wide variety of exciting colors and it is durable, stain resistant, and colorfast.

Design in Fabrics

The color, texture, and pattern in a fabric must be keyed to the basic theme and to the purpose of the room. Certain fabric designs will express very definite characteristics, perhaps a formal type of elegance, perhaps a more rustic kind of charm. For example, intricate patterns woven or embroidered with smooth, lustrous yarns in deep, rich colors will relate the idea of skilled craftsmanship and perfec-tion of detail. Other fabrics with coarse, nubby yarns, earthy colors, and little or no pattern may suggest a more simple kind of hand craftsmanship that is less formal in appearance. Different fabrics are appropriate for different styles of furniture. In general, graceful, delicate patterns are suitable for furniture that is graceful and dainty; the more rugged and forceful designs seem better suited to furniture that is more substantial looking. It isn't necessary always to follow the letter of the law in choosing authentic designs for a particular style. In fact, rooms may become trite and dull if one tries to do so. We have a wide range of choice today. There are many modern fabrics that are extremely adaptable to different types and styles of furnishings. Also, there are lovely adaptations and interpretations of traditional fabrics scaled to our contemporary versions of traditional styles. But because there is such a wide variety from which to choose, it is important to select those that do the most to complement and enhance the expressiveness of the furnishings.

The size of the room will certainly influence the color, texture, and scale of the designs used. When shopping for fabrics, one should look closely at quality, but view the pattern from a distance. Is it subdued or advancing? Does it have a great deal of movement or is it a static type of design? It is often wise to purchase a large enough sample, a half yard or so, to try out at home before making a major investment. The color and the scale of the design may appear quite different in a particular room than in a store. A large design, if it has perspective, may even be quite attractive in a small room, but if it is advancing, it may completely overshadow everything else in the room. Seeing the pattern, texture, and color in one's own home will help in making decisions. One should look at the fabric in both natural and artificial light, and hold it next to the other colors, textures, and patterns in the room to be certain that the effect will be right. Of course, the amount of any particular color or pattern will influence the effect, and this is difficult to visualize even with a fairly large sample. One should drape the sample on the furniture or fasten it to the wall and use the imagination. It should be remembered that strong contrasts will tend to make an area seem smaller whereas related colors will tend to blend and make an area seem larger.

(a) Frontera sculptured polymer has the effect of polished stones embedded in sand.

FIGURE 22-1   A new chemical advancement can create almost any textured surface in any dimension and to any degree of flexibility. (*Courtesy of Tenneco Advanced Materials, Division of Tenneco Chemicals, Inc.*)

(b) An elegant sofa is upholstered with this unique material that looks and feels like suede. It can be readily cleaned with soap and water.

FIGURE 22-2   Fabrics coordinated with wallpaper can create an architectural appearance. (*Courtesy of Waverly Fabrics*)

FIGURE 22-3   A print used in an imaginative manner coordinates a variety of styles in a small bed-sitting room. (*Courtesy of Waverly Fabrics*)

FIGURE 22-4   A crisp, sheer fabric acts as a room divider in a small area. (*Courtesy of DuPont Textile Fibers*)

FIGURE 22-5 A sheer fabric in strong blue and orange is used at the window and on the canopy. Even with strong colors, the lightweight texture seems suitable for a small room. (*Courtesy of Celanese Corporation*)

FIGURE 22-6 A fabric valance and table cloth added to the "folded wall" covered in a matching design serve to unify a small dining area. (*Courtesy of Wallcoverings Council*)

FIGURE 22-7 Another simple way to use fabric as the dominant note is demonstrated in this room. A dust ruffle, canopy, and a laminated window shade dramatize the small bedroom designed for a young girl. (*Courtesy of Window Shade Manufacturers Association*)

FIGURE 22-8 Fabric covered shutters integrate this window and wall in a rather unusual manner. (*Courtesy of Waverly Fabrics*)

CHART 2 Glossary of Fabrics

Antique Satin Nubby yarns are added to give satin or heavy cotton sateen a textural effect.

Appliqué One fabric stitched or pasted to another in the form of a design.

Armure Fabric used for draperies and upholstery. Usually rep or twill background with small raised patterns, often in a satin weave.

Aubusson District in France famous for tapestries and rugs.

Bark Cloth Cotton fabric with uneven yarns.

Batik Method of dyeing fabrics that originated in Java. Wax is applied to certain areas to make them resist dye. After dyeing, wax is removed and may be reapplied in several successive stages to build up intricate patterns in several colors.

Batiste Fine, sheer cotton in plain weave.

Beauvois District in France noted for fine tapestries.

Bedford Cord Fabric with heavy corded yarn.

Block Print Design applied to fabrics or wallpaper with wood or linoleum blocks.

Bobbinet Net fabric with round or hexagonal mesh.

Bouclé Novelty yarn with curly loops on the surface. Imparts a distinctive texture when used in a fabric.

Broadcloth (1) Cotton or silk; a slightly heavier crosswise yarn gives the effect of a very fine rib. (2) Wool: surface is napped and pressed to impart a sheen.

Brocade Woven pattern, made with an extra filling yarn, often resembles embroidery.

Brocatelle Pattern in warp-faced satin weave against plain or twill background. Appears to be embossed.

Buckram Strong plain-weave cotton with glue sizing. Used for stiffening.

Burlap Coarse, loosely woven fabric in a plain weave. Usually made of jute or hemp.

Calico Plain-weave cotton fabric printed with small designs.

Cambric Lightweight fabric of cotton or linen in a plain weave.

Candlewick Tufts of yarn stitched to a plain cotton fabric such as muslin. Used for bedspreads.

Canvas Heavy plain-weave fabric in cotton or linen. May be dyed or printed. Popular for outdoor use.

Casement Cloth Term used for a variety of fabrics made for use in curtains and draperies. May be any fiber. Weave often has a small design on plain, twill, or leno background.

Chenille Special type of yarn made by the cutting of strips of a woven cloth. Each strip has a fuzzy surface that produces a pile when used in a fabric.

Chintz Fine cotton cloth in a plain weave. Often has a printed design. Much of it has a glaze applied to the surface. Unglazed chintz is soft and pliable; glazed chintz is stiff and shiny, but the glaze may gradually disappear in laundering.

Corduroy Cotton fabric with pile in ridges or "wales" running lengthwise. Pinwale has pile in narrow, corded effect.

Crash Term used for various types of fabric that have plain weaves and coarse, uneven yarns.

Cretonne Heavy fabric of cotton or linen in a plain or twill weave. Printed designs are usually larger than those found in chintz; surface is not glazed.

Crewel Type of embroidery worked in various colors of wool yarn on a fabric of cotton or linen in its natural color. Designs often include trailing vines and floral motifs.

Damask Patterned fabric of any fiber, made on Jacquard loom. Design is flat; fabric can often be used on either side.

Denim Heavy cotton fabric in twill weave.

Dimity Plain-weave cotton fabric that is crisp and sheer. Often has stripe or crossbar design formed by heavier threads.

Dotted Swiss Sheer, plain-weave cotton fabric with dots woven or embroidered. Similar-type fabric sometimes has tiny flocked dots.

Drill Heavy fabric, usually cotton, in twill weave. Often used as backing for coated fabrics.

Duck Heavy cotton fabric in plain weave, but it often has a ribbed effect. Similar to canvas.

Faille Plain weave with ribbed effect caused by heavy crosswise yarns. Warp is usually silk, rayon, or other synthetic, and filling is usually cotton.

Felt Fabric formed by matting and interlocking a mass of fibers. Has no yarns.

Filet Lace with a square as the background.

Flannel Fabric of wool or cotton with a napped surface.

Fortuny Prints Cotton fabrics in basic weaves with rich textural effects printed upon them.

Frise Pile fabric with uncut loops. Made of wool, mohair, cotton, and sometimes linen. When the same construction is used with silk, the fabric is called *uncut velvet*. Mohair frise is extremely durable but not very popular at the present time. (Frieze, an Irish coating fabric, is commonly confused with frise.)

Galloon Narrow fancy binding or braid of wool, cotton, or silk.

Gauze Thin sheer fabric in a open weave, either plain or leno; sometimes a combination of the two. Made in almost any fiber. Useful for curtains.

Gingham Lightweight, plain-weave cotton fabric, in which the yarn has been skein-dyed to produce checks, plaids, stripes.

Gobelins Name associated with hand-loomed tapestries produced in France.

Glazed Chintz (See chintz.)

Grass Cloth Fabric made of coarse reeds or other vegetable fibers in a loose, open weave to show texture. Often impregnated to backing for wall coverings or panels on furniture.

CHART 2 (*cont.*)

Grosgrain Ribbed fabric with heavy crosswise yarns and close, lustrous warps. Often made in narrow widths for trimmings and ribbons.

Gros-point (See needlepoint.)

Guimpe Narrow trimming fabric, braid, or edging with heavy cord running through it.

Haircloth Originally made with a warp of wool, cotton, or linen and a filling thread of horsehair. Frequently synthetics are now used in place of hair. May have small patterns.

Homespun Fabrics in a plain loose weave with soft yarns, made to imitate original hand-loomed Colonial textiles.

Honeycomb Pattern in small squares on a plain or twill background.

Indian Head Although this is actually a trade name, the fabric is well known and widely used. A medium-weight cotton in a plain weave. Has a linen-like appearance; available in wide range of colors.

Jaspé Fabric with a streaked or striped effect produced by uneven dyeing of threads.

Lace Fabric produced by various methods of knotting and twisting yarns or threads. Originally laces were always made by hand, but now machines can reproduce some exquisite effects. Some laces are knitted or crocheted; others are made with pins, bobbins, or shuttles. Intricate designs are often worked into an open-mesh background.

Lampas Patterned fabric usually in two or more colors. Design is integral part of the fabric and does not have a raised appearance. Background and pattern formed by a combination of plain, twill, and satin weaves.

Lawn Lightweight fabric in plain weave. May be cotton or linen (handkerchief linen).

Madras Cotton shirting fabric with small woven pattern. Also a curtain fabric in a leno weave with an all-over design.

Marquisette Sheer curtain fabric in the leno weave. Made of cotton, silk, or synthetic.

Matelasse Double cloth in the Jacquard weave. Pattern has a quilted appearance. Used for upholstery.

Moire Finish produced by engraved rollers to give a fabric a watermarked appearance. Usually applied to fabrics with ribbed weaves.

Monk's Cloth Fabric of loosely twisted coarse yarns in a basket-weave construction.

Muslin Plain-weave cotton fabric in a variety of weights and grades. Available in bleached or unbleached state, also in wide widths for sheeting.

Needlepoint A half cross-stitch hand-embroidered with wool yarns on net, coarse linen, or canvas. Petit-point has a small fine stitch; gros-point has a large stitch. Fabrics with similar appearance can be woven by machine.

Net Sheer fabric used for glass curtains. Often appears in plain weave made of rayon, but other weaves and fibers are also used.

Oilcloth Plain-weave cotton fabric coated with mixture of oil, clay, gum, and pigments to provide a waterproof surface.

Organdy Lightweight muslin fabric with crisp finish.

Osnaburg Plain-weave cotton fabric with coarse yarns.

Paisley Design printed or woven to imitate Scotch shawls formerly woven by hand in town of Paisley. Designs adopted from Indian Kashmir shawls.

Panne Pile fabrics that have been steam pressed to flatten the pile and produce a lustrous surface.

Percale Plain-weave cotton fabric. Used in fine-quality sheetings. Also dyed and printed.

Petit-point (See needlepoint.)

Piqué Fabric with raised wales or ridges that usually run lengthwise. Also woven with honeycomb pattern (waffle piqué) and diamond pattern (birdseye piqué).

Plissé Finish applied to fabrics to produce a crinkled surface.

Plush Fabric similar to velvet but with deeper pile. Used for upholstery.

Point d'Esprit Net with small embroidered design.

Pongee Plain-weave fabric of wild silk. Usually appears in natural tan color.

Poplin Fabric in plain weave with crosswise ribbed effect. Heavier than broadcloth, lighter than rep.

Quilted Fabrics Two layers of fabric stitched with padding between.

Ratiné Ply yarn with rough nubby surface. Term also applies to fabric made with these irregular yarns in plain or twill weave and having irregular surface.

Rep Fabric with horizontal ribs produced by heavy filling threads.

Sail Cloth Heavy cotton fabric in a plain weave. Similar to lightweight canvas.

Sateen Cotton fabric in a sateen weave.

Satin Fabric woven in satin weave with glossy warp threads. May be all silk or synthetic. For heavier upholstery weights, a cotton filling yarn is sometimes used.

Scrim Plain-weave fabric with open construction and somewhat coarse yarns. Used for curtains.

Seersucker Plain-weave fabric that has a puckered surface texture caused by warp threads being held under different degrees of tension.

Shantung Fabric with irregular texture produced by uneven yarns. Originally made of wild silk, but heavier than pongee.

Shikii Heavy fabric of silk or rayon with ribs made by thick irregular filling threads.

Swiss Fine, sheer cotton with crisp texture (see dotted swiss).

Taffeta Plain-weave fabric; may be made of

synthetic, silk, cotton, or wool. Crosswise yarns are sometimes slightly thicker than warps to produce fine ridges.

Tambour   Embroidery done on tambour frames. Now reproduced by machine on Swiss, lawn, or batiste for curtains.

Tapa   Cloth made from tree barks in the South Sea islands. Characterized by block-printed designs applied with vegetable dyes.

Tapestry   Fabric frequently made by machine to imitate original hand-woven tapestries. Made with two sets of warps and two sets of filling yarns. Has ribbed effect.

Tarlatan   Thin cotton fabric in an open plain weave. Sized or glazed to make it stiff.

Terry Cloth   Fabric with uncut pile loops, usually on both sides. Made of cotton.

Theatrical Gauze   Open-weave fabric of cotton or linen. Transparent and slightly stiff.

Ticking   Heavy, closely woven fabric of cotton. Twill weave but sometimes varied by satin stripes or small patterns.

Toiles de Jouy   Fabrics made originally in the French town of Jouy with delicate printed designs showing landscapes and figures in monotones of blue on cream-colored backgrounds. Modern adaptations effectively vary the themes and the colors.

Trapunto   A design achieved by the quilting or padding of a specific motif.

Tweed   Broad term applied to fabrics woven from rough, heavy yarns in two or more colors in plain, twill, or herringbone weaves.

Velour   Closely woven pile fabric that resembles velvet but is heavier and has a shorter pile.

Velvet   Broad term for pile fabrics made with the velvet weave.

Velveteen   A cotton velvet made with filling yarns forming the pile. Made on a plain- or twill-weave back. Twill back is stronger and more durable.

Voile   Sheer lightweight fabric with tightly twisted yarns. Plain weave. Made in cotton, silk, wool, and synthetics.

Whipcord   Twill-weave fabric with pronounced wale on right side.

CHART 3 Other Terms and Trademarks*

Agilon   Stretch yarns made by the combining of elasticized thermoplastic filaments with other textile yarns. (Deering-Milliken)

Asbestos   A natural fibrous mineral material from which nonflammable textiles are made.

Avicron   Filament rayon yarn with a component that permanently crimps the yarn during the dyeing and bleaching process. (American Viscose Corp.)

Avisco   Fibers, yarns, and textiles processed by the American Viscose Corp.

Avisco XL   High-tenacity rayons made by the American Viscose Corp.

Avlin   A rayon fiber with unique bonding properties that give bulk, firmness, and a crisp texture to fabrics. (American Viscose Corp.)

Avril   A cross-linked rayon with similarity to cotton that takes readily to being Sanforized, mercerized, and treated with wash-and-wear finishes (American Viscose Corp.)

Ban-Dew   A process for making fabrics mildew-resistant. (Joseph Bancroft & Sons)

Ban-Lon   Garments and fabrics, knitted or woven, made from yarns produced by a hot crimping process that gives a desirable degree of stretch and bulk. (Joseph Bancroft & Sons)

Belfast   A finishing process for cotton that permanently modifies the fibers to make the fabric dry wrinkle-free. (Deering-Milliken)

Briglo   A high-luster rayon yarn. (American Enka Corp.)

Cadon   A specialized type of multifilament nylon yarn. (Chemstrand Corp.)

Carpet Nylon   A heavy denier nylon yarn with crimp and resiliency, designed especially for floor coverings. (du Pont)

Contessa   A yarn made of 70%–30% blend of Corval (rayon) and Orlon (acrylic). (Cohn-Hall-Marx)

Contro   An extruded or cut thread of rubber, usually covered with natural or synthetic fiber and woven or knitted into elastic fabrics for underwear and swimwear. (Firestone)

Coronized   A process for heat-treating Fiberglas cloth to set the weave and release strain in the glass yarn. (Owens-Corning Fiberglas)

Cotron   A yarn that combines cotton and Avisco rayon. (American Viscose Corp.)

Cumuloft   Texturized nylon filament for use in carpets and upholstery fabrics. (Chemstrand Corp.)

Curon   A light, flexible polyurethane foam, usually bonded to fabrics used as linings in outdoor garments and for household uses. (Reeves Bros.)

Cyana   Fabric finishes for various purposes: shrinkage control, spot repellence, resistance to perspiration. (American Cyanamid)

Cygnet   A Dacron and cotton blend. (Standard Bleachery & Printing Co.)

Denier   The size or number of a filament or yarn. The higher the denier number, the heavier the yarn.

Dyna-Wool   A washable woollike fabric made of low-twist blended yarns of 65% wool and 35% Dynel modacrylic. After weaving, the fabric is heat set to stabilize it against shrinkage. (Union Carbide Chemicals Co.)

Everglaze   Designation for various types of fabric with a glazed finish. (Joseph Bancroft & Sons)

Fortrel   Polyester fiber. (Celanese Fibers Marketing Co.)

Frontera   A sculptured polymer that adapts to various textures. (Tenneco Chemicals, Inc.)

Jetspun Solution-dyed rayon fiber and yarn. (American Enka Corp.)

Metallizing A process used in plating plastic film with a continuous film of metal to produce a brilliant reflecting surface. Used on Mylar polyester film to produce metallic yarns for use in textiles.

Milium Coating of aluminum flakes in a resin binder applied to fabrics to make them resistant to wind penetration. (Deering-Milliken)

Mylar Polyester film used with foils to produce metallic yarns. (du Pont)

Perlglo A semidull viscose filament. (American Enka Corp.)

Reymet Plastic films laminated to metallic foils to produce metallic yarns. (Reynolds Metals)

Sanforized A process applied to fabrics to control shrinkage to within 1% in length and width. (Cluett, Peabody & Co.)

Sanforized Plus A term applied to fabrics finished for wash-and-wear performance in a controlled program. The use of the name is rigidly controlled by the trademark owners, and sample yardage must be submitted periodically to be sure it meets the required wash-and-wear standards. (Cluett, Peabody & Co.)

Sangaree A blend of 50% Orlon acrylic with 50% Corval rayon. (Deering-Milliken)

Sanitized A chemical treatment that renders fabrics and leathers hygienically clean and helps to resist the development of perspiration odors and bacteria. (Sanitized Sales Co.)

Scotchgard A fluoro-chemical textile finish used to make fabrics resistant to water-borne and oil-borne stains. (Minnesota Mining & Mfg. Co.)

Sculptured Acetate A filament yarn with a bulked slub. (Tennessee-Eastman)

Silicone A chemical compound in which the element silicon has replaced the element carbon. Textiles finishes of the silicone resins render fabrics water repellent and resistant to water-borne stains.

Skyloft A rayon filament yarn bulked and textured by the application of compressed air. (American Enka Corp.)

Solution Dyeing The coloring of a solution from which synthetic fibers will be formed.

Super-Cordura High-tenacity rayon yarn. (du Pont)

Super-L A rayon carpet fiber with considerable resistance to soiling. (American Viscose Corp.)

Syl-Mer Silicone finish for cottons that makes them resistant to water and water-borne stains. Can withstand machine washing at 160° F. (Dow Corning Corp.)

Taslan A process of bulking and texturizing synthetic and glass filament-fiber yarns by means of air jets. (du Pont)

Tempra High-tenacity rayon fiber and yarn. (American Enka Corp.)

Tycora Bulking and texturing processes applied to filament-fiber yarns to achieve bulk and texture and to eliminate pilling and surface distortion. (Textured Yarn Co.)

Verel A modified acrylic fiber similar to Dynel, but used mostly for household fabrics and synthetic furs. (Tennessee-Eastman)

Zefran A nitrile-alloy fiber assigned to the acrylic group. It has many of the characteristics of the acrylics, but is said to be stronger. Has excellent insulating qualities. (Dow Badische Co.)

Zelan A chemical finish for water repellency used on cotton and rayon. (du Pont)

Zepel Stain-resistant finish for clothing and home furnishings fabrics. (du Pont)

---

* Adapted from *Modern Fibers and Fabrics*, (New York, J. C. Penney Co., Inc.).

The basic functions of walls and ceilings are to provide protection and privacy, but these areas are important for many other reasons. They determine space relationships within the home and they have a tremendous effect on light, heat, sound, and odor. In addition, they make a major contribution from an aesthetic standpoint. Color and texture become an integral part of each room.

Modern concepts of interior design have broadened our ideas about what walls and ceilings should and should not do. Even with the open planning favored in so much contemporary architectural design, walls and ceilings remain major areas. But when walls are not necessary for actual enclosure they are replaced by various types of dividers to separate areas without sacrificing a feeling of spaciousness. Grillwork, panels, screens, open shelves, and cabinets are frequently used in lieu of actual walls. Sliding wall panels and folding walls are used to make rooms more adaptable to a variety of purposes. Storage walls of various types have been utilized to conserve floor space. Wall-hung shelves and cabinets have become decorative as well as functional features. They allow for the maximum expanse of floor area so important in making small rooms seem larger. Also, rooms are easier to clean when furniture does not have to be moved.

Luminescent ceilings that allow for a variety of lighting effects have not yet become part of the average home, but it is quite probable that in homes of the future the ceiling will play a more important role in light control.

23
Walls and Ceilings

Structural Walls

The same substances that are used for exterior walls can provide interesting surfaces inside the home. Almost every conceivable building material is used for both structural and dividing walls. Stone, brick, wood, cement, cement blocks, and various other kinds of masonry are used. Metal, glass, and plastics are also popular.

In exterior walls we are chiefly concerned with materials that will be strong, durable, and easy to maintain. Cost is of course always an important factor, as are insulating qualities. New methods of construction and new materials now make it possible to construct well-insulated homes at moderate cost.

The idea of using structural materials for interior walls has been favored in contemporary design for various reasons. Modern architects like to relate the outdoors to the

FIGURE 23-1 Structural walls adapt to different types of treatment. (*Courtesy of Armstrong Cork Company*)

indoors, and interior walls of earthy materials, such as stone, wood, or brick, help to achieve the purpose. Glass window walls have been a favorite because they reject the feeling of enclosure as well as provide a surface that is durable for both exterior and interior. Glass blocks, sheets of fiberglass and plastic panels are often used for interesting effects.

Wall Finishes

As far back as the time when people lived in caves, walls have been treated or decorated in some way to add to their beauty and importance. Designs and stories painted on the walls of primitive dwellings have been a valuable source of information for scholarly research.

Just as the caveman wanted to express something by decorating his walls, we do too. But we have a wide variety of wall finishes in different colors, textures, and patterns. Modern technology has improved on the old standbys of paint, wallpaper, wood paneling, fabric, and tile, so today we may have wall surfaces that are both beautiful and easy to maintain.

PAINT. Almost any interior wall can be painted in any color. There are many advantages to using paint, especially in certain areas. It is quick and easy to apply and it is relatively inexpensive. Many paints can be washed and some can be scrubbed with soap and water. When it is necessary or desirable to refinish the wall there is no problem of removing the old finish. In addition to the wide range of available colors, paint can be had in different degrees of gloss ranging from a dull mat finish to one with a high degree of luster. Various textural effects can be produced by stippling with a stiff brush, a sponge, or a cloth. Variegated color effects can be produced with mottling or spattering. Also, certain paints have special extra uses—for example, there are paints that contain insect repellent and there are some that are phosphorescent.

There are some tricky problems in selecting colors. It should be remembered that a large area of color will look quite different from a small sample or color chip. Walls will reflect each other and the color will be intensified. Other large color areas in the room will also affect the wall color. The ceiling, floor, large upholstered pieces, and wood tones of furniture must all be taken into consideration in choosing the color of the walls. When mixing paints, one should keep in mind that the colors are different when the paint is dry. Some paints will become darker and others will become lighter when they are thoroughly dry.

The surface to be painted will also affect the texture of the wall. Cracks and serious blemishes may not be easily covered with paint; wallboard and other composition substances may need a sizing coat to prevent the paint from soaking in with uneven splotches. However, the original material of the wall may provide an interesting texture when it is refinished with paint. Brick, wallboard, and fabric are notable in this respect.

WALLPAPER. The romantic history of wallpaper dates back to ancient times, but its popular use can be traced back only to about the seventeenth century. Today the diversity of wallpapers presents a real challenge to the imagination. They may be used to create any atmosphere; they may also be used in new and different ways to create an infinite variety of novel effects. The wide range of textures, colors, patterns, and interesting special designs almost defies any attempt at classification. There are wallpapers that simulate wood, marble, and fabric. Flock designs are used to give motifs a fuzzy, raised appearance that adds interesting texture. In these, the design is applied to the paper with some form of glue or adhesive. Short fibers are then embedded in the design, and the background remains smooth. The result is a design of somewhat felted or woven appearance that often has a luxurious texture.

Some papers introduce architectural features into a room and still others provide scenic effects. The traditional all-over patterns are ever present, but panels and "spot" motifs have become extremely popular. For example, the wall behind a bed may be decorated with an elegant design that simulates a canopy or emphasizes the bed in some way to add dramatic interest. *Trompe-l'oeil* or trick-of-the-eye designs have made it possible to produce interesting three-dimensional effects on a flat wall surface. Sculptured effects that simulate brick or stone are also useful in some areas.

FIGURE 23-2   A bold wallpaper emphasizes architectural features. (*Courtesy of DuPont Textile Fibers*)

FIGURE 23-3 A "new-old" approach is reflected in the setting above. The walls, covered in an English crewel-work design provide an appropriate background for the camel-back sofa covered in gold velvet. (*Courtesy of Latex Foam Rubber*)

FIGURE 23-4 Panels of wallpaper may be attached with velvet ribbon that simulates a decorative molding and dado. (*Courtesy of Wallcoverings Council*)

Wallpaper is no longer confined to use on walls. It may be used on folding screens, furniture, and decorative accessories. Closets and other storage areas lined with wallpaper are often more attractive and may even be more useful. For example, cedar wallpaper may make a closet repellent to moth damage.

Advantages of Wallpaper. There are many advantages and relatively few disadvantages to using wallpaper as a finish for interior walls. Among the reasons why wallpaper is a popular choice, we might include the following:

1. Color, texture, and pattern lend a distinct individuality to the character of the room.
2. There is a wide variety of designs from which to choose.
3. It may be used to emphasize or to minimize architectural features that are either pleasing or unattractive. A large room may be made to appear smaller and a small room may be made to appear larger. The design of the paper may change the apparent proportions of the room; for example, an emphatic treatment of one wall will make it more advancing.
4. Defects and blemishes in the wall surface can be easily covered or camouflaged.
5. A problem area can be made interesting and attractive. A small foyer or a long, narrow passageway can become a dramatic center of interest without the use of furniture. Difficult or uninteresting alcoves can be given importance.
6. Wallpaper can be used both to separate and to coordinate areas when other means are impractical. One end of a small living room can become the dining area without a room divider simply by the use of a different wall covering.
7. One can try large samples of wallpaper taped to the wall to study the effects of pattern and color in relation to the rest of the furnishings.
8. Wallpaper can emphasize a furniture arrangement or make a center of interest more dramatic. A popular application is a panel or spot design at the headboard of the bed in an otherwise plain bedroom.

Disadvantages of Wallpaper. Perhaps the only major disadvantage of wallpaper is that after two or three layers have been applied to a wall they must be removed before a new finish is applied. With professional steam equipment, old wallpaper can be removed quite easily, but sometimes the amateur without equipment must soak the paper with hot water and scrape it off. This can be very time-consuming.

There are some new stripable papers on the market that can be taken off and reused in another area. There may be some difficulties, however, in fitting sections to a new location.

One other possible disadvantage might be mentioned. The wrong choice of pattern may become tiresome and irritating. Of course, the same objection could be raised for the color of painted walls, but repainting may be easier and less expensive than repapering.

Types of Wallpaper. The wallpaper industry has offered to the consumer various kinds of wallpaper at different price levels. With prepasted paper that can be simply moistened and applied to the wall, the do-it-yourself amateur can easily develop sufficient skill to paper complete rooms with a professional touch.

The wide variety of materials that are generally categorized as wallpaper almost defies classification. Designs are printed on different grades and weights of paper. Some colors are applied with water-soluble paints, which would, of course, make them nonwashable. Others have various degrees of imperviousness produced by special finishes that set the colors and make it possible to wipe the paper with a damp cloth to remove surface soil. Still others have the design impregnated or coated with durable protective finishes that can withstand scrubbing.

In addition to the actual wallpapers there are various types of fabric wall coverings and nonwoven plastics that have different degrees of permanency and resistance to soil and stains. It behooves the consumer, therefore, to determine the requirements of any particular area in the home and to make the choice accordingly. For example, a kitchen, a bathroom, or a child's room may require a wall covering that is truly scrubbable. A hallway, a dining room, or a guest room may be papered with a less rigorous material.

For our purposes we may classify wallpaper in the following categories:

1. *Nonwashable coverings.* These are papers that have been printed with water-soluble dyes,

FIGURE 23-5   A small kitchen assumes a new atmosphere with the use of a gay wallpaper and a coordinated texture on the ceiling. (*Courtesy of Wallcoverings Council*)

and any application of water may quickly damage the design.

2. *Washable coverings*. A thin coating on the paper renders it capable of withstanding cleaning with a damp cloth to remove surface dust. More vigorous treatment of spots and stains will remove the coating and possibly damage the design.

3. *Scrubbable coverings*. Some papers are given a finish that makes them quite resistant to spots and stains. This finish is of a highly protective nature and therefore it can usually be washed with soap and water. In addition to the coated papers, there are various coated fabric wall coverings. In general, these tend to be more expensive than the wallpapers, but they are more durable and easier to maintain.

Paper may be given a plastic finish that is quite tough and resistant to scrubbing; however, the more durable scrubbable coverings have a fabric backing. A light-weight canvas may be impregnated with a coating that has the design applied in such a way that it will withstand repeated washings. (Two well-known examples of this type are Sanitas and Wall-Tex.)

Both vinyl coatings on cloth and non-woven vinyl coverings are available. These are resistant to spots and stains and can withstand constant washing with soap and water.

Walls and Ceilings **327**

(a)

FIGURE 23-6   A fabric panel becomes a headboard and creates an interesting wall treatment with relatively little expense. (a) (*Courtesy of* 1969 Rooms of Tomorrow. *Designed by Roland Wm. Jutras, N.S.I.D.*) (b) (*Courtesy of Monsanto Company*)

Walls and Ceilings **329**

FIGURE 23-7 Wall-hung furniture and shelves blend into matching paneling. (*Courtesy of Royal System of Denmark*)

Selecting a Wallpaper. A general rule of thumb is to choose a wallpaper design according to the size of the room—small-scaled patterns for small rooms, medium-scaled patterns for average rooms, large patterns for large rooms. But many other factors must also be considered. In a small room, for example, a dramatic effect can be created with a large-scaled pattern on one wall, or a scenic design can lend perspective and thus increase the apparent size of the area. A large room that has many doors, windows, or other architectural features may have a chopped off appearance if papered with a large pattern.

The theme of the design and the color tones must, of course, blend with the decoration of the room. Small, delicate, or quaint pat-terns seem more appropriate for less formal rooms; large motifs and scenic designs lend themselves better to formal and elegant themes.

WOOD PANELING. The lovely grain textures of woods make an effective wall finish that is both beautiful and easy to maintain. In modern architecture the beautiful colors and grain patterns of the more exotic woods have provided an interior finish that meets the requirements of exquisite texture plus easy maintenance.

Wood paneling seems to meet modern requirements for informality or for formality with richness and warmth. The color, texture, and pattern of wood answers a need for beauty in a natural form. It looks neither contrived nor man-made. This natural form of elegance has, therefore, found its way into modern buildings that are designed for both public and residential use.

Various types of precut and prefinished panels are available for finishing walls. Sometimes a room may have all the walls finished with wood, or one wall in a wood finish may be combined with another wall in paint, wallpaper or a structural material. The familiar pine, walnut, birch, oak, and maple have been popular in various rooms of the home. Now the more exotic patterns of rosewood, teak, and zebrawood are in demand, although they are more expensive than the woods that are more readily available.

LAMINATES. A popular process of bonding layers of various materials together with resins and other plastics has resulted in a number of substances that are extremely useful for wall coverings as well as for counter tops and furniture. These surfaces are usually very durable and resistant to heat and stains. They are easily cleaned with a damp cloth. New techniques of laminating can produce almost any desired effect, so wood grains and marbleized patterns can be simulated with an amazing likeness to the natural product. In addition, laminates offer a variety of novelty textures and patterns that resemble no natural materials. The laminates are still rather expensive wall coverings when compared to paint and wallpaper. However, their permanency and ease of maintenance make them desirable for some areas.

FABRICS. Many types of cloth have been used to add interest and warmth to walls. Fabrics may be tacked on frames, pasted directly to the wall, or glued to heavy paper and applied as wallpaper. Open-weave fabrics on metallic papers provide interesting textures and color combinations.

Felt, grass cloth, burlap, and canvas are popular wall fabrics. Damasks and brocades are also used for rich elegance. There is almost no limit to the variety of color and texture that fabrics can provide. Many of them can be treated or impregnated with plastic so that they will resist soil and can be easily cleaned.

FIGURE 23-8 Pegboard is a popular choice for functional walls in various areas. (*Photograph courtesy of Macy's*)

FIGURE 23-9 Grille work is used to create a wall and ceramic tile is used to emphasize the fireplace. (*Courtesy of Harvey Probber, Inc.*)

CERAMIC TILE. Although it is expensive and time-consuming to apply, true ceramic tile is both durable and easy to maintain. It is a highly desirable finish for floors and counter tops in certain areas, such as the kitchen, bathroom, and utility room. Tile table tops have also become increasingly popular because of their high resistance to heat, alcohol, and moisture.

Mosaic tiles produce surfaces with interesting designs and colors. Because of its durability and easy maintenance, ceramic tile is also a favorite finish for certain wall areas that should be both attractive and easily maintained.

Various plastics have simulated tile finishes at considerably less cost. Although many of these are both durable and attractive, they do not have the intrinsic qualities of the real tile. Sheets of simulated tile may be glued or nailed into place. Almost invariably there is some-

thing ersatz about the appearance, even though the less expensive substitute may well serve the purpose of the original when cost is a major consideration.

LINOLEUM. Perhaps linoleum and other similar materials are more favored as coverings for floors and counter tops than for walls, but they must be mentioned in this section because they are so frequently used for certain sections of interior walls, such as splash boards in kitchens, bathrooms, and laundries.

Ceilings

In some respects ceilings may be considered as the upper wall of a room. The ceiling will affect space, light, heat, and sound as well as the appearance of a room.

Fabrics and wallpapers are sometimes used

to make ceilings more decorative. Acoustical tiles are used to absorb sound, and we have mentioned the contributions that the ceiling area can make toward lighting the room. In general, however, the ceiling has been a somewhat neglected area in modern interior design, particularly in homes of low and average cost. This is understandable because decorated ceilings are expensive. However, the ceiling is a large area that will have considerable influence on the appearance of any room. The height of the ceiling is important in establishing the proportions of the room. It is interesting to note that tall people often feel uncomfortable in rooms with very low ceilings. Although this may seem to be a minor point, it is nevertheless one that should be considered when one is buying or building a permanent home.

Room dimensions may be altered considerably by color applied to the ceiling. Dark colors tend to advance and light colors tend to recede. In addition, the ceiling is usually expected to reflect light. In the small rooms with low ceilings that are so common in modern homes, the practice is to paint the ceilings white or a light tint of the wall color. However, painting a disturbingly high ceiling in a dark color can make the proportions seem more pleasing. Also, if the color scheme of the room permits, a warm color, such as a soft yellow or a pale pink, casts a sunshine glow on the atmosphere of the room without seriously affecting the light reflection.

24

Table

Appointments

Modern living has demanded many changes in the traditionally accepted standards and routines of serving meals. Television, outdoor barbecue pits, prepared foods, and buffet service have all had their impact on our way of life. We have accepted a more casual, informal, and perhaps a much more creative attitute toward both family meals and entertaining. However, the words *casual* and *informal* must never in any sense be confused with *sloppy* and *careless*. Food should always be served with meticulous care and in the most attractive way possible.

Each homemaker establishes her own standards for serving meals, and to a large extent these reflect her outlook on family life. There is an old adage that "manners saved for company soon spoil." The atmosphere and the manner in which everyday meals are served have a strong influence on patterns of behavior as well as on family spirit. It has already been pointed out that the dining area is an important center for family living. For both psychological and physiological reasons, eating should always be a pleasant experience.

Years ago it would have been almost unthinkable to invite guests for a special dinner party without having a regular dining table fully equipped with matched china. Now such traditional standards have been relaxed in several ways. Just as we have come to reject matched suites of furniture in favor of more individual combinations, we have also become more creative about tableware. It is often more interesting to mix and coordinate pieces that harmonize with one another than to use things that exactly match.

We have also become more adventuresome about table decorations. Floral centerpieces are always popular, but more imaginative arrangements and the use of other items to express particular themes are gaining in favor. Colored cloths in a variety of materials and interesting new place mats have also, to a large extent, replaced traditional tablecloths. (Table linens are discussed in Chapter 25.)

334

In many households, buffet service has become a preferred means of entertaining. The modern hostess who uses this method with a delightful combination of simplicity and elegance requires some special equipment. Various chafing dishes, serving bowls, and appliances have been designed to meet these needs.

An artistically planned table and attractive service contribute to the enjoyment of good food and pleasant conversation. There is a wide choice of tableware, and selections must be made with care. The various items should be chosen to harmonize with one another so that the table presents an interesting design.

Dinnerware

The so-called china department in any large store will probably display dinnerware in a variety of materials and in a wide range of prices. Several types of ceramics are widely popular, but plastics, glass, woods, and metals are also used.

CERAMICS. Although the origins of pottery-making are unknown, we do know that in the ancient civilizations of Egypt, Greece, Rome, and China it was practiced as a fine art. Throughout the centuries, various countries not only adapted old methods and designs but initiated new techniques. The history of ceramics is an interesting study of cultural development. In addition, ceramics have provided us with much historical source material, because designs frequently depict the beliefs, customs, and daily activities of the ancient civilizations.

Ceramics are made from a base of clay mixed with other materials, such as flint and feldspar. Water is added to produce a creamy consistency and the mixture is known as *slip*. For fine products, the slip may go through several processes of refining and screening. Excess water is removed and the clay mixture may be allowed to age. Then it is kneaded to remove air bubbles.

Shaping may be done on a potter's wheel or in a mold. This step requires great skill, because the details of final form are determined at this point. The potter's wheel holds tremendous fascination for the amateur craftsman. The skilled "thrower" shapes a mass of clay as the wheel revolves to create a beautiful, graceful form. Most dinnerware is made by the pressing of clay in molds. Finishing is done on a *jigger* machine.

Firing of ceramics is done in a kiln. When the clay form emerges from the firing it is in the *biscuit* stage. Some pottery is used with no further treatment; however, dinnerware and many other ceramics are usually dipped in a milky liquid after the first firing and then fired again in another kiln. This gives the pieces a glaze, providing luster and making the pieces more sanitary. A high-quality glaze fuses with the clay body; it is hard, durable, and resistant to tiny surface cracks (*crazing*).

Decoration may be applied before or after the glazing. When applied on top of the glaze, another firing in a decorating kiln melts the design into the glaze so that it will remain permanent with ordinary care.

It should be obvious that within this rather oversimplified version of pottery-making there is room for a tremendous amount of variation. Perhaps because there are so many different types, there is some confusion about the terms associated with ceramics. For example, the word *pottery* technically refers to all types of ceramics, including fine china. In popular usage, the word designates only opaque wares, usually of the coarser types and the heavier shapes. Also, because the first porcelain was made in China, we have incorrectly referred to all dinnerware as *china*.

Porcelain. Porcelain is the finest type of china. For centuries the making of fine porcelain was a closely guarded secret in China. Europeans prized the exported articles, but failed to imitate them until early in the eighteenth century when kaolin, a white pottery clay, was discovered in Germany. With some experimentation and development of the proper kilns, the discovery led to the manufacture of fine porcelain in several European countries.

When kaolin is used in the clay mixture, a hard-paste slip is produced. Other types of clay were used in the quest for true porcelain but none of these provided the same results. Some of these soft-paste products are still used today for china that is less than top quality.

Porcelain is translucent. When a plate is held up to the light, the shadow of one's hand can be seen through it. It is also nonporous, or *vitrified*. Even without the glaze, high-quality porcelain will not absorb foreign materials to any appreciable degree. For this reason chipped porcelain is not unsanitary even though it may be unattractive.

Bone China. English potters developed a clay mixture by adding bone ash to kaolin. The resulting product was a strong, highly translucent white china that was particularly suitable for decoration under the glaze. Bone ash is used in some china from other countries, but England has several well established firms associated with the manufacture of fine bone china. These include:

Spode
Royal Worcester
Wedgwood
Minton
Royal Doulton
Royal Crown Derby

Earthenware. In general, earthenware ceramics are opaque when held to a light, and they are also more porous than fine porcelain. However, there are many different grades and types of earthenware. It must be noted that at least two distinguished English pottery firms, Spode and Wedgwood, manufacture high-quality earthenware. The term *earthenware* includes materials that have various degrees of porosity from the lowest-grade pottery to a fine quality that almost equals china.

Semivitreous Ware. Semiporous clays have been developed and are sometimes sold in competition with true china. A high-quality semivitreous earthenware may cost more than a poor quality china, but insofar as classification is concerned these semiporous materials must be grouped with earthenware products.

Stoneware. Certain clay mixtures can be fired to high temperatures that cause them to become quite hard and nonporous. Ironstone is such a product.

Pottery. We have mentioned that this term really refers to all ceramics, but the more popular connotation leans toward the heavier forms of earthenware. We also tend to associate pottery with rougher textures and more earthy colors.

Names and Terms. Some well-known names and terms associated with ceramics include:

Arzberg   Bavarian china.
Basalt Ware   Unglazed stoneware, usually black, popularized by Wedgwood factory.
Belleek   Highly translucent ivory-colored china characterized by iridescent glaze.

Appears mostly in tea sets and small decorative objects. Made in Ireland.
Castleton   American china made in various types suitable for home or institutional use.
Coalport   English bone china.
Delftware   Various types of ceramics made in Holland. Usually associated with blue and white coloring.
Dresden   Name of china made in Meissen, Germany. Frequently associated with delicate figurines.
Faience   Term that refers to various kinds of pottery. Usually earthenware with an opaque lead glaze. Name derived from the Italian town of Faenza.
Haviland   China originally made in France but now produced in the United States.
Jasper Ware   Famous Wedgwood pottery made in blue, green, lilac, and other colors. Characterized by Greek motifs in relief designs.
Lenox   Fine-quality American china.
Limoges   Ancient town in France renowned for manufacturing fine china.
Majolica   Faience from Spain and Italy, usually enameled in bright colors.
Minton   Famous family of English potters. Business established at Stoke-on-Trent.
Queen's Ware   Famous cream-colored earthenware made by Wedgwood potteries.
Rosenthal   Fine Bavarian china.
Royal Copenhagen   Fine Danish china.
Royal Crown Derby   English china produced at potteries established in the mid-eighteenth century by William Duesbury. Decoration is rich and delicate, often on ivory-colored background.
Royal Doulton   Ceramic wares of various types, including fine china, made at potteries in Lambeth, England.
Royal Worcester   Wares made at the Lowdin pottery in Worcester, England.
Salt Glaze   Finish used in making pottery.
Sèvres   Fine porcelain named after town in France where it is made. Characterized by delicate but elegant designs.
Spode   Wares manufactured at pottery established in England by Josiah Spode. In 1799 he produced the first fine bone china.
Staffordshire   County in England famous for its potteries district, centered at Stoke-on-Trent. Among famous factories were those owned by Thomas Minton, Josiah Wedgwood, and Josiah Spode.
Syracuse   Fine American china.

(a)

(b)

FIGURE 24-1 **Table appointments should relate to the theme of decoration. (a)** (*Courtesy of Tiffany & Co.*) **(b)** (*Courtesy of The Sterling Silversmiths Guild of America*) **(c)** (*Courtesy of Allied Chemical Corporation*) **(d)** (*Courtesy of Allied Chemical Corporation*)

(c)

(d)

FIGURE 24-2 Melamine dinnerware with gilded rococo curves on a green background is used with gilded stainless steel flatware for a formal setting. (*Courtesy of Allied Chemical Corporation*)

Wedgwood Famous wares made at the potteries founded by Josiah Wedgwood in Staffordshire. Designs are most notable for interpretations of neoclassic motifs in jasper ware, especially the white figures applied to delicate, colored backgrounds.

Plastic Dinnerware. Within recent years, plastics have become more widely accepted for use at the table. Plastics do not break or chip as easily as ceramic dinnerware; however, some do require special cleaning to remove stains.

Most plastic dinnerware on the market today has been improved to overcome some of the earlier objections to its use. It can be washed in automatic dishwashers and the styling of the patterns has become far more glamorous than in the first plastic dishes. Quite probably, the plastics will continue to grow in popularity as consumers become more aware of the wide range of colors, patterns, and styles now available.

SELECTION OF DINNERWARE. Traditional practice called for one everyday set of dishes and another ''good'' set for company meals. Once again the young homemaker breaks with tradition, depending upon her fancy, and may choose one set that can be adapted to different situations. Plain white china, for example, may be as formal or as informal as one makes it with table decorations. Another school of thought leans toward having several types of dinnerware suitable for different kinds of entertaining. The available storage space as well as the pattern of living will influence decisions in this respect. One word of caution might be offered here about choosing several types. There may be times when it is desirable to mix dishes. One should choose patterns and colors that will harmonize if they must be used together. One set with little or no pattern is usually a good choice.

Pattern. Choosing a design in dinnerware is perhaps one of the most difficult decisions for the young homemaker. When one has to look at dishes three times a day one must be sure the pattern won't become tiresome. It should also be remembered that the design of the dinnerware should be in keeping with the spirit of the home.

A beautiful display of china can be most bewildering. Every pattern seems to have a special appeal and it is difficult to narrow down the choice to only one.

One should try to visualize food on each plate. The profusely decorated plates are lovely for display, but the plain, simple designs are more adaptable and more generally appealing for the service of food. Embossed motifs or raised effects provide interesting designs, but they do require extra care in washing to prevent food from sticking in the crevices.

Open Stock. Some patterns may be purchased in open stock as opposed to complete sets. With open stock, one may purchase any quantity. As long as the manufacturer makes the pattern, pieces may be added or replaced. The price may be cheaper by the set, but when breakage occurs, odd pieces will have to replace the broken ones, so selecting an open-stock pattern is advantageous even though one may be initially purchasing an entire set.

Sets may be purchased for four, six, eight, or twelve. These vary in the number of serving pieces included. "Starter" sets for four are popular, and there is sometimes a variety of extra pieces that may be purchased separately.

A popular practice is to buy china in place settings and then to fill in with extra serving pieces. One five-piece place setting generally includes:

1 dinner plate
1 salad plate
1 bread-and-butter plate
1 cup
1 saucer

Glassware

Glass is created by the fusion of silica (sand) and other chemicals into a molten substance that has a thick, viscous consistency. In this stage it may be molded, pressed, or blown into various forms, after which it is carefully cooled by a process called *annealing*.

TYPES OF GLASS. There are hundreds of different kinds of glass produced by variations of the raw materials and the methods of heating and cooling. The term *crystal* is sometimes used to refer to any clear glass, but more traditionally it denotes fine-quality, highly refractive glass. For our purposes here we may consider three general categories of glass in common use:

Lime Glass. Sand, soda, and lime are the basic ingredients of the everyday type known as *lime glass*. It is used for commonplace purposes when high durability and low cost are desirable. Window panes, jars, bottles, and inexpensive glassware for table use are all made of lime glass.

Lead Glass. Far more expensive and far more beautiful is a glass made from a mixture of sand, potash, and lead. These ingredients produce a glass that has luster and sparkle. When gently tapped on the rim, lead glass has a bell-like tone.

Borosilicate Glass. Boric oxide added to the sand and soda mixture for glass produces a substance that is resistant to heat and cracking. This type of glass is useful for cooking utensils. Because glass holds heat and is attractive in appearance, food is often served in a dish in which it has been cooked. Color and decorative motifs have made glass utensils even more adaptable for use as serving dishes.

SHAPING GLASS. Molten glass may be shaped by several methods:

Blowing. It is indeed a fascinating experience to watch a skilled workman blow a piece of molten glass into a beautiful form. On the end of a simple hollow pipe known as a *blow iron*, he gathers a mass of the hot glass mixture. As he twirls and blows into the pipe, the shaping of the glass seems almost miraculous. The experienced artisan shapes the ball of molten glass with unbelievable symmetry and refinement of form.

Machines have been developed for blowing glass for various items including electric light bulbs, some bottles, and miscellaneous containers. Hand blowing in the commercial field must usually be restricted to the production of high-quality objects.

Molding. Some types of glass are molded, either by hand or by machine. Quality products may be *blown-molded*, which means blowing glass into a mold. In some cases mold marks are left on the finished items, but there are methods of rotating the glass within the mold to remove any such markings.

Pressing. Somewhat similar to molding, pressing employs a plunger to shape the inside of the object. It is a fast and inexpensive means of shaping glass items. The molten glass is poured into a mold that forms the outer contours; the plunger presses on the inner surface to shape flat bowls, lids, saucers, and similar forms.

DECORATING GLASS. Many fine examples of modern glassware depend on exquisite form and the intrinsic beauty of high-quality glass for their excellence. A lovely, graceful form fashioned in clear sparkling glass needs little, if any, additional decoration. There are, however, a variety of processes that further enhance the decorative qualities of glass. At almost any stage of manufacture there may be some treatment intended to make the finished product more attractive.

Color may be added to the molten glass by the mixing of mineral salts into the basic blend of ingredients. Milk glass has a colorant that renders the finished product opaque. White milk glass is probably the most widely used, but other colors, especially turquoise, have become popular.

Bubbles injected into molten glass also have a decorative effect. This method is used in manufacturing glass of all qualities, but the "teardrop" designs in some glassware clearly reflect special skills.

Ornamental designs may be applied to glass in the form of enamels or metals encrusted on the surface. Gold, platinum, and silver are favorite forms of enrichment.

Frosted designs are popular for decorating glassware. Clear glass may be given a rough, grayed finish by sandblasting or by treatment with acids. Etching, a widely used means of decorating glass at all levels of quality, employs hydrofluoric acid to produce a frosted effect. Intricate lacy designs may be etched by the coating of parts of the glass surface with wax and leaving other areas exposed to the acid.

Cutting is another popular method of decorating glass. Hand-cut grooves on lead crystal may be polished to sparkling brilliance. On high-quality pieces the cut designs may be extremely complex. However, machine methods of cutting have been responsible for much of the inexpensive cut glass on the current market. These low-cost items attempt to simulate the finer examples, but they lack the brilliant luster, the sharp edges, and the intricate patterns found on cut glass produced by hand craftsmanship.

NAMES OF GLASS. Glassworks in various parts of the world are producing interesting designs that are noteworthy for high quality. In France, the names Daum and Baccarat both represent outstanding firms. Orrefors in Sweden, Leerdam in Holland, and Val Saint Lambert in Belgium are other well-known manufacturers of beautiful glassware. England, Ireland and Italy also produce considerable amounts of high-quality glass. Venetian glass with its intricate shapes and exquisite colors has been extremely popular.

Several manufacturers in America produce fine glassware for a mass market. Perhaps the most outstanding producer in America is the Corning glassworks, which makes Steuben glass. Exquisite examples of Steuben designs are often exhibited in museums or are presented as gifts to foreign dignitaries. Some other well-known names include Blenco, Forstoria, Libby, Westmoreland, and Tiffin.

CHOOSING GLASSWARE. Glass accessories may be found in any room, and of course they should complement the decor. Bowls, vases, pitchers, ashtrays, and the like may be simple or elegant. They may express formality or informality.

Glassware for entertaining and for table use must be chosen with regard for usefulness as well as design. Glasses are made in a wide variety of sizes and shapes, but modern concepts of living demand fewer types then were often demanded in the past, and it is not uncommon to see glasses that are adaptable to different uses—for example, wine glasses that may also be used for cocktails. Figure 24.3 shows some of the popular sizes of glassware.

The formality or informality of the dining area should have some influence on the types of glasses selected for table use. Tall, long-stemmed water goblets are lovely in a full-sized dining room where there is plenty of space at the table. However, they may be a real problem on a small table in a tiny dining area. A short-stemmed glass or some type that is not so likely to tip over would be much more practical.

The design of glassware for table use should harmonize with the other table appointments. Simple china and plain silver usually call for glassware that is unadorned, although it should be beautiful in form. Graceful curving designs on glassware blend with similar designs on china and silverware. Plain surfaces and geometric and abstract designs have a common denominator that produces a unifying effect.

FIGURE 24-3 Basic sizes and shapes in stemware. (*Courtesy of Fostoria Glass Company*)

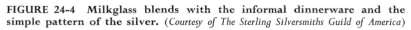

FIGURE 24-4 Milkglass blends with the informal dinnerware and the simple pattern of the silver. (*Courtesy of The Sterling Silversmiths Guild of America*)

Flatware

The various types of knives, forks, and spoons are called *flatware*. Ladles, cake servers, and other special serving utensils would also come under this category.

There is a certain symbolism associated with flatware. Sometimes the family silver is passed down from one generation to another. Or the young bride-to-be may feel that choosing her pattern is the first step toward setting up a household. Whether or not it involves sentiment, tradition, or prestige, flatware is a major item in table decoration and has a peculiar role in representing the spirit of the home.

If one is not fortunate enough to inherit beautiful silver, the choice will probably be either sterling, silver plate, or stainless steel. There are several other variations, such as Dirilite, a gold-colored flatware, and combinations of wood, ivory, and similar materials, which have a more limited appeal.

STERLING SILVER. The most expensive and generally the most prized silver is sterling. Because silver by itself is too soft to be useful, another metal, usually copper, is added for durability. By law, a product marked sterling must have 925 parts of pure silver in every 1,000 parts of the finished metal.

SILVER PLATE. During the eighteenth century it was discovered that a layer of sterling silver could be fused to a copper base. Objects made by this method were first made in the town of Sheffield, England. Old Sheffield plate is prized by the collector today. Plated ware is made by the use of a base metal of nickel, copper, and zinc. Electrolytic methods are employed to fuse a coating of silver to the surface. The durability depends upon the thickness of the silver coating and also upon how carefully the process is controlled. Some manufacturers reinforce the areas that will receive hard use with inlays of sterling silver.

Naturally, silver plate is less expensive than sterling silver. Because there is variation in the quality of plated silver, it is wise to deal with reputable firms that take pride in high-quality products. With proper care, well-made silver plate will give many years of satisfactory service. Poor-quality silver plate will soon become unsightly as the plating wears off.

STAINLESS STEEL. Stainless steel is a solid alloy that must contain at least eleven and one-half per cent chromium or it may not be called stainless steel. Within recent years stainless steel has developed wide popularity for table service. Although it does not carry the same sentimental attachment that silver table service does, stainless steel has several practical advantages. It requires less care than silver. It does not tarnish and therefore does not need polishing, and it resists stains from foods that ordinarily discolor silver. Although it is available in a rather wide price range, stainless steel in general costs less than sterling silver.

Until recently, stainless steel seemed more suitable for contemporary settings. Now, however, there are many traditional designs. In some cases, the same design is made in both silver and stainless steel.

CHOOSING FLATWARE. Pattern is probably the primary consideration when choosing flatware. In silver, the design may be extremely ornate or very simple. It should be chosen to harmonize with other table equipment. There is such a wide range of patterns that the choice is a matter of individual preference, but it is often a difficult decision to make.

Unusual shapes and proportions are sometimes interesting to look at but not as functional as they might be. One should note the balance of each piece while holding it. Well-balanced flatware rests comfortably in the hand when held as it would normally be held. One should also study the types and shapes of serving pieces to be sure they will be functional.

It should also be remembered that silver will tarnish and must be cleaned. Ornate designs require more time for careful polishing in all the crevices, although they do provide an elegant note on the table.

Various designs in both flatware and hollow-ware (see the next section) are intended to blend with particular styles in furnishings. We need not always be consistent in this matter, but usually a design that harmonizes with the general theme of the home will be more attractive. Very modern designs in a home that is

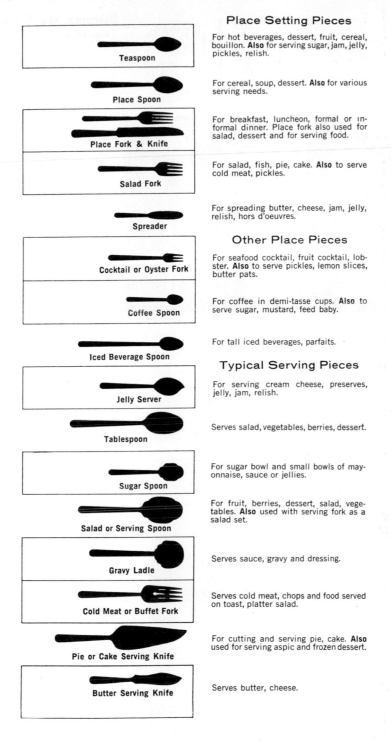

Place Setting Pieces

Teaspoon
For hot beverages, dessert, fruit, cereal, bouillon. **Also** for serving sugar, jam, jelly, pickles, relish.

Place Spoon
For cereal, soup, dessert. **Also** for various serving needs.

Place Fork & Knife
For breakfast, luncheon, formal or informal dinner. Place fork also used for salad, dessert and for serving food.

Salad Fork
For salad, fish, pie, cake. **Also** to serve cold meat, pickles.

Spreader
For spreading butter, cheese, jam, jelly, relish, hors d'oeuvres.

Other Place Pieces

Cocktail or Oyster Fork
For seafood cocktail, fruit cocktail, lobster. **Also** to serve pickles, lemon slices, butter pats.

Coffee Spoon
For coffee in demi-tasse cups. **Also** to serve sugar, mustard, feed baby.

Iced Beverage Spoon
For tall iced beverages, parfaits.

Typical Serving Pieces

Jelly Server
For serving cream cheese, preserves, jelly, jam, relish.

Tablespoon
Serves salad, vegetables, berries, dessert.

Sugar Spoon
For sugar bowl and small bowls of mayonnaise, sauce or jellies.

Salad or Serving Spoon
For fruit, berries, dessert, salad, vegetables. **Also** used with serving fork as a salad set.

Gravy Ladle
Serves sauce, gravy and dressing.

Cold Meat or Buffet Fork
Serves cold meat, chops and food served on toast, platter salad.

Pie or Cake Serving Knife
For cutting and serving pie, cake. **Also** used for serving aspic and frozen dessert.

Butter Serving Knife
Serves butter, cheese.

FIGURE 24-5   Types of flatware. (*Courtesy of The Sterling Silversmiths Guild of America*)

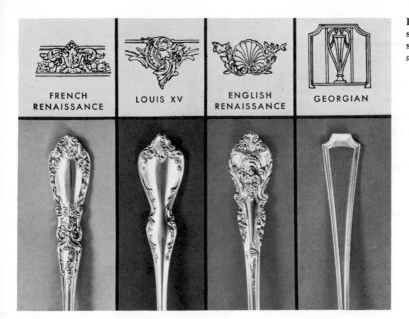

FIGURE 24-6   Some motifs designed to blend with traditional styles. (*Courtesy of The Sterling Silversmiths Guild of America*)

FRENCH RENAISSANCE   LOUIS XV   ENGLISH RENAISSANCE   GEORGIAN

FIGURE 24-7 Stainless steel designed to coordinate with silver in a *Matchmakers* group. (*Courtesy of* Matchmakers, Dover *by Oneida Silversmiths*)

FIGURE 24-8 A basic four-piece place setting can take care of initial needs. Other pieces such as salad forks, butter spreaders, and additional spoons can be added. (*Courtesy of The Sterling Silversmiths Guild of America*)

traditional in all other respects seem incongruous. Ornate traditional designs in a modern home seem equally out of place.

There are several ways to purchase flatware. One may buy individual place settings or a set of four, six, eight, or twelve.

A basic place setting of five pieces would consist of a knife, a fork, a teaspoon, a soup spoon, and a butter spreader. However, a four-piece place setting is sometimes chosen as a starter, with the idea of adding the spreader and a salad fork later. In some of the older patterns, knives and forks are made in both a dinner size and a smaller luncheon size. Newer designs are made in one all-purpose size called the *place* size. Many people find extra teaspoons very useful.

Hollowware

Bowls, trays, pitchers, serving dishes, and the like are classified as hollowware. These do not as a rule match the designs in flatware, but they should harmonize with all table appointments. Silver, silver plate, and stainless steel are used for hollowware, sometimes in combination with crystal.

Designs in hollowware may be as ornate or as simple as they are in flatware, and the same cautions apply to choosing a design. There will not be the same diversified range of patterns to choose from in hollowware, but the general features and characteristics should blend with the china and flatware as much as possible.

25

Household Linens

Today relatively few of the items in the linen closet are actually made of linen. The term *household linens* dates back to a time when linen was widely used for sheets, pillowcases, towels, and tablecloths. Now, although linen sheets are still available, cotton and synthetic fibers are more widely used. Nevertheless, linen is still popular for table coverings and for certain kinds of towels.

Several items that come under the category of household linens are likely to receive hard use, and they should therefore be selected for durability. However, many items have become more glamorous in recent years, and color and styling have become as important as durability in influencing decisions. Nevertheless, frequent laundering does exert wear and tear, so both styling and durability should be important factors in making selections.

Bed Linens

It pays to invest in good-quality bed linens because they wear longer and present a more attractive appearance. Sheets and pillowcases, mattress covers and mattress pads must be laundered frequently. Poor-quality products become limp and sleazy after a few washings.

SIZES. Before buying bed linens it is most important to know the exact size of the mattresses on which they are to be used. There is considerable variation in this respect.

Sheets may be either fitted or the more traditional flat type. The fitted or so-called contour types are shaped to fit the mattress. Bottom sheets are fitted or shaped at four corners; top sheets are shaped only at the two bottom corners. Innerspring mattresses are usually six to seven inches deep; foam rubber mattresses are generally four and one-half to six inches deep. Fitted sheets are made for both types.

Sizes for flat sheets are usually expressed as the torn size before hemming. The actual length of the finished sheet will be several inches less than the measurement on the label. It is important to use a flat sheet large enough for the bed. For a bottom sheet there should be a sufficient amount to tuck under the mattress, at least five inches at the foot and at the head of the bed. For a top sheet there should be sufficient length for a five-inch tuck-in at the foot and an eighteen-inch turn-back over the top of the blanket. A twelve- to fifteen-inch overhang at each side is necessary for comfort. Some standard mattress sizes and recommended sizes for flat sheets are shown in Table 1.

Pillowcases should be large enough to slip over the pillow with ease, but they should fit smoothly; they should be about ten inches longer than the pillow. For a pillow twenty-one by twenty-seven inches a pillowcase forty-two by thirty-six inches should be used. Larger sizes (forty-five by thirty-six inches and forty-five by thirty-eight and one-half inches) are available for larger pillows.

TYPES OF SHEETS AND PILLOWCASES.

The difference between fitted and flat sheets has been mentioned. Fitted sheets provide a smooth, wrinkle-free surface, which many people find most comfortable. Because they stay in place, less time is required for making the bed. They may require no ironing because they stretch taut over the mattress and wrinkles disappear. However, they are more expensive and may not be adapted to beds that vary slightly from standard sizes.

Sheets are available in a variety of fabrics—some woven, some knitted. Cotton is the most widely used fiber but the man-made fibers are becoming more important. Nylon tricot sheets have a silky texture and they are easy to launder. The blends of cotton and polyester are becoming very popular because they require little or no ironing. Combinations of 50/50 per cent cotton/polyester and 65/35 per cent cotton/polyester have produced fabrics that seem to meet the demands of durability and easy care.

Cotton sheets may be muslin or percale. The basic differences between the two types are weight, type of yarn, and texture. Muslin sheets are heavier and woven with thicker carded yarns. The thread count, or the number of threads in one square inch of fabric, is one way of designating different types of sheeting. A heavy muslin would have 140 threads to the square inch; a medium weight would have a thread count of 128. Lightweight muslin with a thread count of 112 is available but not generally recommended.

Percale sheets are lighter in weight and generally made of smooth combed yarns. Percales vary in the quality of yarn and the closeness of the weave. Fine-quality percale has a thread count of 180; an even finer quality has a thread count of 200 or more. Top grade percale is expensive, but it has a smooth, luxurious texture.

The choice between muslin and percale may depend on several factors. A medium-weight muslin sheet is strong, long wearing, and economical. Good-quality muslin stands

TABLE 1 Sheet Sizes

Type of Bed	Standard Mattress Size (inches)	Recommended Flat-Sheet Size (inches)
Crib	27 × 52	42 × 72
Standard Twin	39 × 76	72 × 108
Long Twin	39 × 80	72 × 108 or 72 × 113
Three-quarter	48 × 76	81 × 108 or 81 × 113
Standard Double	54 × 76	90 × 108 or 90 × 113
Long Double	54 × 80	90 × 108 or 90 × 113
Queen Size	60 × 80	90 × 113 or 90 × 120
King Size	72 × 84	108 × 122

up well in commercial laundering, but when charges are based on pound rates, the upkeep of a heavy muslin sheet will be comparatively high. If sheets are laundered at home, percale may be easier to handle because of its lighter weight.

Well-made sheets will have strong taped selvages at the side edges. Hems will be smooth and evenly stitched with small firm stitches. It is customary to have a one-inch hem at the bottom and a three- or four-inch hem at the top. However, some sheets are made with equal-sized hems at the ends, which makes it possible to reverse the position of the sheet. If these hems are narrow, however, they are not usually as attractive as the one deep hem at the top.

Knitted sheets require little or no ironing; nylon, in either woven or knitted constructions, is easily laundered. Of course, the textures of such sheets will be different from the textures of traditional woven cotton sheets.

If one has sheets of different sizes and different types in the linen closet it is helpful to have some identifying label stitched at a bottom corner. Many manufacturers provide some sort of a marking, or sheets can be easily marked with a bit of colored tape, thread, or a laundry marking pencil.

DESIGN. Color and pattern have become important style features of bed linens. In most cases reliable manufacturers use dyes that stand up well even with commercial laundering. However, in poor-quality sheets the colors may fade. Bright, fresh designs on bed linens often contribute to the attractiveness of a bedroom, but this is another matter of personal preference. Of course the design and the color scheme should blend with the decor of the room for the most charming effects.

REQUIREMENTS. Specific needs for bed linens will vary for each household, depending on the number of beds, the number of different sized beds, the types of sheets (flat or fitted; white or colored, and so on.), and how the laundry is done. A good basic rule to follow, however, is to allow six sheets for each bed and three cases for each pillow. Thus there will be two sheets in use, two in the laundry, and two in reserve. Linens will wear longer if they are rotated in use, so the reserve supply should be used as frequently as the others.

Many homemakers like to protect mattresses with heavy muslin covers and pads. These are especially desirable in times of illness when food or medicine may spill and spot a mattress.

FIGURE 25-1 Sheets and pillow cases are accessories in the bedroom and should be selected to emphasize the theme. (a) (*Courtesy of West Point Pepperell*) **(b)** (*Courtesy of J. P. Stevens & Co., Inc.*) **(c)** (*Courtesy of J. P. Stevens & Co., Inc.*)

(a)

(b)

(c)

Blankets

Comfort, appearance, and durability are major factors in choosing blankets. To be comfortable, the blanket should be of desirable weight and provide adequate warmth. Most people prefer lightweight blankets. A deep fluffy nap will encase many little air spaces that provide good insulating qualities. A firmly woven heavy blanket may not be as warm as a well-made lighter type.

SIZES. Blankets range from small crib sizes to extra-large sizes designed for kingsized beds. For a standard twin bed a blanket should be 65 by 90 inches; a standard double bed requires a blanket 80 by 90 inches. Blankets that measure 90 by 108 inches are more comfortable on beds that are longer and wider than the standard double size.

TYPES. Blankets are available in a variety of weights and in several fibers. In addition, comforters filled with feathers and down are sometimes used in place of blankets.

Good wool blankets are warm and durable. The nap remains fluffy if the blanket is properly cleaned. Synthetic fibers, including nylon, Acrilan, Orlon, and Dynel, have become popular in blankets and are often used in blends. If well constructed, blankets made of synthetics retain their light fluffy qualities. They are easy to launder and require no special care to prevent moth damage.

Thermal blankets, constructed so that tiny pockets of air provide excellent insulating qualities, have become very popular. They are very light in weight and easy to care for.

Various finishes are used on the ends of blankets. A machine-made blanket stitch is sometimes used on lightweight blankets. If the thread is firm and the stitches are close together this may be a durable finish. Binding is usually a more attractive and more luxurious finish. Bands of silk, rayon, nylon, or cotton sateen are used to bind edges. These should be of good quality and firmly stitched. They should not interfere with the launderability of a washable blanket.

DESIGNS. Most blankets depend on soft fluffy texture and rich colors for their beauty. However, some do have designs woven into the fabric, and printed designs have become extremely popular. Quilts and comforters may have coverings of printed fabrics or they may be decorated with appliquéd motifs. Some comforters are covered with smooth taffeta or satin. Although rather elegant in appearance, this type of covering tends to slip and slide more than a fuzzy blanket.

REQUIREMENTS. In some climates at least two blankets may be needed for each bed— one lightweight summer blanket and one heavier-weight winter blanket. Some people prefer more. Electric blankets have become popular for several reasons, but especially because the one blanket can be regulated for various degrees of warmth. Thus they are always comfortable and the homemaker does not have the problem of storing extra blankets.

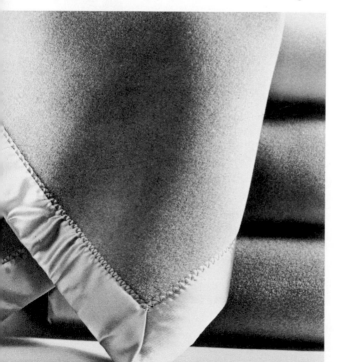

FIGURE 25-2 A non-woven blanket made by bonding nylon yarns to a core of urethane foam. The result is light, soft, and warm. (*Courtesy of West Point Pepperell*)

FIGURE 25-3 Good quality terry towels have a close, thick pile; the underweave is firm and hems are stitched with close, even stitches. (*Photo courtesy of Fieldcrest*)

Towels

New fashions in towels have added glamour to both the kitchen and the bathroom. Style trends in both types have followed the prevailing tastes in color and pattern. Towels, therefore, have become important accessories in the decorative scheme, especially because they are always on view.

SIZES. There is a wide range of sizes in towels. In the bathroom we might find tiny fingertip towels nine by fourteen inches as well as huge oversize bath sheets thirty-six by seventy-two inches. In between these two extremes are the more popular sizes. For hand towels sizes range from fifteen by twenty-five to eighteen by thirty-six inches. Bath towels from twenty by forty up to about twenty-seven by fifty inches are more widely used than the extra-large sizes, which are better for outdoor use as beach towels. Washcloths should be at least twelve by twelve inches.

Today the trend is toward larger sizes in bath towels. Big people usually find a large bath towel more comfortable and convenient to use.

Kitchen towels usually measure about sixteen by thirty inches. They should never be any narrower, but some people prefer them wider.

TYPES. Cotton terry cloth is the popular choice for toweling. It is used exclusively for bath towels and for many hand towels. It is also used for kitchen towels. However, other fabrics are used for some face and hand towels. Huck in either linen or cotton is widely used. Sometimes rayon and cotton mixtures are used. Linen is a preferred fiber for kitchen towels because it is so absorbent and because linen towels do not leave lint on dishes and glassware. Some kitchen towels made of cotton are specially constructed and treated to make them lint free.

Judging quality in towels requires careful observation and comparison. In terry cloth the underweave should be firm and close for strength and durability. The loops of yarn that form the pile provide absorbency and they should be closely packed. More loops mean greater absorbency and a more luxurious texture. Long loops also increase absorbency. The twist of the yarn will influence texture and absorbency. Loosely twisted pile yarns soak up more moisture and feel softer to the touch. However, some people prefer a towel with a slightly hard, rough texture for mild stimulation of the skin.

It is important to compare terry towels of different weights, textures, and qualities to observe the differences before making selections.

The side edges of a towel may be finished in different ways. A woven-taped selvage should be firm and sturdy. An over-edged selvage uses an overcast stitch, which should be close and tight for maximum durability. A hemmed selvage should be stitched with small firm stitches.

FIGURE 25-4 Solid colors coordinated with a bright pattern add an attractive decorative note to the bathroom. (*Courtesy of J. P. Stevens & Co., Inc.*)

The stitching at the hemmed ends of the towel is a good indication of quality. Small stitches and backstitching at the corners provide sturdy hems. The towel should be free from loose thread ends.

DESIGNS. Pile loops are responsible for absorbency in terry cloth. Any pattern that reduces the area of the pile will make the towel less functional; for example, some designs are woven with flat areas, and other towels are decorated with large appliquéd motifs. Metallic yarns are sometimes used for added glamour. In most cases these are quite durable. Nevertheless any added decoration should not interfere with the chief function of the towel.

Coordinated colors and patterns often add interest in the decoration of the bathroom. Various solid colors may be combined with related prints or stripes for added interest.

REQUIREMENTS. Minimum quantities of towels are difficult to determine, because requirements vary with individuals. Also, if the laundry is done at home in an automatic washer and dryer there will be less need for large reserves. However, there should be a supply adequate to meet extra demands should there be illness in the family or should one entertain overnight guests. Also, towels wear better if they are rotated in use. A suggested estimate includes:

Six face towels per person
Six bath towels per person
Four washcloths per person

The bathroom linen closet should also include at least two bath mats.

Table Linens

In the selection of table linens there is far more freedom of choice than for other household linens. It has already been pointed out that each homemaker sets her own standards

FIGURE 25-5 Select a tablecloth in relation to the size and shape of the table. (*Courtesy of Simtex—J. P. Stevens and Co., Inc.*)

FIGURE 25-6 A lively daisy pattern in a permanent press linen cloth by Fallani & Cohn permits an elegant look with minimal work. (*Courtesy of Belgian Linen Association*)

with respect to meal service. With the vogue for more informal service and many easy-care materials on the market, there is no reason why table settings should not be both attractive and functional.

Some young homemakers question the use of any table linens at all. With laminated table tops that require only wiping with a damp cloth, and with paper napkins, there may be no need for any kind of table covering. This kind of table service, however, lacks a certain warm and gracious quality. Various place mats and tablecloths require little or no care, yet they lend a charm and an aura of hospitality to meal service. This is an area where individuality may certainly be exercised, but today it requires no effort at all to set tables that are gracious and inviting.

SIZES. Place mats are available in new and interesting shapes, but the traditional rectangle measures about twelve by eighteen

inches. A cloth that covers the entire table should usually extend about six or eight inches beyond the edges of the table. Naturally the size and shape of the table will determine the size of the cloth. Popular standard sizes for small tables include 36″ × 36″ for a card table, 54″ × 54″ for a dinette table, and 54″ × 72″ for a dinette table with leaves extended. Regular dining tables usually require wider cloths. Popular sizes are 64″ × 72″, 72″ × 90″, and 90″ × 108″. Cloths for round tables are available in a variety of sizes.

Napkins range in size from small cocktail napkins to large dinner napkins. Tea or luncheon napkins may be 12″ × 12″ or 15″ × 15″. Dinner napkins are more usually 18″ × 18″, 22″ × 22″, or 24″ × 24″, although other sizes are available.

TYPES. There is such a wide range of table coverings on the market that it is difficult to classify them in any useful manner. Perhaps the use, the appearance, and the amount of care required will be the most important factors in making a selection.

Place mats and even tablecloths in plastic or plastic-coated fabrics have become more glamorous and more sophisticated in styling. Lovely textural effects and interesting color combinations are rapidly removing the stigma that has for so long been associated with plastic. If these are chosen with care and discretion, there should be no objection to their use even on special occasions. For everyday use, especially for breakfast and lunch, they are attractive and require minimum care.

The more traditional mats and cloths are made of linen, cotton, and rayon, and now the synthetics have entered the field. Linen damask cloths have, for many years, been the most desirable cloths for rather formal, elegant settings. The lovely texture of linen provides a suitable background for beautiful china, glassware, and silver. Linen cloths do not become fuzzy with use, they do not absorb stains quickly, and they launder easily. Cotton and rayon have been widely used in damask cloths because they are less expensive, but neither of these fibers offers the beauty and the lasting quality of linen.

Damask refers to various kinds of construction. In table linens, the terms *single* and *double* damask are often used. In double damask a yarn floats over seven threads, which allows for a more lustrous texture. In single damask, the yarn floats over four threads. Double damask often has more threads per square inch.

Because of the long floats of yarn, the pattern of double damask is often more distinct. However, many factors must be considered in judging quality. A poor-grade double damask will be less durable and probably less attractive than a high-grade single damask.

Lace is often used for tablecloths that may be either formal or informal. A good lace cloth has many practical advantages. It can be laundered easily, it requires little or no ironing, and it is elegant enough for very special occasions. Spots do not become immediately prominent. A lovely handmade lace cloth is indeed a family treasure. Machine-made lace cloths, although not usually as beautiful, do offer similar advantages.

The synthetics in modern table coverings present beauty and elegance with the appealing little-care features. Most of the synthetics do not spot easily and require little or no ironing. All of these characteristics are making them more important in the field of table "linens."

REQUIREMENTS. Naturally the requirements for table linens will depend on how family meals will be served, the kind of entertaining that will be done, the size of the tables, and the general decor of the home. However, table linens might be considered as accessories in that they will complement the decorative scheme. From this standpoint, they should be chosen with care so that they will provide a suitable background for the other table appointments.

Section VI
Home Projects

There seems to be renewed interest in the various types of needlework that can provide attractive accessories for almost any room. Kits with all the necessary materials are readily available for hooked and braided rugs, needle-point, and embroidery, especially crewelwork. In many cases designs have become modernized or highly stylized.

A sewing machine will soon pay for itself if one enjoys making lovely things for the home. Many women prefer working on decorative items rather than clothing, because in general the sewing of these items is quick and easy. There is a wide variety of beautiful fabrics and exciting trimmings. Also, the many simple labor-saving devices help to provide a custom-made appearance with relatively little expense.

General Hints

Naturally, every new trend in home decoration won't be suitable for every home, but magazines and department stores are full of ideas that can be adapted. Rooms need never be dull or monotonous, nor need they be static. Often just a simple little change, such as new chair covers or a few new decorative pillows, will add fresh interest and sparkle. New curtains and slipcovers need not be expensive to be interesting.

PLAN CAREFULLY. Successful decoration does require careful and long-range planning. Before investing time and money in sewing for the home, one should be sure to select colors and textures that are exactly what is wanted. Even with inexpensive fabrics, mistakes are costly. If possible, when buying any new fabric it is wise to take samples of the colors already in the room. If that is not possible, it's worth investing in one-third or one-half yard of fabric to try out at home. In a

26

Sewing for the Home

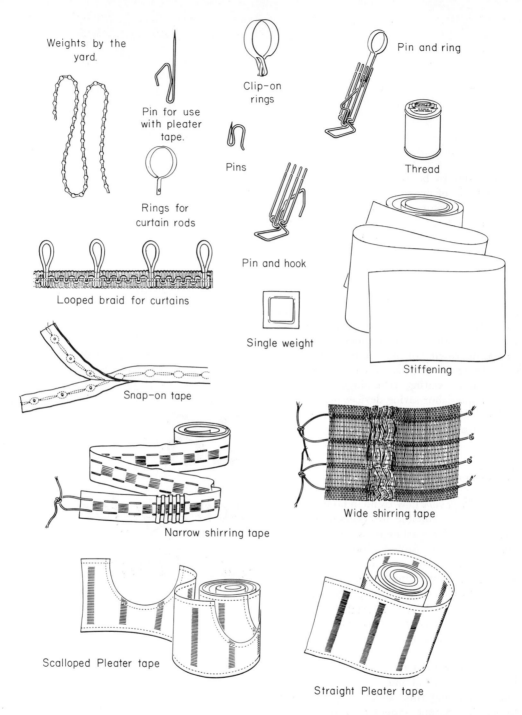

Weights by the yard.

Pin for use with pleater tape.

Rings for curtain rods

Clip-on rings

Pins

Pin and hook

Single weight

Pin and ring

Thread

Stiffening

Looped braid for curtains

Snap-on tape

Narrow shirring tape

Wide shirring tape

Scalloped Pleater tape

Straight Pleater tape

FIGURE 26-1   Various tapes and supplies that simplify sewing for the home.
(*Courtesy of Conso Products, Inc.*)

different setting, the colors may look altogether different than they did in the store.

One should think in terms of the amounts of each color and pattern to be used. It should be remembered that large areas of brilliant colors tend to decrease the apparent size of the room. So does too much bold pattern and too much contrast. Also, repeating certain colors, textures, and prints tends to unify the effect. But too much repetition can be monotonous. Thus, one must try to visualize the room as a whole and plan the areas of color and pattern for a pleasing result.

SHOP CAREFULLY. One should compare qualities very carefully before buying, and check information about shrinkage, colorfastness, and care. One should also deal with stores that will stand behind their products.

It may be necessary to look around in several stores to become familiar with all the different types of curtain rods, drapery hooks, and trimmings. There are also many useful notions and patterns that will make projects easier, such as corded shirring tape, snap tape, press-on tape; there are various uses for all of these.

MEASURE CAREFULLY. One must be sure to have complete and accurate measurements for any decorating to be done. Projects like draperies and slipcovers often require large amounts of fabric, and one can get into serious difficulties by not knowing the exact dimensions of windows, sofas, chairs, and so on. Ample fullness in curtains, draperies, bedspreads, and slipcovers should be planned for. Rather than skimp with a costly fabric, it is better to be generous with one that is less expensive. Also, calculations should be generous, allowing for full ruffles and deep pleats, headings, and hems.

Most decorative fabrics are forty-eight to fifty inches wide, but some are only thirty-six inches wide. The exact width must be known before the yardage can be figured. If the fabric has a printed or woven design, the size of the motif is important. (This is spoken of as the *repeat*.) When several lengths of fabric are seamed for draperies, the motifs must be evenly matched and they must be placed exactly alike at both sides of a window. When a large motif is used for slipcovers, the design must be attractively placed on the chair, otherwise it will appear chopped up. The larger the motif, the more fabric will be required for matching and placing the design.

Ruffles, skirts, and pleated flounces are usually cut on the crosswise grain of the fabric. For adequate fullness in gathering fabric should usually be at least twice as long as the finished measurement; lightweight, sheer fabrics may require two-and-a-half to three times the finished measurement for ample fullness after gathering.

Curtains and Draperies

Only a few simple hems are needed to make plain, tailored curtains, but they can be taken out of the ordinary class with a little trimming, such as a few tucks parallel to the bottom hem, or bands of braid or fringe for a border effect. It's all simple, straight stitching with no complicated fitting. Even the measuring is easy. With the use of lots of fabric and interesting colors, in no time at all a dowdy room can be converted into one that has character.

Curtains and draperies should be planned so that they can be used on either side of the window. This is just a matter of making all the side hems the same depth. Light weakens some fabrics, so they will last longer if the panels are reversed once in a while.

The window must be measured accurately. In a patterned fabric, the panels should be cut so that the motif will be spaced the same way across all windows. The lengths of fabric should be cut allowing for headings and bottom hems. A three-inch hem at the bottom may be enough, but on some fabrics a deeper hem looks more attractive and hangs better. Six inches, or even nine inches, may not be too much for a nice solid look at the lower edge. A double hem is sometimes used to add body and to allow for shrinkage. One should be generous with hem allowances, because it's much easier to cut fabric off if the hem is too deep than it is to add on if the curtains have to be lengthened.

Weights are sometimes used at the bottom edges of curtains and draperies to make them hang nicely. There are tiny weights that come by the yard. A length of this type of weighting can be inserted in the bottom hem and tacked in place. Larger single weights can be covered with fabric and tacked on the inside at the lower corners.

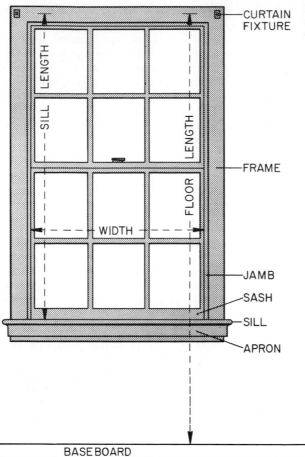

FIGURE 26-2 Measure from the fixture for the desired length. Allow ample fabric for headings and hems. (*Courtesy of Conso Products, Inc.*)

The required fullness in the width of the curtain or drapery depends on the weight of the fabric. Sheer, lightweight fabrics should be cut with greater fullness. One should seam together as many lengths as will be needed to give the desired width. If selvages pull or draw, they should be clipped every four or five inches. They may have to be cut off completely and the seam edges finished with a machine stitch to prevent fraying.

The side edges of each curtain should now be hemmed. About one to two inches for this hem is enough, but that depends on the fabric and the width of the whole panel.

HEADINGS. The way the top of the curtain should be finished depends on the kind of rod and hooks to be used. If the curtain or drapery will be covered by a cornice or valance, one can turn a simple hem, leaving both ends open so the rod can be inserted. If the

top will be exposed, it is usually more attractive to have some decorative type of heading. For a simple one, one can turn a deep hem, then put in another row of machine stitching to form a casing and a heading at the top of the curtain. When measuring for this type of finish, one must remember that the top row of stitching will rest on the rod. The heading will be in addition to the length of the curtain from rod to hem.

Pleater Tape. Pinch pleats at the tops of curtains and draperies provide a more finished, custom-made appearance, especially on curtains or draperies that will be mounted on traverse rods and on those that will be exposed at the top.

One could use a strip of stiffening, such as buckram, at the top of the curtain, then measure and stitch the pleats. However, there is on the market a pleater tape, which makes the whole process very simple. The tape is

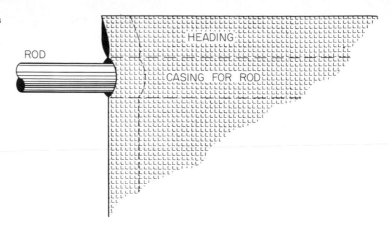

FIGURE 26-3 Allow ample amounts for casing and standing heading.

ROD

HEADING

CASING FOR ROD

made with narrow pockets or casings at regularly spaced intervals and special hooks are inserted to form the pleats.

About three quarters of an inch of fabric should be allowed for turning under at the upper edge. Then the pleater tape is stitched to the wrong side of the fabric. The top edge of the tape must be at the top edge of the curtain so that the pockets will be in the proper position. Then one inserts hooks to form pleats, spacing the pleats by skipping one casing between pleats. Single hooks should be used at the ends. (Note: The pleats may also be spaced with two casings in between if desired. However, this results in fewer pleats and the effect is not quite as attractive.)

This method of making pinch pleats has several advantages. The tape is easy to apply and requires no complicated measurements. Also, when the hooks are removed the curtains spread out flat, which simplifies cleaning, pressing, and storage.

Shirring Tape. Another interesting finish for the tops of curtains is possible through the use of shirring tape that has woven-in cords. The tape is stitched to the top edge of the curtain on the wrong side. The cords are then drawn to provide the desired fullness and tied back at the ends. They can be released so that the curtain will spread out flat for laundering. Regular drapery pins are used for mounting the curtain on the rod.

VALANCES AND CORNICES. The top of the window may be covered by a valance or a cornice to lend a more interesting decorative note. The type of finish and trimming chosen will, of course, be influenced by the style of the curtains or draperies. There is almost un-

limited variety and we shall suggest only a few simple ways to achieve interesting effects. The depth of the valance will also be determined by the proportions of the window. A tall, narrow window will seem shorter if a deeper valance is used.

Cornices are usually made of wood or metal, but there is available a special stiffening that can be covered with fabric and mounted on a curtain rod. It can be cut to any desired shape and trimmed to give the effect of a cornice. Wide tape should be stitched across the top on the inside to hold the rod.

A simple valance can be made with a plain hem at the top or with a standing heading such as is used for curtains. The lower edge may have a plain hem or some form of trimming to match the curtains.

Pleater tape can be used at the top of the valance. For a more formal and elegant valance, vertical strips of shirring tape might be used. In this case about three times the length of the finished valance should be allowed when the fabric is measured and cut.

CAFÉ CURTAINS. Short curtains are very popular, and attractive ones can be made quickly and easily. Although café curtains are in general rather informal in appearance, they have been adapted to more formal rooms in some interesting window treatments.

Various finishes can be used on the top edges of the curtains. One can make a plain hem and a casing for the rod just as for plain tailored curtains. There is also a tape with loops that will slide over the rod. Loops of braid or tape can be stitched to the top of the curtain at intervals.

Pleater tape and special hooks are also

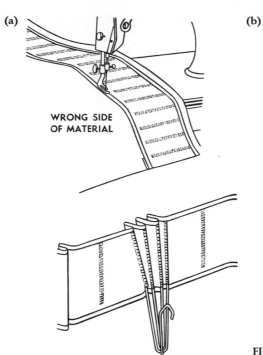

(a)

WRONG SIDE
OF MATERIAL

(b)

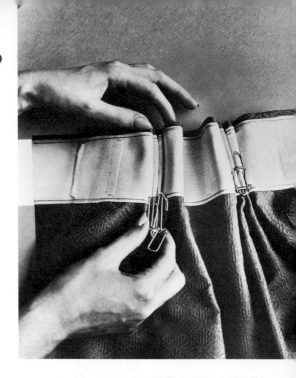

FIGURE 26-4 Stitch pleater tape to tops of curtains or draperies. Insert hooks for even, professional looking pleats. (*Courtesy of Conso Products, Inc.*)

(a)

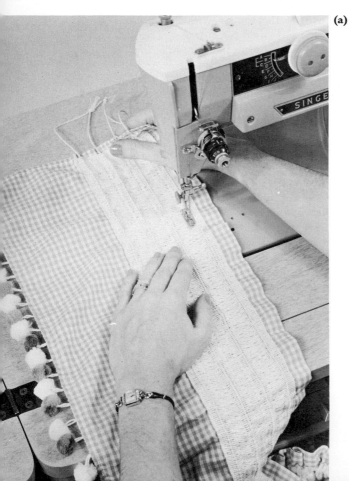

FIGURE 26-5 Shirring tape may be used at the tops of curtains, draperies, or valances. (*Courtesy of Conso Products, Inc.*)

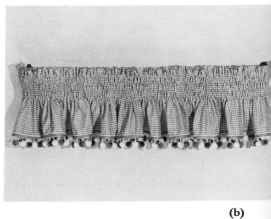

(b)

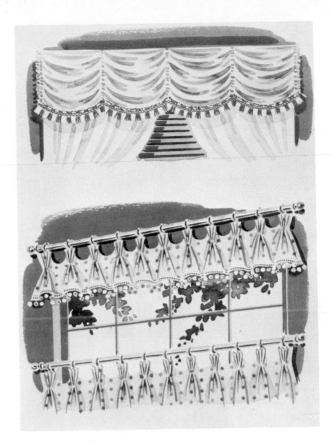

available for café curtains. This tape for short curtains is not quite as deep as that used for long curtains and draperies.

Some pleater tape also comes in a scalloped design. With this one must allow for side hems and stitch the right side of the tape to the right side of the curtain. The top edge should be trimmed close to the line of stitching, and the tape should be turned to the wrong side. When the hems are finished, the lower edge of the tape should be stitched to the curtain, and hooks should be inserted to make pleats between the scallops.

Café curtains are often plain, but a simple trimming frequently adds an interesting touch. Tucks, ruffles, decorative stitching, braid, fringe, or appliqué might be used.

LINED DRAPERIES. Drapery fabrics will usually hang better at the windows if they are lined. Cotton sateen is the popular choice for drapery linings because it lends body without being too stiff. Other fabrics that have a coating of metallic powder are also used, and they act as insulators. For a large

picture window that gets a lot of sun these treated fabrics should be investigated. They will make the room cooler in the summer and warmer in the winter.

It isn't difficult to line draperies. One makes the drapery panel the desired width by seaming together the required number of panels. The lining should be about three inches narrower and about one inch shorter than the drapery panel. The hems are then turned on the lower edges. With the top edges even and the right sides of the two fabrics together, the two pieces should be seamed together. The panels should then be turned right side out and pressed along the lengthwise edges so that the drapery fabric folds over to form a hem on each side.

If one is not sure about the depth of the hem at the lower edge, the side seams may be left free at the bottom and the hems on the drapery fabric and on the lining may be turned after the side edges have been seamed. The lining should be slip-stitched to the drapery at the lower end after the bottom hems are turned.

FIGURE 26-7 Nearly all the items in this room were made on the sewing machine. Rug is flowery swirls of coating remnants appliqued to heavy cotton and backed with rug canvas. Curtains are white cotton organdy with vertical strips of fashion-stitching. "Painting" on wall is appliqued felt, mounted on poster board. Ottoman is two slip-covered foam cushions on a felt-covered wooden platform. Pillows are appliqued. Couch cover and cushions are slip-covered to match draperies. (*Courtesy of The Singer Company*)

FIGURE 26-8 A tiny sleeping alcove has a regal appearance created by imaginative use of fabric and trimming. (*Courtesy of DuPont Textile Fibers*)

FIGURE 26-9 Draperies and café curtains trimmed with braid lend an elegant touch to this window treatment. (*Courtesy of Conso Products, Inc.*)

FIGURE 26-10 **A new press-on fringe adds a smart decorative finish to the window treatment shown above.** (*Courtesy of Window Shade Manufacturers Association*)

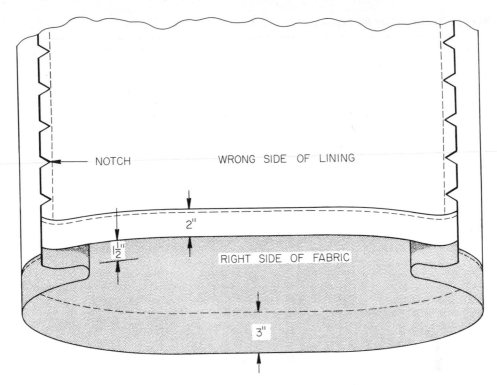

NOTCH

WRONG SIDE OF LINING

2"

1½"

RIGHT SIDE OF FABRIC

3"

FIGURE 26-11   Cut lining narrower and shorter than drapery material.

At the top edge, the lining should be stitched to the drapery fabric after they have been turned right side out and pressed. Then one turns under one-half inch along the top edge, presses the crease, and applies pleater tape as it is applied for unlined draperies.

Slipcovers

For both functional and decorative reasons, slipcovers play a major role in furnishing a home. They protect upholstered pieces, they are easy to keep clean, and they provide for a variety of effects. Some people use slipcovers all year round with one set for winter and another for summer. Others prefer to cover the upholstered pieces only at certain times of the year.

Actually, slipcovers are not difficult to make, but they do require time, patience, and accuracy. With some experience in clothing construction, one can make a beautiful cover for any type of chair. Of course, the techniques for cutting and fitting slipcovers are quite different from those used in making clothes. Here we shall present a few of the

basic techniques, but the references in the bibliography can be used for more detailed instructions. The extension service in your state will probably have some pamphlets that will be helpful.

Because the first slipcover will be a new experience, it is wise to keep the project as simple as possible so that the results will be letter perfect. The beginner should note the following suggestions.

1. Choose a simple, basic-type chair with straight lines, if possible.
2. Select a fabric in a solid color or one with a very small all-over pattern. Large motifs, stripes, plaids, and so on must be either placed in a special way or matched.
3. If possible, work first with an old sheet or inexpensive muslin. Using the test pieces as a pattern will increase confidence in cutting the fabric.

STUDY THE CHAIR. Furniture varies so much in design that one must plan a cover that will fit well and enhance the contours of the chair. In general the seams of the slipcover will follow the basic lines of the chair, but at

TABLE 1 Yardage Chart for Slipcovers*

| Type | Cushions | 48" Wide | | 36" Wide | | Welting or Trimming |
		Plain	Figured or Striped	Plain	Figured or Striped	
Sofa	2–3	14	15$\frac{1}{2}$	21	23	36
6–7 ft.	1 LC	13$\frac{1}{2}$	15	20$\frac{1}{2}$	22$\frac{1}{2}$	33
	0	10	11	15	17	21
3-ft. Sectional						
1 arm	1	6$\frac{1}{2}$	7$\frac{1}{2}$	12	12$\frac{1}{2}$	25
no arm	1	5	6	11	11$\frac{1}{2}$	20
4-ft. Sectional						
1 arm	1	9$\frac{1}{2}$	10	13	13$\frac{1}{2}$	28
no arm	1	8	9	12	12$\frac{1}{2}$	22
5-ft. Sectional						
1 arm	1	10$\frac{1}{2}$	10$\frac{1}{2}$	14	14$\frac{1}{2}$	31
no arm	1	9	9	13	13$\frac{1}{2}$	24
Sofa Bed	2	14$\frac{1}{2}$	16	20	21	40
Love Seat	2	10$\frac{1}{2}$	12	15	16$\frac{1}{2}$	24
	1	10$\frac{1}{2}$	11	15	16$\frac{1}{2}$	23
	0	8$\frac{1}{2}$	9$\frac{1}{2}$	13	14$\frac{1}{2}$	14
Arm, Club, Lounge,	1	7$\frac{1}{2}$	8$\frac{1}{4}$	11$\frac{1}{4}$	12$\frac{1}{4}$	18
and Cogswell	0	6$\frac{1}{2}$	7	8$\frac{1}{2}$	9$\frac{1}{2}$	13
Fanback, Wing,	1	8	8$\frac{1}{2}$	12	13$\frac{1}{2}$	18
and Barrel	0	7	7$\frac{1}{2}$	10	11	13
Boudoir	1	5	6$\frac{1}{2}$	8	9	15
	0	4$\frac{1}{2}$	5$\frac{1}{2}$	6$\frac{1}{2}$	7$\frac{1}{2}$	12
Chaise Longue	2	11$\frac{1}{2}$	12$\frac{1}{2}$	16	17	23
	1	10$\frac{1}{2}$	11	13	14	20
	0	8	9	12	13$\frac{1}{4}$	16
Ottoman	0	2	2$\frac{1}{2}$	3	3$\frac{1}{2}$	6
Cushion	1	1$\frac{1}{4}$	1$\frac{3}{4}$	2	2$\frac{3}{4}$	5

* With 54-inch goods, yardage should be reduced 10% for solids and 5% for prints. If the repeat is over 24 inches, the salesgirl should be consulted for yardage.

* *Courtesy of Conso Products, Inc.*

the back and the sides of the seat, the cover must be tucked down into the crevices to be held in place. It will therefore have to be larger in this area than the chair itself.

PLAN THE COVER. How should the lower edge of the chair look? Most slipcovers have a flounce that may be pleated at the corners, pleated all around, or gathered. However, the chair to be covered may be more attractive if the lower edges of the cover are carried under the chair, giving it an upholstered look.

An opening must be provided either at the side seam or at the center back so that the slipcover can be easily removed and replaced. A zipper or snap tape is usually used for the closure. The cover for a separate cushion will have an opening along the back, and possibly it will extend a few inches along the sides to allow for easy removal.

The exposed seams of slipcovers are usually reinforced with a welting or some form of trimming, such as fringe. Cable cord can be bought and covered with bias strips of fabric, or welting may be bought ready made in a solid color that blends with the fabric.

PREPARE THE FABRIC. One must be sure the fabric has a true grain line before cutting it. One can straighten ends by tearing across or pulling a crosswise thread, always working with the lengthwise thread perpendicular to the floor. Grain line is just as important for the proper appearance of slipcovers as it is in garments.

CUT THE FABRIC. First the length of fabric needed for each major area of the chair should be measured, allowing for at least one-inch seams wherever sections must be joined and for a generous tuck-in at the back and sides of the seat. A minimum of five inches on each piece is recommended, but a more generous allowance is sometimes advisable to provide for a better fit.

When planning some sort of a flounce at the lower edge of the slipcover, one should pin a tape or a cord around the chair to mark a line for it. A depth of about eight inches is usually attractive for a plain or a pleated flounce; one with gathers might be slightly deeper.

FIT EACH SECTION. While the fabric is held wrong side out, each piece should be smoothed in position. The lengthwise grain line must be kept perpendicular to the floor and the crosswise grain line parallel to the floor. A bit of care here will make the sewing much easier and will also yield better results.

Each piece should now be placed in position on the chair. Whenever possible, pins should be placed exactly at the seam line, and the seam line of one piece should be matched to another. One should pat and smooth the fabric while working, and trim the fabric, allowing for generous one-inch seams.

A few tricky points require special care. Where the inside arm section joins the back section, there is usually a curved seam that must fit smoothly on the arm of the chair. It tapers outward to form the tuck-in at the base of the seat. The seam line should be pinned and the fabric trimmed. Making notches in the seam allowance will make it easier to manipulate the fabric in this area.

FIGURE 26-12 Smooth each section into position. Allow for generous seams and tuck-ins.

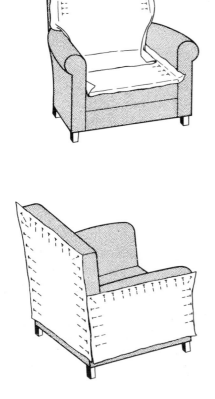

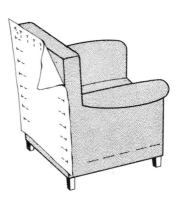

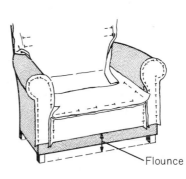

Flounce

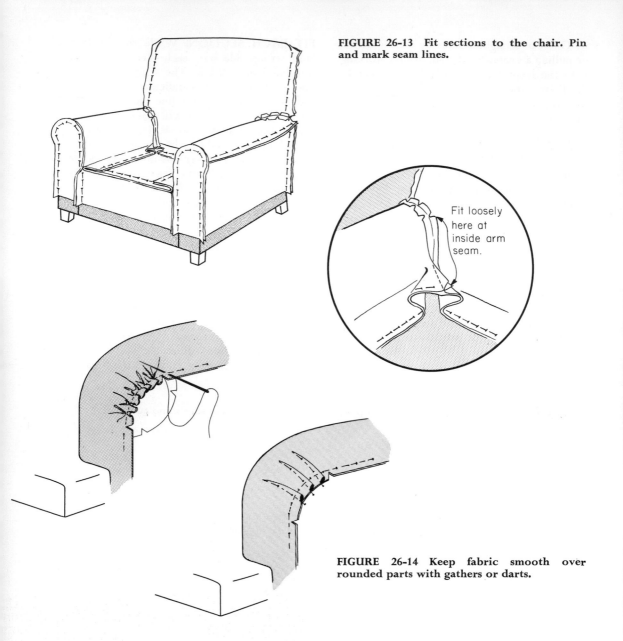

FIGURE 26-13 Fit sections to the chair. Pin and mark seam lines.

Fit loosely here at inside arm seam.

FIGURE 26-14 Keep fabric smooth over rounded parts with gathers or darts.

The tuck-in allowance at the seat will taper off toward the front on most chairs. Then the seam line must exactly meet the front arm-panel. Some chairs or sofas have rounded contours or T-shaped cushions that require different fitting.

When fitting the fabric over a rounded edge, one must make notches in the seam allowance and distribute the fullness with either gathers or darts.

MARK SEAM LINES. Using a colored pencil or chalk to mark all seam lines, one should make definite marks that will not rub off during work with the different sections of fabric.

STITCH THE SEAMS. The seams of the tuck-in allowance will not have any cording or trimming. These seams should be joined first, and should be trimmed and pressed as one goes along.

For other seams it is easier to stitch the welting or trimming to the right side of one section of fabric before joining the seam. It is best to baste it in position, completing one

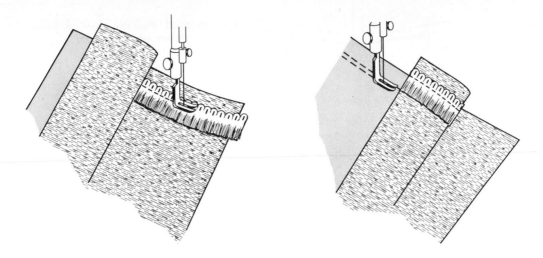

FIGURE 26-15 Stitch welting or fringe to right side first. Join seams.

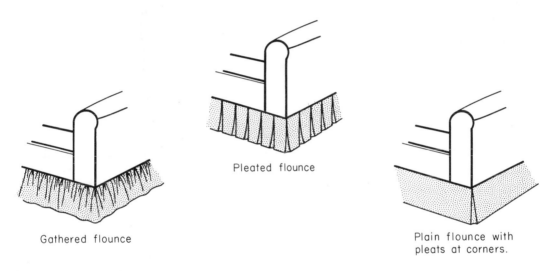

Pleated flounce

Gathered flounce

Plain flounce with pleats at corners.

FIGURE 26-16 Various treatments of the skirt provide different effects.

section before attempting to join it to another. On the back seam left free for the opening, the welting should be applied along one edge so that the finished effect will be consistent with the other seams.

MAKE THE SKIRT OR FLOUNCE. The sections of fabric that will form the skirt should be joined with plain seams, and the lower edge should be hemmed. A hem of about one or one-and-a-half inches is usually attractive. The skirt should now be pleated or gathered as planned. A kick-pleat at each

corner of the chair should have an allowance of at least eight inches. The skirt should be joined to the chair cover with a reinforced seam similar to the other seams. This seam should begin and end at the line of the opening so that the zipper or snap tape may extend to the lower edge of the cover.

FINISH THE OPENING. The raw edges can now be turned under along the lines of the opening. The two finished edges should meet along the seam line. The zipper or the tape can now be stitched into position.

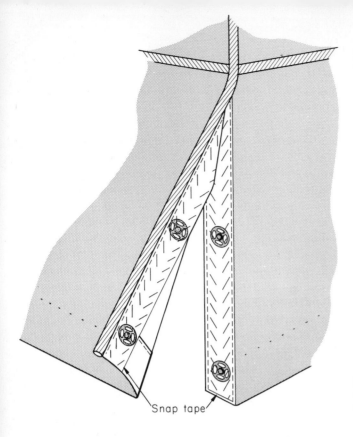

FIGURE 26-17 Plan the opening. Snap-tape or zippers are usually used.

FIGURE 26-18 Cover the cushion. The opening should be long enough to allow for easy removal of the cover.

Snap tape

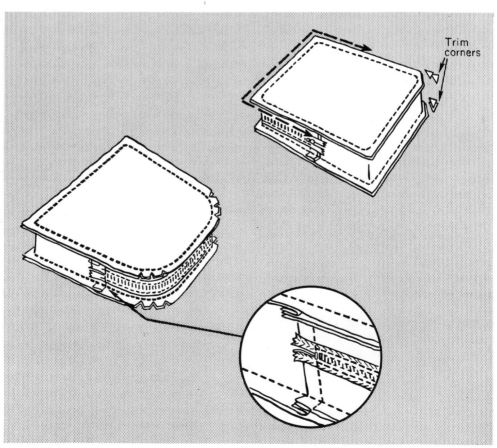

Trim corners

COVER THE CUSHION. The cushion should be placed on a double thickness of fabric and the outline marked with chalk. One-inch seams should be allowed in cutting the sections for the top and the bottom. Bands should then be cut for boxing the cushion. The band that extends along the front and sides of the cushion should be cut the depth of the cushion plus two inches for seams. Four inches should be added to the length for finishing ends. Some opening along the back band must be provided so that the cover may be easily removed. One method of doing this is to cut two bands the length of the back edge, keeping each band the same width as the front band. Each one should be folded lengthwise and pinned along the fold. One band should be sewn to the cushion top and the other band to the cushion bottom along the back edge. The zipper is then inserted between the folded edges and the under ends of the front band are turned under one inch. These ends should overlap the ends of the back bands. The band should then be seamed to top and the bottom of the cover as shown in Figure 26-18.

The finished cover should fit smoothly and follow the lines of the chair.

Bedspreads

It is possible to make lovely coordinated ensembles for the bedroom with curtains, bedspreads, and a dressing-table skirt. Closet accessories that go with the bedroom decoration lend a real custom-made touch.

PLAN THE SPREAD. Because the fabric used will probably be either thirty-six inches or fifty inches wide, some seams on part of the spread that goes on the surface of the bed may be necessary, such as one section of fabric down the center and another length for the two side sections necessary to cover the surface of the bed. A pleasing proportion should be planned for these sections, even if the fabric must be cut narrower for the center section. For example, if the bed is fifty-four inches wide and a fifty-inch fabric is being used, the center section might be cut thirty-four to thirty-eight inches wide. Some fabric may be wasted, but very narrow strips on either side of the fifty-inch width would not provide pleasing proportions.

FIGURE 26-19 The finished product should be trim and smooth.

Some decorative finish may be used, such as cording, piping, braid, or bands of fabric for the seams. Lace insertions or French seams turned to the outside may also be used. With a striped fabric, one might cut the middle section short and plan a border with mitered corners.

There are various ways of treating the pillows on the bed. The spread can be cut long enough to cover them and tuck in under the pillow edges, or a separate pillow cover can be made to match the spread.

FLOUNCES. The skirt or flounce of the spread is usually attached to the top section with decorative seams. Welting, fringe, or French seams can be used. The flounce may be straight, pleated, gathered, or circular.

Pleated skirt. The fabric is cut on the cross-wise grain. The measurement for the depth of the skirt must allow for seams and a hem at the lower edge. Enough strips should be joined to give ample fullness. After the lower edge of the skirt is hemmed, the sewing machine's ruffler attachment can be used to pleat the top edge, or box pleats can be folded with the use of a gauge to keep the pleats uniform and evenly spaced. There should be a pleat at each corner of the bed. This is a pretty effect but it does require patience and arithmetic.

Gathered Skirt. The fabric is cut on the crosswise grain with allowance for hems and seams. At least twice the finished measurement

FIGURE 26-20 A small room looks more spacious when it is decorated in white. In this teenage girl's bed-sitting room, café curtains, daybed cover and cushions are fashioned of white cotton corduroy, trimmed with gold and white braid. Walls are pale yellow. Although the room is light and bright, everything in it can be easily washed or wiped clean. (*Courtesy of The Singer Company*)

of the bed is needed for sufficient fullness. Hem the lower edge. The sewing machine's gathering foot or ruffler attachment should be used on the top edge.

TWO-PIECE SPREADS. The unique attractiveness of a two-piece spread is that the lower section, or dust ruffle, stays on the bed. The top section, or coverlet, covers only the mattress and extends over the dust ruffle about two or three inches. The two parts may match, but often they are made to contrast with each other.

First a pleated or gathered flounce is made for the dust ruffle. There are several ways of attaching it to the bed. One may use preshrunk muslin or cut an old sheet to fit the top of the box spring and seam the dust ruffle to the edge of this piece. One may also fasten

the ruffle to the box spring with snap tape, attaching one side of the tape to the spring and the other side to the inside of the dust ruffle.

Dressing Tables

Almost any ordinary small table or even a simple shelf can be converted into an attractive vanity with a few yards of fabric. It can be as tailored or as frilly as desired, but it should add an interesting note to the decoration of the room. The top of the table should be covered with mirror, glass, or a plastic that will not be marred by perfume and cosmetics.

On a plain table or shelf that has no drawers, one might cut a piece of fabric to fit the top,

FIGURE 26-21 A simple dressing table can become a center of interest in a small area. (*Courtesy of The Singer Company*)

FIGURE 26-22 Fabric and trimming add a decorative note to an ordinary bathroom. (*Courtesy of Conso Publishing Company*)

and seam a flounce or even a simple ruffle, to the edges. Also, snap-on tape can be used to hold the skirt in place. One side is tacked to the table and the other side is sewed to the inside of the skirt.

A regular vanity table usually has drawers and swing-out arms, so the skirt must be made with a center front opening. One can use either snap-on tape to attach the skirt as already suggested or stitch a plain strip of tape inside the top edge of the skirt and tack it to the table.

The top of the skirt can be pleated or gathered. The ruffler or the gathering foot may be used to stitch a firm cotton tape to the inside.

Shirring tape also provides an attractive heading. The cords at the back of the skirt should be pulled but not cut off. If they are rolled and then tacked to the bottom of the table, the fabric can be drawn out flat when it is laundered.

A bench or stool that matches the table will emphasize the pretty effect.

Bathroom Decoration

Plastic film is available in widths up to seventy-two inches and in some very attrac-tive colors and designs. However, other fabrics are frequently used for decorating bathrooms, and can be used with plastic under-curtains for the shower.

The window curtains might be tailored, tiered, café, or ruffled. If plastic film is used, the edges of ruffles can be pinked instead of hemmed because there is no danger of fraying. Curtains can also be trimmed with braid, tape, or fringe.

Shower curtains should be made with ample length and fullness. If the shower is over a tub, the curtain should extend at least eight inches below the top of the tub. Nar-row felled seams should be used to join panels of fabric if the curtain requires more than one panel.

One-inch side hems are made first. The top hem can be finished with a special tape made with eyelets, or with metal eyelets that can be bought and are easily applied.

If the shower curtain will hang inside the tub the bottom hem should be turned to the *outside* of the curtain so that water running down the curtain does not catch in the hem. A two- or three-inch hem is usually sufficient.

A vanity shelf or table in a bathroom is also useful, and it can be made quite attrac-tive with trimming that blends with the other bathroom decorations.

"Do-it-yourself" projects often require time, patience, and energy, but there is a certain satisfaction that comes with turning something unattractive into something beautiful. With a little imagination and ingenuity, one can sometimes work wonders with what seems like an impossible situation. Whether it be painting a room, reconverting an old piece of furniture, or making a simple table, one's efforts may be well repaid. Many people find this kind of activity so interesting that it actually provides a very rewarding hobby.

Not all such projects have to be time-consuming. Some may require only a few hours or even just a few minutes to produce interesting results. At first, such activities should be simple ones that do not require special skills and equipment. New "antiquing kits" and paint in spray cans are fairly simple to use.

One should try to find a local paint store that is well stocked. The dealer will probably be able to offer advice and assistance. A good hardware store will probably have a variety of interesting drawer pulls, knobs, furniture legs, and other equipment for rejuvenating furniture. The new adhesive-backed plastics are also available in most paint and hardware stores. These have many uses and are particularly suitable for projects that are quick and easy.

As one works up to the somewhat more complicated processes, such as refinishing furniture, he should be sure to do a little preliminary research on the proper methods. Extension services often have very useful pamphlets along these lines. The local library will probably have books on the subject. Many paint manufacturers publish directions for using their products.

Types of Paints and Finishes

There is such a wide variety of paints, wood stains, and finishing materials on the

27

Paints and

Finishes

FIGURE 27-1 An old sewing machine cabinet and an inexpensive mirror bought in a second-hand store were "antiqued" to produce a more attractive and useful vanity. (*Courtesy of Allied Chemical Corporation*)

market today that the novice may easily become confused. However, paint manufacturers have recognized the interest in home projects among amateurs and have developed products that are easy to use. It always pays to buy good-quality materials: one can be more certain of achieving perfect results.

Essentially, paint is a mixture of three basic ingredients: pigment, binder, and solvent. The pigment determines the color and the binder holds the pigment particles together to form a film. The solvent or thinner must be volatile substance that acts as a carrier. It allows the coating to be applied in liquid form and it then evaporates, leaving the solids affixed to the surface.

Various paints are designed to meet different requirements; for example, a paint for exterior use must be rather heavy and particularly resistant to the elements of weather. Certain paints are made for special surfaces—metal, concrete, wood, or plastic. Also, different degrees of gloss are required for various purposes.

The beginner should understand that paints require different thinners. Some must be thinned with turpentine or mineral spirits, others may be thinned with water. This difference will also determine how one cleans brushes and equipment. It is easier to use a paint that permits the washing of tools in soap and water.

Some of the important terms include:

OIL-BASE PAINT. Several kinds of oil may be used as vehicles for binding the pigment particles together and for giving strength to the paint. Linseed oil is most commonly used. Oil-base paints are available for different purposes and in varying degrees of gloss. They are usually thinned with turpentine or mineral spirits.

ALKYD PAINT. Several synthetic resins may be used as vehicles for paint, the usual ones being the alkyds. These have been a most important development in the paint industry and to a large extent have replaced oils in some types of paint. Alkyd paints are usually thinned with turpentine or mineral spirits.

LATEX PAINT. Another synthetic resin has become extremely popular for interior use. Latex is a resin dispersed in water. As the water evaporates, the extremely fine particles of resin produce a film that is strong and durable. Latex paints have good covering powers, they dry quickly, and they have little or no odor. After drying they become resistant to water and most of them can be scrubbed. The tools used in painting can be washed easily in soap and water.

ENAMEL. Somewhat similar to an oil paint, enamel is a special type made with varnish or lacquer to produce a tougher and more durable finish. Much enamel has a high gloss, but it is available in semigloss and low-gloss (or flat).

VARNISH. In general, varnish is a transparent protective coating that allows natural surface textures to show through. It is widely used on wood because it does not hide the grain pattern. Various types of varnish are available for different purposes. Some have a high gloss whereas others have a dull sheen or a satin finish. Certain types of varnish are resistant to moisture and alcohol stains.

A varnish stain has a colorant mixed with the protective coating. Although these are easy to apply, the results are not usually as attractive as when wood is stained first and then treated with a protective coat of clear varnish.

SHELLAC. Somewhat similar to varnish, shellac is also a protective coating. However, it is generally less durable and will show water spots. It dries more quickly and is often useful as a primer or wood sealer. Shellac must be thinned with alcohol, and brushes must be cleaned after using this solvent. Different types are available in a clear or an orange finish. The surface to be coated will determine the type to be used. Clear shellac will not darken light-colored surfaces.

LACQUER. A smooth, glossy finish can be obtained by the use of lacquer, which dries quickly to a durable coating. However, lacquers are not easy to apply with perfect results and they may require special thinners.

STAIN. Various types of colorants are available for use on bare wood. These may change the color of the natural wood or merely emphasize the grain pattern. Oil stains penetrate the pores of the wood and must usually be covered with some other protective coating. A stain will react in different ways on different types of wood. It is wise to test the results on some inconspicuous area before staining a piece of furniture.

SEALERS AND PRIMERS. New surfaces of plaster, wood, or wallboard sometimes require a preliminary coating that will make the final finishing appear more uniform. Shellac is often useful for this purpose, but paint or special preparations may be used.

General Suggestions

A few hints and suggestions may be useful in getting off to a good start.

ASSEMBLE THE PROPER EQUIPMENT. Each project will require specific items, and the work will be more enjoyable if one has the right equipment.

Newspapers or Drop Cloths. Floors and furniture are protected from spattered paint if they are carefully covered. Cloths are more satisfactory than newspapers, which tend to crumple and tear. Old plastic table-cloths are good for this purpose. Paint stores sell large plastic or canvas cloths that are very useful.

Mixing Pails. Large, clean cans or paper buckets can be used for mixing paint. They must be large enough to allow one to stir the paint easily.

Paddles. Smooth, flat wooden paddles are good for mixing paint. Paint-store dealers often give these to customers. An old ruler or some other piece of flat wood will also serve the purpose.

Clean Rags. These are used to wipe up spills and spatters.

Brushes. It pays to invest in good-quality paint brushes and to take good care of them. They will not shed bristles and will probably provide a less streaky effect than cheaper brushes would. One should use a brush that is a convenient size for the job. A three- or four-inch brush is good for walls, but a narrower one will be needed for trim and edges. A width of one and one-half or two inches is usually good for furniture projects.

Rollers and Pans. For large flat areas such as walls and ceiling, rollers make a job easier and faster. They come in a variety of sizes and with different types of covers. The paint dealer can help in the selection of the proper roller.

Gloves. Old gloves or properly fitted rubber gloves should be worn to protect the hands.

Ladder. A sturdy ladder is essential to the painting of a room. A good one will have a shelf near the top for holding paint cans.

Putty Knife. The broad, flat blade of a putty knife is useful for scraping loose flakes of peeling paint before a fresh coat is applied. It is also essential for removing old finishes when furniture is to be refinished.

Screwdriver. A screwdriver is handy for opening paint cans, removing switch plates, and taking knobs or handles off furniture.

Sandpaper. Sandpaper comes in various degrees of coarseness and it is important to select the proper grade for the purpose. For most projects a medium-coarse (#4/0) and a fine (#6/0) paper will be sufficient.

Steel Wool. For some purposes steel wool is more useful than sandpaper, In refinishing furniture, the initial preparation may be done with sandpaper but a final smoothing with fine steel wool (#00) provides a more pleasing surface.

CHOOSE THE PROPER PAINT. It has been mentioned that the wide variety of paints may be confusing. It is important, however, to use the material that best suits the purpose. When in doubt, one can consult a paint dealer. He will also be able to give advice on amounts to buy if he is given measurements of the surface to be covered.

Some paints are washable whereas others are not. Also, certain paints are available in spray cans, which may be useful for some projects.

PREPARE THE SURFACE. Much of the success in any home painting project will depend upon how well the surface is prepared for its final finishing. This may be the more tedious part of the work, but the end results will reflect such efforts.

Before painting a wall, one should repair cracks, holes, and rough spots with plaster so the surface is smooth and free from blemishes, and remove peeling or cracking paint with a putty knife, sandpaper, or steel wool.

Switch plates, covers of electrical outlets, and any other removable fixture plates should

FIGURE 27-2 Assemble the proper equipment before starting. (*Courtesy of Benjamin Moore & Co.—Paints*)

FIGURE 27-3 A roller and a tray simplify the task of painting large flat surfaces. (*Courtesy of Benjamin Moore & Co.—Paints*)

be removed. Handles and knobs that can't be removed can be covered with masking tape to prevent paint spatters. A little care in this matter makes the cleaning up easier. A paint liner is a gadget with a metal edge that is sometimes useful in the painting of window frames. It can be used to keep paint off the glass.

Refinishing furniture is quite another problem. When old finishes or several layers of paint must be removed, a commercial paint and varnish remover can be applied. This should be applied with an old brush and allowed to remain until the surface blisters or crackles. One should have a can or a paint bucket handy and use a putty knife for removing the scum that forms, then use steel wool or a blunt instrument to remove the old finish from corners and crevices. It may be neces-

sary to sandpaper the remains of the old finish or to use a fine steel wool to get down to the bare wood.

All surfaces should be completely free from dust, wax, or grease before any painting or refinishing is attempted. In some cases, merely wiping with a damp cloth will be enough. Greasy kitchen walls may have to be scrubbed with detergent and then rinsed with clear water. Wood surfaces that have been sandpapered should be wiped with a cloth dampened with turpentine. The surface must be completely dry before the new finish is applied.

Paint will adhere better to a surface that is slightly rough. One should sandpaper any very smooth surface and wipe away the dust to be sure the surface is absolutely clean.

APPLY THE FINISH. When using paint one should dip the brush into the paint and wipe it against the can to remove the excess. Smooth even strokes will make the paint flow from the brush to the surface. On walls, an up-and-down stroke should be used. On wood, the direction of the grain should be followed. It takes a bit of practice to apply a smooth even coat that will dry to a uniform finish. With a little practice one can eliminate streaky runs and drips.

Some wood stains should be applied with a cloth or a sponge. One should allow them to penetrate according to directions on the can and then wipe off the excess with old rags. It may be necessary to experiment a bit to obtain the desired color. This should be done on some inconspicuous part of the piece.

After staining, wood may be finished in a variety of ways. Several coats of wax might be all that is needed. Varnish or shellac may be more desirable in some cases. To develop a beautiful finish several coats of varnish are often used. One should let each application dry thoroughly, then rub it down with fine steel wool. The surface should be wiped with a clean cloth dampened with turpentine and allowed to dry. Then another finishing coat should be applied. The rubbing and polishing between many applications develops a beautiful mellow patina that is far more attractive than the application of one thick coating.

With all painting and refinishing it is important to follow carefully the directions on the label. It may be necessary to experiment a bit on the surface to be refinished, but it pays to develop proper techniques before working on major areas.

Wallpapers

It is so easy to produce interesting and unusual effects with wallpaper that this is one of the most useful means of decorating. One does not always have to paper a whole room to get the desired effect; sometimes papering just an alcove or one wall will do the trick. Wallpaper can also be used in an interesting manner on folding screens, shelves, accessories, and even on some furniture. Once having tried a wallpapering project, one will probably feel very creative and very proud of the results.

TYPES OF WALLPAPER. Two basic types of wallpaper are available, the prepasted variety and the kind to which one must apply the paste oneself. It may be necessary to experiment with each type before deciding which one is preferable.

Prepasted papers have a dry paste applied to the wrong side. A strip must be soaked in water for a few seconds until it is thoroughly wet; then it is applied directly to a surface. Many dealers sell special cardboard troughs or trays designed for the soaking process, but any tub or vessel that is larger than the width of the roll of paper can be used.

When using a paper without paste, one will need a large table on which to lay the strip and apply the paste. A supply store may rent a special folding paste table. When using a dining room table or two card tables placed together, one should cover the surface with heavy brown paper to protect it from the paste.

Most wallpaper sold today is pretrimmed. This means that the selvage edges are already cut off and do not have to be trimmed. A few special designs may have a protective edge that must be cut off before the paper is hung. One should check this point with the dealer before working with the paper.

The type of design should be carefully studied, especially for a first project. It is easier for the beginner to work with small all-over patterns or textures or with panels that match straight across. Certain designs have "drop-match" patterns with motifs in alternating positions. These require more skill in cutting and applying the paper because the pattern repeat is staggered. With this kind of pattern the motifs on every other strip must be placed at a certain level while those on the in-between strips are dropped to a lower level. This is another point to check with the dealer before one buys the paper.

ESTIMATING AMOUNTS. It takes a bit of figuring to determine how much wallpaper will be needed to decorate a specific room or area. With large motifs there may be considerable waste because of the problems of matching the design. Also, the number and sizes of openings in the room will influence the requirements.

Wallpaper is sold in various widths, usually eighteen, twenty and a half, twenty-four, twenty-eight inches, and so on. A single roll of paper contains about thirty-five square feet (there may be about only thirty square feet of usable paper because of matching problems). The actual length of paper in one roll will vary with the width. Thus the narrower papers will have greater length per roll than the wider ones.

Ordinarily one will have to buy a "bolt" of paper, which contains either two or three single rolls, depending on the width of the paper. One bolt usually provides five or six floor-to-ceiling strips of paper.

One should approximate the amount of paper needed by determining the square feet of wall space to be covered, multiplying the length of each wall by the height and totaling the walls to be covered.

A single roll of paper eighteen inches wide and eight yards long will cover about thirty to thirty-five square feet of wall area. On this basis, a room ten feet wide by fourteen feet long will require about thirteen single rolls. One single roll should be deducted for every two doors or windows of average dimensions.

One should be generous with the estimates. Leftover paper can be used for other purposes; sometimes an unopened package can be returned to the dealer. It is frustrating to run out of paper in the middle of a project and to have to wait until more can be obtained.

EQUIPMENT. It has been indicated that equipment needs will depend to some extent upon the type of paper used. With prepasted papers one will not use the large table but will need a vessel for moistening the rolled strips of paper. When applying the paste oneself, one will need a wide brush and a paste bucket. With either type of paper a yardstick will be needed for measuring and shears for cutting. A wheel knife or plenty of sharp razor blades will be necessary for trimming edges. A smoothing brush is used to smooth the paper on the wall. A sponge and cloths will also be needed for wiping away paste drips. A roller or chair caster is useful for pressing edges if one overlaps them at the seams.

PREPARING THE WALLS. New plaster may require a sealer before any finish is applied. A smooth, slick surface is easier to hang paper on than a rough one. Old plaster walls may require patching. A scraper or steel wool should be used to remove rough spots caused by crackling or peeling paint. Holes and cracks should be filled with plaster and the surface should be smoothed.

If a previous layer of wallpaper is firmly attached to the wall, one may apply new paper over it. However, if there are several layers on the wall it is advisable to remove them by soaking and scraping. Some paint and hardware stores rent steaming machines, which make the process easier.

PREPARING THE PAPER. Because wallpaper is usually tightly rolled, each strip that is cut may curl quite a bit. The paper will be easier to handle if one draws it over the edge of a table, pattern side up by holding a hand firmly on the paper as it is drawn over the edge. This should be done several times to make the paper lie flat.

When working with a large motif, one should decide how it is to be placed on the wall. A light pencil mark should be put on the paper at the point where the strip is to start at the ceiling or molding. Allowing about four inches above this mark, one cuts across, then measures the full length of paper needed from ceiling to floor and, allowing another four inches below this point, cuts the strip. The four inches above and below is a generous allowance, which may be reduced once one gets started hanging the paper. A yardstick should be used to mark a line where the paper is to be cut.

For the second strip, the paper should be drawn from the roll and held next to the first strip. The pattern should be matched and the top edge marked. The second strip should be cut the same length as the first. Several strips of paper should be cut before the paste is applied.

PASTING. The paste should be mixed according to the directions on the package. It should be about the consistency of cream and entirely free of lumps. One should use a large container so that the wide brush can be easily dipped into the mixture. With the pattern side down, one should place one strip on the table with the edge of the paper along the table edge nearest him. The paste should be applied about two thirds of the way down from the top of the strip. About an inch or so should be left unpasted at the top edge. This section should be folded in half with the pasted sides together. Now paste

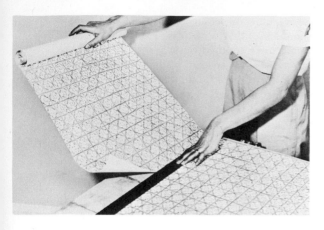

(a) Cut strip desired length.

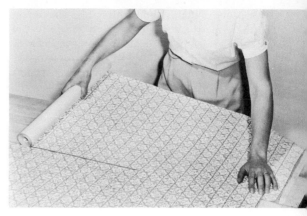

(b) Match design when cutting next strip.

(e) Position the first strip.

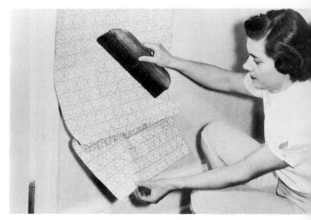

(f) Smooth strip in position at lower level.

(i) Slide second strip into position.

(j) Use trimmer to cut paper around outlets.

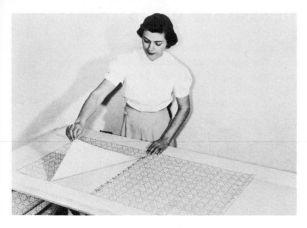

(c) Apply paste and fold paper.

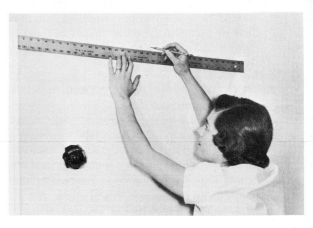

(d) Measure line for first strip.

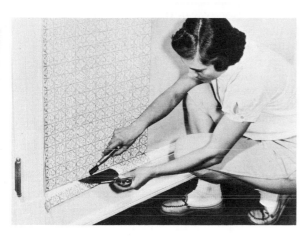

(g) Trim excess at lower edge.

(h) Trim excess at door frame.

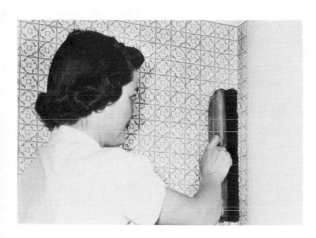

(k) At corners allow a small extension onto next wall.

FIGURE 27-4 Steps in applying wallpaper.
(*Courtesy of Wallcoverings Council*)

should be applied to the remaining one-third and this section should be folded in a similar manner. This folding makes the long strip easier to handle.

HANGING THE FIRST STRIP. It is important to start a papering project with the first strip in a perfectly vertical position, and using a plumb line is the only sure way to accomplish this. The architectural lines of a room are often tilted at a slight angle and may complicate the job unless one uses the plumb line.

One should plan to hang the first strip next to a door or window casing, measuring from the point chosen to a distance about one inch *less* than the width of the pasted strip and placing a tack near the ceiling line at this point. A string is then tied to the tack and a weight is attached to the end of the string near the floor. This line of the string will be a vertical guide for the first strip of paper. One can chalk the string and press it against the wall to mark the vertical guide line.

One should apply the pasted strip of paper by grasping the top edge (about one inch has been left free from paste), unfolding the upper section, and positioning the paper so that the line marking the upper edge is at the ceiling (or molding). The right edge of the strip must follow the plumb line exactly.

The left edge of the strip will extend beyond the starting point about one inch. This will allow for any inaccuracies in the door or window casing.

Holding the right edge in line, one smooths the paper on the wall with a few strokes of the smoothing brush. Working downward, one should be particularly careful to keep the right edge of the strip accurate on the plumb line.

The fold at the lower end of the strip is then opened and the paper is smoothed in place.

When the whole surface is smooth and free from any wrinkles, the top and bottom edges should be trimmed. A *very sharp* razor blade or wheel trimmer must be used. This will make the work easier and help prevent tearing.

At the left edge where the paper overlaps the window or door casing, the brush should be used to press paper firmly into the joint. The trimmer or razor blade should then be used to cut away the excess.

HANGING THE SECOND STRIP. The procedure outlined above should be followed in pasting and folding the next strip.

If the paper is pretrimmed, as most of them are, one should butt the seams. This means that there is no overlap; the two edges meet.

Now one is more interested in the left edge of the strip, making sure the pattern matches that of the strip already applied. One slides the paper into place, smooths the surface with the brush, and trims the edges as before.

If the paper should have selvage edges, before applying the paste one must trim the edge that will be on top and lap it over the selvage of the preceding strip. The overlap will be less obvious if the seams are gone over with a wallpaper roller.

CORNERS. When approaching the corner of the room, one should measure the distance from the last strip to the turn of the corner, adding one-half inch to the measurement and cutting a strip that wide. For example, if the last strip ends ten and a half inches from the corner the next piece should be cut eleven inches wide. One should apply the strip with the one-half-inch excess extending to the adjoining wall and use the brush to press the paper into the corner.

Next the excess that was cut off should be applied as the next strip. There will be a slight overlap and a mismatch at the corner, but in most cases this will not be obvious. Hanging a new plumb line at the corner will help to keep this strip in proper alignment.

SPONGING. Any excess paste should be removed from the surface of the wallpaper and woodwork very quickly. If paper is water-resistant, one should use a damp sponge; otherwise a dry cloth will do.

SPECIAL HINTS FOR PREPASTED PAPERS. There will be directions for moistening the strips before they are applied. Each strip must be thoroughly wet before one attempts to apply it. Also, plenty of *sharp* razor blades must be available for trimming the edges. Wet paper is more likely to tear. Allowing it to dry a few seconds before attempting the trimming process may solve the problem.

One should sponge the surface of prepasted papers with clear water to remove all traces of paste.

range a collage on heavy cardboard or thin plywood and paste the pieces in place. Apply two coats of orange shellac for an "antique" finish. Mount the collage with an appropriate mat and frame.

4. Choose an illustration of some room that appeals to you. Analyze it in terms of how the principles of design have been applied. Choose another illustration that you believe violates the principles of design and indicate why you think so.

Suggested Activities

Section I—Planning a Home

1. Assume that you are about to set up your first household. Write a paragraph or two in answer to each of the six basic questions pertaining to your situation.
2. Select several house plans from magazines and analyze each one as to how it might meet the needs of a family composed of the following members: father, mother, teen-age son, and three younger daughters.
3. Investigate the available houses and apartments in your community. Assume that you had to choose one of these as a place to live. Explain how you would arrive at a decision.
4. Select a house plan from a magazine. Analyze it in terms of your own needs. What are the most desirable or attractive features of the plan? If you were going to have the house built, are there any changes you would want to make? Why?

Section II—Design

1. Select several designs, represented in fabrics, wallpaper samples, prints, ceramics, and so on to illustrate the different types of design.
2. Select pictures from magazines to show particularly pleasing use of each of the elements of design.
3. Collect samples of interesting textures, colors, and designs from magazines. Ar-

Section III—Styles of Furniture

1. Select one style of furnishings for more intensive study. Use the library to find out all you can about the style and collect illustrations from newspapers, magazines, museums, and so on to show various interpretations of it.
2. If possible visit a museum or a restoration and write a report on the styles of furnishings displayed.
3. Visit local department and furniture stores to see how many styles of furniture you can identify.

Section IV—Decoration

1. Draw a scaled floor plan of some room with which you are familiar. Show the furniture arrangement as it exists. Make another plan of the room and try a different arrangement of the same furniture. Explain why your new arrangement is or is not an improvement.
2. Draw a scaled floor plan of some room that presents a particular problem in arranging furniture. Plan a furniture arrangement that you think solves the problem in the best possible manner. Explain why you think this is the best solution.
3. Select a floor plan of a house or an apartment in which you would like to live. On a scaled drawing, plan a furniture arrangement for each room. Explain how you have considered both function and design in making your plans.
4. Plan a color scheme for each room in the home selected for Number 3 above. Use paint chips, swatches of fabric, wallpaper, and magazine pictures to show the colors and textures you would select.

5. Collect illustrations of window treatments that you find particularly interesting and attractive. Explain why they appeal to you.
6. Select a room in which you might want to change the type of window treatment. Take measurements of the windows. Visit local stores to study shades, blinds, shutters, and fixtures. What would you select and how much would the project cost?
7. Use old wallpaper sample books and select motifs that might be suitable for framing. If possible, purchase inexpensive frames and mount wallpaper samples and prints to form an interesting group of pictures.
8. Assemble a variety of decorative accessories. You might borrow some from the home economics laboratories or ask each member of the class to bring in one or two small items. Experiment with different groupings that might be suitable for a mantel, a bookshelf, or a whatnot shelf.
9. Collect magazine illustrations that show interesting lighting effects.
10. Visit a local store to study the variety of lamps and lighting fixtures. Assume that you are going to buy all the lamps and fixtures needed for your home. Which ones would you select? Explain why you made these choices. Estimate the total cost.

Section V—Consumer Buying

1. Assume that a young couple about to be married have an annual income of $8,000 and plan to furnish a three room apartment. Select a floor plan and list all the items they would have to provide to make the home functional. Allowing for only a few gifts, plan a budget that they might follow.
2. Visit local stores and compare prices on some major item of furnishing. You might select sofas, mattresses, floor coverings, dining tables, chests of drawers, desks, and so on. Evaluate quality, function, and design in low, medium, and high price-brackets.
3. Select a floor plan for a house and note the dimensions of the kitchen and the living room. Visit local stores to determine how much the floor covering you would like to use in each area would cost.
4. Collect pictures of dinnerware, flatware, and glassware. Assemble combinations that you think are in harmony.
5. Visit local stores to compare different qualities of terry-cloth towels. Analyze quality and design at different price levels.
6. Make a study of the blankets available in local stores. Note the information on the labels and the price range. If you were going to purchase one, which would be the best selection? Why?

Section VI—Home Projects

1. Select a room in your home for which you might make new curtains or draperies. Measure the windows and estimate the yardage that would be required in fabrics of two different widths.
2. If possible, visit a local lumberyard to look at the types of wood, moldings, hardware, and so on that are available.
3. Visit local stores that sell paint, wallpaper, and hardware. Note the various types that are available.
4. Select a simple project to improve some area in your home. You might make a pair of café curtains, construct a simple table, cover seat cushions, antique an old piece of furniture, or redecorate a closet. Keep a record of the costs and the time involved. Evaluate results as to whether or not the project was worth the time and money involved.

Bibliography

General References

Ball, Victoria Kloss. *The Art of Interior Design*. New York: The Macmillan Company, 1960.

Craig, Hazel Thompson, and Ola Day Rush. *Homes with Character*. Boston: D. C. Heath and Company, 1962.

Faulkner, Ray, and Sarah Faulkner. *Inside Today's Homes*. New York: Holt, Rinehart and Winston, 1968.

Macmillan, Donald. *Good Taste in Home Decoration*. New York: Henry Holt and Company, 1954.

Obst, Frances Melanie. *Art and Design in Home Living*. New York: The Macmillan Company, 1963.

Rockow, Hazel Kory, and Julius Rockow. *Creative Home Decorating*. New York. H. S. Stuttmann Company, 1953.

Rutt, Anna Hong. *Home Furnishing*. New York: John Wiley and Sons, Inc., 1961.

Van Dommelen, David B. *Designing and Decorating Interiors*. New York: John Wiley and Sons, Inc., 1965.

Whiton, Sherrill. *Elements of Interior Design and Decoration*. New York: J. B. Lippincott Company, 1963.

Section I—Planning a Home

Agan, Tessie, and Elaine Luchsinger. *The House*. New York: J. B. Lippincott Company, 1965.

Beyer, Glenn H. *Housing and Society*. New York: The Macmillan Company, 1965.

Gottlieb, Lois Davidson. *Environment and Design in Housing*. New York: The Macmillan Company, 1965.

Rogers, Kate Ellen. *The Modern House, U.S.A.: Its design and Decoration*. New York: Harper and Row, 1962.

Varney, Carleton. *You and Your Apartment*. Indianapolis: Bobbs-Merrill, 1967.

Pamphlets

American Public Health Association (1790 Broadway, New York, N. Y. 10019): *Basic Principles of Healthful Housing* (also other pamphlets).

Better Business Bureau: *Facts You Should Know About Buying or Building a Home*.

Small Homes Council (University of Illinois, Urbana, Illinois): various booklets on home planning and construction.

U.S. Government Printing Office (Washington, D.C. 20402): *F.H.A. Home Owner's Guide* and *Minimum Property Standards When You Buy a House*.

Section II—Design

Anderson, Donald M. *Elements of Design*. New York: Holt, Rinehart, and Winston, 1961.

Beitler, Ethel Jane and Bill Lockhart. *Design for You*. New York: John Wiley and Sons, Inc., 1962.

Bevlin, Marjorie Elliot. *Design Through Discovery*. New York: Holt, Rinehart and Winston, 1970.

Goldstein, Vetta, and Harriet Goldstein. *Art in Everyday Life*. New York: The Macmillan Company, 1954.

Graves, Maitland. *The Art of Color and Design*. New York: McGraw-Hill, 1951.

Itten, Johannes. *Design and Form*. New York: Reinhold Publishing Corporation, 1964.

Randall, Reino, and Edward C. Haines. *Design in Three Dimensions*. Worcester, Mass.: Davis Publications, Inc., 1965.

Warner, Esther S. *Art: An Everyday Experience*. New York: Harper and Row, 1963.

Section III—Styles of Furniture

Aronson, Joseph. *The Book of Furniture and Decoration*. New York: Crown Publishers, 1952.

————. *The Encyclopedia of Furniture*. New York: Crown Publishers, 1961.

Boger, Louise Ade. *The Complete Guide to Furniture Styles*. New York: Charles Scribner's Sons, 1959.

————. *Furniture Past and Present*. New York: Doubleday, 1966.

Moody, Ella. *Modern Furniture* (paperback). New York: E. P. Dutton and Company, Inc., 1966.

Nutting, Wallace. *Furniture Treasury*. New York: The Macmillan Company, 1954.

Wanacher, Ole. *The Art of Furniture*. New York: Reinhold Publishing Corporation, 1967.

Wolsey, S. W., and R. W. P. Luff. *Furniture in England*. New York: Frederick A. Praeger, 1969.

Pamphlets

Good Housekeeping Bulletin Service (57th Street at Eighth Avenue, New York, N.Y. 10019): *Furniture Charts* (35 cents). (Also pamphlets on other topics.)

Section IV—Decoration

Birren, Faber. *Creative Color*. New York: Van Nostrand Reinhold Company, 1961.

Burnham, Robert W. *Color, A Basic Guide to Facts and Concepts*. New York: John Wiley and Sons., Inc., 1963.

Halse, Albert O. *The Use of Color in Interiors*. New York: McGraw-Hill, 1968.

Hicks, David. *David Hicks on Decoration*. New York: The Macmillan Company, 1967.

Itten, Johannes. *The Art of Color*. New York: Van Nostrand Reinhold Company, 1961.

Kira, Alexander. *The Bathroom*. Ithaca, N.Y.: Cornell University Center for Housing and Environmental Studies, 1966.

Kornfeld, Albert. *The Doubleday Book of Interior Decorating and Encyclopedia of Styles*. New York: Doubleday, 1965.

McCall's Decorating Book. New York: Random House, Inc., 1964.

Pahlmann, William. *The Pahlmann Book of Interior Design*. New York: Studio-Crowell, 1955.

Seventeen Book of Decorating, (Editors of *Seventeen*). New York: David McKay Company, Inc., 1961.

Smith, Charles N. *Student Handbook of Color*. New York: Reinhold Publishing Corporation, 1965.

Steidl, Rose E. *Functional Kitchens*. Ithaca, N.Y.: Cooperative Extension, Bulletin 1166, New York State College of Human Ecology, Cornell University, 1969.

Wilson, Jose, and Arthur Leaman. *Decoration U.S.A.* New York: The Macmillan Company, 1965.

Section V—Consumer Buying

Gillespie, Karen. *Home Furnishings*. New York: Prentice-Hall, Inc., 1951.

Logan, William B., and Helen M. Moon. *Facts About Merchandise*. New York: Prentice-Hall, Inc., 1962.

Margolius, Sidney. *The Consumer's Guide to Better Buying*. New York: Pocket Books, Inc., 1963.

Reist, Janet Aston. *Elegant Decorating on a Limited Budget*. New York: The Macmillan Company, 1965.

Pamphlets

Household Finance Company (Prudential Plaza, Chicago, Ill. 60601): *Your Home Furnishings Dollar* (15 cents).

Marsh, Betty. *All About Furniture*. High Point, N.C.: Southern Furniture Manufacturers Association, 1969.

The Seng Company (1450 North Dayton Street, Chicago, Ill. 60622): *Furniture Facts* (50 cents).

Section VI—Home Projects

Grotz, George. *The Furniture Doctor*. New York: Doubleday, 1962.

Hicks, Eula (ed.). *Singer Home Decorations Sewing Book*. New York: Singer Sewing Machine Company, Singer Education Department, 1961.

McCann, Karen Carlson, and Sue T. Garmon. *Creative Home Decorations You Can Make*. New York: Doubleday, 1968.

O'Connell, C. B. *Home Furnishing Self Help*. Metuchen, N.J.: Scarecrow Press, 1968.

1,001 Decorating Ideas. Consolidated Trimming Corporation, 27 West 23 Street, New York, 10011.

Painting and Decorating Craftsman's Manual and Textbook. Painting and Decorating Contractors of America, Inc., 2625 Peterson Avenue, Chicago, Ill. 60645.

Appendix

Publications

American Home
300 Park Avenue
New York, N.Y. 10022
Antiques Magazine
601 Fifth Avenue
New York, N.Y. 10017
Better Homes and Gardens
Meredith Publishing Company
1716 Locust Street
Des Moines, Iowa 50303
Budget Decorating
Maco Publishing Company
757 Third Avenue
New York, N.Y. 10017
Curtain and Drapery Department Magazine
230 Fifth Avenue
New York, N.Y. 10001
Daily News Record
7 East 12 Street
New York, N.Y. 10003
Floor Covering Weekly
350 Fifth Avenue
New York, N.Y. 10001
Flooring
116 East 16 Street
New York, N.Y. 10003
Furniture Manufacturer
342 Madison Avenue
New York, N.Y. 10017
Furniture Retailer Magazine
804 Church Street
Nashville, Tenn. 37203
Giftwares
111 Fourth Avenue
New York, N.Y. 10003

Home Furnishings Daily
7 East 12 Street
New York, N.Y. 10003
Home Modernizing Magazine
383 Madison Avenue
New York, N.Y. 10017
House and Garden incorporating *Living*
420 Lexington Avenue
New York, N.Y. 10017
House Beautiful
572 Madison Avenue
New York, N.Y. 10022
Interiors
18 East 50 Street
New York, N.Y. 10022
Linens and Domestics
111 Fourth Avenue
New York, N.Y. 10003
Modern Floor Coverings
630 Third Avenue
New York, N.Y. 10017
National Furniture Review
666 Lake Shore Drive
Chicago, Ill. 60611
New Homes Guide
383 Madison Avenue
New York, N.Y. 10017
Southwest Furniture News
Box 4667
Dallas, Texas 75206
Western Fabrics, Curtains and Draperies
1516 Westwood Boulevard
Los Angeles, Calif. 90024
Western Furniture Manufacturing
Suite 102
1516 Westwood Boulevard
Los Angeles, Calif. 90024

Other Sources of Information

American Carpet Institute
350 Fifth Avenue
New York, N.Y. 10006
Committee of Stainless Steel Producers
633 Third Avenue
New York, N.Y. 10017
Fine Hardwoods Association
666 Lake Shore Drive
Chicago, Ill. 60611
Glassware Institute of America
19 West 44 Street
New York, N.Y. 10036

Home Furnishings Council
P.O. Box 262
Flossmoor, Ill. 60422
Illuminating Engineering Society
345 East 47 Street
New York, N.Y. 10017
The Melamine Council
60 West Street
New York, N.Y. 10006
National Paint, Varnish, and Lacquer Association
1500 Rhode Island Avenue N.W.
Washington, D.C. 20005
National Retail Furniture Association
666 Lake Shore Drive
Chicago, Ill. 60611
National Retail Hardware Association
964 North Pennsylvania Street
Indianapolis, Ind. 46204

J. C. Penney Company, Inc.
Educational And Consumer Relations
1301 Avenue of the Americas
New York, N.Y. 10019
Sears, Roebuck and Company
Consumer Information Services
Chicago, Ill. 60607
The Society of the Plastics Industry
250 Park Avenue
New York, N.Y. 10017
Southern Furniture Manufacturers Association
High Point, N.C. 27261
The Sterling Silversmiths of America
551 Fifth Avenue
New York, N.Y. 10017
Wallcoverings Council
969 Third Avenue
New York, N.Y. 10022
Window Shade Manufacturers Association
341 Madison Avenue
New York, N.Y. 10017

Index